DISTANT THUNDER

Contents

For beloved friends who have helped so much with this and other ventures of mine:

Cooper Blankenship, Monique Duroc-Danner,
Raja Sidawi, Dominique Sumian, Nikki Thomas

William R. Polk
Vence, France 2010

William R. Polk studied at Harvard and Oxford and taught at Harvard until 1961 when President J. F. Kennedy, McGeorge Bundy, then director of the National Security Council, and former Governor Chester Bowles, then Under Secretary of State, put him on the newly reorganized Policy Planning Council. There he was responsible for much of Africa, the Middle East and Central Asia. He was one of three members of the Crisis Management Committee during the Cuban Missile Crisis; headed the American task force that helped to end the Algerian war; and later he negotiated the Egyptian-Israeli cease fire on the Suez Canal. In 1965, the resigned to become Professor of History at the University of Chicago where he founded the Middle Eastern Studies Center, and subsequently President of the Adlai Stevenson Institute of International Affairs. He is author of scores of essays and 17 books on world affairs. In 2012, he organized and chaired the conference on "Affordable World Security" that has been called the best meeting of its kind ever held in Washington.

And swiftly forming in the ranks of war;
And the deep thunder peal on peal afar;
And near, the beat of the alarming drum
Roused up the soldier ere the morning star;
While thronged the citizens with terror dumb,
Or whispering with white lips — The foe!
They come! They come!
Byron, *Childe Harold*

~

Their rising all at once was as the sound
Of thunder heard remote
Milton, *Paradise Lost*

~

First Witch. When shall we three meet again
In thunder, lightning , or in rain?
Second Witch. When the hurlyburly's done,
When the battle's lost and won.
Shakespeare, *Macbeth*

FOREWORD

Over the last sixty or so years, I have written scores of accounts of events I have observed or people I have encountered. Often, particularly in my earlier days, these papers took the form of letters to my family, but increasingly I found that I expressed my thoughts best in a form of essay that enabled me not only to describe but also to analyze. This style seemed almost to force itself upon me as I focused on such great patterns of events as the wars in Vietnam, Iraq, Afghanistan and Somalia and anticipated the dangers of further wars in Iran and Pakistan. From these essays, I have chosen a few for this volume. Since I have also written books on some of these topics, I have not duplicated here what I wrote there and have not attempted to bring the essays up to date.

I

I begin with Afghanistan which I first visited in 1962 while I was a Member of the Policy Planning Council. Afghanistan is the "Wild East" of Central Asia, and like many travelers I fell for its rugged charms, its stark and dramatic scenes and its proud and valiant people. I was fortunate in finding a remarkable guide in the late Louis Dupree and with him made a trip by jeep, horseback and airplane to almost every part of the country.

My trip came about because I had accompanied the then Under Secretary of State, former Governor Chester Bowles, on a trip to Africa and Asia. When we reached Afghanistan, we interviewed the staff of the American embassy and were horrified to find that they not only had hardly ever got out of downtown Kabul but that they knew almost nothing about the country and appeared to care even less. So Bowles suggested that I go off to see for myself and return to Washington to write a national policy paper on the country. I reprint that paper here.

Sadly, I found no interest in Washington. Secretary of State Dean Rusk was polite and even complimentary but frank in suggesting that I was wasting my time: Afghanistan was not and never would be a significant country.

The reforming government I had encountered – and whose prime minister had become a friend – was subsequently overthrown in a palace coup d'état and murdered in prison. The coup was a pyrrhic victory for Prince Daoud and the reactionary forces. Their excesses soon spurred a second coup that opened Afghanistan for the very Soviet invasion against which I had warned, correctly but prematurely, in my policy paper. Then followed in the 1980s a decade of savage guerrilla and counterinsurgency war in which the Russians lost 15,000 soldiers and killed or contributed to the deaths of roughly a million Afghans while driving some 5 million into exile before giving up and leaving. In the end, it was Afghanistan that virtually killed the Soviet Union.

In the years after 1989 when the Russians withdrew, the country was convulsed by civil war in which local strong men – the word "warlords" has entered our common vocabulary – committed every possible permutation of theft, kidnap, rape and murder. Arising in reaction to these terrible events was the religious fundamentalist movement of the Taliban. Many things about their regime were ugly. (Later, in this book I reprint my account of religious fundamentalism.) But the sin they committed in the eyes of the Bush administration was not their social policy, their brutality or their intolerance but their act of granting sanctuary to the leader of the anti-Western al-Qaida movement, Usama bin Ladin. After his group attacked the World Trade Center and the Pentagon in September 2001, America invaded and overthrew the Taliban government.

Having seized the country and destroyed its government, America found itself in the position of the fox with Tar Baby in the old Southern children's story: it had "won," was in total control, but could not let go. So the American occupation settled down to a decade of increasing Afghan fury and rising cost to America. It was in response to this situation that in 2009 I wrote a memorandum to the newly elected President Barack Obama on what I thought his administration should do. I had planned to deliver it in person, through the good offices of my dear friend Senator George McGovern, but we never got to see him. So I published it as an open letter in *The Nation* magazine.

The President then opted for a military "solution" which I was sure would not work. Our senior civil official in the country, our ambassador, General Karl Eikenberry, was enthusiastic about my analysis of why, which ultimately I also published and here reprint, "the legitimation crisis in Afghanistan."

But, once again, the critique that I and several others have offered was brushed aside and the war has gone on – with, of course, increasing casualties on both sides, vast wastage and diversion of resources so needed for the truly important tasks of the world, health, food, protection of the Earth and security. As I finish this volume, there is no end in sight.

II

Already committed in Afghanistan, the "younger" Bush administration picked up in 2003 where the "older" Bush administration had left off in its 1991 attack on Iraq. On these events, I wrote dozens of articles, testified twice before a Congressional caucus and lectured all over America and in Berlin, London and Oxford. Here I present a few of my reflections and admonitions. I begin with a trip to Iraq in 1983, the midst of the Iraq-Iran war, and in subsequent articles come up to the present.

On Iraq, I have also written several books. In *The United States and the Arab World*, I put Iraq in the larger perspective of the Middle East. That book appeared in the American Foreign Policy Library which had been founded by Sumner Wells at the end of the Second World War. When the first edition of my book appeared in 1965, the Library was edited by Professor Crane Brinton and later, as the book when marched through five editions until 1991, by Professor/Ambassador Edwin Reischauer. Years later, in 2005, I portrayed the long reach of Iraqi history and culture in *Understanding Iraq* and, together with Senator George McGovern, described a means we could have used to end the disastrous war and get out of Iraq safely, with dignity and with due care for the desperate needs of the Iraqi people in *Out of Iraq*.

My experience in Iraq goes back even further than my time in Afghanistan. I first visited the country in 1947 and returned many times over the years. It was the first place I made a serious attempt to understand the Middle East. My study began in 1951 when, the Rockefeller Foundation generously afforded me the first of four fellowships just as I left college. I then spent only six months there but gathered enough information and insight to write a modest booklet with the rather grand title, *What the Arabs Think*. Published by the American Foreign Policy Association, it was my first venture into print. Despite the pretentious title, it was based on substance: it grew out of a sort of salon that took place in my Baghdad living room every week. As the only neutral ground in the capital and not associated with any embassy, it was the place and occasion where the critics of the regime (and of each other) could safely gather to argue. Without intending to do so, they became my teachers. Our time together was thus a sort of self-generated research project that enabled me to understand what the Arabs thought.

Together with Richard Nolte, a fellow student at Oxford and later our ambassador to Egypt, I used these experiences also to write an article that argued that we were seriously misunderstanding Iraq and other Arab countries and that Secretary of State John Foster Dulles's "Baghdad Pact" was really just a house of cards. *Foreign Affairs* published the article just weeks before the 1958 coup d'état gave substance to our argument. The dean of the Harvard faculty and later director of the National Security Council, McGeorge Bundy, told me that this article was the beginning of the new look at the Middle East by what would become the Kennedy administration.

After the coup d'état that overthrew the old regime, I was apparently the first foreign private citizen to arrive to find many of my "teachers" had become cabinet ministers. Over the next couple of years I assisted the great architect Walter Gropius and his colleagues in their project to design Baghdad University.

At the request of President Kennedy, Governor Bowles and Bundy I then joined the Kennedy administration in 1961 to be responsible for planning policy in the Middle East, North Africa and Central Asia.

Visiting friends in Iraq was always like a throw of the dice: one never knew in advance whether they would be in the Cabinet or in the prison. Saddam Husain finally clarified that question: almost everyone I had known was first in prison and then in exile. So it was in his time that I visited and wrote a report on a visit I made to his, not my, Iraq during the war with Iran in 1983. That is the subject of my first paper on Iraq.

The second paper concerns my visit on the very eve of the American invasion in 2001 when I made a doomed attempt to head off the war. In subsequent papers I sought to show both the differences from the Cuban Missile Crisis in which I played a minor role and the similarities to Vietnam, to show the faulty intelligence evaluation that was used to justify the invasion, to analyze the terrible costs and to argue for leaving.

III

No one dealing with the Middle East can avoid the great and continuing tragedy of Palestine. It is the political "cancer" at the heart of the Middle East. No matter where one looks, from Morocco to Afghanistan and from Turkey to Nigeria, Palestine intrudes.

Nor is it solely a Middle Eastern problem. Probably no topic is more sensitive in American politics than Israel. The Holocaust has been the subject of thousands of books, pamphlets and articles. Hardly a week passes without the publication of some new account of the tragedy of European Jewry. Half a dozen "think tanks" and journals in America are devoted to Israeli/Jewish/Zionist affairs. And with large numbers of America's best scholars and writers being Jewish and being supported by large, well-financed and active advocacy groups, the Palestine "problem" sounds large throughout the land.

Within limits, the lobbying for Israel has enriched American political discourse. But, there is a dark side: the charge of anti-Semitism is used in a way reminiscent of the charge of Communism in the 1950s with which Senator Joseph McCarthy poisoned American intellectual life and nearly crippled public service; indeed, the residues of McCarthyism almost kept me in 1961 from serving in the State Department. Today, the similar charge of anti-Semitism is among the most lethal and loose innuendos in political and intellectual affairs. Anyone seeking even to understand Middle Eastern affairs is unlikely to escape it. I certainly have not. While my writings have drawn wide praise, I have been attacked in ways that echoed both Southern racism and anti-Semitism. The charge of anti-Semitism has been used to besmirch even Jewish Zionists – most notably and most recently the distinguished South African jurist, Judge Richard Goldstone, who reported honestly and fairly to the UN Human Rights Council on the Israeli invasion of Gaza. As Judge Goldstone found, this is dangerous territory.

I first trod that territory in 1946 with my brother, George Polk, then the chief CBS news correspondent in the Middle East. And, like most visitors, began what would be a very long "learning curve." Palestine was the subject of three of my books, *Backdrop to Tragedy,* which in 1957 I edited and wrote with two dear friends, David Stamler, an English Jewish Zionist teacher, and Edmond Asfour, a Palestinian Arab economist; *The Elusive Peace: The Middle*

East in the Twentieth Century, in which I tried to explain both Zionism and Arab nationalism and clarify why peace had not come; and *The United States and the Arab World* in which I laid out the history of the whole Middle East and American relations with it.

My involvement with the issue of Palestine has been more than academic. I headed the US government task force on Arab-Israeli affairs, worked out a negotiating agenda to approach a settlement, advised various of our emissaries on how peace or at least a surcease of violence might be achieved, and in 1970 at the request of Israeli Prime Minister Golda Meir negotiated with President Gamal Abdul Nasser a ceasefire to end the costly but inconclusive battles along the Suez canal.

In the course of years of such activities, I have often drawn back from Middle Eastern affairs to look at the larger, humane, issues, because it has always seemed to me that these, rather than technical, diplomatic or strategic issues, are at the heart of the dilemma.

The key issue is where it all began: how Europe created the problem. Of course, everyone knows about and focuses on the German Nazis with their "Final Solution," but that is only the most obvious and most recent part of the story. Beginning in medieval Europe, Jews were exploited but hated, always ostracized and often expelled. When Pope Urban II proclaimed the First Crusade in 1095, those who responded began their bloody work with attacks on Jews in Europe (and, upon reaching Jerusalem, showed a fine spirit of ecumenicalism by burning alive local Christians in their church); the lovely little university city of Cambridge drove them away; the Magna Carta, which to most of us is the flagship in the armada of freedom, was more concerned with protecting Christian barons from Jewish money lenders than enlarging liberty; the concept of the ghetto arose in Venice; and the "Most Christian" rulers of Spain, Isabella Católica and Ferdinand, not only sent Columbus to the New World but also in 1492 expelled Spain's Muslims and Jews. And on and on. The anti-Jewish crusade was picked up by the Russians particularly in the late Nineteenth century in the form of vicious pogroms that set in motion the Jewish desperate quest for a sanctuary – which is the essence of Zionism.

In the Nineteenth century, nationalism was the most powerful ideology, and one people after another cast their aspirations in its terms. Along with the

Italians, Greeks, Bulgarians, French, Poles and Germans, Jews were striving to find for themselves a nationality. Some, particularly in Austria and Germany, did it through assimilation, but the more radical or prescient realized that assimilation was unlikely to protect them because, as one said, "Jews carry anti-Semitism on their backs wherever they go." Reaction to them accelerated when large numbers of relatively poor Jews began to arrive in Western Europe. It was in the 1880s that the thrust toward the concept of Jewish nationhood gained favor. Theodor Herzl led the way toward the concept of Zionism in *Der Judenstaat*.

For many in Russia, Germany and France, Zionism was welcomed as a way to get rid of their Jews. There has always been an element of anti-Semitism in the favor outsiders show for the exodus of Jews to somewhere else. For Christians then, as for many still today, the idea of the Jewish "return" was tied to Old Testament prophecy or promise that once in Palestine, the Jews would convert to Christianity. Today, these threads come together in a form of Christian Zionism.

While the European governments little cared what happened to the Jews after they left, for the British government, two new elements were added to these impulses: imperial aims and the transformation of domestic society by the rise of Jewish politicians and financiers. Around 1900, Zionism was beginning to seem politically attractive and strategically useful. If Anglicized or at least pro-British Jews could be set up in some dangerous part of the British empire, both domestic goodwill and imperial stability would be enhanced. So the British experimented with or at least discussed various African settlement schemes. Through the fortunes of war, as I describe in the essay in this volume, these trends led to the establishment of the Jewish community in Palestine at the end of the First World War.

The thirty years of British rule over Palestine saw a steady increase in Jewish migration to Palestine. At first the numbers were small and mostly ideologically driven, but as Jews began to realize the looming danger of Nazi repression increasing numbers began to arrive. The British, as the ruler over Palestine, made sporadic efforts to keep a demographic balance, but found that what earlier had seemed a confluence of imperial and domestic politics were, in fact, in sharp conflict. The English Jewish community insisted on the "right of return" regardless of imperial interests. Then, after the Second World War, the victorious Allies found that they had also won a large, poor and desperate new society: displaced persons who could not be ignored. What to do with or about them was not totally under the control of the Allied authorities, but they do not appear to have even considered their options.

One they did not consider was to make the Germans pay for what they had done. Despite the fact that it was Germany that had killed millions of Jews, Gypsies and others, and had done its best to destroy the European states and peoples, no one suggested that the Germans be made to donate a suitable territory – say the Ruhr or Bavaria – for a Jewish *heimstaat* or "homeland." The reason, I think, is that in the context of the Cold war, which was already beginning to shape the thoughts and worries of the western leaders in the later stages of the Second World War and soon became paramount, the US and British governments were determined to bring the Germans quickly into an anti-Soviet alliance.

But, if not Germany, where? It certainly did not occur to either the English or the Americans to offer them a piece of their own lands. I have often shocked audiences that professed concern about the Jewish tragedy by suggesting that, if they really cared about the fate of the Jews, they should offer – say Texas or Utah as the Jewish homeland. Compassion has its limits!

The default answer was a place whose people really didn't matter in world politics and who were unable to defend themselves. Thus, ironically, the Christian and Muslim Palestinians, who had no role in persecution of the Jews, were to pay for Western intolerance. Guilt for the Palestine tragedy stains Western hands.

To the Zionists there was no tragedy at all. The Arabs certainly counted for them no more than the Native Americans had for the incoming American settlers or the aborigines had to the Australians. To incoming Jews, Arabs were just gypsies, nomads, a rootless people with no attachment to Palestine or any other land. As Arthur Koestler called them, echoing the Bible, in a novel set in the 1930s, they were hapless victims to lose out to the "Thieves in the Night." Indeed, some Zionists continued to maintain in the face of all evidence that Palestine was, as Israel Zangwill proclaimed "a land without people." Prime Minister Golda Meir went even further: there weren't any arab Palestinians.

The Jews were the real Palestinians.

The Arabs were set up for their decline and fall by historical forces not only in Europe but also in the Middle East. First, unlike the Jews who had caught the wave of nationalism, the Palestinians had no sense of shared nationhood for which Arabic did not even have a meaningful word. As throughout Asia, Africa and even much of Europe, villages remained the nexus of all social and cultural life. Second, that way of life was severely undercut by the impact of Western commerce from the middle of the Nineteenth century. Palestinians, like other Middle Easterners, Indians and other Asians found that they could no longer sell their manufactured goods to Europe and even began to import basic needs from Europe. As tastes changed, they put aside the locally made turban in favor of the French-supplied fez and began to drink English-supplied tea from glasses made in Bohemia. But far more important, in trying to protect itself against Europe, the Ottoman empire, of which Palestine was a province, was "modernizing." To acquire the means to do so, it sought to increase its tax revenue. To this end, in the 1880s, Ottoman reformers imposed upon the villagers a new concept of land ownership. Thus the traditional owners, the "real tillers of the soil," as the contemporary Zionist historian Richard Gottheil called them, legally lost their rights to absentee officials and rich merchants who could pay the government for them. The "real tillers of the soil" did not even know of this change for half a century; they kept on plowing and harvesting. But what the Ottomans decreed shaped Palestinian-Zionist relations. The Zionists were able to buy much of the agricultural land from "owners" who had never set foot upon it.

Anyway, the Jews proclaimed that they were entitled to the land. They could prove it with the Old Testament, which among other things is the national myth and manifesto of the Hebrews: Myth has it that having been driven out of Egypt by "Old Pharaoh" (incidentally, there is not a shred of archaeological evidence that any Jews ever even visited Egypt in ancient times), they invaded Palestine and, on the orders of their tribal god, Yahweh, slaughtered the Canaanite and other inhabitants. As Deuteronomy 7/2 instructs, "And when the Lord thy God shall deliver them before thee; thou shalt smite them, and utterly destroy them; thou shalt make no covenant with them, nor shew mercy unto them..." Exodus 23 goes on, "...thou shalt utterly overthrow them [for] I will send my fear before thee, and will destroy all the people to whom thou shalt come...I will drive them out from before thee, until thou be increased, and inherit the land." It was by conquest and extermination that the new Hebrew arrivals established their right to the country. Joshua 6/21 tells how they did it: "And they utterly destroyed all that was in the city [Jericho], both man and woman, young and old, and ox, and sheep and ass, with the edge of the sword." And so the Hebrews took over the possessions of the natives as Deuteronomy 19/1 puts it, "When the Lord, thy God hath cut off the nations [that is the villages of the natives], whose land the Lord they God giveth thee, and those succeedest them, and dwellest in their cities, and in their houses..." But, to the Jewish Zionists and today's Christian Zionists, this was not a bloody conquest, as the Assyrians, Persians, Macedonians or Romans practiced it, but an act of God. Thus, moral, legal and mandated.

Jews today believe that over the next 2,500 years their ancestors retained their presence in the Land of Israel. Historically, we know that their "presence" was composed only of small, religious colonies. In the middle of the Nineteenth century, they reached, perhaps, 10,000 and were only about 50,000 by the First World War. Recognizing this reality, Jews traditionally have divided themselves into Ashkenazi (East European), Sephardic (Spanish, Portuguese and North African) and Bene Ha-Hizrah (Oriental) communities. These diverse groups were enriched by the conversion of large numbers of Turks, Arabs, Berbers, Indians, Chinese and Africans just as even greater numbers of foreign peoples converted to Christianity. All this was understood and has been documented by Jewish scholars over the last two centuries. But, in the face of Jewish historical scholarship, today's Israeli Radical Right clings to the myths: the Jewish people are one, "pure" and God-chosen and the land of Palestine is theirs by Divine Right. The myth itself, as violently asserted particularly by the settler community in the Jordan valley and the Likud and other Rightists, is among the most powerful barriers to peace.

The Israelis are not the only devotees of myth. Every Palestinian I have ever known believed, not only sincerely but passionately, that before the "Catastrophe," as the Arabs call the 1948-1949 war, Palestine had been a land of milk and honey, in which every village was a little kingdom of happiness and every acre of rock, thorn bush and scrub, a verdant, sweet-smelling garden.

Mingling with myth is today the hard edge of reality: the milk and honey are in the cups of the Israelis, many of the villages have been razed and the gardens have been seized by the government or even by the settlers. The West Bank is sliced through by walls and restricted roads; farmers are cut off from their farms; and unarmed Palestinian villagers are threatened or killed by Jewish settlers. Gaza today is a vast concentration camp whose people have been diminished into one of the poorest societies on Earth. Overall, the lives of over a million people, now in the third or fourth generation, have been blighted, shortened, distorted by war after war and a seemingly endless and certainly brutal occupation.

How to end this misery is one of the most serious challenges of our times. The first step toward that goal is to understand it in all its painful dimensions. That understanding is what I have approached in my essay here.

IV

From wars in progress and tragedy replacing peace, I turn to another potential disaster: the possibility of a war against Iran by either or both America and Israel.

Iran is surely one of the most fascinating countries in the world. I admit to great prejudice as each time I went there – the first being in 1957 with my dear friend and Harvard colleague, Khodadad Farmanfarmaian – I was swept up in the brotherhood of his vast family. The Farmanfarmaians were the descendants of the Qajar dynasty which had ruled Iran until the First World War. Their father, himself an occasional prime minister, had found time and energy to father 55 children. One or other of the brothers was engaged in virtually everything of any significance that was happening in the country. So my time with them was an endless round of poetry sessions, arguments over politics and that all-consuming love of Persians (and historians) gossip. I think that one of the problems I later had with Muhammad Reza Shah was that he regarded me (as I certainly regarded myself) as an honorary brother of the Farmanfarmaians.

I was not surprised by the Muhammad Reza Shah's overthrow. Along with government colleagues, Kenneth Hansen (then deputy director of the Bureau of the Budget) and Robert Komer (then deputy director of the National Security Council) I had predicted it. If he did not, like the great butcher of Iran Timur

(Tamerlane), make pyramids of skulls, the Shah harmed a great many people and deeply offended Iranian sensibilities, particularly in matters of religion. But, ironically, it was the disparity between what he did beneficially (economic development) and what he adamantly refused (political participation) that created the revolutionary condition. (I explain why this happened in my essay analyzing social change in Part V.) We Americans were remarkably insensitive to this process and complicit in the worst of his activities as well as involved in the best of them. I had kept up a running fight on many of these issues since I had become responsible for planning American policy toward the Middle East in 1961. But, I was literally out-gunned both then and particularly after I left government service in 1965. At the urging of American officials and the connivance of Secretary of State Henry Kissinger, the Shah went on a binge of militarization and repression of his society; doing so, he almost literally dug his own grave.

While I had no impact on American policy and little on Iranian-American relations during the years after 1965, I had developed a love affair with Iran and in my book, *Understanding Iran*, I try to show why.

The last part of the story is not attractive: as in other revolutions, the incoming government proved itself at least as tyrannical as the one it displaced. But that was to be expected. What was required was time to achieve a workable synthesis of the old and the new. International and American politics has made this even more difficult than it would otherwise have been. We have skated close to war. Today we are not far from it. The breakdown of our relationship and the danger of war are the subject of my single essay in his section.

V

The reader will have gathered that trying to understand other peoples and their cultures, their ambitions and their fears, has been a life-long quest of mine. One of my exemplars and stimulators in this effort was the great Fourteenth century North African scholar Abdur Rahman ibn Khaldun whose work I first read when I was plunging, vicariously and at distant remove but nonetheless intensively, into his world as a student in the Oriental Studies program at Oxford.

The Oxford program aimed, and in some senses succeeded, in forcing me to duplicate the medieval curriculum that Ibn Khaldun had followed. For him it was total emersion; for me it was at least deep emersion as I plowed my way through pre-Islamic Arabic poetry, the Quran with commentaries, chronicles, the corpus of later Arabic literature and the exacting grammar and syntax of Arabic. The aim, both in medieval Andalusia and North Africa and in at least the medieval cloisters of Oxford was less to comprehend than to absorb. To this day, more than half a century later, I can still recite chunks of poetry and Quran. Ibn Khaldun could, of course, do so far more extensively and sensitively than I, but for both of us, the task of mastering the essence of a great culture was like plunging into a sea. I don't know about his reaction, but often I felt in danger of drowning. Arabic syntax and grammar are stern masters, and the vocabulary, already incredibly rich even in the most primitive times and evolving as it did over a millennium and a half, could never be fully mastered.

Already in my twenties, I was undertaking this study years too late whereas Ibn Khaldun began, as one should, as a child. I was also compressing the normally three-year Oxford program into two. The results showed. I became a passive consumer whereas he became a prolific producer. In the hands of a craftsman, as he certainly was, Arabic has an exactitude that rivals Greek and German and a native richness in range and nuance of vocabulary that exceeds Russian.

So rich indeed was the essence of the culture, the language, that both Arabs and Europeans found it to be all-encompassing. Some never rose above language to think about what it expressed. For example, in my first serious plunge into the study of the Quran, under the guidance of a man who was reputed to be the foremost European scholar, I never heard him comment on what was actually being said. The verses we read dealt with the law, but for him the only serious issue was whether a particular word was in the jussive or the accusative. Linguistics had become mind-numbing. For Ibn Khaldun it was even worse. His first serious "post-graduate" occupation was to copy with a quill pen government documents. I shudder to think how often drops of ink forced him to discard hours of painstaking labor.

Not surprisingly, both of us fled when we could. For him, it was harder in medieval Fez; for me in only partly medieval Oxford, there was the more stimulating environment of the Institute of Social Anthropology, whose director

Professor Evans Pritchard became a dear friend, and the rambunctiously argumentative and gossipy sessions at pubs that inevitably followed the Institute's seminars. Like Ibn Khaldun, I was finding, that my real interest was history: what really happened, why it happened, what were the results and whether there was some sort of pattern or rationale in the flow of events? For both of us, these questions were becoming a life-long quest. In seeking answers to them, both of us set out to study how contemporary peoples managed their lives. For him, the "field" was a group of Berber villages in what became Algeria and for me a cluster of Druze villages in Lebanon.

I am not sure how his mentors regarded this quest, but mine certainly thought it was a diversion from serious study. Professor Sir Hamilton Gibb, my teacher and patron, was deeply disappointed that I wrote my doctorate thesis on the modern Druze village of Ammatour. (He showed his disdain by spending, I once calculated, a total of seventeen minutes supervising the preparation of my thesis which was later published by Harvard University Press as *The Opening of South Lebanon.* And when I went on to write the first of my books on modern Palestine he told me I was throwing away not only all I had learned of Orientalism, the really serious academic study rather than the trivia of social anthropology, but also my future career. I "took refuge," as the Arabic expression has it, in Ibn Khaldun: he would have both understood and approved.

Ibn Khaldun and I also shared a tumultuous and wide-ranging exposure to the great events of our times. Fortunately, I did not share his sojourns in prison, but I did share his immersion in politics and foreign affairs. This led both of us into contact with some of the fascinating figures of our times: he moved from the court of the nominally Christian but actually barbarian king of Spain, Pedro I, who gloried in the name "Pedro the Cruel," through the princes, pashas and deys of North Africa to the governors of Mamluk Egypt to the command post of the great Chaghatai Turco-Mongol conquer Timur (Tamerlane) Shah outside the walls of Damascus while I observed, negotiated with and got to know Muhammad Reza Shah, President Gamal Abdul Nasser, and the prime ministers, presidents or warlords of a number of countries from the Sudan, Yemen, Iraq, Afghanistan, Turkey and Greece to Russia.

So it is that from our similar if not quite parallel experiences, I have long felt that I knew and understood Ibn Khaldun in a more than an academic way, and my first essay in this collection is my appreciation of him and his "Introduction to History," *al-Muqaddimah.*

My own analysis of social change in the process development follows my appreciation of Ibn Khaldun. In it, I seek to provide a more exact way of analyzing what happens when a government sets out to modernize. I focused on Egypt in that essay, but the process has now been repeated in India and China whose governments are also and on a far grander scale, embarked on programs to create the "new men" I found in Egypt while leaving aside the mass of their traditional societies.

In a final essay in this part, I look at what happens when the "social contract" is overthrown by invasion or revolution. This is precisely the problem that has arisen in Iraq, Afghanistan and Somalia and may arise if America thrusts into other lands. I liken the social contract to "Humpty Dumpty" in the old English rhyme and point to its moral: that when it is broken, "all the king's horses and all the king's men cannot put it together again." With all our horses and men, we are painfully learning this truth in Iraq and Afghanistan. We have given up trying in Somalia.

VI

The Cold War made profiting from the thoughts of the Russians on the great issues of our times difficult, but I was fortunate to be invited twice to the Soviet Academy of Sciences twice to lecture and so was able to get to know and to exchange experiences and ideas with that institution's remarkable scholars.

This opportunity grew out of the fact that during my time as President of the Adlai Stevenson Institute of International Affairs, it hosted the 20th meeting of "Pugwash." Pugwash was a non-governmental assembly of representatives of the world's academies of science. The aim of the organization was to provide a forum and an occasion for major threats to world peace to be ventilated in a frank and constructive manner. I served as co-chairman of its committee on the Middle East along with Yevgeni Maximovich Primakov who was then deputy director of the Soviet Academy's Institute of World Economy and International Affairs, and we began a life-long friendship. (Primakov would subsequently become Foreign Minister, head of external intelligence and Prime Minister of

Russia.) It was at his invitation that I visited Russia. In my essay, I provided a guide for American scholars wishing to get to know their Russian counterparts.

VII

Very different was my visit to China which is the subject of two short essays. I was then the senior director of the W. P. Carey Foundation which was dedicated to education and which, in conjunction with Arizona State University, established an advanced training program in management for the chief executive officers of a number of the Chinese banks, airlines and manufacturing organizations. To look over this program, I twice was invited to China and had the opportunity also to travel around the country and meet a number of senior officials. I recount a small piece of this experience – the financial revolution shown by the former vegetable garden of Shanghai, Pudong, and the example given by China's real-life version of Shangri-La, Lijiang, on how tourism can make traditional society profitable to the state.

VIII

In conclusion, I come back to America where I look at the neoconservative movement that has been responsible for our wars in Iraq and Afghanistan and which would happily lead us into "the long war" in Asian and African country after country. In getting at why this extremist group has managed to effect so much of its program, I also examine the rise of American religious fundamentalism. Then in a talk before the Progressive Caucus of the House of Representatives I discuss what the Congress needed to know and should have done about overseas policy. And, finally, I give my thoughts on the obligations and privileges of citizenship as I expressed them to the student body of Bennington College in Vermont.

Now, to paraphrase Samuel Pepys, "and so to the essays…"

DISTANT THUNDER

PART I

AFGHANISTAN

SECRET

S/P:WRPolk
March 27, 1962

this document consists of 16 pages
No. 23 of 28 copies, series A

ELEMENTS OF U.S. POLICY TOWARD AFGHANISTAN

1. The pre-eminent U.S. policy objective in Afghanistan is maintenance of Afghan neutrality and independence.

2. Should Afghanistan fall within the Soviet orbit or move significantly closer to Soviet control, U.S. policy objectives in Iran and Pakistan would be seriously threatened.

In Iran, the Shah, who is already anxious to devote an excessive amount of Iran's limited resources to military expenditures, might curtail the economic development program. Such curtailment would eventually lead to internal dislocation and upheaval and, perhaps, eventually to the growth of Soviet power and influence in Iran.

Pakistan would come under heavy pressure from Soviet presence on the Khyber Pass. Soviet exploitation of the Pushtunistan issue could subvert the concept of Pakistan. The Pak Government, already enjoying little more than popular acquiescence in West Pakistan and faced with considerable opposition in East Pakistan, would probably be forced to come to terms with the Soviet Union. In these circumstances it is doubtful that U.S. would be able to continue to utilize its facilities at Peshawar. Thus, maintenance of Afghan neutrality is vital to the preservation of U.S. policy objectives in Pakistan.

3. Soviet goals in Afghanistan are less clear. Construction of roads from the Soviet frontier through Herat to Kandahar and through Kunduz to Kabul, Soviet provision of a large-scale airlift for the exportation of 18,000 tons of Afghan fruits during the closure of the Pak-Afghan frontier, and Soviet trade policies all indicate a desire to draw Afghanistan into the Soviet market.

In the military field the Soviet Union is actively training Afghan officers and men in Afghanistan and the USSR. The missions in Afghanistan not only control training but also the entire maintenance of the air force and mobile units of the army. Upwards of 200 Afghan military cadets, some as young as sixteen years of age, have left for the Soviet Union for training of two to five years' duration.

In cultural affairs the Soviet Union applies considerable pressure on the Afghan Government to send students and teachers to the USSR and to accept Soviet professors in Afghanistan. Powerful radio stations in the Soviet Union beam an intensive barrage of programs in Farsi, Pashto, Uzbek, and other Turkic dialects to Afghanistan. Through emphasis on its superior technology and respect for traditional culture, the Soviet Union seeks to establish a scale in which the Afghan can evaluate his own present condition and the ineffectual efforts made by this government on his behalf.

To date, however, U.S. intelligence has discovered no case of Soviet political subversion and Afghanistan has no Communist Party.

If the objective of Soviet activities is maintenance of Afghan friendship toward the USSR, the U.S. has no necessary clash with it: Afghanistan must live, as it traditionally has, in the fissures of the great power blocs. U.S. fostering of active hostility toward the USSR can only weaken the Afghan ability to survive. However, the U.S. must seek to provide the wherewithal for Afghanistan to maintain an independent position. The key, however, is the Afghan will to survive.

4. The Afghans are a proud and sturdy nation. They are actually and historically a mosaic of ethnical, religious, and linguistic groups who share the characteristics of mountainous life, are inured to hardships and are proud of a glorious past. The Hazarahs, who inhabit the central mountain region of Hindu Kush, may be descendants of Chingis Khan's legionnaires and the inhabitants of Nuristan claim descent from the Macedonians of Alexander the Great. The Pashtuns (aka Pathans), who are scattered all over the country as nomads but whose main settled concentration is in the south justly earned the respect of the British in over a century of fighting on the northwest frontier. The Uzbeks and other Turcoman groups in the north fled from the Soviet Union in a desperate attempt to preserve their independence after the failure of the Pan-Turanian movement in the 1920's. All of these folk have a dignity

and hardihood which is striking.

5. The Afghan Government is ruthless, devotes a large proportion of its energies to countersubversion activities, is adept in a tradition of wily diplomacy and recognizes the extreme delicacy of its position. The Government puts loyalty above all virtues and ruthlessly weeds out potential opposition — the Prime Minister personally examines the dossier of each student before he is allowed to go abroad for training. Even promotion in the Army depends on security rather than on ability.

The Government is beginning to understand the importance of economic development to its survival. As needs dictate, it is slowly allowing the creation of a generation of trained men. It obviously distrusts and narrowly restricts the foreign contacts of these men (I, for example, was not introduced to an Army Colonel in the town of Balkh and my host subsequently explained that to have met me might have meant the officer's arrest). For the most part they are encouraged to deal with their foreign "counterparts" but not to mingle excessively with foreigners. This restricts contacts of the Army to the Russians and allows Westerners more scope among civilians. There in an undeniable prevalence of fear and suspicion throughout the country. All non-governmental organizational activities are banned.

Yet, there are also positive elements of loyalty. There is certainly more to "Afghanistan" than a collection of peoples. The Pashtun form the main cadre of the officer corps and are the source of provincial officialdom. The extensive royal family, of Pashtun origin, is actively engaged in government and army command at all levels and is closely bound together by the custom of family conferences and apparently by an awareness of common interests.

6. The major divisive element is the nature of the country. Stretching across Afghanistan is the mighty wall of Hindu Kush. In the winter most of the passes are blocked by snow. Communication between the northern towns of Mazar-i-Sharif, Pul-i-Khumri and Kunduz and the capital, Kabul, is over a 9,800 foot pass. To travel from Kabul to Herat, 400 airline miles, one must drive far to the south to Kandahar, 800 miles over-all, to avoid the mountains. A deep gorge cuts the mountains between Kabul and Jalalabad but only recently has a fair motor road been built. Large areas of the country are virtually out of touch with the capital. This is true of the northeast and the southwest as well

as the bulk of the mountainous center. Much of the country is accessible only on horse or camel. Other areas are reachable by jeep but at speeds at less than six miles an hour and at terrific cost in equipment. Even the main "roads" are little more than trails: 318 miles from the capital to Kandahar require 15 hours of hard driving and the 168 miles from Farah to Herat takes seven hours. From Kabul to Mazar-i-Sharif, 390 miles, is about 20 hours. Air traffic is frequently interrupted by bad weather over the passes through the Hindu Kush. There are no railroads. All POL must be imported.

In these circumstances it is natural that the areas north of the Hindu Kush should be linked, economically, with the neighboring regions of the USSR, and that the south, politically divided by the Durand line, should be closely linked, culturally as well as by regular nomadic transit, with Pakistan. Iran is separated by vast deserts and China by even more vast mountainous wastes. Internally, the country is divided into hundreds of discrete valleys and oases which are virtually autarkic.

7. Afghanistan is one of the world's less-developed nations. Statistics are, of course, little more than guesses and vary alarmingly from one source to another. An order of magnitude, however, is provided by these. The population is approximately 13 million of which one to two million are Nomads. Literacy is perhaps five per cent. Per capita GNP is about $50. Life expectancy is probably as low as 20 years. Infant mortality may be as high as 500/1000. There are very few public services. For example, in Badakhshan Province, with a population of approximately 350,000, there is one doctor and in Kataghan Province, with a population of one million there are seven doctors. Malnutrition is almost universal and the diet is seriously lacking in protein. The staple is wheat bread and tea with rice regarded as a luxury. Nowhere in Afghanistan, even in the capital, is there a safe supply of water which is everywhere taken from open ditches. Spot checks by the WHO representative in the north indicates that tuberculosis affects over 50 per cent of the people and intestinal diseases are almost universal. An indication of the problems of health is given by the consideration that an antibiotic pill costs three-days wages for a laborer.

8. Afghan programs to strengthen the economy and society are now entering their second phase. The first five-year plan, which was actually little more than a series of announced goals, ended in September of 1961. At this

time the following are the main points of Afghan economic picture.

a) The major export is Karakul skins valued at $14 million. Karakul is the product of the north center. There are an estimated five million Karakul sheep in the country. At the present time almost the entire production is shipped through the Soviet Union although the Soviet Union, itself a producer of Karakul, is a natural competitor.

b) The second major export of Afghanistan is cotton. Approximately 80 per cent of the cotton is sold in the Soviet Bloc and 20 per cent in the West. The exports are approximately $7.5 million.

c) Fruit is the third major export of Afghanistan. Its regular marketing in the Indian sub-continent was disrupted by the closure of the Pak-Afghan frontier and the industry was threatened with ruin. To meet the desires of the Afghan Government the Soviet Union provided a large-scale and most efficient airlift of 15 daily flights which took out 18 thousand tons of grapes, pomegranates and raisins. An Indian airlift removed an additional 1,000 tons. Two major effects of this were to change the direction of export from the Indian sub-continent to the Soviet Union to save the fruit producers from ruin.

9. The next five-year plan calls for an annual growth rate of almost 11%. Major emphasis will be placed on agriculture and irrigation to which approximately 350 million dollars will be devoted. Transportation and communications will take approximately 300 million dollars and industry and mining, approximately 250 million dollars and health and education, approximately 100 million dollars.

Subsequent to the development of the new five-year plan the Afghan Government has devoted increasing emphasis to the generation of foreign exchange by an increase in the value and volume of exports.

Assisted by Mr. Arthur Paul of the Asia Foundation, the Government is taking steps rapidly to increase the production of cotton. The amount which each farmer is required to plant in cotton has in the past been a loss to him because of the Government's policy of paying a very low price for raw cotton. Now, however, the Government plans to raise the cotton price and to begin a program of incentives for the use of fertilizers. Cadres of people trained on the Helmand Valley Project are to be devoted to the cotton program. The Government hopes that through this scheme it can realize approximately

$18 million of extra annual income of which about 12 million would be in convertible foreign exchange. (This would be more than 50% increase on the hard currency earnings from all exports in recent years).

The reason for this policy is primarily political. The Afghans do not want to be forced to increase their dependence on the Soviet Union and/or the West in their development program. In their view, the past has demonstrated that the West lacks a sufficient concern with the future of Afghanistan to assure the Afghans of an alternative to the Soviet Union as a source of capital. Any withdrawal of Soviet assistance would cause a virtual collapse of their foreign exchange position. Therefore, the Afghans plan to devote a major share of their own efforts to increase the value of their cotton export.

Present cotton production is about 60% of the U.S. per acre yield. So the Afghans hope by the use of fertilizers and better sowing methods to increase their yield without devoting excessive areas of land to cotton production.

Similarly, by better methods of sorting and dyeing the Afghans hope to increase the value of the karakul skin exports and to find new markets for karakul.

10. To assist in Afghan development plans the Soviet Bloc has offered to make available at very generous terms large amounts of Soviet credits. Precise figures do not seem to exist but at various times the Soviet Union has spoken in terms of as much as $400 million. Recently, however, the figure most discussed is approximately half that amount. The October 1961 agreement is for c. $200 million over a five-year period.

The major Soviet projects are in transportation and power facilities. As mentioned above, the Soviet Union is building highways from the Soviet frontier southward by tunnel through the Salang Pass to Kabul and through Herat to Kandahar. Both of these highway projects are being actively undertaken at the present time and both involve use of Afghan labor with Soviet equipment and technicians.

The Soviet Union is also assisting in various other projects notably in the field of energy. A Soviet Bloc mission is undertaking an oil and gas exploration and development program near Mazar-i-Sharif and a Czech team is assisting in coal production near Kunduz. Russian missions are constructing a 10,000 kw hydroelectric installation and irrigation project at Darunta near Jalalabad, a 9,000 kw hydroelectric plant at Pul-i-Khumri and a 60,000 kw hydroelectric facility near Kabul.

The Soviet Union has reputedly offered to take over the entire development program of Afghanistan. If this is true, the Afghan Government has wisely refused.

11. German assistance to Afghan development has a long commercial background. The Siemens Company and other German enterprises have been active in Afghanistan since long before the Second World War and German technician are assisting in industrial projects in Kunduz, Pul-i-Khumri, and Gulbahar. The Germans are also developing a hydroelectrical installation and assisting in some road work. The able and cooperative German Ambassador has disposal of approximately $50 million in credits for Afghan development.

12. The U.S. has provided a total of $193 million in grants and loans since 1952. There is now no commitment on future U.S. expenditures. Unlike the Soviet and German programs, U.S. activities are not based, according to Afghan understanding, on an over-all commitment but develop from project to project. Some of these projects have been impressive contributions to the Afghan nation. Some have not. For our future benefit we need to make a critical evaluation of our past efforts.

13. A major U.S. commitment is the undertaking to build a road on the 318 miles from Kabul to Kahandar. When first projected, this road was estimated at $16 million by a U.S. engineering firm. Subsequently and apparently largely for political reasons, the U.S. decided to upgrade the quality to the road and the cost is now expected to rise to over $50 million.

As now projected the road is, by domestic U.S. standards, extravagant in the extreme. The use factor is now and for the near future will probably continue to be low. In my 15-hour drive over this road I passed four trucks and two cars. If one projects in the near term a multiple of this, say a hundred vehicles a day, the road should be planned to some order of this figure. This would put it in the category of a "farm to market road" at a domestic U.S. cost of $10 to 20,000 a mile.

This category of road is adequate for up to 1,000 vehicles a day with gross loads of approximately 12,000 pounds. A "farm to market road" is normally 20 feet wide, has a gravel base and a 1/2 to 3/4 inch inverted-penetration surface.

It is all-weather and good for any foreseeable future Afghan use. But, our present plans may eventually cost us nearly $200,000 a mile.

14. A second major U.S. commitment is construction of airports. Those built at Kunduz, Jalalabad and Herat will handle Convairs and DC-4's. The Afghan Airways, Ariana, now uses DC-3's for domestic runs and lands these on a dirt strip at Mazari-Sharif as well as on the more elaborate airports. Except for its low ceiling and slow rate of climb the DC-3 is an ideal aircraft for Afghanistan, as the traffic pattern and freight control are rudimentary. Thus the existing airports are at least adequate for the foreseeable future.

The Kandahar airport, labeled an "international jet airport", which is said to have cost upwards of $25 million, is a monument to poor planning. Kandahar will never be an international jet center. It is a town of 80,000 people in a pastoral and agricultural district without major attractions for tourism. Modern long-range aircraft do not need the port for refueling en route from Tehran to Karachi or Delhi. Furthermore, since all POL must be imported by truck across the mountains, the airport is not economic even as a refueling point.

15. Both the roads and airports provided useful guides for future U.S. policy decisions.

a) Since the Afghan Government has not known for certain the over-all U.S. commitment to assist developing its economy it has sought to get the most it could in each individual project. If one is offered a car why not ask for a Rolls even if a Ford will do. The result is that the projects have been the most expensive from our point of view and not necessarily any more useful from the Afghan point of view.

If, on the other hand, we would be prepared to say, in effect – "we intend to spend $50 million on road construction in Afghanistan. Now let us work together to see that this money does the maximum good for the Afghan economy." – There are strong indications that the Afghan Government would have cooperated to use funds more wisely. Since only two of six projected contracts have been let on the Kabul to the Kandahar road it may still be possible to salvage some of these funds. They are needed for other projects in the country and the Afghan Government realizes this.

The same is true of the airports but unfortunately the money is already spent. Our aim now should be to maximize use of the airports in ways which will be discussed below.

In our future aid efforts we should offer an over-all commitment and then critically examine each project within the over-all commitment. This approach has been successfully used by the Germans in their efforts in Afghanistan. The Germans gave an over-all commitment to Afghan development of $50 million and within that figure have been extremely selective in the choice of projects. If they did not wish to undertake a project they simply raised their requirements for the Afghan portion of the over-all expenditure and let the Afghan Government quietly shelve the project.

b) Roads and airports are inert and neutral. There is little to distinguish a Soviet from an American road or airport. While appreciation for American activities is not now and should not become an overriding consideration, we should recognize that we create little "presence" by a strip of concrete with which we were once associated.

More important, we should seek in our future projects to use our aid funds to create organizations and cadres of people to maintain what we have helped to build and to perpetuate our method of approach. We should make no attempt to use these organizations for short-term political benefits but rather should hope that they will grow and develop within Afghan society. Examples of such organizations will be given below.

16. The Helmand Valley Authority, as the obvious pattern of the initials indicates, was begun as a major social engineering project. The Helmand Valley for over a thousand years supported flourishing civilizations but invasions, depopulation and neglect have led to the breakdown of its ancient canal system. While the area is not capable of sustaining a vast TVA-like development it offers the only major area of potential growth of Afghanistan. Reclamation of the land and draining of the swamp areas could significantly boost Afghanistan's productivity, would allow the Afghan Government to achieve its objective of increasing its earning of foreign exchange and, if properly devised, could foster the growth of a stratum of small holders which would give the country more stability.

To date only the upper Helmand Valley has been subjected to intensive development. The project, on which the U.S. has spent more than $100 million has been the butt of much criticism and has experienced obvious short falls:

since it was begun on inadequate studies of water and salt conditions some land has been lost while other land has been reclaimed at exorbitant cost. Insufficient studies were made of the social conditions and agricultural training of the farmers so that certain of their mores were uselessly violated and their skills have proved inadequate to the tasks they faced. Land plots, about 15 acres each, are too small to foster the growth of a prosperous farming group and do not allow sufficient income for the purchase of fertilizers. As a result there is a tendency to allow land to lie fallow on alternate years. Water is not sufficiently controlled and the water-starved peasants naturally have used excessive amounts — "they were like alcoholics given the key to package store". Credit facilities are non-existent and loans are obtained at rates as high as 100%. No cooperatives were created and even such activities as 4-H clubs which were inadequately understood by the Government were banned. Land was not fully leveled or sufficiently reclaimed when turned over to the farmers. Nor is the project self sustaining: there are no taxes or charges for water so any government crisis- as in the closing of the border- programs in the Helmand are sharply curtailed.

Yet, for all this, the scheme is making progress and by Afghan standards is a major achievement. In my opinion we should remedy its mistakes and capitalize on its virtues rather than wasting time in bemoaning its weaknesses. Ways in which this can be done will be discussed below.

17. Various other smaller American projects take up the energies and ambitions of the rest of the American mission. In some cases these are important, useful and practical programs. A good example of this is the Darr-i-Suf coal mine, 107 miles into the Hindu Kush mountains from Mazar-i-Sharif. In other cases our projects seem to represent merely a scattering of our shots and an excessive growth of administrative fat.

Many members of the AID mission deserve special awards for selfless and determined efforts against heavy odds to carry out their tasks. This is particularly true of the officials at the Darr-i-Suf coal mine and the agriculture and reclamation officers in the Helmand Valley. Certain non-governmental Americans are notable for their effectiveness and are highly praised throughout the Afghan Government. This is especially true of the official of the Asia Foundation and the representative of the American Universities Field Staff.

However, as in Iran, there is reason to question the size of the U.S. mission.

The introduction of large numbers of relatively extremely highly paid Americans in a small town like Kabul causes considerable irritation to Afghans and others. The high standard at which they live and a relatively low-visible-performance are both widely commented upon.

In the countryside Americans have made little impact because they are rarely seen outside of Kabul. I was the first State Department officer to visit some of the areas in which I traveled and the first since May of 1961 to travel north of the Hindu Kush mountains.

Nor have we done an efficient job of capitalizing on our achievements. Even those cases in which U.S.-Afghan cooperation has been most effective have not been communicated to the Afghan public with sufficient vigor.

18. Since our aim is to preserve Afghan independence, in developing our future program we should be certain that we have correctly identified the areas of the greatest Afghan weakness and those methods of approach which will enable us to win Afghanistan's confidence.

As I identify them the areas of greatest Afghan need are the following: transportation, energy, agricultural assistance, and the creation of cadres of trained personnel.

As the Afghan Government identifies them the priorities are much the same. However, the first priority is loyalty from those who are allowed to acquire the means of changing the internal balance of power, and the generation of sufficient foreign exchange to assure a modicum of flexibility in the next development plan.

19. Roads are mere trails throughout much of the country. It is difficult to imagine any considerable economic growth until major improvement is made in transportation. A great deal can be done locally. For example, the Governor of Mazar-i-Sharif Province turned out 20,000 men, villagers who were seeking to pay off taxes, to build a passable dirt road of 75 miles in 28 days. The men worked by hand without a grader and since they supplied their own food and shovels the road cost was practically nothing.

Roads are badly needed in many areas of the country. The use factor on these roads, however, will be relatively small for many years so it is possible to rely upon extremely low-cost methods of road construction.

Due to the severe climatic conditions and particularly the lack of rain, gravel roads do not hold up well as the "blinder" dust is blown away in any heavy traffic.

At the same time since rainfall in much of the country is less than four inches a year, dirt roads are adequate for many areas. While Afghanistan clearly does not need $200,000-a-mile superhighways it needs a great many miles of asphalt "farm to market" roads and many more miles of passable dirt roads.

What is even more lacking than the roads themselves, however, is any system of maintenance. In my 2,000 miles of driving in Afghanistan, I averaged 16 miles an hour because almost every road was an endless collection of pot-holes, ruts and bumps. Thus, any road building program should put first priority on the creation of a highway maintenance service. This should be an extremely inexpensive organization to create as most of the maintenance could be done by hand.

A road building program would serve to open up large areas of the country particularly in the lower Helmand Valley.

As a part of the Helmand development scheme, we should consider building a road from Lashkar Gah down the Helmand to Chahar Burjak and northward to Nad-i-Ali. This road, approximately 300 miles, is partially built at its upper end and could be paved and completed for c. $3-5 million. It would open the entire Helmand Valley to the country's market. It should not be undertaken, however, except as part of an over-all scheme for the development of the lower Helmand in such fashion as to avoid the mistakes of the first phase.

A "farm to market" road should be planned from Mazar-i-Sharif to Herat. This would enable the cotton and the karakul of the north to be shipped to the West through Iran. At present, these products would have to go by way of Kabul-Kandahar-Herat to Iran and this route could cost c. $25 per ton more than via the USSR.

We should undertake an improvement project on the Herat-Islam Qala-Mashed road. This would link the Iranian RR and also the proposed Bandar-i Abbas port with the Soviet-built Herat-Kandahar and the US-built Kandahar-Kabul road and provide a usable outlet for Afghan heavy goods. On the Herat-Meshed road, I passed about 75 trucks of which only a dozen of those traveling from Iran to Afghanistan were loaded. The existing road is 238 miles and needs only maintenance to be serviceable in dry weather. Should we undertake a project to upgrade the road, we should do so on a modest scale since the traffic is and probably will continue to be light. By using the existing Herat bridge, we could build a good, all-weather road for c. $2.5-$5 million.

Most important, we should inform, by graphic means if possible, the Afghan Government's senior officials of the effects of overloading of trucks on road surfaces. A 12,000 lb. axle load should be made the limit or our roads will not long hold up, and the equipment we have given the Afghan Government, much of which is now "side lined", will be destroyed.

At the same time it is important to recognize that in Afghanistan roads are not necessarily the best or only answer to the transportation problem.

In the Hindu Kush mountains south of Mazar-i-Sharif is the Darr-i-Suf coal mine. The road from Mazar-i-Sharif to Darr-i-Suf is 107 miles of eight hours of very hard driving. This road, over which coal is now being hauled, fords a river eight times, is almost totally lacking in maintenance and contains numerous hairpin curves, one of which on the face of a cliff, 1500 feet over a river bed, is so narrow that a jeep station-wagon must stop and back up to finish the turn. There is no gasoline en route so all must be hauled in jerry-cans. Some of the grades are 25 per cent.

Even if this road were to be repaired and put in good condition the energy required to lift a load of coal over the mountains into Mazar-i-Sharif, which is about 1800 feet above sea-level, and then back over the Hindu Kush at nearly 10,000 feet, is such as to make coal production extremely uneconomical. However, since there is a river at the mine it should be possible to convert the coal into thermo-electricity and send this directly over the mountain by high-tension lines to the three main centers of industry in Afghanistan, Mazar-i-Sharif, Pul-i-Khumri and Kabul since the coal mine is located at the hub of these three cities.

Additionally, we should encourage the growth of air freight service. This would bring into use the airports in which we have already put a great deal of money and would provide an almost immediate avenue to the west for Afghanistan's two major exports, fruit and karakul. Such a freight line could go from Mazar-i-Sharif or Kandahar to Bandar-i-Abbas or Khorramshar. When one considers the cost of maintenance of trucking equipment and the importation of POL, air freight may prove to be an economically competitive means of transportation.

20. Energy is in critically short supply all over the country. The whole of Afghanistan is practically denuded of timber. The only trees one sees are cultivated and guarded from the ubiquitous herds of sheep and goats. Deforestation produces serious erosion, rapid run-off of water, and forces the people to burn the animal dung needed by their lands to warm themselves. It has also led to the rapid silting of hydroelectric storage reservoirs.

Gas and oil deposits are still in the proving stage. Rumanian technicians have discovered some small producers of lightweight oil (of which 54% is kerosene) and gas rated at three to four million cubic feet. The Afghan Government apparently believes that it is possessed of huge reserves. Several ministers, for example, have built new houses with oil furnaces and the new Ministry of Mines building is to be heated by oil. However, the President of the Petroleum Industries in Mazar-i-Sharif told me that this is wishful thinking from the evidence he now has.

Hydroelectric power is tapped at several places in Afghanistan but almost everywhere it faces rapid silting of its reservoirs due to the rapid rate of erosion. The German Ambassador told me that his technicians think that the new Russian project near Jalalabad faces silting of its reservoir in about eight years. The existing dam down the gorge from Kabul toward the Khyber Pass is nearly choked already. Dams at Pul-i-Khumri and Kunduz supply small amounts of power for the local textile and cement factories. Another small plant operates near Kunduz to supply the town and the combined cotton company.

Coal reserves are rapidly being depleted at the mine near Pul-i-Khumri and much will depend on the new Darr-i-Suf field which is being developed with American assistance. As mentioned above, however, the location of this mine makes it difficult to conceive of the coal ever being economically transported to Kabul.

21. Agricultural needs rank extremely high in priority and relatively little is now being done about them in most of the country. For example, I visited two agricultural "extension and experimentation" farms in the Kataghan Province north of the Hindu Kush, which turned out to be merely rose gardens for the summer leisure of officials. The director of agricultural extension in Kataghan Province, who was trained in India, was scathing in his criticism of his own

department and of the Afghan Government for its lack of effort in this field. Obviously, however, he had simply given up in his job.

An agricultural school in Baghlan is projected for 1,000 students of whom 150 will board at the school. The school is intended to provide trained personnel for the whole northern part of Afghanistan, but it is actually a primary school with a bit of agricultural work tacked on. Realistically, due to the social structure of the country, even if upgraded, it will little affect the rural farming areas. The Director of the school and the Governor both told me that they are hoping for some UN assistance which had been promised but which had not yet materialized.

Farmers are understandably conservative because, living on the edge of ruin themselves, they cannot afford to experiment on unproven reforms. However, from all reports I heard, they can be encouraged to use better methods once they see results. Even a minor failure would pose a serious danger. The Afghan officials to whom I spoke in various parts of the country feared that someone would start a large program and fail to show results, thus making it more difficult for the modest efforts of existing programs to pay off.

After a good look around the rural areas, I found this a somewhat academic problem. Farmers are untouched by any modern notions of agriculture. They need warmth and so burn their only possible source of fertilizer. They cannot afford new seed and so use bad seed and poor cuttings. Their stick plows only scratch the soil. And they are desperately short of water. Much potentially rich land is now waste although water is available in good supply (due to run-off of the snow-covered mountains) at various depths above 200 feet.

Farm animals are miserable. I saw cattle the size of a Mexican burro and chickens as tough as an eagle. At little cost we could make a useful contribution in this field. I believe, however, that except for occasional exceptions, we should concentrate such small-scale activities in our large-scale Helmand project. If we were able to develop a widely-accepted, disease-resistant and hardy breed of cattle, for example, it should be associated with the US-sponsored Helmand scheme.

An exception, which could produce useful local results would be the importation of about 5,000 eggs to the Darr-i-Suf coal field. When chickens are hatched, they could be swapped for the miserable chickens of the valley. The villagers' chickens could be used to feed the coal miners while the better new stock could provide eggs which the villagers could sell to the miners. This would not only provide a considerable U.S "impact" at small cost on the villagers and on the nomads for whom this is the main route from winter and summer grazing areas but would also provide a means of raising the productivity of the area.

Afforestation should be an extremely high priority project. Wood for fuel is the only conceivable substitute for dung. It would be useful to consider the feasibility of introducing a tough fast-growing tree such as mesquite into the mountain and foothill area of northern Afghanistan.

Equally important is the development of a fertilizer industry. It is difficult to imagine any way in which the U.S. could more effectively reach people throughout the country than in assisting in providing them with more to eat. A fertilizer plant is included in the next five-year plan.

Since water is in short supply throughout the country, the U.S. should consider assisting in the development of pilot projects based on windmill-run tube wells. These projects should be large enough to be fully integrated with some method of agricultural credit and cooperative being available. One such project could be put in the north near the boundary between the provinces of Mazar-i-Sharif and Kataghan. A second in the plain at Kabul to be evident to the people of the capital.

Of overwhelming importance, however, is the potentiality of the Helmand Valley for agricultural growth. With this project the American reputation in Afghanistan is completely linked. There is an area of possible extension into the south of a third of a million acres (165,000 is in the Upper Helmand project) by drainage and leveling of land. Sufficient experience has been gained from work on the upper Helmand that many of the earlier pitfalls can be avoided. Marginal lands can be bypassed and the cadres of Afghan officials, many of whom greatly impressed me during the five days I spent with them, can work toward a more centralized and efficient control of the project.

In the context of a strong and well-planned over-all American effort, it should be possible to insist on remedy of the various faults of the old program — farm plot sizes should be raised to at least 20 acres; provision should be made for the establishment of cooperative societies and credit facilities; and tighter control over water including charges for water should be instituted.

We should recognize that not all of the failure of the Helmand scheme are due to Afghan inefficiency. Our own efforts have been highly erratic. For example, when one of our technician is relieved, he may not be replaced for as much as two years. Since April of 1961 we have had no irrigation expert in the area despite the fact that the Helmand is an irrigation project; similarly, a dairy is about to be started without the services of a veterinarian. Etc. In insisting on higher Afghan performance, we must be prepared to accept criticism ourselves and to remedy our obvious faults.

A Peace Corps mission, preferably composed of former 4-H club members, would be an extremely valuable addition to the project to push extension work.

A modest road-building program of $3-5 million should allow the creation of a nucleus of a highway construction and maintenance department, which could eventually spread over the rest of Afghanistan; as this happened, it would open to the national market potentially rich areas in which subsistence farming is now the rule. In my trip from Lashkar Gah through Chahar Burjak, through Nad-i-Ali to Juwain (that is, the whole sweep of the Helmand Valley), I encountered only one vehicle, a truck loaded with people. A road through this area would be approximately 500 kilometers in length and of this amount 112 kilometers exits now in reasonable condition.

Events outside the Helmand will impact powerfully on the project there. Because of the dispute between Pakistan and Afghanistan over Independent Pushtunistan," Pakistan has closed its frontier to the customary migration of the Pathan nomads (aka "Kuchis"). As a consequence, they have been forced northward. This year, many thousands have moved into the Helmand valley. They and their animals are in very bad shape as little rain has fallen. Many animals are expected to die during the foaling season. For them, the Helmand is a short-term refuge and a long-term hope. Many will undoubtedly become settlers.

Ironically, what the Afghans call "Pushtunistan" (and the Pak call "Paktunistan") is a dead letter. I spoke to dozens of Afghans all over the country and not one of them raised the issue with me. Other Americans, who get outside the capital, have had the same experience. When the radio begins discussing Pushtunistan, it is usually turned off. Nonetheless, the dispute has caused a major migration into the Helmand that will change its demography forever.

22. A number of small items will serve to spread the impact of our larger programs throughout the country. Many of these at first glance may seem trivial in comparison with such major projects as the Helmand Valley. But a number of them offer the only feasible and efficient avenues of American activity:

a) USIS activities should give top priority to fostering an Afghan sense of confidence. The Afghan Government would doubtlessly appreciate activities which engender this spirit. For example, it should be possible to produce a film on the project to develop a coal mine at Darr-i-Suf. This is a startling effort at "boot strap" nation-building. American involvement in the project could be played in very low key and major credit given to the Afghan Government for its activities to help its people. A similar project on the Helmand Valley would pay a great dividends.

A major useful activity would be the further inculcation of pride in the Afghan national past. Afghanistan is a colorful country. Its people have an intense interest in their folk tradition. Therefore, activities promoting knowledge of Afghan history and culture would be more productive to the basic American objectives in Afghanistan than abstract and little understood propaganda about the American way of life.

b) A major Afghan problem is protein deficiency. Since the Soviet Union has already invested much money in dam building, the U.S. should consider stocking the resulting lakes with fish. Selfishly, we could gain much good will at probably less than 1% of the cost of the Soviet effort.

c) Through careful sub-contracting of jobs, e.g., in auto and truck maintenance, we should gradually foster the creation of a middle class. There is a large body of men in the country who were trained by Morrison-Knudson International in auto repair and we might consider using our activities to convert them into active businessman. We might further assist in this by providing surplus tool and blacksmith shops from Pentagon stocks.

d) Generation of local currencies will continue to be a major problem. We should not let lack of local counterpart hinder us from those projects we consider important. We could, however, expand our activities in low-bulk goods such as edible oils and protein high products. Due to shipping restrictions we should perhaps cut down on wheat importation.

e) Our powdered milk program, now run by UNICEF and CARE, is not well handled outside Kabul. In the north, the milk is sold and does not reach the children while in the Helmand, the program has been discontinued due to lack of supplies. Where milk is available, it should be provided, in liquid forms, at schools and hospitals and consumption should be on the premises.

f) Since intestinal diseases are prevalent and medicines expensive, the U.S. might want to send a non-Government public health group from Johns Hopkins, Harvard or the Rockefeller Foundation to explore means by which an attack could be made on the public health problems.

g) School enrollment increased 85% during the first five-year plan but there are less than 1/4 million pupils in school, of whom only about 100 each year go on to graduate from college.

Due to the lack of facilities we must seek imaginative approaches to train or retrain people for productive employment. No U.S. project should be contemplated without major emphasis on in-service training. Furthermore, due to the sensitivity of the Afghan Government on sending Afghan nationals abroad for study, we should only rarely bring students to the U.S. Rather, we should place major emphasis on conducting training programs in Afghanistan. This is the only way in which significant numbers of the best qualified students and trainees may be reached.

h) Since the Soviet Union has pre-empted the field of military training, the U.S. can make no significant inroads in military affairs. Our efforts to date in this field have been largely unsuccessful. There is, however, one area, of a paramilitary nature, in which the U.S. might undertake a useful program. This is in the Labor Corps. Young men who are inducted into the army are normally put into the Labor Corps to serve out their conscription period. This Corps is used for road construction and other heavy activities. Members of the Corps are paid approximately fifty cents a month in salary and are subjected to a discipline reminiscent of the chain gang.

Our normal inclination is to have nothing to do with such a group but it would be useful to explore the possibility of taking a small group of this Labor Corps and, under the supervision of the Afghan government, creating from it a disciplined, well paid, properly-uniformed Corps of Engineer-type organization. It should be possible to experiment in this way on any of the major U.S. projects. It would be difficult for the Afghan Government to refuse to allow this experimentation in view of the Soviet pre-emption of the rest of the military field.

23. We should work with and encourage further participation in the development of Afghanistan of non-Communist nations. The Germans have available some $50 million of which a large part is not yet committed. We should develop the closest relationship with the Germans so that our efforts are complementary.

Similarly we should encourage the Italians, who are said to be interested in an alabaster mine near Chahar Burjak, and the Japanese, who have sent technicians to assist in the pottery industry, to take a larger part in the development of Afghanistan.

24. Various aspects of our efforts need careful attention:

a) Our staffing pattern has been erratic and rapid changeover is a block to the close man-to-man relationship upon which hard-won confidence depends.

b) While some members of our mission have earned the highest praise from the Afghans, we must be extremely careful to minimize the ostentation of our mission in the capital. The Russians, who travel to work in busses, at an early hour, are favorably compared with American chauffeur-driven personnel. If the Government pays for cars to be shipped to Afghanistan we should not also need a large fleet of cars and drivers. This aspect of Kabul life is demoralizing to the hard-working personnel in the outer areas of the country.

c) Many of the U.S. activities have gone unappreciated since the reports on them are written in English and the Afghans lack the facilities to translate these. No official consideration (at the Cabinet level) is ever given without a Farsi or Pashto translation. Thus, a study which may have cost $100,000 to do is ignored or buried for lack of a $100 translation. We should provide translations of all our studies.

d) A relatively trivial action which could gain the U.S. a tremendous amount of good will would be the provision of Polaroid cameras for all traveling officials who, upon being entertained in the Afghan manner, could provide their hosts with photos as mementos of the visit. Two or three Americans have done this on their own and have earned a great deal of good will by their efforts.

e) Due to the difficult road conditions, the Ambassador should be supplied with a helicopter capable of climbing over the Hindu Kush range. His attaché plane, a DC-3, which now is mainly used to access the post exchange in Pakistan, would restrict him, even if he chose to visit them, to a few major centers whereas he could make quick and efficient visits throughout the country in a helicopter.

f) We should consider the provision of a small-scale radio transmission facility for outlying posts such as the coal mine at Darr-i-Suf which now lack communication with the outside world.

g) Good equipment for our personnel is essential. In the outlying districts our people are virtually immobilized by poor equipment. The only vehicle we should send to Afghanistan is the Jeep Station Wagon with 4-wheel drive. At the present time many of our vehicles are Corvairs which are useful only on some of the streets in downtown Kabul. Existence of many different types of vehicles also makes maintenance extremely difficult and spare parts unobtainable except after long delays. Furthermore, a single vehicle readily identified as American would be useful in indicating an American presence throughout the country. The Russian "Jeep" is exactly this for the Soviets. Conclusion:

Afghanistan has the will to survive and a carefully thought-out intelligently pursued U.S. policy can greatly increase its chance of doing so.

To achieve maximum benefit from our expenditures in Afghanistan, we should make an over-all five-year commitment. Within that commitment, however, we should exercise a very hard-headed approach in our choice of AID projects.

We should demand that our AID funds be used with discrimination and creatively.

We should undertake no construction project which does not include the creation of a cadre of people capable of maintaining it.

We should concentrate our activities on major projects and then, through the development of better person-to-person relationships, make certain that our major activities are understood and appreciated throughout the country.

We should be extremely cautious to not overplay our hand in Afghanistan. The Afghan ability to survive depends in large part on Soviet acquiescence so a policy which the Soviet Union perceives as threatening will be self-defeating. The spectrum of profitable U.S. action is small. Our goal is not to "win" but to enable the Afghans to retain their freedom.

Similarly, we must be careful not to embarrass the Afghans. By pushing too hard we will create Soviet countermeasures and by too intrusive a relationship with Afghan officials we may undermine their effectiveness within their own government or create suspicion of their loyalties.

At the same time, however, we can capitalize on the genuine Afghan desire for independence. In my talks with a dozen provincial governors throughout the country, I found their feelings on this subject to be extremely encouraging and vigorously held.

What needs to be developed is the muscle of the Afghan economy and a feeling of self-confidence.

A piecemeal, short-term approach by the U.S. will be a waste of our resources and opportunities. If we drift as we are now doing, Afghanistan is likely to slide into the Soviet orbit over the coming decade or so. But if we wish to do so, and act intelligently, we can maintain this buffer, which is how the British always regarded Afghanistan, and so protect our important interests in Iran and Pakistan. Doing so successfully will depend far less on money than on intelligence and tact.

SECRET
(Declassified November 1, 1962)

GREEN UPRISING IN COAL COUNTRY

THE Nation.

'I see an opportunity to accomplish American objectives in Afghanistan while avoiding a course of action that could derail plans for your presidency, just as the Vietnam War ruined the presidency of Lyndon Johnson.'

OCTOBER 19, 2009
TheNation.com

AN OPEN LETTER TO PRESIDENT OBAMA

WILLIAM R. POLK

Open Letter to President Obama

Dear Mr. President,

Although we were separated by more than a decade, we lived a few steps apart in Hyde Park and were both professors at the University of Chicago. There I established the Center for Middle Eastern Studies and was also president of the Adlai Stevenson Institute of International Affairs. Before going to Chicago, during the Kennedy administration I was the member of the Policy Planning Council responsible for the Middle East and Central Asia. A Democrat, I was an early supporter of yours. So I hope you will accept the following analysis and proposals as being from a friend as well as a person with considerable experience on Afghanistan and Pakistan.

In recent events I see an opportunity to accomplish American objectives while avoiding a course of action that could derail plans for your presidency, just as the Vietnam War ruined the presidency of Lyndon Johnson.

According to press accounts, you are being told that America can win the war against the Taliban by employing overwhelming military power. Just like President Johnson's generals, yours keep asking for more troops. You are also being told that we can multiply our power with counterinsurgency tactics. Having made a detailed study (laid out in my book *Violent Politics*) of a dozen insurgencies, ranging from the American Revolution to Afghanistan, and fought by the British, French, Germans and Russians in America, Europe, Africa and Asia, I doubt that you are being well advised. When I was in government, we were told we could achieve victory in Vietnam by the same combination of force and counterinsurgency recommended by your advisers in Afghanistan. But as the editors of the Pentagon Papers concluded, the "attempt to translate the newly articulated theory of counter-insurgency into operational reality.... [through] a mixture of military, social, psychological, economic and political measures.... [were] marked by consistency in results as well as in techniques: all failed dismally."

What actually brought all the insurgencies, including the one in Vietnam, to a halt was the withdrawal of the foreigners. Some foreigners left in defeat, but others left in ways that achieved their most important objectives. I believe you have an opportunity to achieve America's important objectives in Afghanistan.

In Vietnam we never understood the Vietnamese and were defeated; so here I lay out the essential features of Afghanistan, Pakistan and Kashmir and then show how they set the context for a successful policy. I begin with Pakistan.

Pakistan has long been obsessed with Kashmir, frightened of India and favorably inclined toward its Pashtun ethnic minority. To help Pashtun "freedom fighters" in the 1979-89 war against the Soviet Union, we funneled billions of dollars into Pakistan. Opposition to the Soviet Union was our motivation, but Pakistan had a different motivation: to protect Islam. This necessarily involved it not only in Afghanistan but also in Kashmir. Since Pakistan's capital, Islamabad, is about as close to the Indian-held capital of Kashmir, Srinagar, and to the Khyber Pass, which leads into Afghanistan, as New York is to Hartford, both Afghanistan and Kashmir appear to the Pakistanis to be nearly domestic issues.

Kashmir is one of those legacies of the age of imperialism that still blight international relations. Today's problem was created in 1846, when the British sold Kashmir and its Muslim population to a Hindu who became its maharaja. Cruel and rapacious, he and his descendants were bitterly hated by Kashmiris. When the British were leaving South Asia in 1947, they assumed that because the people were mainly Muslim, Kashmir would be folded into what became Pakistan. But the maharaja opted for India. Despite a promise from Jawaharlal Nehru, then prime minister-designate of India, to Lord Louis Mountbatten, then viceroy of India, that a plebiscite would be held to ascertain the wishes of the Kashmiris, it has never been held. Ever since, the Indians have occupied Kashmir with half a million troops as a conquered enemy country. Under Indian rule, thousands of Kashmiris have been imprisoned, hundreds "disappeared" and almost everyone afflicted by lesser tyrannies. In shorthand terms, Kashmir is the Palestine of Central/South Asia. Pakistan and India have fought three wars and innumerable bloody engagements over Kashmir. The drain on the resources of both India and Pakistan has been immense. In part because of the destabilizing effects of this conflict, Pakistan has never developed a durable, coherent government. The only really solid Pakistani organization is the army. Civilian governments have been marked by massive corruption, ineptitude and fragility.

There are many reasons for Pakistan's problems, but one stands out: it is an amalgam of ethnic/cultural nations. The British ruled the Punjab and Sind directly, but sought merely to divide and weaken the Pashtuns. That was the purpose of the Durand Line, which they drew in 1893 along the mountainous frontier. The effect of the line is that today about 25 million Pashtuns live in Pakistan and roughly 14 million live in Afghanistan. The Pashtuns wanted to form an independent nation-state in 1947 but were prevented from doing so. Until its recent military campaign against the Taliban in Swat, the Pakistanis made little attempt to integrate the Pashtuns, but because of them Pakistan has always been deeply affected by Afghanistan.

Afghanistan has always baffled foreign invaders. After three attempts from 1842 to 1919 to rule it, the British gave up; at the end of a decade of costly war, the Russians did as well. Neither understood the complex social and political makeup of the country. Without doing so, we cannot hope to accomplish our objectives, so let me highlight the main points.

When I first went to Afghanistan, in 1962, to prepare a US National Policy Paper, I found a good analogy for the land and the society to be a rocky hill sliced by gullies and covered by 20,000 Ping-Pong balls. The balls represented the autonomous village-states. Politically and economically divided, they shared a common adherence to a blend of primitive Islam and even more primitive tribal custom (varying throughout the country but known in the south as *Pashtunwali*). During their occupation, the Russians crushed many Ping-Pong balls, but they could not defeat enough of them to win. At any given time, roughly 80 percent of the country remained outside Russian control; so the Russians won all the battles but lost the war. Afghanistan became the graveyard of the Soviet Union.

The brutal Soviet occupation shattered the Afghan social structure.

Nearly one in ten Afghans was killed or died, and more than 5 million fled the country. Living wretchedly in refugee camps, mainly in Pakistan, hundreds of thousands of young Afghan men were "reshaped." Like the biblical Children of Israel after forty years in the wilderness, these Afghans emerged very different from their fathers. The new generation kept their stern code of belief, but they lost touch with the humanizing aspects of growing up in families. Living apart from mothers and sisters, many of the young men, mostly Pashtuns, were incorporated into male-only madrassas in which they were housed, fed, armed and radicalized. They emerged as the foot soldiers of the Taliban.

When they were in power, the Taliban enforced an ugly, repressive regime, but it was no worse than some other regimes in Asia and Africa. And, as we can observe, societies and regimes evolve. Look at what has happened in postwar Vietnam. No one in my time in government could have guessed that the Communist regime would evolve into a relatively open and indeed capitalistic society. In Afghanistan there are signs, still faint to be sure, that while the stern code remains intact, at least the Taliban leadership is beginning to modify its program. As I will point out, we can encourage this trend.

But as insurgents, the Taliban remain formidable foes. Our chances of defeating them are poor. Indeed, some independent observers believe they are becoming more popular while we are becoming less popular. They, and many non-Taliban Afghans, regard us, as they regarded the Russians, as foreign, anti-Muslim invaders. Moreover, they see that the government we are backing is corrupt and rapacious. Observers report that it is deeply involved in the drug trade, stealing aid money and even selling US-supplied arms to the Taliban (as the South Vietnamese government did to the Vietcong). Moreover, it is ineffective: its writ hardly runs outside Kabul. Most of the country is in the hands of brutal, predatory warlords. The Karzai government will not last long after our withdrawal — that was the fate of the Soviet puppet government there and of our puppet government in Saigon. Forced to choose between the warlords and the Taliban, Afghans are likely to choose the Taliban. As Gen. Stanley McChrystal has said, "Key groups have become nostalgic for the security and justice Taliban rule provided." Thus, we are courting long-term strategic defeat.

Even in the tactical short run, I believe, trying to defeat the Taliban is not in America's interest. The harder we try, the more likely terrorism will be to increase and spread. As the history of every insurgency demonstrates, the more foreign boots there are on the ground and the harder the foreigners fight, the more hatred they engender. Substituting drone attacks for ground combat is no solution. Having been bombed from the air, I can attest that it is more infuriating than a ground attack.

Our principal objection to the Taliban is that it has given Osama bin Laden and his immediate entourage a base of operations. The two groups, however, are very different: the Taliban are a national political organization, anchored in Afghanistan's largest ethnic group, while Al Qaeda is a loose alliance of dissidents from many countries, united only by their belief that their legitimate aims of ethnic/national self-determination and religious culture are being denied.

For us, the overlap of the two groups comes when we try to get the Taliban to surrender Osama. We have offered what to poor tribesmen is an astronomical reward for him "dead or alive." This ploy has failed. In the Afghan code of *Pashtunwali*, to fail to protect someone who has been given sanctuary (*melmastia*) is a mortal sin, so our attempts to get the Pashtuns to do this insults their sense of honor.

So what, realistically, can we do, and what can we not do? Let me be specific.

On the nuclear issue, Pakistan and India are locked together. The only effective course of action is precisely the one you've recommended: reduction of nuclear weapons everywhere, beginning with us and the Russians. Once momentum is established, we should be able to move toward regional arms control with security guarantees, economic incentives and revocation of the neoconservative-inspired first-strike doctrine. From having served on the Crisis Management Committee during the Cuban Missile Crisis, I can attest that nuclear weapons anywhere are a danger to people everywhere. Your policy is literally vital to us all.

Regarding Al Qaeda, what is important to US security is not capturing Osama bin Laden but disabling him. That is achievable. Here's how: he now enjoys the protection of the Pashtuns. *Melmastia* is a sacred obligation, but the *Pashtunwali* limits it. Osama's Pashtun hosts can insist, with honor, on his stopping actions that endanger them. That could be a key element in a truce that either we or, preferably, Pakistan makes with the Taliban. From that necessary first step, we can move toward dealing with the motivations of the disparate components of Al Qaeda. Since terrorist attacks can be mounted from many places, the only effective long-term defense against them is to deal with their causes.

On the drug trade, it would be convenient if the Afghans solved our drug problem for us, but if we are realistic we must admit that drugs are ultimately our problem. Heroin is proof that market forces really do work. We can make minor adjustments, subsidizing the planting of other crops, buying up what is grown, engaging in defoliation, etc., but as long as people are willing to pay a high price for drugs, producers and distributors will supply them. To put our attempt to stop them in perspective, imagine a foreign invader trying to stop the French from producing wine. We cannot expect any Afghan government to solve our problem, but if we leave, the Taliban would probably again combat the drug trade, as they did in the 1990s.

On our occupation, we need to consider three issues. Does our presence lead toward a sustainable result after our withdrawal? Can the occupation be maintained without turning a large part of the Afghan population and others against us? And can we afford it? I think the answer to all three is no. Consider these factors:

First, it is rare that insurgencies end with the establishment of a regime favored by the occupier —that was the experience of the British and Russians in Afghanistan, the Americans in Vietnam, the French in Algeria. Governments acceptable to the foreign occupier may last a short while, but almost always, those who fought hardest against the foreigner take over when he leaves.

Second, US military intervention in Afghanistan has not only solidified the Taliban as an organization but has also created increasing public support for it. There is much evidence in Afghanistan, as there has been in every insurgency I have studied, that foreign soldiers increase rather than calm hostility. The British found that to be true even in the American Revolution (where the two sides were "cousins," shared the same religion and spoke the same language).

Third, the cost in casualties may not rise to the level of Vietnam or even Iraq, but the financial cost is unlikely to be less. My hunch is that the real cost to the US economy will be $3 trillion to $6 trillion, calculating overall, not just Congressional appropriations. So the Afghan campaign could derail your plans for America, as Vietnam derailed Johnson's Great Society.

On Afghan government reform, there is not much we can do. Corruption runs from top to bottom. As I witnessed in Vietnam, if a government wishes to steal itself to death, foreigners can't stop it. We had an opportunity in the 1960s to help a reforming Afghan government but failed to do so; indeed, we welcomed the man who overthrew it, Mohammed Daoud Khan, because he was anti-Communist. To be realistic, we must assume that even an elected Hamid Karzai will probably not last long after our army departs.

On the Pakistani government, there is even less we can do. There also, massive corruption begins at the top. President Asif Ali Zardari, who is described as "our man," is said to be disliked by the vast majority of Pakistanis and has a long record of mind-boggling dishonesty. I think Zardari's administration will be replaced fairly soon by a military government. If so, we must roll with the punch but try, modestly and unobtrusively, to help encourage the growth of compensating civic institutions.

On Kashmir, as with many world problems, the logical solution is probably not practical. If India and Pakistan could agree to hold a plebiscite, the Kashmiris would probably accept modestly enhanced autonomy under India. Neither Pakistan nor India wants an independent Kashmir, but the current situation is costly for both, so they have established a back channel to inch toward accommodation. We should stay out of this problem.

On Islam, you have set the only intelligent, humane course for our diverse world. The legacy of the neoconservatives and the Bush administration can be overcome, but it will take time for the marvelous speech you gave in Cairo to convince Muslims that we are willing to live with them in a multicultural world.

On getting started, we have been given what I think is a major new opportunity by the Pakistanis. The Taliban are, after all, Pashtuns, Muslims and either Afghans or Pakistanis, while we are none of these. Thus Pakistan can fight the Taliban more acceptably than we can, and because of its longstanding support of their movement, Pakistan can more easily bring the Taliban to the negotiating table. If we are smart, we will take advantage of its attack on the Taliban in Swat by backing out as quickly and as gracefully as possible. How to get out is something former Senator George McGovern and I laid out in our book *Out of Iraq*, which with suitable changes can provide a template for Afghanistan. But as long as we are there, the war will continue, with disastrous consequences for all the things you want to do and we Americans need you to do. We must not follow Britain and Russia into Afghanistan's quicksand.

Respectfully yours,
William R. Polk

LEGITIMATION CRISIS IN AFGHANISTAN

IN THE MEDIA CELEBRATION of our "victory" over the Taliban in the Helmand Valley, little attention has been given to the nature of insurgency: the proper tactic of guerrillas is to fade away before overwhelming power, leaving behind only enough fighters to force the invaders to harm civilians and damage property. This is exactly what happened in the recent fighting in Marja. Faced with odds of perhaps 20 to 1, helicopters, tanks and bombers, the guerrillas wisely dispersed. Victory may not be quite the right description.

That battle will probably be repeated in Kandahar, which, unlike the agricultural area known as Marja, is a large and densely populated city. Other operations are planned, so the Marja "victory" has set a pattern that accentuates military action. This is not conducive to an exit strategy – it will not lead out of Afghanistan but deeper into the country. Indeed, there is already evidence that this is happening. As *The Washington Post* reported shortly after the Marja battle ended, not far away "the Marines are constructing a vast base on the outskirts of town that will have two airstrips, an advanced combat hospital, a post office, a large convenience store and rows of housing trailers stretching as far as the eye can see."

Since the Helmand Valley is the focal point of the military strategy, it is important to understand its role in Afghan affairs. The Helmand irrigation project, begun in the Eisenhower administration as a distant echo of the TVA, was supposed to become a prosperous island of democracy and progress. As a member of the Policy Planning Council in the Kennedy administration, I visited it in 1962. What I found was deeply disturbing: no studies had been made of the land to be developed, which proved to have a sheet of impermeable rock just below the surface that caused the soil to turn saline when irrigated; the land was not sufficiently leveled, so irrigation was inefficient; nothing was done to teach the nomad settlers how to farm; plots were too small to foster the social engineering aim of creating a middle class; and since there were no credit facilities to buy seed, settlers were paying 100 percent interest to moneylenders.

In short, after the buildup of great expectations, disappointment was palpable.

Was it a portent? It seems likely. At the least, it's striking that precisely where we carried out our first civic action program is where the Taliban became most powerful.

So what should that experience have taught us? That we should learn about the Afghans, their country and their objectives before determining our policy toward them. There is much to be learned, but I will here highlight what I believe are the three crucial issues that will make or break our relationship.

The first issue critical to evaluating US policy is the way the Afghans govern themselves. About four in five Afghans live in the country's 20,000 plus villages. During a 2,000-mile trip around the country by jeep, horseback and plane half a century ago, as well as in later trips, it became clear to me that Afghanistan is really thousands of villages, and each of them, although culturally related to its neighbors, is more or less politically independent and economically autarkic.

This lack of national cohesion thwarted the Russians during their occupation: they won many military victories, and through their civic action programs they actually won over many of the villages, but they could never find or create an organization with which to make peace. Baldly put, no one could surrender the rest. Thus, over the decade of their involvement, the Russians won almost every battle and occupied at one time or another virtually every inch of the country, but they lost about 15,000 soldiers – and the war. When they gave up and left, the Afghans resumed their traditional way of life.

That way of life is embedded in a social code (known in the Pashtun areas as *Pashtunwali*) that shapes the particular form of Islam they have practiced for centuries and, indeed, that existed long before the coming of Islam. While there are, of course, notable differences in the Pashtun, Hazara, Uzbek and Tajik areas, shared tradition determines how all Afghans govern themselves and react to foreigners.

Among the shared cultural and political forms are town councils (known in the Pashtun areas as *jirgas* and in the Hazara area as *ulus or shuras*). The members are not elected but are accorded their status by consensus. These town councils are not, in our sense of the word, institutions; rather, they are "occasions." They come together when pressing issues cannot be resolved by the local headman or respected religious figure. Town councils are the Afghan version of participatory democracy, and when they act they are seen to embody the "way" of their communities.

Pashtunwali demands protection (*melmastia*) of visitors. Not to protect a guest is so grievous a sin and so blatant a sign of humiliation that a man would rather die than fail. This, of course, has prevented the Afghans from surrendering Osama bin Laden. Inability to reconcile our demands with their customs has been at the heart of our struggle for the past eight years.

As put forth in both the Bush and Obama administrations, our objective is to prevent Al Qaeda from using Afghanistan as a base for attacks on us. We sharpened this objective to the capturing or killing of bin Laden. That is popular with US voters, but even if we could force the Afghans to surrender him, it would alienate the dominant Pashtun community. Thus it would probably increase the danger to us. It is unnecessary, since a resolution of this dilemma in our favor has been available for years. While *Pashtunwali* does not permit a protected guest to be surrendered, it allows the host, with honor, to prevent the guest from engaging in actions that endanger the host. In the past, the Taliban virtually imprisoned bin Laden, and they have repeatedly offered – provided we agree to leave their country – to meet our demand that Al Qaeda not be allowed to use Afghanistan as a base. Although setting a withdrawal date would enable us to meet our objective, we have turned down their offers.

<u>The second crucial</u> issue in evaluating our policy is the way the people react to our civic action programs.

Afghanistan is a barren, landlocked country with few resources, and its people have suffered through virtually continuous war for thirty years. Many are wounded or sick, with some even on the brink of starvation. The statistics are appalling: more than one in three subsists on the equivalent of less than 45 cents a day, almost one in two lives below the poverty line and more than one in two preschool children is stunted because of malnutrition. They are the lucky ones; one in five dies before the age of 5. Obviously, the Afghans need help, so we think they should welcome our efforts to aid them. But independent observers have found that they do not. Based on some 400 interviews, a team of Tufts University researchers found that "Afghan perceptions of aid and aid actors are overwhelmingly negative." We must ask why this is.

The reason, I think, is that the Taliban understand from our pronouncements that civic action is a form of warfare. The Russians taught them about civic action long ago, and Gen. David Petraeus specifically proclaimed in his Iraq days, "Money is my most important ammunition in this war." Thus many ordinary citizens see our programs as Petraeus described them – as a method of control or conquest – and so support or at least tolerate the Taliban when they destroy our projects or prevent our aid distribution.

To get perspective on this, it is useful to look at Vietnam. There too we found that the people resented our efforts and often sided with our enemies, the local equivalent of the Taliban — the Viet Minh, or, as we called them, the Vietcong. The Vietminh killed officials, teachers and doctors and destroyed even beneficial works. Foreigners thought their violence was bound to make the people hate them. It didn't. Like the Kabul government, the South Vietnamese regime was so corrupt and predatory that few supported it even to get aid. When we "inherited" the war in Vietnam, we thought we should sideline the corrupt regime, so we used our own officials to deliver aid directly to the villagers. Aid got through, but our delivering it further weakened the South Vietnamese government's rapport with its people.

Is this relevant to Afghanistan? Reflect on the term used by Gen. Stanley McChrystal when his troops moved into Helmand: he said he was bringing the inhabitants a "government in a box, ready to roll in." That government is a mix of Americans and American-selected Afghans, neither sent by the nominal national government in Kabul nor sanctioned by local authorities.

How will the Afghans react to McChrystal's government? President Karzai was at least initially opposed, seeing the move as undercutting the authority of his government. We don't yet know what the inhabitants thought. But we do know that when we tried similar counterinsurgency tactics in Vietnam, as the editor of the massive collection of our official reports, The Pentagon Papers, commented, "all failed dismally."

If we aim to create and leave behind a reasonably secure society in Afghanistan, we must abandon this failed policy and set a firm and reasonably prompt date for withdrawal. Only thus can we dissociate humanitarian aid from counterinsurgency warfare. This is because once a timetable is clearly announced, a fundamental transformation will begin in the political psychology of our relationship. The Afghans will have no reason (or progressively less reason, as withdrawal begins to be carried out) to regard our aid as a counterinsurgency tactic. At that point, beneficial projects will become acceptable to the local jirgas, whose members naturally focus on their own and their neighbors' prosperity and health. They will then eagerly seek and protect what they now allow the Taliban to destroy.

If under this different circumstance the Taliban try to destroy what the town councils have come to see as beneficial, the councils will cease to provide the active or passive support, sanctuary and information that make the Taliban effective. Without that cooperation, as Mao Zedong long ago told us, they will be like fish with no water in which to swim. Thus, setting a firm and clear date for withdrawal is essential.

This leaves us with the third issue, the central government. We chose it and we pay for it. But as our ambassador, Gen. Karl Eikenberry, has pointed out in leaked reports, it is so dishonest it cannot be a strategic partner. It is hopelessly corrupt, and its election last year was fraudulent; General Petraeus even told President Obama that it is a "crime syndicate." It is important to understand why it lacks legitimacy in the eyes of its people.

For us, the answer seemed simple: a government must legitimize itself the way we legitimize ours, with a reasonably fair election. But our way is not the Afghan way. Their way is through a process of achieving consensus that ultimately must be approved by the supreme council of state, the *loya jirga*. The apex of a pyramid of village, tribal and provincial assemblies, the *loya jirga*, according to the Constitution, is "the highest manifestation of the will of the people of Afghanistan."

Like the Russians, we have opposed moves to allow Afghanistan to bring about a national consensus. In 2002 nearly two-thirds of the delegates to a *loya jirga* signed a petition to make the exiled king, Zahir Shah, president of an interim government to give time for Afghans to work out their future. But we had already decided that Hamid Karzai was "our man in Kabul." So, as research professor Thomas Johnson and former foreign service officer in Afghanistan Chris Mason wrote last year, "massive US interference behind the scenes in the form of bribes, secret deals, and arm twisting got the US-backed candidate for the job, Hamid Karzai, installed instead.... This was the Afghan equivalent of the 1964 Diem Coup in Vietnam: afterward, there was no possibility of creating a stable secular government." An interim Afghan government certified by the *loya jirga* would have allowed the traditional way to achieve consensus; but, as Selig Harrison reported, our ambassador at the time, Zalmay Khalilzad, "had a bitter 40-minute showdown with the king, who then withdrew his candidacy." We have suffered with the results ever since.

Could we reverse this downward trend? If we remove our opposition to a *loya jirga*, will the Kabul government respond? Probably not so long as America is willing to pay its officials and protect them. But if we set a clear timetable for withdrawal, members of the government will have a strong self-interest in espousing what they will see as the national cause, and they will call for a *loya jirga*. Indeed, President Karzai already has.

Would such a move turn Afghanistan over to the Taliban? Realistically, we must anticipate that many, perhaps even a majority, of the delegates, particularly in the Pashtun area, will be at least passive supporters of the Taliban. I do not see any way this can be avoided. Our attempts to win over the "moderates" while fighting the "hardliners" is an echo of what we tried in Vietnam. It did not work there and did not work for the Russians in Afghanistan. It shows no sign of working for us now. As a 2009 Carnegie Endowment study of our occupation and the Taliban reaction to it laid out, even after their bloody defeat in 2001, "there have been no splinter groups since its emergence, except locally with no strategic consequences."

Nor, as I have shown in my history of two centuries of insurgencies, *Violent Politics*, are we likely to defeat the insurgents. Natives eventually wear down foreigners. The Obama administration apparently accepts this prediction. As The Washington Post reported this past fall, it admits that "the Taliban cannot be eliminated as a political or military movement, regardless of how many combat forces are sent into battle."

A *loya jirga* held soon is the best hope to create a reasonably balanced national government. This is partly because in the run-up to the national loya jirga, local groups will struggle to enhance or protect local interests. Their action will constitute a brake on the Taliban, who will be impelled to compromise. Today the Taliban enjoy the aura of national defenders against us; once we are no longer a target, that aura will fade.

If we are smart enough to allow the Afghans to solve their problems in their own way rather than try to force them to adopt ours, we can begin a sustainable move toward peace and security. Withdrawal is the essential first step. Further fighting will only multiply the cost to us and lead to failure.

April 1, 2010

Changing the Guard. Keeping the Drill

ON JUNE 24, the *International Herald Tribune* published an editorial from its parent, *The New York Times*, entitled "Obama's Decision." Both the attribution – printing in the two newspapers which ensures that the editorial will reach both directly and through subsidiary reprinting almost every "decision maker" in the world – and the date – just before the appointment of David Petraeus to succeed Stanley McChrystal – are significant. They could have suggested a momentary lull in which basic questions on the Afghan war might have been reconsidered.

That did not happen. The President made clear his belief that the strategy of the war was sound and his commitment to continue it even if the general responsible for it had to be changed.

The editorial sounded a different note arising from the events surrounding the fall of General McChrystal: Mr. Obama, said *The Times*, "must order all of his top advisers to stop their sniping and maneuvering" and come up with a coherent political and military plan for driving back the Taliban and building a minimally effective Afghan government."

In short, Mr. Obama must get his team together and evolve a plan.

Unfortunately, the task he faces is not that simple.

First, consider the "team." It has two major components, the military officers whom McChrystal gathered in Kabul. As they made clear in the *Rolling Stone* interview, they think of themselves as "Team America" and hold in contempt everyone else. Those who don't fully subscribe to their approach to the war are unpatriotic, stupid or cowardly. Those officers are not alone. Agreeing with them is apparently now a large part of the professional military establishment. They are the junior officers whom David Petraeus and Stanley McChrystal have selected, promoted and with whom they take their stand.

The other "component" is not a group but many groups with different agendas and constituencies. The most crucial for my purposes here are the advisers to the President; they were dismissed out of hand as "the wimps in the

White House." Most, but not all, were civilians. Other senior military officers, now retired, who are not part of "Team America" anzd its adherents were also disparaged. Famously, General Jim Jones, the director of the National Security Council staff, was called a "clown."

These were the comments that forced Mr. Obama's hand and were what the press latched upon to explain the events. But many missed the point that McChrystal had just a few days before his dismissal written a devastating report on his mission. Confidential copies of it were obtained by the London newspaper, *The Independent on Sunday*, which published it today, but of course the President had seen it earlier. Essentially, its message boiled down to failure.

McChrystal pointed out that he faced a "resilient and growing insurgency," with too few troops and expected no progress in the coming six months. Despite expenditures of at least $7 billion a month, his politico-military strategy wasn't working. Within weeks of the "victory" over the Taliban in the agricultural district of Marja, the Taliban were back and the box full of government he had announced proved to be nearly empty. As the expression went in the days of the Vietnam war, whatever happened during the day, the guerrillas "owned the night." As he described it, Marja was the "bleeding ulcer" of the American campaign.

Behind McChrystal's words, the figures were even more devastating: Marja, despite the descriptions in the press is not a town, much less a city; it is a hundred or so square miles of farm land with dispersed hamlets in which about 35,000 people live and work. Into that small and lightly populated area, McChrystal poured some 15,000 troops, and they failed to secure it.

To appreciate what those figures mean, consider them in context of Petraeus's counterinsurgency theory, on which McChrystal was basing his strategy. As he had explained it, Marja should be taken, secured and held. Then an administration – McChrystal's "government in a box" – should be imposed upon it. Despite all the hoopla about the brilliant new strategy, it was hardly new. In fact it was a replay of the strategy the French General Lyautey called the *tache d'huile* (the oil spot) and applied in Indochina over a century ago. We also tried it in Vietnam, renaming it the "ink spot." The hope was that the "spot," once fixed on the Marja, would smudge into adjoining areas and so eventually spread across the country. Clear and simple, but unfortunately, like so much in counterinsurgency theory, it never seemed to work.

Petraeus's counterinsurgency theory also illuminated how to create the "spot." What was required was a commitment of forces in proportion to native population size. Various numbers have been put forth but a common number is about one soldier for each 50 inhabitants. Marja was the area chosen for the "spot." The people living there, after all, were farmers, wedded to the land, and so should be more tractable than the wild warriors along the tribal frontier. Moreover, it was the place where the first significant American aid program, the Helmand Valley Authority, had been undertaken in the late 1950s. So, if an area were to be favorable to Americans, it ought to be Marja. But, to take no chances, General McChrystal decided to employ overwhelming force. So, what is particularly stunning about the failure in Marja is that the force applied was not the counterinsurgency model of 1 soldier for each 50 inhabitants but nearly 1 soldier for each 2 inhabitants.

If these numbers were projected to the planned offensive in the much larger city of Kandahar, which has a population of nearly 500,000, they become impossibly large. Such an attack would require at least four times as many US and NATO as in Marja. That is virtually the entire fighting force and what little control over Marja and most other areas, perhaps even the capital, Kabul, that now exists would have to be given up or else large numbers of additional American troops would have to be engaged. Moreover, in response to such an attack, it would be possible for the insurgents also to redeploy so the numbers would again increase.

The more fundamental question, which needs to be addressed, is why didn't this relatively massive introduction of troops with awesome and overwhelming fire power succeed. Just a few days before he was fired, as I have mentioned, General McChrystal posed, but could not answer, that question. I hope President Obama is also pondering it.

For those who read history, the answer is evident. But, as I have quoted in my book *Understanding Iraq*, the great German philosopher, Georg Willhelm Friedrich Hegel, despaired that "Peoples and governments never have learned anything from history or acted on principles deduced from it" and, therefore, as the American philosopher George Santayana warned us, not having learned from history, we are doomed to repeat it. Indeed, it seems that each generation of Americans has to start all over again to find the answers. Who among our leaders and certainly among college students now really remembers Vietnam?

So, consider these simple facts:

The first fact, whether we like it or not, is that nearly everyone in the world has a deep aversion to foreigners on his land. As far as we know, this feeling goes back to the very beginning of our species because we are territorial animals. Dedication to the protection of homeland permeates history. And the sentiment has never died out. Today we call it nationalism. Nationalism in various guises is the most powerful political idea of our times. Protecting land, culture, religion and people from foreigners is the central issue in insurgency. The former head of the Pakistani intelligence service, who has had unparallelled experience with the Taliban over many years, advised us that we should open our eyes to seeing the Afghan insurgents as they see themselves: "They are freedom fighters fighting for their country and fighting for their faith." We agreed when they were fighting the Russians; now, when many of the same people are fighting us, we see them only as terrorists. That label does not help us understand why they are fighting.

Instead of asking why they are fighting, counterinsurgents think they can overcome aversion to foreign invaders by "renting" the natives. In Marja, we not only put in a large military contingent but, as Rajiv Chandrasekaran reported this month in The *Washington Post*, we offered to employ virtually the entire adult population, some 10,000 people. Unquestionably such efforts do persuade some of the people for some of the time. But not all or permanently. In Marja, only 1,200 people signed up for the jobs we offered.

Why so few? After all, the Afghans, as I wrote in an earlier article, have suffered through virtually continuous war for thirty years. Many are wounded or sick, with some even on the brink of starvation. More than one in three subsists on the equivalent of less than 45 cents a day, almost one in two lives below the poverty line and more than one in two preschool children is stunted because of malnutrition. They are the lucky ones; one in five dies before the age of 5. Obviously, the Afghans need help, so we think they should welcome our efforts to aid them. But Marja shows that they do not. Nation-wide, independent observers have found that attitude is common: most do not want us there, even giving them aid. And even those who do are fairly easily dissuaded by the insurgents.

Threats or attacks by the insurgents have brought them into our gunsights. In Afghanistan, as in Vietnam, we have tried to so weaken the insurgents that they cannot effectively block our programs. Our "body counts" in Vietnam showed that we killed off the entire Viet Minh several times over and today we are told that the ranks of the Taliban have been severely depleted. But, because the motivation that energized the first group of insurgents is widely shared, and is usually intensified by foreign military action, which by its nature is regarded by many of the natives as unjustified and brutal, new insurgents as well as supporters of the temporarily evicted insurgents will emerge from among the inhabitants of the oil/ink spot. Outsiders may have come in, but, according to US military intelligence about three in four insurgents fight within five miles of their homes. They were "home" and taking up arms within a month in Marja.

Indeed, the campaign may have been, to use that cumbersome locution of governmentese, "counter-productive." According to the former British counter-terrorism chief and current head of the UN monitoring mission, Richard Barnett, as cited in *The Guardian/The Observer* last week, "Attempts by British and American forces to expand their control over Afghan territory over the past 12 months have been counter-productive and led to a worsening security situation."

The second fact is that those insurgents who don't get killed are the ones who have learned three simple ways to defeat the counterinsurgents.

The first of these ways to defeat counterinsurgents is to use appropriate tactics – never stand and fight. Insurgents can see that their enemies outgun, and usually far out-number, them so they should hit and run – lay mines, ambush patrols, disrupt logistics but never get caught. Drawing on a Kenyan fable, this has been termed "the war of the flea and the lion." The flea bites and jumps away. The powerful lion swats, occasionally hits, but eventually tires and moves away. Lions don't defeat fleas.

The second way insurgents can defeat the counterinsurgent is a form of jujitsu – using his strength against him. His strength is his superiority in weapons. So the insurgent seeks to incite him to use them. Inevitably, caught in the middle, the people – who are after all the "spoil" in insurgency warfare – get hurt. And when they get hurt, they naturally come to hate those who fire the weapons. In Vietnam, insurgents would sometimes enter a "neutral" village, shoot at an American airplane and then steal away. The attacked airplane would call in troops or gunships. The villagers would suffer and would be confirmed in their hatred of the Americans. It was brutal but very effective.

Counterinsurgents think they can avoid this problem by withholding as much as possible of their lethal power. But doing so is very difficult. Their soldiers also get hurt and angry. And they come to hate the locals – wogs, gooks, rag heads, untermenschen – who appear to them dirty, slovenly, corrupt and cowardly. No one can be trusted when even children act as spies or carry bombs. Soldiers make bad neighbors to civilians in the best of circumstances and insurgency is not one of those circumstances. As I have pointed out in my book, *The Birth of America*, it was the presence of even superbly disciplined British troops in Boston that touched off the American Revolution.

The third way insurgents can defeat invaders is by destroying their local puppets. Ruling another country is, of course, expensive and difficult so foreigners have almost always and everywhere enrolled willing natives to help. In the American Revolution we called those people "the Loyalists." In Vietnam, they were the government of the South. In Afghanistan they are the "Kabul government."

So the insurgents regard collaborators – "Quislings" as we called them in the Second World War – as their prime target. In America, the colonists threatened, tarred and feathered, lashed, imprisoned, hanged or drove away tens of thousands of the Loyalists. In Vietnam, French police records show that in the 1950s, the Viet Minh virtually wiped out the administration of the southern government, murdering policemen, postmen, judges and other civil servants as well as teachers and doctors. And today in Afghanistan, as Rod Nordland reported in *The New York Times* on June 10, "The Taliban have been stepping up a campaign of assassinations in recent months against officials and anyone else associated with local government in an attempt to undermine counterinsurgency operations in the south."

One Afghan told Nordland, "I know many people who are afraid to take jobs with the government or the aid community now. It's a very effective and very efficient campaign; the armed opposition are using this tool because it works." Even from a nationalist perspective, this is very rough justice. But many Afghans appear to believe it is both "justice" and Afghan justice.

To validate their actions, the insurgents must themselves supply what the foreigners and their local supporters offer. We have full records of how insurgents did this in Yugoslavia and Greece during the Second World War. The records are not so open for Afghanistan as yet. But, we know from a study by the US Government Accountability Office (GAO) that the Taliban has set up a "widespread paramilitary shadow government...in a majority of Afghanistan's 34 provinces."

One of the things these shadow governments do is administer the law. For years, I have read reports contrasting what happens in a government court and a Taliban court. In the government court, cases languish for months or years while bribes are collected. A UN study found earlier this year that officials shake down their fellow citizens for an amount that is nearly a quarter of the country's gross domestic product. In a Taliban court, there is no bribery and no delay: Islamic law as defined by Afghan custom is immediate. From our point of view, this too is very rough justice, if justice at all, but in insurgencies, people appear willing to put aside the niceties of peaceful life. In our Revolution we did too.

So where are we?

For some years I have been reading every study, poll, government release, press report and assorted other documents I could find. What I see is a decline, accelerated in the last two years, of "security." In 2009, there were 8,159 "incidents" involving bombs (IEDs), and in the first four months of 2010 there have already been almost half that many. But, more important than "security," I think, is the widely held belief that America is not moving toward anything that can be considered success. And certainly not on anything like President Obama's reëlection-related timetable.

I have been taxed with being severe in this judgment, but listen to General McChrystal's Chief of Operations, Major General Bill Mayville. Having described the war as unwinnable, he said "It's not going to look like a win, smell like a win or taste like a win. This war is going to end in an argument." Even his choice of the word "argument" may be unduly optimistic. In Vietnam, the disgraceful scene of the helicopter taking a few people off the roof of our embassy – while abandoning others of our supporters to the rough justice of the Viet Minh – is hard to put out of mind.

But, I am astonished to find how many Americans today do manage to put not only the now-distant Vietnam war but also the wars in Iraq and Afghanistan out of their minds. In lecturing around the country, I find little interest among the American public in the growing number of wounded – now over a hundred thousand – or the casualties. Based on informal talks with members of my audiences, I have come to attribute this is to the fact that, whereas in the Vietnam war, our army was made up of draftees who were drawn from our families, today our army, and therefore our casualties, come in high proportion from the disadvantaged, minorities and foreigners. As a man in one lecture I gave in Arizona put it bluntly, "they just aren't our people." The pain does not reach most of us. Recent polls show a different view in Europe. Some 72% of the citizens of our principal ally, Great Britain, want their troops home immediately and 62% of the Germans agree.

Surprisingly, the vast expenditure of money on the war does not seem, at least yet, to worry Americans either. As a people, we seem far more ready to spend money on warfare than on our own health, housing, jobs and education.

But, worry about the course the war is taking appears strongest in precisely those places where it is most crucial – the ruling circles of Afghanistan. Recognition of this development was apparently what motivated Afghan President Hamid Karzai at least to talk about a new peace initiative: he must see that not only his regime but his life is in danger. Closer to it than we, he must know that the war is being lost.

So what can America do?

We can begin by being realistic. We were sold a phony policy in counterinsurgency – one that essentially tried to substitute technique for politics, enthusiasm for wisdom, money for knowledge. As I have shown in my book on insurgency, terrorism and guerrilla war, *Violent Politics*, there is no record that counterinsurgency ever worked anywhere, and it is certainly not working now in Afghanistan. The neoconservatives also sold the Bush administration on the quixotic idea of "regime change." Whole cultures and the regimes they embody are not phantoms to be whisked away, overthrown, replaced by foreign mandate. Trying to do so may be quixotic, but we should remember what Cervantes tells us the real windmill did to Don Quixote.

But, can we just "cut and run?" That question is meant to turn off intelligent analysis. So the proper answer to it is 'No, but unless we come to a realistic policy, we are likely to be forced eventually to do something like our disgraceful exit from Vietnam. Therefore, let us think carefully and move prudently before it is too late.'

So what should be included in a realistic policy?

The first thing is to go beyond merely saying that a solution may ultimately and under certain unidentified circumstances involve negotiation to actually working to bring negotiation about. Astute commentators have pointed up the obvious: we have opposed negotiation at every opportunity and still do so. We complain that we don't think the Taliban now want to negotiate. Were I Mullah Umar, I would not either.

Why not? Is it just because he is a bad man? A narrowminded ideologue? Or because he is driven by a hatred of freedom and democracy? Otherwise sober and intelligent people have adduced each of these. They don't get us very far. So let us examine the "negotiating climate."

We have repeatedly said that we want to bloody the insurgents to make them more amenable to our terms. So our concentration has been, and still is, on killing enough of them to weaken their movement. Suppose we manage to do that, what do we then offer?

One proposal under discussion is "reintegration," which the US favors. Under this rubric, we have said that we are willing to forgive those low-level Taliban footsoldiers who defect. Even more, we have espoused a new order for them in the "Afghan Peace and Reintegration Plan." As Joshua Partlow summarized in *The Washington Post,* the defector who renounces violence and promises to support the constitution is then set out on a trajectory that he is bound to regard as humiliating: first, he must be fingerprinted and given a retinal scan; then he must get his fellow tribesmen to vouch for his sincerity; next he must submit to a course in Islam given by an appointee of the government. Because he is likely to be at least a graduate of a religious school, and may be a man of religion himself, this is no mean psychological hurdle. But, never fear, if he does, there is a pay-off: As Jon Boon reported in *The Guardian*, he will be offered a manual job in such things as carpet-weaving. In Afghanistan, that is a task for children. There is not a great deal of incentive in this plan. One is tempted to ask: did those who designed it want it to fail?

The other proposal, which America opposes, is aimed at more senior insurgents. "Reconciliation" holds out only the prospect of eventual but limited participation in the existing Karzai government for those judged innocent of any serious crime. Excluded, of course, are the commanders. Again think back to Vietnam: could anyone have seriously thought that the Viet Minh would have accepted a minor role in the despised Saigon government, when they thought they were winning. And today, are the terms offered in this proposal likely to be even vaguely attractive to the Taliban? It is hard to imagine.

But, if they are not acceptable, why can't these proposals at least be discussed? Under discussion they might be modified in ways that would make them acceptable. The answer is a wonderful example of "Catch-22."

The "22nd catch" is that American military command maintains a secret list of insurgents who can be shot on sight. Because the list is secret, no Talib can know if he is on it. So, he is apt to suspect that the offer of negotiation is really a trap. It is very hard to negotiate with anyone when you are trying to kill him. As Steve Coll pointed out in a perceptive article in *The New Yorker*, even President Karzai is "powerless to offer the Taliban a secure place to negotiate." Moreover, Coll identified a joker in the American strategic hand which presumably, Mullah Umar and his comrades will also have spotted: "Whether talks succeed or fail," Coll points out, "the very act of opening serious negotiations could touch off divisions and confusion within the Taliban leadership."

Thus, if we are honest with ourselves, we can understand at least part of what makes the Taliban reluctant to deal with us or our Afghan proxy. We don't start with a hand outstretched, as President Charles DeGaulle did with his October 1958 proclamation of the "Peace of the Brave," in a move to start the process of ending the Algerian war. We start with a hand hidden behind our back that may contain at least a handcuff and perhaps a gun. It will take time and effort to change these appreciations. That process can happen only if there is a change in the reality of our policy.

President Obama has said that a change in our policy is not in the cards. So is there another way that negotiations might be begun?

This might be the place where Pakistan and/or other neighboring countries, including Iran, could be helpful. We are told that we should not trust Pakistan because it has its own (not our) policy toward Afghanistan. Of course it has. As I have pointed out elsewhere, the Khyber Pass between Pakistan and Afghanistan is about as close to Islamabad as Hartford is to New York. And the two countries share millions of Pashtuns as their citizens. To imagine that Pakistan does not and should not have an Afghan policy is criminal naïveté. But that it could play a useful role is surely evident.

Iran is now our favorite whipping boy. We are furious with it and it is fearful of us. I won't dilate on that dangerous situation here as I have dealt with it in length in my book, *Understanding Iran*. Let us just say, it is doubtful that the Iranians would want to do us any favors.

But we should keep in mind two things: the one is that an end to the war in Afghanistan would be to the national interest of Iran as meetings between Karzai and Ahmadinejad have already made clear. So apart from their feelings about America, the Iranians might play a useful role in Afghanistan. The second is a precedent: Iran actually has furthered American interests in Afghanistan in the past. At a critical point, it helped us to overcome in the Taliban in the Western, mainly Shia Muslim, area around Heart. Apart from these ventures, Iran also deployed a significant part of its army and police force to try to interdict the drug traffic. Since it is Afghanistan's neighbor, we cannot exclude Iran from Afghan affairs. And, of course, if we could work out even a minimal accommodation with Iran, it could be a major force for peace in Afghanistan.

So what is really up for negotiation with the Taliban?

Apart from timetables, reparations, further aid, and such technicalities, the core issue is the internal social/political/religious balance of the country – not the longevity or composition of the Karzai government.

It isn't only that the Karzai government is corrupt, weak and almost universally hated – all of which is true – but that its inner circle and hangers-on have already begun to jump ship. With their hands deep in our pockets – as a recent Congressional study ("Warlord, Inc.) documented for just one activity, road transport, and as others have charged for years in virtually every other area – and in the pockets of their poorer citizens, whom they fleece with apparent abandonment, they are moving hundreds of millions of dollars out of the country and, at the same time, many have put their families abroad. All this apparently has been documented by, among other things, wiretaps on senior officials. We saw the same flight of money to foreign bank accounts and people to safe havens during the war in Vietnam. It was personally smart but governmentally disastrous. So, the collapse of the Karzai government is already underway. Saving it is probably beyond our capacity. Nor, in the opinion of most observers, would the government's collapse be a major loss. But it would be beneficial to us and to the Afghans if, as in Vietnam, it could last for a while. That is, it would be beneficial if it could help to get negotiations underway and if we are smart enough to use the time we are given to get our policy in order.

What would be a tragic and dangerous loss would be for the civil war to recommence or for the rapacious warlords to give up the pretence of legality and revert to raping and pillaging.

How to avoid these two outcomes is what negotiations must be all about.

We don't do ourselves a favor with wishful thinking. We were not able to prevent the Viet Minh from taking over all of Vietnam. Their takeover was initially a horrible ordeal. Many people suffered and many were killed. I think we might be able to leave Afghanistan in better condition if we act intelligently and soon and if we get others to help us. And we can take hope from what subsequently happened in Vietnam. Finally, the Afghans are a resilient people and may, themselves, also have learned by their ordeal.

June 27, 2010

PART II

IRAQ

Return to Baghdad

FROM FAR OUT IN THE Great Syrian Desert, the amber glow of Baghdad, its lights mixed with the dust of the Mesopotamian Plain, announced the city. How different, already, it appeared from the darkened town into which I drove 30 years ago in 1951. Thus, even before I arrived, the theme of my visit seemed set: I would see much that was totally new, look for places that no longer existed, but find themes and issues which were hardly changed.

Since Iraq is locked in a furious if stalemated 3-year-old war with Iran, I hardly expected to see the warm glow on the horizon and then to be able to pick out thousands of lights as the city took shape below the plane. It might have been Denver or Hartford. If ever a country sought a military target, Baghdad was a perfect gift: each street, each factory, each house was brilliantly etched against the dark ground.

The ironic contrasts were not merely on the ground. In the plane was a returning contingent of diplomats from the still functioning Iraqi Embassy in Tehran, nervously and happily talking of relatives and homes, friends and colleagues, the prospects of new assignments and the dangers of recent experiences, while just beyond the runway lights, as I later saw, gunners sat day and nights on the hard iron seats of anti-aircraft cannon.

When the plane pulled up to the terminal gate, I walked into a gleaming white corridor that connected the plane directly to a huge entrance hall. Down an escalator the passengers filed to the immigration booths. "Most welcome to Baghdad, Sir," said a tall uniformed official as he checked and then stamped my passport. In no more time than it took to write about it, I was through the barrier and, walking a few steps, I found my often-lost luggage already on the conveyor belt. Was this Baghdad or Singapore?

And as I was to do so often in the days ahead, I remembered an earlier passage. Shortly after the 1958 coup d'état, I was leaving from the "old" airport, then just two shacks on a lightly tarmaced strip, without conveyor belts and with only minimal activity of any kind, when out of the "other" shack emerged two dozen young women. One sat down beside me on the plane to tell me her sad tale: signed on as a cabaret dancer, she had "opened" in Beirut to accompanying gunfire as the civil war there began. Moving over to Cyprus, she watched the first live rounds of the war against the British. Retreating to Baghdad, her show got in one night before being closed by the coup. Her tale of woe complete, with obvious effort waving her golden, heavily braceleted arms, she lamented, "And since then I have had absolutely nothing to do."

Those days of frivolity seemed like memories of the Middle Ages in the puritanical and suspicious Iraq of today's Baath Government. But life, even that kind of life, obviously goes on. Now, not in the sense of pleasure, but of today's currency shortage and tomorrow's development. Topless swimming and décolleté gambling are in — mainly for the Gulf Arab brothers at the huge new Sheraton Hotel.

Three weeks before, I had made arrangements to visit Iraq, but, in the long interval, I had been unable to confirm my arrival time. From long experience, I was sure that the arrangements (and I) would have been forgotten. I planned to jump in a taxi. But, to my surprise, even the immigration officer knew I was expected. "Two escort officers of the Foreign Minister were here to meet you," he explained, "but when they were told that the plane was taking the Iraqi diplomatic mission to the other side of the airport, they raced over there, thinking you might get off. Sorry for the delay. They will be right back."

That was a sign of changed times. A new efficiency, a new seriousness, was evident everywhere. Particularly, as I would see, this was true at the front.

In just a few minutes, the escort did indeed arrive. Together, we shook hands and walked out of the air conditioned hall into the close, thick, warm air of the Baghdad night. Again a flashback: one August noon, years ago, the airplane door opened and an oven blast hit me like a slap in the face. Of course, that was August and noon, but even discounting for the September evening, Baghdad already seemed gentler.

Driving out of the airport, with its many tiered parking garage, we were immediately on double, divided highways, clean and well lit. Twice on the way to the city, we passed a highway cleaning truck. My memories flooded past me. On my visit, in 1951, from about as far out as the airport now is, I had had real trouble finding the city, so dark and unmarked was the collection of pot holes and ditches that served as a road. Now, at 150 kilometers an hour, we shot past scores of partially finished new building complexes, crossed the Tigris by the new bridge, and once into the real Baghdad, confronted the huge bas-relief my old friend Jawad Salim had designed to commemorate the 1958 coup d'état.

The Iraqi Baath regime is still proud of the 1958 coup from which it derives some of its mythology, but the then "sole leader," General Abdul Karim Qasim, has long been, as Lenin would have said, "consigned to the dust bin of history." Cult lives on but Qasim's name and face have been replaced on every wall by portraits, in every conceivable pose and style of dress, by President Saddam Husain.

A Baghdad joke puts it well: 'if you go down the street, turn right, go into the first shop, and look up, what will you see ?' Answer: the same thing you will see if you walk up the street, turn left and go into the first house, the smiling face of the leader.

At an earlier time, it was the boy king, Faisal; still earlier, his handsome but insane father, Ghazi. Yet, no one seems – or ever seemed – to object. No picture I saw was scrawled on or disfigured as they would have been in New York or Rome. It was only, apparently, in foreign eyes that the personality cult seemed excessive. And to the superficial observer no sign was evident that anyone reflected on the sequence of leaders or on the likelihood that Saddam Husain may not be the last.

Twenty stories of the Sheraton loomed over the road. It was saved from excess by the near parallelism of the Meridien. Inside, minus the dress of some of the guests, one might have been in Atlanta: six floors up, the lobby was glassed over and on one wall exposed passengers shot heavenward in silent glassed-in elevators. The lobby was jammed. Scores of businessmen and engineers from Japan and Korea, France and Germany, mingled with Iraqis in from the countryside and with Kuwaitis and Saudis up from their more prudish and drier lands. A large staff of Egyptians and Filipinos registered me, carried my suitcases heavenward, made my bed and brought tea. Conspicuous in their absence were Americans and Russians.

As I passed, I glanced in at the bar. It was "hotel bar, type universal, expensive." How different from my first Baghdad hotel, the old Zia, immortalized by Agatha Christie as the "Tia" in *They came to Baghdad.* At the Zia, when I drove in, dusty and exhausted from 700 miles of desert, Mike Zia and his even more ponderous brother, both dressed in shiny white suits, looking like suntanned Sidney Greenstreets, gravely but warmly greeted me as they did each new arrival. Guests were few and each coming was an event. Most were not new and many were old friends with whom tales were swapped and gossip compared. A drink and a yarn always took priority over getting the bags up to the room. And, hanging on the fringe of the "management" was Jesus.

Jesus, the barkeep, was a great figure. A kind and gentle man, he inadvertently made alcoholics of many a visitor. Around him, Agatha Christie hung a shroud of mystery, but my favorite tale rested on firm foundations: during the 1952 crisis over ownership of the oil in Iran, the Abadan Crisis, as we then naively thought, American families were evacuated from that scene of potential violence to the softer climate of Baghdad. One American family was put up at the Zia and it fell to Jesus to entertain their twin boys. By the hour Jesus told them tales and made them expurgated copies of his normally lethal drink, the "Desert Dream."

After some weeks, the crisis subsided, as all crises – even this one – eventually do. Their exile over, the family returned to Tehran. The twins were disconsolate. They had lost their great and good friend, Jesus. To cheer them back into the pleasures of normal life, their parents put them into a Sunday School. Perhaps the inspiration was psychic but the occasion was chance: On their first day, the teacher told the story of the Resurrection. The twins fidgeted. Annoyed, the teacher turned her cool and pious gaze onto the nearer of the twins. What was bothering him? Did he need to go to the toilet? No, the embarrassed little boy stammered. Well, then, what was wrong? An answer had to be found. The little boy screwed up his face, seemed about to cry, but finally with great effort asked, "how did Jesus get to heaven?"

Patiently and serenely, the teacher wove a beautiful scene of clouds, harps and angels wafting Jesus upward. The other children were spellbound, but the second twin looked even more worried. When the teacher gave him a chance, he blurted out his question, "if Jesus is in heaven, who is taking care of the bar at the Zia hotel?"

History does not record the form of punishment.

* * *

Once in my room, I could see far down the bank of the river. Immediately below was the old British club, last bastion of a lost (British) Indian Empire, where a vile curry could be had only at Sunday lunch – so, it was generally believed, one could recover before having to return to work on Monday – and which then afforded a chance for cricket to the select few. Today, I learned, it caters to over 14 thousand members and is so jammed that invited guests are not allowed even to see the swimming pool for fear, it was said, that they might be pushed in by the crowd.

Baghdad is no Cairo, but it is today a city of over four million or roughly ten times the size it was when I lived there. And, like the club, it suffers from the numbers. In every direction, it has spread across the flat Mesopotamian plain. Suburb has conceived suburb. The highway system, radiating out from the old center, along Rashid Street, is jammed like any European or American city with commuters. And plans are being made for a subway.

Plans are still the order of the day. When I was in Baghdad with Walter Gropius and Robert McMillan with the drawings for Baghdad University, we daily visited the Ministry of Planning. On a certain, particularly hot July day – long before the now ubiquitous air conditioning was available – I complained to one of the officials about the slowness of getting decisions. "Let me show you something," he angrily replied. Leading me into a bare and dusty store room, about twice the size of a two-car garage, he pointed to stack after leaning or fallen stack of papers and books. "Those are all plans!" He shouted. "We are going to be buried in plans. We could practically build our city out of the plans themselves without any bricks or mortar."

But, remarkably, the plans are being implemented. Gropius's Baghdad University is rising on the river bank as he hoped it would. His mosque, still today a remarkably bold and "modern" design, a dome unsupported by walls but touching down on three points directly in a pool of water, is nearly finished. Gropius had lovingly researched the "idea" of the mosque, and concluded that it required only two elements, a minaret and a dome. Always the minimalist, he designed just that, no more, and daringly conceived the mosque as a delicate concrete bubble. For all his genius, he left behind few manifestations of his style so I found it particularly poignant to see his dream coming into being. Seeing it, I fondly thought of our long walks and talks together in Baghdad, Cairo and Rome. He had a wonderful eye and always brought new visions from each new vista. Even without him, I was happy that this, virtually his last creation, will soon come into being.

"Coming into being" is now a slow process because of the war. Invisibly and soundlessly, the war affects every minute of life in Baghdad. It has stopped all development, stopped foreign tourism, stopped most Iraqi travel abroad and served as an excuse for every problem faced by the country. Men on crutches advertise it on the streets. And it was also to see the war that I returned to Baghdad.

My visit coincided with the third anniversary of the beginning of the war. Actually, of course, the conflict and the war are not quite the same. Skirmishes and artillery bombardments had been going on for months from the spring of 1980 and these became intensive on September 9. At that time, President Saddam Husain reached the calculation that he could break what Khomeini had not already broken of the Iranian military organization. Convulsed by revolution, Iran appeared an inviting target and Saddam hoped to "liberate" Khuzistan, the Arabic-speaking area in the south (which more or less coincides with the oil producing area) and dictate a peace. For weakening or destroying Khomeini's revolutionary regime, he thought, the whole world would thank him.

Later, in Cairo, the foremost Egyptian journalist Mohamed Hassanain Heikal, told me that he had visited Saddam and Khomeini at that time, in the spring of 1980, when everyone was talking of the possibility of a war. What he said to Khomeini I do not know, but he said he had urged Saddam to be more realistic about the relative size and strength of the two countries. Saddam deprecatingly told Heikal that it would all be over in three months; Heikal says that he prophesized a 30-year war.

At first all went well. Armed with their new Soviet arms, the Iraqis invaded on September 22 and quickly seized much of the southwestern part of the country. They were coolly received, however, even by the Arabs of Khuzistan and soon a combination of their own inexperience and the Iranian zeal broke their offensive. Abadan became their Stalingrad. And, in retreat, they gave up about 50 thousand prisoners. Today, their army holds no Iranian territory but is strung out along the old international frontier.

A "minor", "unknown" or "forgotten" war, as the newspapers have variously called it, the Iraq-Iran war has been savagely fought. In addition to the loss of 50 thousand men, now captive in Iran, the Iraqis have lost roughly an equal number of dead and a equal number of wounded. In a country of 14 million, few and families have not lost a husband, father or brother. Meanwhile, the much-more-numerous Iranians have suffered nearly three times the dead and wounded. But Iranian zeal – or fatalism – has left less than 10 thousand prisoners in Iraqi hands.

One night during my stay, I was getting ready for dinner and turned on the television. I caught the Baghdad equivalent of a "talk show" and was treated to a very polite interrogation, with interpreter from Farsi, of three "defectors" who told why and how they quit Khomeini's Iran. Their very casualness, dressed as they were in new sport shirts, and the happy face of the questioner, somehow made what was probably a fairly innocent interview seem both artificial and vaguely sinister. It is fairly standard fare on the television, I was told, but no one I spoke to admitted watching.

In terms of economic costs, as Foreign Minister Tariq Aziz later emphasized to me, the costs are triple. Iraq has lost about $25 billion in anticipated revenues (largely because Syria, which is sympathetic to Iran, closed the pipeline through which Iraqi oil used to reach the European market), spent an unknown or undisclosed amount of its own money on the war (perhaps $40 billion) and has had to borrow an addition $30 billion from Kuwait, Saudi Arabia and the United Arab Emirates.

What Iran has lost is not known, but it cannot be much less.

More visible in Baghdad is the development cost: buildings by the hundreds, stopped in mid-construction, crowd the landscape. Less visible is the derailment of the ambitious social and economic plan by which Iraq was well on the way to becoming the most advanced of the Arab states. Projects abandoned, talents unused, enthusiasms unstimulated, there is no way to measure these things. The war has become a way of life as my visit to the front was to make clear.

Iraq must be one of the few battlefields of its kind in history. One can, as I did, breakfast in an air conditioned modern hotel, go out, get in an air conditioned Mercedes Benz sedan and drive down a superhighway for three hours to the front. Indeed, the most striking single feature of the war was the massive infrastructure built to support it.

At 420 kilometers from Baghdad in the city of Amara is the headquarters of IV Corps under the command of L. General Hisham Sabbah Fakhri. His office had to be my first stop.

Long before we reached Amara, however, we saw signs of the war. No devastation, no burned out vehicles, but concentrations of armored vehicles and well-placed cannon and missiles. Every bridge was squared by anti-aircraft guns, manned and at the ready. Parks of tanks carriers were discreetly placed off the highway and army camps, still marked as the British long ago taught the Iraqis they should be, advertised the support services of a modern army. Just before Amara a palm garden sheltered row after row of boat-fronted armored personnel carriers, and then, across another bridge, the huge, wire enclosed Corps headquarters loomed before us.

By this time, I had two escort officers. Ambassador Hisham al-Khudhairy had been my constant companion, and a more intelligent, thoughtful and helpful person I have rarely met. A member of a distinguished "old" Iraqi family of remote bedouin origins, he was, without being a bit less loyal to his government, a figure who would have been at home in the "old days." In this "battlefront Iraq" he was almost as much an alien as I so we were joined by a new kind of Iraqi, a Baath Party political officer, Major Saad Abdul Wahhab.

Major Wahhab was born in Baghdad, of recent bedouin ancestry and attended the military academy. From his student days, he was marked for intelligence work. Later he shifted into a position that was more or less what the British called a political officer and the Russians a political commissar. Like the other political officers I met, he wore an olive-colored uniform without distinguishing patches or identification. Unlike the regular officers, neither he nor his colleagues carried side arms.

With me, he was relaxed and self-assured, willing to discuss even subjects which appeared sensitive, and he was obviously well able to arrange whatever we needed. Being an army man, regardless of rank or role, he assumed that he took precedence over his civilian colleague and, as a matter of course, took a seat in the back of the car.

As we drove, we all dozed, then chatted, watched the scenery go by and dozed some more. The flat plain was hypnotizing. But, though we talked of many things, curiously we never once discussed the nature of the regime. I was surprised but decided to let the conversation take its course. What I already knew was that Baathism, bitterly split between its Syrian and Iraqi manifestations, is essentially a sort of corporate form of Arab nationalism. It had grown out of a French-oriented or at least French inspired, student movement. I used to know its founders, Michel Aflaq and Salah Bittar. A Syrian, Alflaq is no longer persona grata in Iraq and his ideas have been pushed into limbo. They never once came up un a conversation during my visit. I ascribe this to the growing pragmatism of the regime although it is fashionable among the many "experts" to blame it on his Syrian connections.

Once through the guarded barrier to the camp, Major Wahhab guided us to a low set of buildings which doubled as office and dormitory for the senior command. There, another political officer joined us, and after a cup of coffee in the staff dining room, led us into the office of General Fakhry.

General Fakhry made a short, set welcoming speech and then asked if I had any questions. Not having seen anything up to this time, I had few. But I began by asking what the chance was to end the fighting.

Fakhry was incisive, direct and, I thought, candid. "Not much," he replied. Iraq would need outside help to stop the war, he went on. It had made every effort, used every intermediary, offered the carrot and used the stick. Nothing had worked. Iran wanted the war to continue, needed it to continue, for domestic reasons. But stopping it was imperative. Iraq was ready even to discuss paying compensation but would not, of course, cede one centimeter of its territory.

Did he see any cracks on the other side of the line? Some, he thought, in recent months, since soldiers were defecting not singly but in small groups, and the Iranian army seemed no longer to be able to mount "human wave" attacks as, he said, they had learned from their North Korean military instructors.

Was there any contact across the lines? I paused and said that I understood that this must be a sensitive issue, but I believed that only answers not questions were sensitive and of course he need not answer. "Not at all," he immediately replied. "I am a political man and a senior official of our Party. I have no hesitation in answering. But you will see that this would be very difficult on this front. "

I pushed the point, remarking that in my study of history, I found that often armies which faced one another over long periods often grew not only to understand one another well but even to develop elements of sympathy leading to fraternization. That had happened during the First World War in Europe.

Emboldened by his answer, I moved into even more sensitive territory: It seemed to me, I said, that if I had to pick a spot to look for a potential successor to Khomeini, I might pick the headquarters opposite his.

The general thought this over for a moment, looked down at his desk and then replied in a measured voice that he and his colleagues had been struck by how few regular of professional officers they encountered among the troops on the other side. In the early period, they had cut off and forced the surrender of a substantial Iranian force only to find that in a regiment there remained only one regular officer. The revolutionary purges had decimated the officer corps. With the revolutionaries, he implied, no such sympathy as I had expected could exist nor was a person like to favor a return to the old regime likely to have remained alive.

What of his own troops, I asked. They must be jaded by months, now years, of relative inactivity. How could he keep their attention to such boring tasks as sitting at anti-aircraft guns waiting for planes that never came?

A problem, he conceded, but not a major one. In fact, the war, he argued, had educated and vitalized the army. Today, it was a wholly new organization, dramatically different from the one with which Iraq began the war. And, now that the role of the army was to defend the nation, sitting on its recognized frontiers, the soldiers had no doubts as to the rightness of their cause.

"Go see for yourself," he suggested, and I took my cue.

❧ ❧ ❧

After a few minutes wait in the orderly room, as transport was organized, we traded our Mercedes Benz for two Toyota land cruisers and headed out of the camp. Again, the roads were superb and obviously expensive, double divided highways, but as the city fell away behind us, the scenery became more bleak. Ten-foot-deep, square-cut trenches knifed through the desert at right angles from the highway. Like the highway, one trench was double so that a tank, getting across the first, would crumble the middle ridge and plunge helplessly into void. Shallow but spiked and probably mined barbed-wire barriers appeared at regular intervals. On both sides of the highway, I could see carefully spaced parks of partially dug-in tanks and tank carriers, surrounded by anti-aircraft guns. Then a battery of 12 large Russian-built SAMs. When I asked if these were manned by Soviet personnel, the indignant answer was a flat no: Iraqi soldiers were now highly competent.

At this point, we were 15 kilometers into the front from Corps headquarters and turned off the road into yet another fenced-in area. It proved to be the regimental headquarters of the Fakah front. Again, we went into an air conditioned staff room and again, as in each office and assembly area, right up to the most forward positions, I saw a television set hard at work. If television in America made Vietnam a "living room war," the Iraqis have reversed the process, bringing the "home front" into the trenches. I found it disconcerting to see every eye in each room shifting constantly back and forth from the speaker to the screen. But no matter what the topic or who the speaker, no one moved turn down, much less off, a single program.

At regimental headquarters, Colonel Abu Ubaid entertained me to lunch. He apologized that the commanding officer had gone home for the holidays but answered all my questions – more or less the same ones I had asked his general – and gave me the best bread I ate in the Middle East along with fresh fruit, meat and rice, a good soup, and chicken. I laughingly asked how they had time to fight with all that food. He professed not to understand the question and turned to the political officer for a translation of my Arabic into his Arabic. The compliment was unappreciated and the joke fell somewhat flat. But the food was good so I just ate until it was time to get back into the Toyotas.

As a sign of the new seriousness, the fact that we were now in a danger zone, subject to bombardment and possible sniper fire, we were then joined by an MP officer in a brand new English Range Rover. He led the way and soldiers at each barrier sprang to attention and saluted as we covered the last

2 kilometers to a company headquarters right on the old frontier. There, we drove into a sort of gulley that was partly natural and partly scooped out by bulldozers. A group of officers and soldiers with Kalashnikovs in proper battle gear then led us underground into the command post.

Again the television set. This time, in an unconscious self-parody, an Egyptian version of a soap opera. The trials and tribulations of a young man and his girl friend, his kind but prudish mother and her tyrannical father had everyone's eyes riveted to the screen. No one even looked up when a shell whistled overhead. What did I want to do? I think they half expected me to say, sit down and watch, of course. So reluctantly, they took me up to the forward observation post.

There, through binoculars, we looked across a further two kilometers into the Persian line. As the hazy heat of the early afternoon rose off the desert, I could not see perfectly, but, the company commander said, on a clear and cool day – obviously a dim Memory after the long and fearfully hot and dusty summer – one could easily see the Iranian soldiers going about their chores.

Back in the dug out, I noted that a huge picture of Saddam Husain, this time taken right in the dug out with all the same officers, graced the room near the television set.

How, I asked, did they keep up the morale of the soldiers. The commanding officer, to the obvious satisfaction of his colleagues, said "well, you know, we are fighting what we have been told is the seventh most powerful army in the world and we beat them. We don't have any morale problem."

As I walked through the deep dust of the front trench and thought about what the soldiers must have felt in July and August, I found doubt in my heart.

I was surprised to see civilian trucks at the front and when I asked why they were there, I was told that they belonged to the People's militia which serves along side of the army and under its command. The militia volunteer enrolls for a more limited period and is more political, I was told, than the soldier. The force is somewhere, I gathered, between a national guard and an arm of the Baath Party. But on this point, my questions seemed to get rather spongy answers.

After curiosity began to seem rude, I got back in the Toyota and back we sped to our waiting Mercedes Benz at Corps headquarters. Then four hours later, we were deep in the rush-hour traffic of Baghdad.

❧ ❧ ❧

I awoke very early the next morning, perhaps still buzzing with the excitement of the front, and having read all the books I had brought with me, decided to go out for a walk along the river bank. The early morning was clear and cool so it was delightful to watch the city shake off its sleep. In each of the waterfront coffee houses, each now also focused on a television set, the waiters were bedded down on iron cots and snuggled under heavy blankets more useful to ward off the sun and flies than the non-existent cold. Soldiers guarding the turgid waters were stretching and scratching as they slowly moved from cot to chair. Dogs were exploring the wide dry bottom of the Tigris and forming into playful packs while doves moved heavily and carefully among the volunteer plants.

Scenes of the river have always been as much a part of Baghdad life as canal life in Amsterdam or Venice. The Iraqis, before air conditioning and television, thought God's finest gift to mankind was a fish fry, known as masguf, enjoyed in the cool of a summer evening when the Tigris made Baghdad livable. At the Zia Hotel, all meals were served on a terrace overlooking the river, and it was an accepted part on the city lore that the huge population of cats had read the menus, knowing accurately when the fish course was being served at each hotel. Some travelling British officer from India had given Mike Zia a mongoose – "best thing to run cats off" – he advised. And it was true, the mongoose hated cats, but poor fellow, he was outnumbered. Just as the Iraqi soldiers suffered from the human waves of Iranian soldiers, in their feline waves, the cats overwhelmed him.

As the sun burst forth in the eastern sky, sending everyone scurrying for shade, I found myself far along the river to the south toward the Karada suburb. There a new kind of Baghdad is taking shape in the form of town houses. Nearly a mile of them. Each is surmounted by a solar heating unit but each, I was told, was inspired by traditional architecture – meaning, I gather, that each door was enclosed in an arch – and so, presumably more satisfactory than the faceless, boxlike, not-quite-finished and empty apartment buildings which march down the streets nearer the center of town.

While it is easy to find fault with the lack of style and the lack of social acceptability in the new housing, there is no denying that it is a vast improvement over the kind of housing known to most Iraqis in the old days. With the shanty towns along the canals one could see in 1958, there is simply no comparison. And even in comparison to the relatively good old-fashioned housing, the level of comfort has improved enormously. So conscious of the improvement is the Government that is maintains a museum to remind people of what their lives or the lives of their parents had been. Its display is simply an old Baghdad house, filled with crude but evocative figures portraying "the old days." Every visitor I was told is captured by the graphically arranged scene of a circumcision. Ouch! I was stopped by the realistic sight, from the attic window, of an old crone, soundlessly screaming down at the cavorting young people on the second floor. And in the main rooms, the televisionless women sewed while, apart from them, the bored men smoked their nargilas and played backgammon.

Baghdad's main museum, of course, houses Iraq's magnificent collection of Sumerian, Babylonian and Assyrian art. Hundreds of cylinder seals reveal why the Harrapan Indus River cities copied them. They are treasures of an almost microscopic art. Opposed to them in size and spirit are the vast wall sculptures and political proclamations of the Assyrians. And, in glass case after case, the libraries and archives of the first law givers alternate with clay tablet love letters and dunning demands for payments of overdue debts. The museum not only is a great deposit of ancient lore but symbolizes the move of this Government toward a greater sense of localized (wataniyah) – as distinct from and supplementary to pan-Arab (*qawmiyah*) – nationalism.

It is in quest of that localized identify that this government is experimenting with such vast and unconvincing buildings as the "martyrs' monument" and the tomb of the unknown soldier, as though from the concrete symbol, they could find their ways back to the historical reality of their separate existence. Again, it is the war which has thrust upon them the question and has given an excuse for the symbol.

❧ ❧ ❧

The war, fittingly, was the issue in the main talk of my visit. That was with Foreign Minister Tariq Aziz. Aziz, a former secondary school teacher, is the ideologue of the Iraqi Baath leadership. A bright-eyed, alert, hard working man, he was also that rare human being, a good listener. It was Sunday morning, in the midst of the Islamic religious holidays when most of this colleagues were at the lake-side resort at Habaniyyah or home resting that he invited me to his office.

Like most of the government buildings, the Foreign Ministry is protected by the tire-puncturing spikes, arranges on a movable, wheeled steel span, like a low gate. As each car approaches, the barrier could be rolled out of the way, but if the car tries to crash the carrier, it wouldn't get far. The great fear is Iranian suicide squads driving in cars equipped as bombs like the one that gutted the Ministry of Information two years ago.

Past the barrier, the Ministry was a pleasant building. My friend the Egyptian architect Hassan Fathy would have been delighted to find that the designer of its domed entry hall got the Islamic symbolism of fountain (the Earth of female principle) and skylight (the Heaven or male principle) right. Less governed by aesthetics, I was amused that it made utilitarian the required heroic photograph of Saddam Husain by embedding a clock in it. We both would have agreed that its cool marble floors and walls would have charmed the ancient Sumerians.

I had only a minute for these thoughts when I was joined by the two under secretaries of foreign affairs. Ismet Kittani is a former president of the

U.N. General Assembly and deals with "multilateral affairs," while Mohammed Said as-Sadat deals with the rest of the world. After shaking hands, I reviewed my impressions of the battle front, and we talked about the prospects for peace. Then we were ushered into the office of the Minister.

Tariq Aziz appeared in the same uniform as the political officers, a sort of olive-green safari suit. But, unlike them, he wore a pistol on his hip, looking a bit like General Patton. As with Patton, I gathered, the pistol was not so much for protection as for image: Aziz, a civilian, a Christian and physically not a large man, seemed to use the pistol, a cigar and a large gold Rolex to say, "I too am a tough guy." But Aziz's toughness was mental and I found it impressive.

"The war is the unfortunate fact," he said. "The Iranians needed it. It explained the appalling tyranny of Komeini. In the old days, when the Shah was killing scores of people, Iran was not less imperialistic and was the puppet of America, but Iraq got along with him. However, in 1980, getting along with Iran became impossible. At first the war was bloody and terrible, but now it has settled into a way of life, costly, inconvenient and futile, but stable."

Iraq, he continued, had lost much in the war but had achieved a sense of security and purpose, a sense of itself, and a realization, with Syria and Libya actively helping the anti-Arabs, that Arab unity is still only theoretical. It is harder, he remarked, for Arabs to travel to – much less to work in – other Arab countries than in Europe.

The major economic cost, he underlined, was the loss of revenue: "Figure it out for yourself. We used to export 3.6 million barrels of oil and now export 1 million." In addition, he went on, many of the hoped-for benefits of investment were stopped, like the fertilizer plant, just short of completion so, while most of the money has been spent, none of the benefits had been gained.

What about your neighbors, I asked. I particularly wondered about Turkey which is Iraq's natural trading partner. I had meant, of course, that I thought Iraq could seek new regional allies. To my astonishment, Aziz replied, "we have no aims on Turkey." He must have noted my surprised look for he went on to say, "we are not partners of the Soviet Union to be afraid of a NATO country like Turkey." And, now, with Saudi money, he pointed out, Iraq is building an alternate oil pipeline through Turkey to Europe. In the future, he said, he hopes for more cooperation.

And Kuwait? I ventured. "With them our relations are warm and close." Again, he noted my expression and continued. "We resent the suggestion, one occasionally hears, that they are not." I ducked the barb and went on: Why then have you not settled your frontier dispute. "It is being worked out," he replied. Then why, I pressed, have the Kuwaitis cut their aid program? "They have already given us $10 billion and continue to support us as they can, but they too have been hurt by the fall in the price of oil. They will keep on helping us because, at base, they know that they are not supporting us but helping us to fight for our common defense. No we are quite sure of the Kuwaitis."

Later, in Cairo, Heikal was to quote a poem recited to him by the late King Khalid of Saudi Arabia on the benefit to third parties when the snake and the scorpion go to war. Despite Mr. Aziz, there is no doubt that no one of the Arab neighbors wants to see either a defeated Iraq or a victorious Iraq. A defeated

Iraq would put their regimes face-to-face with the powerful combination of Iranian social revolution and messianic religion while a victorious Iraq would be an only slightly less unpleasant neighbor.

When I suggested that such thoughts might have occurred to the Kuwaitis, Aziz retorted, "Nonsense…There is no such thing as victory or defeat. If we could defeat Iran, we could certainly not pick up the pieces. Someone else would. To seize Iran is not only beyond our desire but far beyond our capacities. But, of course, they cannot defeat us either. We just want to settle the war so we can get about our business."

And, anyway, he continued, "We don't need Kuwait or anyone else. Once the war is over, Iraq will have again, as it had before, plenty of money. In 1979, before all this happened, the President told every minister that he could have whatever he could absorb. There was no lack of money, only a lack of capacity to absorb. That will be our situation again when we can sell our oil. Remember that before the war, in the years between 1973 and 1980, we passed out, mainly in Africa, $9.5 billion in aid."

"Who really wants to end the war?" I asked. "I do not see that anyone other than you really wants an end that badly: Kuwait and Saudi Arabia, I still believe, are not keen on an end to the war; Syria does not want you to win but probably would not be very happy to have Iran as a neighbor. The Russians presumably don't want either anti-communist regime – yours or Iran's – to "win," but presumably is waiting for its opportunity in Iran. And Iran certainly does not want the war to end in a humiliating way and, even if Khomeini were overthrown, the only way an Iranian successor could win legitimacy would be to fight against you."

Aziz listened carefully and without comment. Then he launched into what was worrying him the most: the American role.

"How could Iran stay in the war for three years? Of course it has had help. North Korea gave military equipment as did South Africa and Israel, Syria and Libya. But I know the Libyans. They are misers. And the Syrians couldn't do much. The Israelis have given advanced technical assistance and some military equipment as have the South Africans. But Iran depends on money. And that you give it."

Again, my astonished look.

Seeing it, he went on. "Yes, you sell its oil. The Seven Sisters (the major oil companies) have kept it in the war. To the amount of $15 to $20 billion. It is a dirty game. You Americans don't want the war to end. We hear about your 'destabilizing' regimes in other parts of the world, and we see your hand here too. You want to keep Iraq bleeding and not to let either side lose."

"Oh, of course, [US Secretary of State George] Shultz denied it to [Iraqi ambassador Ismet] Kittani when I sent him to Washington, but I am not impressed by official denials. It is a dirty game, a dangerous game, but the scenarios being planned in Washington and Moscow are not going to be implemented in our area...we have the capacity to stop the war. And, if we must, we will."

While the Minister did not explicitly say so, I gathered that what he meant by 'stopping the war' was using the Super Entendarde jet fighter-bombers and Exocet missiles which Iraq has purchased from the French to knock out the Iranian oil loading facilities at Kharj Island in the Persian Gulf. This, the Iraqis believe, would finally bring the Iranians to their knees economically and so enable Iraq to force a peace settlement. Of course, other "scenarios" are possible. The Iranians have said that they would, in retaliation, "block" the outlet of the Persian Gulf. Then Iraq too would be in jeopardy.

The effects of such moves are difficult to predict but they might include a major dislocation of the petroleum markets, a serious armed confrontation of the United States and Iran, with possible Soviet involvement, in the Indian Ocean, or even more dire consequences.

Thus, the Iraqi desperation, inability to conclude a peace and means to precipitate a crisis are not an idle threat.

Message conveyed, we talked pleasantly, *lente ma non troppo*, about my trip to the front – "thank heavens you didn't get shot," he shook his head – and his forthcoming trip to New York – "don't wear your six shooter," I laughingly cautioned, "or they might think you are a cowboy." We chatted about his New York venture (where he was to speak at the UN General Assembly) for a few minutes until I was taken off to lunch by the two Under Secretaries.

They, like Ambassador Hisham al-Khudhairy, were warm and friendly and we talked without the slightest hesitation, as one always had done in the Baghdad of the old days.

In those far-off days, my little apartment had been a salon, the scene of a continuous seminar on the destiny of Iraq and it was on the basis of that seminar that I had written *What the Arabs Think.* Today, I could not have done it. Outside of official contacts, there were no contacts.

My arrival had coincided not only with the third anniversary of the war but also with the Muslim equivalent of Christmas, Eid al-Fitr, the feast that ends Ramadan, so most of my appointments has been cancelled. Some Middle East expert I turned out to be! Naively, I had assumed that the determinedly secular Baathists worked on religious holidays. Not a bit of it. So Hisham very kindly invited me to a feast with his large and extended family. I was surprised since I had heard that few foreigners were any longer invited into Iraqi houses. Yes, he assured me, he had checked with his cousins and all was well. I should be ready the next day at noon.

About 11:30 the next morning, I was not exactly surprised when Hisham called from the hotel lobby and asked if he could come up. Openly and correctly, he then said he was sorry and embarrassed, but his cousins had asked him not to bring me after all. It seems that they had made a further check and found solid opposition. Coming to the party, explained Hisham, were not only some army officer cousins but even two judges.

Apparently, I might have encouraged a military revolt or suborned Iraqi justice.

He then insisted on staying with me, despite my request that he spend the day with his relatives, and we drove out to the lakeside resort of Habaniyyah, there to observe Saddam Husain's children, like Sadat's children I had seen in Egypt a few weeks before, frolicking in the water, which had been cleared for their exclusive use. There, under the watchful gaze of heavily armed security guards in their black Mercedes Benzes, they roared about in their motor boats.

That night at dinner with the American chargé, I heard the British, French, Greek, Australian and even the Austrian ambassador each confirm that none could lure a single Iraqi to a lunch or dinner. They even asserted that this was also true of the Arab ambassadors. Never, even in Moscow, had I seen so isolated a group as the Baghdad diplomatic corps. They really never saw Iraqis. As we talked through the evening, I came to the conclusion that, as a group, they knew almost nothing about the country. Only the French ambassador, helped by the extensive trade, particularly in armaments, and the development projects of French companies, seemed to get out and see very much.

Somewhere, under the bright and modern surface, fear had ambushed the traditional warmth and hospitality, far and away the most charming aspect of the old Baghdad. Yet with almost no contact, each side projected to the other both sinister designs and vast intelligence. Both believed itself to be completely transparent to the other. And twice I heard the story of all-pervasive Israeli intelligence. According to the story, when an Israeli pilot was captured, his Iraqi interrogator pressed hard for information. Within days, everyone heard Jerusalem Radio in Arabic announce the name of the Iraqi security officer, give his address, the name of his child, her school address, and warn that if he caused further discomfort to the Israeli pilot, he could expect dire consequences.

Yet, despite the war, the fear of subversion, and the halting of the moves toward the good life, the natural exuberance of the Iraqis remains. If anything, it seems to me even more evident in the streets than in past years. Probably, in part, this is because the city is now so much larger and better lit. But it is far from the somber place I had expected. I had thought that the expulsion of foreign communities, particularly the large Iranian community, would have dampened the spirit of the night life. But, to the contrary, I found the city much more lively than its near neighbors Kuwait, Amman or Damascus.

I wondered if this had something to do with the fact that over one million Egyptians have moved to Iraq. But it had more to do, I think, with the "street orientation" of the Iraqis themselves: every night I was in Baghdad, I saw dozen processions of relatives and brides rushed through the streets in honking cars and buses, announcing weddings, and the brightly lit and music-blaring shops were jammed with throngs of shoppers every night until midnight. Under the film of dust from the Mesopotamian Plain, Baghdad remains a vibrant, open city.

"If only the war can be ended…" is the theme of every conversation, the conditional clause of each thought, and, one hopes, the way in which the two Baghdads might be fused into one better than either.

It remains Iraq's big if.

April 2, 1983

Weighing the Iraq War in the Scale of Vietnam

WATCHING DAY-BY-DAY the build-up to war against Iraq, my thoughts keep wandering back to the Cuban Missile Crisis. Since I was a member of what was essentially the "2nd tier" of the 30 or so people fully involved in the American government activities relating to the war – I was a member of what was rather pompously called "the Crisis Management Committee" – I had a certain perspective on the unfolding of that crisis.

Comparisons and contrasts of that crisis and the way we handled it are, I believe, significant as we attempt to make sense of the pronouncements and actions of the Bush administration. I begin with the issue of the reality of the two crises.

<u>The reality of the crises</u>: During the Cold War, both the United States and the Soviet Union had probed one another's capacities and intentions. Many of the actions were highly provocative and dangerous. As is now well known, the United States had for years penetrated Soviet airspace with aircraft. A number of these planes were shot down by Soviet air defenses. Meanwhile, the Russians flew aircraft along the American coast but did not penetrate American airspace. The Russians did, of course, blockade Berlin and subsequently built the Wall, both of which the US regarded as provocative acts. Both of us built military alliances (NATO and the Warsaw Pact) and when the Soviet alliance was challenged internally in 1956, the Eisenhower Administration was on the verge of parachuting American personnel into Central Europe to face the Russians with the danger of war with the US. The Suez Crisis (the British-French-Israeli attack on Egypt) made the move impossible. But constantly, both the US and the USSR sought to enhance their positions, and to undercut one another, in the "Third World" through provision of arms and development aid. More

pointedly, America regarded the Communist take-over of Cuba under Castro as tilting the balance of security and the Russians apparently so regarded the placement of US nuclear-armed missiles in Turkey.

The Missiles in Turkey were more significant than many then realized. What was significant about them was that they were liquid-fired. Consequently, they took a relatively long time to be launched. So, viewed in the arcane world of nuclear strategy, there were "offensive" rather than "defensive." Thus, they were provocative; ironically, they were also redundant. We then had nuclear-armed fighter bombers (F-100s) stationed in Turkey on constant alert and programmed for targets in the Soviet Union. In my capacity as the member of the Policy Planning Council responsible for Turkey, I had urged that the missiles be removed. Military planners, always reluctant to give up any "advantage," were strongly opposed. The missiles were still in place at the time of the Cuban Missile Crisis.

If we attempt to understand the motivation of the Russian in deploying missiles in Cuba, we must take into account our shared concern with "balance." Since we regarded our having missiles on the Soviet border in Turkey as right and proper, they presumably thought it right and proper for them to have missiles on our border in Cuba. We, of course, did not: we trusted ourselves and not them, and we regarded ours as defensive and theirs as offensive. In the jargon of the day, we felt that missiles in Cuba would "tilt" the balance of power whereas ours in Turkey, already in place, were by then a part of that balance.

Whatever our views of one another's actions, and motivations, we agreed that the potential damage of nuclear confrontation was overwhelming. In the vivid phrase of my former colleague at the University of Chicago, Albert Wohlstetter, we lived in a "balance of terror." Simply put, we each had the capacity to destroy the other. The trick was to avoid doing so.

If we weigh Iraq in the Soviet scale, disproportion is evident, indeed almost laughable: The Soviet Union was a vast part of the world, comprising well over 200 million people, with a huge and well-equipped army and air force, producing its own nuclear weapons and the means to deliver them and run by an experienced, capable and centrally-controlled military and civil bureaucracy.

In contrast, Iraq is a tiny country about 2/3rds the size of Texas of which 70% is desert or steppe inhabited by less than 20 million people who are deeply divided religiously and ethnically. Moreover, 1/3rd of the country (Kurdistan) is now, de facto, a separate state. Under boycott, Iraq's revenue (particularly in foreign currency) has been drastically reduced, and its small and comparatively obsolete armed forces, badly mauled in the 1991 war, have never been fully rebuilt. There is no indication (despite vague accusations) that Iraq has – or could have in the foreseeable future – access to nuclear weapons. Finally, unlike the Soviet Union, Iraq is ringed with actual or potential foes: Iran to the east, Turkey to the north, Israel to the west and Kuwait and Saudi Arabia to the south. Each of these has more modern armed forces; Turkey and Israel have much larger armed forces; and Israel has, it is believed, about 400 nuclear bombs and the means to deliver them. So how did we respond?

The nature of the response: Whatever provocative actions it may have taken before (attempts to assassinate Castro and to sponsor an invasion by Cuban exiles), the US government's reaction to the Cuban Missile Crisis was essentially defensive. We sought to avoid war. True we were prepared, if necessary, to invade or bomb Cuba to destroy the missiles, and quickly mobilized forces to do so, but from the opening of the crisis throughout the critical days, everyone in the circle around the President was attempting to find ways short of military action to end what we all perceived to be an unacceptable threat.

Moreover, our objective was limited. While we did not approve of the Castro government, we sought only to remove the missiles. "regime change" or occupation of Cuba was never, to my knowledge, considered. This was crucial to the success of American actions since only if Chairman Khrushchev could back down without unacceptable loss of prestige could he withdraw his missiles. In short, the aim was limited, discrete and achievable without destruction of Cuba or the replacement of its government.

Turn now to Iraq. First, consider our objectives insofar as these have been disclosed: They are to rid Iraq of nuclear weapons; to prevent Iraq from engaging in terrorist actions; and to prevent Iraq from endangering its Neighbors.

Second, are these real dangers? There is no credible evidence that Iraq has (or could have for many years) the capacity to produce nuclear weapons and no evidence of any likely source for acquisition abroad that cannot be otherwise controlled by America and its allies. Despite attempts to link Iraq to the al-Qaida organization, there is no evidence of such a link; indeed, we know that Usama bin Ladin was so strongly opposed to the Iraqi regime that in 1990 he offered to form an international brigade to attack it; and Iraq today has very limited military capacity. The only weak point on its frontier is Kuwait which is under an American guarantee. Saddam moved against it in 1990 only when the first Bush Administration gave him what he took to be (and which an independent observer would agree was) a green light to do so.

Third, what means of action are contemplated? The Bush Administration has announced its intent to invade the country and overthrow the government. Rather than seeking to avoid military action, as we did in the Cuban Missile Crisis, its announced intent is to undertake it.

This is a critical point and requires announcing an ancillary analytical consideration: Looking at the way nations interact, we often fail to distinguish "national interest" from "interest of government."

In the Cuban Missile Crisis, the national interest of the USSR was to avoid being destroyed while the interests of its leaders was to not be overthrown. Thus, we tried not to so humiliate (and therefore endanger) the Soviet leadership that it could not do what we wanted it to do. That is, we tried to make the Russian national interest (to avoid a destructive war) coincide with the interest of government (to keep from being overthrown as unpatriotic). In this way, we were able to accomplish our key objective which was to get the missiles out of Cuba.

Some months after the Missile Crisis, senior officials of the American government played a war game to try to understand it more fully. At the usual crucial point in war games, action is precipitated: In this case, "Blue Team" (the Americans) "took out" a Russian city; then "Red Team" (the Russians), to whom I was acting as political adviser, had, within 7 or 8 minutes (the time set by the constraints of nuclear exchange), to decide what to do. We identified three options:

The first option was to retaliate in kind and destroy one American city of comparable size. We quickly decided this would accomplish nothing since no American leader could accept this tit-for-tat as an end to the confrontation: he would be forced to "escalate" and we would have to reply and so on until one side or the other went to general war.

The second option was to do nothing. But we concluded that such a policy would result in the overthrow and murder of the Soviet leaders. They obviously would not adopt that policy.

The third option, the only other alternative, was to strike with everything we had in the hope of so disabling or discouraging "Blue Team" that it could not inflict unacceptable damage on us. Thus, a very experienced team of senior military, intelligence and other officials opted for general war.

The important lesson was that in a conflict between "national interest" (Red Team having a national interest in receiving as little damage as possible) and "interest of government" (Khrushchev and company having a governmental interest in staying alive), it was often interest of government that won out. History is full of examples of that lesson.

Turn back to Iraq. We have told Iraq that even if it allows us full access to ascertain that it has no nuclear potential, that is insufficient; we insist on the overthrow of the existing government. If those in power are almost certain to be "replaced," that is, killed, they have no incentive to allow inspection or to reduce their military potential or otherwise conform to our desires. Quite the contrary, they may conclude that their best chance of survival lies in adopting the very policies we want them to put aside.

They do not, of course, have the option adopted by "Red Team," to strike us with overwhelming power, but they probably will try to deter us by making our attack unacceptably expensive. Thus, they have a strong incentive to try to acquire nuclear weapons (from the Russians, or its mafia, the Chinese or the Pakistanis), to produce as much chemical and biological material as they can, to develop means of delivery and to engage in, encourage or position themselves to be able to carry out terrorist acts. We may regard these policies as irrational or ugly, but, if we are honest, we must admit that they are policies we also adopted vis-à-vis the USSR. We can, I presume, be sure the Iraqi leadership is aware of this. In short, our current Policy appears likely to produce exactly the result we should seek to avoid.

To summarize: our handling of the Cuban Missiles Crisis was certainly not perfect – we made mistakes, we misread Russian intentions and our information was sometimes faulty – but we accomplished our objective and we made the maximum effort to avoid endangering our society whereas the policy now announced by the Bush Administration certainly does endanger the American way of life and, moreover, it could be self defeating.

Now consider the modalities of government action in the Missile crisis: as I remember it, four features stood out: the first was that, although the number of people in the inner circle was very small, it was diverse. The President was, of course, a Democrat; his Ambassador to the United Nations (Adlai Stevenson) was a liberal Democrat; his Secretary of State (Dean Rusk) was a very conservative Democrat; both his Secretary of Defense (Robert McNamara) and Director of the National Security Council (McGeorge Bundy) were Republicans; he drew in as advisers men with impressive records of service in previous administrations from both parties.

The second feature was that consultation with and granting full information to America's overseas allies was emphasized. Elaborate measures were taken to ensure that the British, French and German governments were kept abreast of thinking in Washington and the unfolding of events in Cuba and elsewhere.

The third feature was that, beginning with the President's speech on the Monday of the crisis week, in the writing of which I played a minor part, the American public was given an honest, fairly complete and up-to-date account of the crisis and the dangers inherent in the action the President proposed.

And, fourth, the government did not feel itself beholden to or constrained by any domestic lobby or pressure group. Although there was a vociferous community of Cuban exiles in Florida, and although they felt traduced by the Administration's failure in the Bay of Pigs fiasco, they exercised no discernible influence on decision-making.

The contrast today in the handling of the Iraq "crisis" is telling with each of these items:

First, to judge by press reports, the only people who exercise any influence in the presidential circle are men to the far right of the Republican Party. To the best of my knowledge not a single Democrat is among the President's advisers. Nor have experienced statesmen of former regimes been coopted.

Second, with the single exception of the British Prime Minister there seems to be no serious attempt to consult with any other government. Except, that is, for Israel which appears not only to have been consulted but to have played a key role in setting American policy. This is, ironically, far more openly discussed in Israel than in America; indeed, Israeli accounts suggest that even joint military action against Iraq (and Iran) has been extensively discussed between the American and Israeli governments.

Third, while speeches and press releases are a daily occurrence, surprisingly little "hard" information has been given by the Bush Administration to the American public; they have been told that all information is "highly classified" and so unavailable. Whereas Kennedy released aerial surveillance photographs of Cuba, showing precisely what the danger was, Bush has not released any comparable materials. In a previous essay on secrecy, I pointed out that, if such materials actually exist, they will hardly surprise the Iraqis, who not only know what they have and what they are doing but also are quite familiar without satellite reconnaissance since, during the first Bush Administration we shared the results with them. In short, the Bush administration has no discernable reason for its policy.

Fourth, whereas Kennedy was able to operate on the sole criterion of his (and his adviser's) best judgment of what was in the American national interest, this Bush Administration has been quite open in catering to the powerful and dedicated lobby with whose representatives he has staffed his administration and on whom he relies for support.

❧ ❧ ❧

Consider the motivation of political leaders: Even President Kennedy's strongest critics have never suggested that in his policy on the Cuba Missile Crisis, electioneering played any role. Indeed, it could hardly have done so since the crisis was not of his making and came upon us suddenly and without warning. I do not recall during the crucial week anyone ever considering the impact if what we were doing on the chances of reëlection of the Democratic party.

I would like to think that the same could be said today, but there are indications that make one doubt. First, as mentioned, the Bush administration has restricted itself to the far right of the Republican party and has excluded from the councils all others. Second, it is widely discussed, even in that group, that George Bush Sr. lost his election over Iraq and that, therefore, "grudge" figures into calculations on Iraq. Third, there has been widely publicized calculation, by no means restricted to Bush's opponents, on the timing of an attack on Iraq: should it be before the November Congressional elections or afterwards, near to or well before the presidential elections in 2004? Fourth, the President has himself fueled speculation by taking the position that we are in a war and that failure to support him is unpatriotic. There are those who believe that this will be his strategy for the election. And, finally, since considerable doubt as to the necessity of confronting Iraq has been expressed by former senior (Republican and Bush Sr.) officials (Brent Scowcroft, Henry Kissinger, and others) and by military men (General Wesley Clark, former NATO Supreme Allied Commander, for one), there is doubt that any military action is justified. In short, it is widely believed that a major motivation of the build-up to war in Iraq has more to do with American politics than with Iraq's threat to the United States.

Competence is always a serious and questionable issue in governments. Since I have identified myself as one of the Cuban Missile Crisis team, let me say only that I found those members of the team with whom I worked the most able, experienced and dedicated group I have ever known. In contrast, the group today seem more ideologically motivated than informed. That is a subjective opinion, but consider four objective points:

First, there is a report, unsubstantiated but from very good sources, that the White House has disbanded the office of the State Department charged with Iraqi affairs and scattered its professional officers. If this is true, it suggests that those in charge of American activities do not want to listen to professional advice; second, there is a similar report that the former head of the C.I.A. counter-terrorist office has been told to keep quiet and not venture his opinions; third, while virtually every former senior professional from the CIA and the State Department believes our current policy to be wrong-headed, none has been consulted whereas almost always in the past the incumbent administration has sought a variety of opinion and particularly those of former senior officials; and fourth, there are persistent reports that the Secretary of State has disagreed strongly enough to have twice offered his resignation.

Negotiation is always a valuable option: In conflict situations today, we often act like merchants did in the ancient "silent trade" where gesture rather than words was the medium. As the expession goes, "we send a signal," taking care not to have any move appear either as a sign of weakness or of bellicosity. The one major exception during the Missile Crisis, and the one most worrying to me at the time, was Kennedy's decision to board Russian ships. In international law such a move is considered an act of war, but, to everyone's relief, Chairman Khrushchev chose not to so regard it. At the same time, moreover, the President's Brother created a "back-stair channel" to the Soviet Government through a Russian emissary in which at least some of the key issues could be discussed verbally.

Neither negotiation by gesture nor by discussion is being used with the Iraqi government. That government has been told, in fact, that we will not negotiate with it but intend to destroy it.

The only other time in my experience when something like this happened was under President Lyndon Johnson during the 1967 war. I had been brought into the White House and given the task of writing a draft peace treaty. When I submitted it, McGeorge Bundy, to whom I was acting as policy adviser, handed it back, saying "the President does not intend to negotiate with Nasser. Please draft a peace of treaty that does not require his participation." I remonstrated that is was impossible to make an agreement when the other party was not to be allowed to participate. Bundy did not argue the logic but simply repeated that the President had made up his mind and that I should not "fight the issue." I tried to comply but could not produce anything within that restriction that had a chance of success. So I left the White House and returned to my post at the Adlai Stevenson Institute.

It is perhaps worth emphasizing, however, that while Johnson would not negotiate, he also did not attempt, to the best of my knowledge, to do what the Bush administration has proclaimed its intent to do, to overthrow a government.

Putting all this together, it seems to be that what is happening today is indeed shooting craps with destiny. Actions are not carefully or professionally considered, Thus, what is likely to happen will probably result in the needless death of thousands of people. Moreover, it may well create conditions not only in the Middle East but throughout the world in which terrorism will flourish. Since they are either kept in the dark or are unconvinced by our lack of logic, even our allies are likely to regard us as a "rogue" state. In short, our current policy is likely to cause enormous internal damage to our country and particularly to our tradition of civil liberties, democracy and the rule of law.

September 11, 2002

Baghdad on the Brink of Destruction

FIRST IMPRESSIONS OF BAGHDAD are the same one gets starting to read a mystery novel: superficial calm masking anticipated danger.

Life here is deceptively normal. The streets are so jammed with cars that trucks and buses need special permission to invade from the suburbs; some streets have become virtual pedestrian malls as thousands of peddlers set up their tables or lay out their wares on rugs. Large wooden carts laden with gunny sacks full of grain, potatoes or dates are manhandled adroitly through the swirling crowds while sweating, yelling porters manhandle impossible loads or silently trudge under huge refrigerators or boxes that would tax the capacity of a small truck. Crowds are everywhere, moving about in what Kipling would have called typical Oriental splendor. There are more people now – since my first visit in 1947 Baghdad has grown from a little town of 50,000 or so to a city of more than 6 million – and certainly far more cars, but in many ways it is still the Baghdad I saw first fifty years ago.

What is different is not the energy and frenzy of street life but the purposefulness of activity. Building cranes are busily at work on mammoth public buildings and even substantial private houses. Baghdad's people are not just surviving; they are moving hectically toward some sort of future. Just what that future might be would be terrifying if everyone were not so busy keeping out of the way of cars and pushcarts as he rushes through his daily chores.

Although I was easily identified as an American, even though I spoke Arabic, not one person made the slightest reference to the conflict between our countries. That is, with one exception, as I drove across the frontier from Jordan, I stopped to buy some dates, long the premier agricultural product of Iraq, and the shop keeper crossed the index fingers of his hands, the sign of hostility, as he said "Bushi, Iraq," but he immediately laughed. Each person I met, even the normally dour taxi drivers, said, "welcome, most welcome to Baghdad."

Under that calm and friendly facade, however, there are abundant signs of tension. I expected fear, but that is not the word that comes to mind. Rather, tension is what I felt. Perhaps that is surprising. After all, the Baghdadis know war far more than most of us. What happened to New York in the September 11 attacks was a small taste of what hit Baghdad in the furious month-long American air strikes of 1991. In comparison, the Blitz of London was a sideshow and the famous devastation of Rotterdam hardly counted. The Guernica that Picasso immortalized as the essence of war was a mere outing. When the Baghdadis read their press or listen to their radios, they are in no doubt of the real meaning of statements that America intends to shower this city with 300 or 400 cruise missiles a day. For them, that is not a statistic; it is a mortal threat. And it is not the worst possible vision of the immediate future. There is also talk of using tactical nuclear weapons, so-called "bunker busters," which even children here know would spew out clouds of radioactive dust.

Although it was not fully understood at the time and has been little discussed since, the first Gulf War had a nuclear component too. Artillery used depleted uranium shells which, in the intense heat of impact, mutated into an aerosol of. U_3O_8, an extremely potent neurotoxin which results in genetic defects like cancer and malformation in developing fetuses. In the Gulf war, some 300 tons of such shells, some of which apparently also contained over 4,500 grams of solid uranium, which, being heavier than iron, was considered more effective against armored vehicles. In the Gulf War, some 300 tons of such shells, some of which apparently also contained plutonium, were fired. Unfortunately, they were effective not only against armor. And not only against those actually hit. Wherever they were used, they set in motion a process that resulted in a marked increase of malignancy among adults, both soldiers and civilians. Children were particularly vulnerable; worst of all, infants were sometimes born with horrible defects. Little as we Westerners have heard of these things, they are common talk in Iraq.

Reports in the Western press that power stations, water purification plants, transport grids and even sewage treatment facilities are projected targets are also openly discussed here. I asked shopkeepers, taxi drivers, and people I met casually in the street about the guess of disaster relief agencies that upwards of a million people may flee their homes, without access to food or clean water. Almost all echoed the sad reflection of a taxi driver. I mention him because having access to a car, he had the option. "What," he said, shaking his head, "leave my house? Where would I go? If I went to [the town of] Hilla or Kut, how could I get anything to eat or a roof over my children's heads. No, I will stay in Baghdad. It is better, after all, to die at home."

Later I asked the deputy prime minister, Tariq Aziz, about the much touted "option" of the government to hie off to some place of exile. He looked sternly at me and said, "Iraq is my country. I was born here. I will die here."

So, why, one must ask, the calm? Of course, it is largely deceptive. Teachers and doctors report a marked increase in the consumption of calming drugs, especially among children, while social workers say that, during their rounds, they witness much private anxiety. But still the outward calm is astonishing. Do the Iraqis expect the war to be averted, Saddam and his team to run away to some gilded exile or the United Nations investigators miraculously to prove that no more weapons of mass destruction exist? None of the above. No one I have spoken to thinks what is called here the "Bushi war" will be averted. They expect the worst. The words "humanitarian disaster" have become part of daily speech.

Then, could the apparent calm come from the Islamic fatalism which Western observers always profess to find in the "mysterious East?" I find no evidence for this. Islam sits lightly on the average Baghdadi, far more lightly than upon the Kuwaiti, Saudi or Jordanian. Iraq has been a secular state from the beginning, and secularism, except for the occasional public show, has been the rule of this regime. The regime is proud of its liberation of women and is bitterly hostile to the Muslim fundamentalists, the mutasalafin. To call someone a Wahhabi, like the followers of Usama bin Ladin, is to insult not only him as a person but his intelligence. It is to say that he is a backward, uneducated, a sort of country bumpkin. Like people everywhere, few Iraqis are really resigned to fate: they keep working and hoping even when faced with overwhelming odds.

And the odds are certainly overwhelming. Iraq had trouble, even in its better days, matching the power of neighboring and much more populous Iran. And during the 1991 "Bushi war" it lost most of what had given it an edge over Iran. Its "air force," now reduced to a handful of aging planes, is almost unable to take off; what remains of its tanks and armored personnel carriers are as battered, rusty and patched together as Baghdad's taxi fleet and its now much smaller army has lost its élan. What America did not do to it, purges accomplished. Iraq now has a ghost army, suitable for television performances but almost certainly unable to move in any coordinated fashion or to project significant force. Fight, it may, in desperation, or as its leaders proclaim from house to house, all the while knowing that it will be futile and horribly costly and making no visible preparations for such a conflict.

So what underlies the apparent calm? My impression is that Baghdadis, like most of us, have learned to live on two levels: the immediate reality takes precedence over the future possibility. Getting dressed, fixing breakfast, going to work, performing the myriad chores of daily life, these all have to be done right now; worrying about the future, which, after all may or may not finally happen, can wait.

And so, Baghdad is waiting. Its 6 million people have taken on a corporate existence. One can feel it in the air. It is expecting the full horror of war as each person in it tries to keep his eyes fixed firmly on the comforting tasks of daily life.

This air of impending doom became evident even before I reached Baghdad. On the way here, I stopped in the capital of Jordan, Amman, and spoke to several old friends about what they expected to happen. They were, they said, absolutely convinced that, no matter what happens at the United Nations Security Council and no matter what further reports the observers make, the Bush Administration will attack Iraq, as President Bush put it, "within weeks." Nothing, they felt, could be done to avert the attack. The decision had been made months ago; some pointed to studies and statements made by the now-senior officials of the current Bush administration years ago. It was not a matter of Islamic predestination but of American policy. And so, Jordan will "keep its head down, trying to minimize the damage done to it." It will try to maintain a neutral stance even if Israel joins in the attack on Iraq. That will be difficult, or perhaps even impossible, particularly if Prime Minister Sharon uses the war to push the Palestinians further off the West Bank or closes down completely what remains of the Palestinian national authority. But Jordan is determined to try.

As I got ready to drive across the 1,000 kilometers of desert to Baghdad, I was struck by how much in evidence arms were in Amman. Soldiers were everywhere. Jordan is today, as it has always been, a "soldier state." And despite great improvements in the streets, the erection of imposing new buildings, a vast influx of people (Amman now numbers well over a million inhabitants) and a high degree of commercial prosperity, Jordan remains a military outpost on the desert frontier.

Its link with Iraq is fragile. The most evident part of that link is mobile: every day upwards of 1,000 giant oil tanker-trucks make the same drive I made, racing along at 120 kilometers an hour, heavily laden from Iraq to Jordan and returning empty to refill. The highway told the tale: the westward lane, used by the fully loaded trucks, was worn almost to the foundations whereas the eastward lane, used by the returning empty trucks, was as new.

As we drove along, I lost count at over 400 tanker-trucks in the 500 kilometers before we reached the half-way point at about the Iraqi frontier. There the highway divides with the trucks shunted aside from the double six-lane Iraqi highway to an auxiliary road. That road is the slender and fragile blood vein of Iraq's economy.

Politically, the link is more fragile than the road testifies. Jordanians do not like Saddam Husain. While Jordanians, like all the Arabs, indulge in "personality cults," they scoff at the excesses to which the Iraqi regime has carried the cult of Saddam. Reach the frontier and you understand the Jordanian remarks. Everywhere one's eyes fall, there is a poster or picture of Saddam, dressed for each separate occasion as a soldier, a typical amiable uncle, a school teacher, a businessman, a farmer or a bedouin; he appears as the portly model for some exotic fashion designer. Reach Baghdad and you find that the posters and pictures are augmented by colossal statues. In one, outside the university, he is appropriately dressed as the rector while at the city "gate," he is the guardian of his people, holding aloft a rifle.

What the reaction of Iraqis is to these displays is hard to fathom because people prudently turn away from such questions, but to visitors the displays appear either amusing or frightening. However, they are in character, not only of Saddam but also of each of his predecessors. I well remember the same poses on grandiose posters featuring the kings and dictators who went before him. Arabs, and particularly Iraqis, have an abiding weakness for the vanity of their leaders.

Visitors are one of the curious features of this city on the brink of war. The UN weapons survey team has grown to impressive size and its members can be identified by their dress, obviously purchased from some mountaineering store. They mostly keep to themselves in a separate hotel, but are as avidly pursued by flocks of photojournalists as movie stars used to be in Rome by the *paparazzi*.

Even more striking are another group of visitors, the peace activists.

Hundreds of peace activists have streamed into Baghdad to offer their protests against the announced American invasion and their bodies as human shields. Despite their diverse origins – Americans, various Europeans, Africans and Asians – they too have their distinctive dress and badges. I saw one group from Ohio who were dressed as though for a trip to a mall or a football match but around their necks, they wore signs proclaiming their purpose in large letters: "STOP THE WAR ON IRAQ." Most carry unusual (and for Iraqis, outlandish) back packs, presumably laden with lunch boxes and drinking water. In the evenings they lounge around the hotel lobby, tired from the day's movement, which consists mainly in being seen and in accosting journalists, and bored from having already visited every shop in the hotel. Their mecca is the alcoholless bar which features an internet site with twenty or so new computers primed and ready to go and, undoubtedly, well recorded by various security services.

The Iraqis to whom I have talked are grateful for the peace activists' gesture but are not quite sure what to make of them. Such up-welling of genuinely emotional and obviously anti-government protest would be unimaginable here. It thus presents a curious contrast in attitudes: the peace activists are protesting in a thoroughly American fashion against American policies in a way that Iraqis who feel themselves to be the victims of American policy could not imagine doing themselves.

Mingled with them, often to their annoyance, are the journalists who were lucky enough to get visas. I have counted about thirty in this hotel alone. They come from all over the world, are well looked after by the Ministry of Information, pampered but watched, usually "assisted" by official "minders" who facilitate (and report on) their movements. The Iraqis, this time officials, are even more nonplussed by them than by the activists. To be a journalist here is to be the recipient of and reproducer of government hand-outs. To demand the right to go see for oneself, to write critical pieces and to cast doubt on the official line is as shocking a departure as the inspectors' insistence on the right to snoop at will. The Iraqis are trying to get used to both practices, but it is certainly taxing their patience.

However much the UN inspectors, the journalists and the peace activists differ from one another, all are astonished by one common experience: money. The Iraqi dinar which I remember from past visits as the equivalent of about three American dollars is now trading at between 2,000 and 2,500 to the dollar.

When I cashed a $50 bill I was awarded a stack of bills that would have supplied a couple of dozen games of Monopoly. The larger bills, with a face value of 250 dinars, were worth 10 to 15 cents each. Perhaps the best thing about Baghdad today is that almost any visitor can become an instant millionaire.

Prices are low but few people earn much. The most astonishing is the price of gasoline: four liters (roughly a gallon) of high-test gasoline costs the equivalent of one cent. (My driver from Jordan had a specially equipped car that would hold 160 liters so he could fill it in Iraq for his round trips). But even at a penny a gallon, a Baghdad taxi driver earns only $5-10 a day because his car and its tires have to be imported at great cost. The low man on the economic pole, a draftee in the army, earns the equivalent of about $3 a month and is poorly dressed. A school teacher does better but not much. To feed his family, he is helped by a rationing system that distributes food at low cost, but if he wants to supplement his diet, he finds meat costing $2.50 a kilo. Hard as he finds it to sustain his family, he is still "privileged." Unemployment is certainly widespread but hard to gage; underemployment is the more common experience. Driven by need, almost everyone becomes a peddler, hawking everything he can get his hands on. As I walked down the central street, which has changed little from my first visit, I saw little clots of people squatting by the gutter, selling bars of soap, used clothes, candles, each person having a stock that could not have been worth more than a few dollars. Even selling out his stock completely could hardly have made up a day's needs.

As I walked along, an old man stopped me. Looking at my shoes and seeing that I was a foreigner, he asked if I had a second pair. When I said yes, he offered to buy the ones I had on. Later, one of the drivers outside my hotel asked me to finger the sleeve of his jacket. He mentioned the name of a well-known European designer and almost proudly explained that he had bought it second hand. Like many poor countries, Iraq has a thriving market for European and American secondhand clothes. One wonders where jobbers find the vast quantities that end up here.

Poverty and want also promote a thriving exchange market: one man doesn't need all the rice he gets in his ration (at 15 cents a kilogram) and swaps some of it for part of another person's cooking oil (worth 20 cents a liter) and so on. Barter is the grease of the poor man's economy, but most of his transactions still depend on money; so even shoeshine boys have learned to flip through piles of bills with the eye and speed of an experienced money changer. The good thing about even nearly worthless money is that it gives an illusion. And Baghdad needs illusions.

The worst thing in Baghdad, of course, is the guessing about what tomorrow will bring. I asked a taxi driver, every city's gossip, what he was doing about it. He shrugged. Have you, I probed, laid in a stock of food? He shrugged again, but admitted that he had stored in his *sirdab* (the half-cellar that serves as the poor man's air conditioner in the scorching summer months) sacks of rice, wheat, beans and other dried vegetables. How about water? I insisted. Water, I pontificated, is the absolutely vital emergency supply. No, he replied "it is too expensive." A six-pack of bottles costs about 3,000 dinars or roughly 15 cents. "My children would drink me out of everything I own in a week," he waved his hands in a futile gesture. I was about to lecture him on this improvidence when I remembered my own reaction to the Cuba Missile Crisis. As I sat in my Washington office closely observing the events of that dreadful week, there came a particular moment on the Thursday when I was reasonably sure we had lost it, that war was upon us. I vividly remember reaching for the telephone to tell my wife to leave town. I pulled my hand back from the telephone, feeling like that Baghdad taxi driver: if hell really does descend on earth, why bother.

February 5, 2003

As War Approaches

BOTH THE IRAQI AND AMERICAN governments now regard war as inevitable. President Bush has said that even the destruction of all remaining prohibited or questionable weapons by Iraq will not deter him; only Saddam Husain's removal might. On Iraq's part, Deputy Prime Minister Tariq Aziz told me in a two-hour meeting I had with him in Baghdad that his government would continue to do all in its power to comply with United Nations resolutions but that it did not intend either to flee the country or to commit suicide. "America has long since decided to attack Iraq," he said, "and nothing Iraq could do would prevent it."

In a visit to Washington, I found knowledgeable people split into two camps so divergent from one another that they seem to be seeing different worlds. The U.S. Government position, well reported in the press and shown hourly on television, portrays an Iraq hell-bent on the destruction of America through the use of its store of chemical, biological and even nuclear weapons. Secretary of State Colin Powell provided the U.N. Security Council on February 5 with what President Bush said was "irrefutable and undeniable" proof of Iraqi deadly capacity and determination to wage war against America in concert with Usama bin Ladin's al-Qaida.

Much of that "proof" has been disputed by former and current State Department and CIA officials. One senior CIA officer, who declined to be named, even categorized the evidence as worthless "garbage." Worse, some allege that the pro-war officials knew that they had no worthwhile evidence but withheld that knowledge from the public. Critics pointed out to me that the evidence rested on two foundations: what defectors reportedly said and what satellite photos allegedly showed.

The most important defector, Lt. General Husain Kamil, (Saddam's son-in-law whom he executed for treason in 1996) was reported by Newsweek on February 24 as actually having said the opposite of what the American government quoted him as saying. He said, "All weapons – biological, chemical, missile, nuclear – were destroyed" but was quoted as saying that Iraq had hidden them.

The British government's contribution to the evidence, purportedly based on secret intelligence sources and described by Secretary of State Power to the Security Council as sophisticated and accurate, was laughed out of court when it was shown to have been based on an essay by a university student from Baltimore who had never visited Iraq and some several-years-old articles published in the English press.

At best, these briefing leave much in doubt. Doubts about them have not been reported extensively in the major American media, but they have occasioned a flurry of e-mails and speeches all over America, England and Europe.

Apart from the sensational reports, critics of the pro-war American government policy point out that Iraq is a small, poorly-armed country, isolated by distance and surrounded by far-stronger neighbors, unable to harm America today but, if attacked, potentially the source of a new generation of America-hating terrorists.

But they too agree that war is almost inevitable.

What are we to make of the divergent views of the Bush-Blair camp, the highly experienced diplomatic and intelligence experts and officials of Iraq and other Arab states?

As a historian and former planner of American policy, I have been trying to understand three things: first, is war really inevitable? Second, if America attacks Iraq, what is likely to happen? And, third, what are the long-term consequences?

Although these questions are of fundamental importance not only to Iraq but also to the health and well-being of Europeans and Americans, they are rarely asked. Many people in both Baghdad and Washington have told me that it is too late even to ask them. To the contrary, we should have learned from the Vietnam War that we will spend years, perhaps decades, wishing we had answered them. Here are some of my answers.

War is almost certain; indeed it has begun. Knowledgeable Americans in close touch with the White House and Pentagon even put a date on the major campaign: the third or fourth week of March. Journalists have discovered, and the American military has admitted, that not only is the move toward the frontiers of Iraq of sufficient forces nearly complete but that special troops and undercover espionage agents are already operating in Iraq authorized to kill Saddam and to overthrow the regime. British and American aircraft started three weeks ago to bomb Iraqi antiaircraft installations in the south of Iraq. Unannounced, war has actually started.

The "wild card" in what many see as a game of high-stakes poker is what the Turkish government will do. Until last night (March 2) the American government assumed that the Turkish parliament would agree to let American forces operate from Turkish territory (in return for a payment of roughly $30 billion and a free hand in Kurdistan). It had already positioned supply ships off the main southern Turkish port ready to equip an American division. And it had warned its terrified Kurdish allies that it was dumping them. The Americans were stunned when the Turkish Parliament voted down the proposal. If the Turkish parliament cannot be persuaded to change its vote, the planned campaign against Iraq will have to undergo a fundamental revision.

In Baghdad, despite having said that doing so was a virtual "death warrant" for his regime, Saddam began yesterday the destruction of Iraq's medium range missiles. His act was purely symbolic, Tariq Aziz told me. Iraqis knew it would not stop an attack. "The only reason the inspectors are here," he said, "is to give an excuse for what American has already decided to do. The war will come. We will not run away. But America may find a nasty surprise."

Aziz would not elaborate that "nasty surprise." So consider my second question, what is likely to happen when America attacks.

The small group of men identified as advisers to whom President Bush listens say that Iraqis so hate Saddam that they will be out in the streets, even in front of their demolished houses, waving American flags when the troops arrive.

The Baghdadis of all walks of life know war as few Europeans or Americans – and certainly neither Bush nor Blair who have never heard a shot fired in anger – do. Realists, Iraqis know that buried under demolished houses will be the bodies of mothers and fathers, aunts and uncles, husbands and wives and many children. And they know that they can do almost nothing to protect themselves. Stunned by reports of hundreds of missiles, thousands of "smart bombs" and, perhaps, tactical nuclear weapons American government advisers have told them it would hurl at them, no one I saw or talked with was digging trenches, piling up sandbags or even storing emergency rations. They are strangely mute, even seemingly obvious to the coming storm.

My third question is what then? Both the Anglo-Americans and Iraqis, I think, have missed the likely course of events. American military planners believe that a house-to-house guerrilla war is unlikely. The most wildly optimistic assessment holds that 99 out of each 100 Iraqis will welcome the Americans with smiles on their faces. But in Baghdad alone, a city of 6 million, that will leave at least 60,000 people who, thinking of dead and dying relatives, lying under the rubble of their houses, will be consumed with hatred for America.

Their numbers will quickly grow. Even in the best of circumstances, armies make poor neighbors to civilians. Power breeds contempt for powerlessness and powerlessness breeds hatred for power. More important, nationalism will assert itself: natives will want the foreigners to get out. This is not just an Arab-American phenomenon. America experienced it in Vietnam in the 1960s. Indeed, the stationing of British troops in Boston, long ago and mostly forgotten today, was one of the main causes of the American Revolution in 1775. No matter how benign the Americans will think themselves to be as they "restructure" Iraq, the Iraqis will quickly come to see American soldiers as heirs to British imperialists. Americans may be oblivious to that piece of recent history, but Iraqis are not.

It is, of course, for this reason that Usama bin Ladin has urged the Iraqis to fight America. He hates the Iraqi "Socialist infidels," as he called them," but an Anglo- American invasion will give his cause a whole new generation of potential recruits. Thus, the real winner in the American policy is likely to be Usama bin Ladin.

March 3, 2003

Dark Matter

LIKE MOST CONCERNED PEOPLE, I have spent a large chunk of my waking hours in recent months trying to understand how and why we have arrived on the brink of war. In my quest I have been stimulated and guided by years spent as a historian and analyst of international affairs including four years in one of the most privileged places in the American government. Yet these advantages have not enabled me satisfactorily to resolve the ambiguities. Here I explain why and then offer a different interpretation.

I

First, what is the crisis? In my experience in government and in my reading of history, it was nearly always possible to answer that question "objectively" or logically. In the Cuban Missile Crisis, we felt that the stationing of Russian nuclear-tipped missiles in Cuba not only posed a new threat to the continental United States but would also "destabilize" the world balance of power. We determined not to allow these changes to occur. True, we were reacting in part emotionally and even asymmetrically: we had far more nuclear-armed missiles placed close to the Soviet Union, some right on the frontier in Turkey, than the Russians intended to put in Cuba. But, we argued, ours were already in place and so the balance of power had already adjusted to them whereas the introduction of missiles into Cuba was new and therefore unbalancing. Unsaid, of course, was our assumption that what we did was right and what the Russians were doing was wrong. Yet, overall, there was a logic to our actions and the Russians accepted it. They concluded that Cuba was in our orbit and we recognized that our having missiles in Turkey was provocative. So we struck a deal. We both removed them.

As I have tried to add up the factors in Iraq, in part with the Cuban Missile Crisis in mind, they just do not compute. Compare the two situations: Russia had a sophisticated population of about 250 million living on a vast land mass and led by an experienced government, able to field a huge army equipped with full arsenal of weapons of mass destruction. If Russia threatened, the threat would be real.

In contrast, Iraq is a small country, two-thirds the size of Texas, but with a use-able area (that is minus the desert that takes up 3/4ths of the land) about the same size as West Virginia. The population numbers about 23 million, but, like the land, much of it is "unusable" by the government. Roughly a quarter are Kurds who are guided by a different culture, aspire to independence and live in what is virtually an autonomous state. Nearly half the total Iraqi population are Shi'a Muslims who are strongly influenced by Persian culture and who are viewed with suspicion by the Sunni Muslim government. What is left, the "Iraq" now in our gun sights, amounts to less than the population of Massachusetts, roughly five million.

Powered by oil, Iraq had become by 1990 the most progressive and modern state in the Middle East other than Turkey and Israel. Per capita income then reached about $2,000 which enabled a large and thriving middle class to come into being. Today, after a decade of depression created by the economic sanctions (imposed on August 6, 1990), gross national product has collapsed and the middle class has been reduced to poverty. In industry, in the army and even in Baghdad's taxis, the results are evident: to keep some machinery working, old equipment has been cannibalized. Few new pieces of equipment could be imported. The result, obviously, is a rapid run-down of numbers, capacity and performance.

II

While the real power of a nation-state is only superficially a question of the size and modernity of its military force, one must take it into account. So what do we get? The army is smaller than in 1990-1991, numbering today about 400,000, but, like the land and population, much of it is of little value. The loyalty or at least the élan of about 80% of the troops is questionable; its equipment is both worn and now largely obsolete or at best obsolescent; it does not have the command-and-control capabilities that make armies like ours, the Russians, the Israelis and a few others superior; and, finally, it has no long-range capability: it cannot move men and equipment over distances more than a few hundred miles; it has virtually no air force; the few missiles it still has are short range, able to reach only a hundred miles or so. In short, it has nothing dangerous that can reach anywhere near America.

Moreover, unlike the Soviet Union at the time of the Cuban Missile Crisis, Iraq is not only isolated but is surrounded by countries stronger than it. Iran has a much larger population, is vastly richer and can field a far larger army; Turkey has Europe's second largest army (after Russia) and is equipped and trained to NATO standards; Israel has one of the most powerful armies in the world and has a full arsenal of chemical, biological and nuclear weapons which it has announced that it is willing to use. It nearly did use nuclear weapons against Syria and there is evidence that, at least once, in February and March 2001, it did use the toxic chemical weapons it manufactures at Nes Ziona.[1] Certainly it would use them against Iraq, if it perceived an Iraqi threat.

Does Iraq have an ace in the hole, that is, weapons of mass destruction? So much attention has been focused and so much fear generated by this topic that we lose sight of the realities. The realities are not impressive. Everyone agrees that Iraq does not now have, and never had, nuclear weapons. Building nuclear weapons requires not only the money and technical skills that Iraq did have but also both a sizable industrial plant and space for testing.

We can see the importance of the mix of these prerequisites in other situations: Germany could not develop atomic weapons during the Second World War because it had no suitable place to make or test them. With the help of France, Israel could do the preliminary work at Dimona in the southern desert, but, in the vital testing period, it had to ally itself with South Africa. France tested in the Algerian desert; similarly, America, India, Pakistan and China used their deserts. Where North Korea will test its weapons is not yet evident. But the crucial factor is that Iraq has been steadily, virtually hourly, under observation for the last ten years and could import nothing and certainly could test nothing without us and others learning of it.

I am not, of course, the only one to evaluate these facts. Others have recognized that they do not accord with the fears now driving public opinion. So attempts have been made "by persons unknown" to augment them or simply to manufacture new "evidence."

A few weeks ago, the fact that Iraq imported special aluminium tubes, thought to be intended for nuclear weapons manufacturing, was taken as the "smoking gun." Then as that episode was shown not to be meaningful, another was floated.

This fraud was elaborate and highly dangerous. As reported by the head of the International Atomic Energy Authority (IAEA) to the UN Security Council, some organization, presumably a government organization having access to sophisticated techniques, forged a set of documents designed to show that Iraq had sought to import uranium from Niger. The documents were examined by the US and British governments which turned them over to the UN inspectors. When UN experts examined them, they concluded that the documents were bogus.

What is disturbing is that the British and American experts almost certainly knew that the documents were not genuine. Why did they, by turning them over without comment, lend credence to them? Did they know their provenance? Did they have a hand in their manufacture? This classic example of espionage "dirty tricks" fits the American Constitutional definition of a "high crime" since it could have been, and may still be, the trigger that sets off the American invasion of Iraq. As citizens of a democracy, we deserve to have been told both that the story was a fake and also who concocted it.

Turning now to biological weapons, we do not need to be scared into buying duct tape; what we need is a rational evaluation of the danger. I admit to being somewhat out of date, but when I was in our government I was "cleared" for information on these weapons. While a few refinements have been made since I was fully briefed, the basics have not changed. They are the following: biological weapons are more terrifying than lethal. Relative to other weapons, few people have ever been hurt by them and few are likely to be hurt. They are difficult to use, much less "efficient" than comparable quantities of explosives and highly limited in their impact. Given the choice of weapons, a rational enemy would not pick them except, as I said, for their psychological effect. This is why the government should not scare the public, as it has been doing, but should inform it while carrying out such programs as will reduce or eliminate the danger.

Does Iraq have biological weapons? And if it does can it use them? Will it hand them over to independent terrorist organizations? I think the short answer is no.

While it is true that Iraq did have them – in fact got seed stocks along with the industrial equipment to "weaponize" them from America and Britain[2] – biological weapons, like bread on a supermarket shelf, grow stale and lose their effectiveness. What Iraq had was destroyed along with the equipment needed to make new batches.[3] Any that was hidden would now be useless. Moreover, we have ample means to ensure that no new stock or equipment has been imported.

Suppose the many inspectors we and others have sent to Iraq are wrong and that Iraq does have some biological weapons left over and miraculously kept fresh, can it use them? Theoretically, yes, but note that when it really did have them, in the 1990-1991 war, it did not use them. Why? Because it knew that if it did, all stops would have been pulled and we (or Israel) would have demolished the whole country. That is to say, Iraq was "contained" by what Albert Wohlstetter (the mentor of Paul Wolfowitz) termed "the delicate balance of terror." Containment, we learned in half a century of confrontation with the USSR, worked.

Moreover, to be useful, such weapons must be delivered. In delivery systems, considerable technological advances have probably been made since 1991, but to my knowledge, well over 90% of viruses are destroyed if they are dropped from aircraft. So vast quantities must be transported to cause significant results.

Iraq does not have delivery capability except in two categories: first, months ago, when we began to threaten to invade and topple his government, Saddam Husain could have pre-positioned biological materials abroad, perhaps in ordinary shipping containers. But such materials would have begun to deteriorate from the day they were packed up and months or years later would not work. The government should tell this fact to the public rather than scaring it.

Second, if it has them, Iraq could use biological weapons in its own country. So, if there is a danger of their use, it is to invading troops. Obviously, the best way to avoid this danger is not to invade.

What about turning them over to some terrorist organization? As has frequently been pointed out by senior officials of both the FBI and the CIA, great pressure has been brought to bear on both organizations by Secretary of Defense Donald Rumsfeld, Deputy Secretary Paul Wolfowitz, NSC director Condoleezza Rice, NSC deputy director Stephen J. Hadley and others to prove a link between Iraq and the al-Qaida organization. Despite attempts to do so, no link has emerged. As one FBI official told *The New York Times* (February 2, 2002), "We've been looking at this hard for more than a year and you know what, we just don't think it's there." Attempts have been made "by persons unknown" to manufacture links, but one by one they have fallen apart in the hands of the reporters. The most famous was the alleged meeting in Prague of an Iraqi intelligence agent with Muhammad Atta (one of the men implicated in the World Trade Center attack). This was touted as the "smoking gun" that would justify an attack on Iraq. After investigating it on the spot, President Vaclav Havel called President Bush to warm him that the information was spurious. And CIA Director George Tenet confirmed his message.

As various commentators have remarked, the Bush administration is the most secretive in our history – as one observer said, "its instinct is to release nothing;" Vice President Dick Cheney refused even to allow the Congress access to the records of his energy task force; and even the Department of Agriculture and the Environment Protection Agency, for the first time, were given power to stamp documents secret. In what it reveals, the administration exhibits a frightening habit of playing fast and loose with facts.[4]

Annoyed by the lack of "responsiveness" of the CIA and even of the Defense Intelligence Agency (DIA) to what the administration wants to show, Defense Secretary Donald Rumsfeld decided to set up a new and separate intelligence office under Undersecretary Douglas Feith, who is a strong advocate of attacking Iraq.[5] Presumably, Rumsfeld thought, an in-house agency would be responsive where independent agencies would not be. This move violates the cardinal rule of intelligence evaluation, that it must be independent if it is to be accurate.

What one learns in evaluating intelligence is that most events have certain logic; sometimes, of course, governments act irrationally or out of character, but analysts are enjoined to exercise extra care and to demand clear proof when they suspect an abnormal act. Such an act would be cooperation between an authoritarian state and a nongovernmental group. So we should ask, what is the Iraqi government likely to do with Islamic Fundamentalists (Arabic: *mutasalafin*).

Start with what we know. What we know is that Usama bin Ladin has consistently attacked Saddam Husain as an infidel (Arabic: *kafir*) which is the strongest denunciation a Muslim can use and which proclaims that the person can be legally assassinated. Bin Ladin even offered to organize a military unit to attack Iraq in 1990. On his side, Saddam has done all the things that the Fundamentalists hate: he has liberated women, even put them in the army, secularized the state and society and attacked the most conservative Muslim leadership in the country, that of the Shi'is. It would take a major transformation of both men and their teams for them to find common cause.

What might common cause be? Obviously, hostility to America. So far it has not happened, and it would be unlikely except in extreme circumstances. If Saddam were in imminent danger of losing his life, I can imagine him doing virtually anything including embracing Bin Ladin's organization. And Bin Ladin? For him, as I have been pointing out for months, nothing could be better than a war between Iraq and America since it will almost certainly provide a new source of recruits to al-Qaida and the many similar organizations that will spring up from its ruins. To defend Islam against what he sees as an American crusade, an emotionally-charged word President Bush himself injudiciously used, Bin Ladin would presumably even work with an infidel or, preferably, with the angry fellow-countrymen of a dead infidel.

The two critical points here are that short of war, cooperation between Iraq and any terrorist organization is unlikely and so far none has been shown to exist. It follows, obviously, that pushing Saddam and Bin Ladin together in fear of us is not smart. Predictably, wounded, angry and humiliated in a war with us, Iraqis as a whole, not just the government, may come to support activities we will see as terrorism but which they will see as patriotism.

What about chemical weapons? They are easier to store than biological or nuclear weapons. Does Iraq have them? The Bush administration tells us that it has. The proof, it says, has been provided by defectors. The star witness was Lt. General Husain Kamil, a son-in-law of Saddam Husain who was executed for treason after he defected in 1995. While abroad, he was extensively interviewed by the CIA and other security agencies. Both Secretary of State Colin Powell and Deputy NSC Director Stephen Hadley told us that General Kamil said that the Iraqis had hid them. In fact, as recently released U.S. Government documents prove, he said[6] "that after the Gulf War, Iraq destroyed all its chemical and biological weapons stocks and the missiles to deliver them."

Secretary Powell was sent to the Security Council with what President Bush called conclusive evidence on how Saddam Husain was hiding prohibited weapons and was working with terrorist organizations. Despite high-tech staging, the evidence fell apart upon examination. Worse and more amateurish, the contribution of the British, supposedly from the famous Secret Intelligence organization, 007 James Bond's MI-6, actually was plagiarized from old copies of Jane's weapons reports and from a paper written by an American of Shi'i Muslim background from Baltimore who had never been in Iraq[7] Ibrahim al-Marashi, then a student at the Monterey (California) Institute of International Studies, later published his paper in an Israeli magazine. This pathetic mishmash, apparently the best that could be cobbled together, was characterized by Secretary Powell, who allowed his usual good manners to overcome his good intelligence, as "fine."

As citizens of a free society, we deserve more from our paid civil servants. Without access to the facts, we cannot possibly perform adequately our duties as citizens. If Iraq poses a threat to the United States, it certainly has not been demonstrated.

III

Yet we are being rushed into a war that may —

1. throw our society (and much of the rest of the industrial world) into a depression. In the first week of March, the Congressional Budget Office wrote down its estimates for the coming decade from a revenue surplus of $5.6 trillion to a deficit of $1.8 trillion; Other estimates predict at least twice that deficit; the shortfall for 2003 is expected to be driven by the war to about $400 billion;

2. cause further hardships for poorer Americans as the unemployment rate rises. Since 2001 nearly 2 million jobs have been lost.

3. force a cut-back in social welfare (unemployment benefits, support for schools, etc.). State schools (and even jails) are being forced to cut budgets. In Texas, for example, school financing has already hit a 50 year low and is expected to go lower; some states are even being forced to release prisoners because they cannot afford to keep them in jail;

4. put further pressure on public health where 40 – 45 million Americans are already without insurance;

5. jeopardize retirement safeguards among the middle class through the loss of savings when companies go bankrupt as financing becomes increasingly expensive and consumer spending falls. Fear of the consequences already, before any hostile action has actually taken place, has led to a drastic fall in the index most people regard as the test of the health of the economy, the stock market. The Dow Jones Average has fallen from 11,522 on January 3, 2001 to 7,552 today or down about one third.

6. accentuate or bring about deep and bitter splits and cause profound confusion and fear within our own society;

7. lead our government to alter, in some cases radically, traditional American concepts of law (as with imprisonment of resident suspects in harsh conditions without access to counsel[8] and in some cases torture[9] or killing of men we are legally required to treat as prisoners of war[10]); a draft of to-be-proposed legislation entitled "the Domestic Security Enhancement Act" of January 9, 2003, would allow the Attorney General to strip Americans deemed threats to our "national defense, foreign policy or economic interests" of their citizenship and deport or incarcerate them without review;

8. separate America from what President Eisenhower, quoting Thomas Jefferson, called "a decent respect for the opinion of mankind." As I write, it appears that even America's closest ally, British Prime Minister Tony Blair, is close to "jumping ship" for fear of losing his party and Parliament. Such allies as the Bush administration can count upon are either bribed with billions of dollars (like Turkey, Jordan, Israel and Egypt) or driven by local agendas which are not necessarily conducive to American national interests (Turkey against the Kurds and Israel against the Palestinians) or subject to irresistible diplomatic or commercial pressures. Some of the new allies are countries the American government hardly noticed in previous times. NATO, so patiently built over

decades, is in shambles and the European Community, which many of us sought to help come into being over the last half century, is fractured, perhaps fatally. And even in America's closest neighbors, Canada and Mexico, both public and government opposition to American policy is now palpable.

9. fail to learn from the past. It was Secretary of State, then chief of the U.S. General Staff, Colin Powell who in 1992 in an article in *Foreign Affairs* underlined the lesson America should have learned from the Gulf War. "The Gulf War," he wrote, "was a limited-objective war. If it had not been, we would be ruling Baghdad today at unpardonable expense in terms of money, lives lost and ruined regional relationships." Yet, today, the Bush administration has announced plans that will incur all three of these costs.

In short, there must be, somewhere, compelling reasons for a policy that has so many obvious disastrous consequences. The Bush administration's senior men are certainly not stupid. So we must ask, if not fear of Iraq's attacking the United States, which as I have shown has no rational basis, what could the motivation for such an obviously costly and perhaps ruinous policy be?

IV

A prominent candidate, one widely discussed, is oil. The American economy now uses a high portion, roughly 30%, of the entire world's production of about 20 million barrels a day. Even during my time on the Policy Planning Council, "acquisition of oil on acceptable terms" figured as one of the four key objectives of American policy in the Middle East. Since then, American domestic reserves have virtually run out. Because the Bush administration has decided not to implement the standards set of the Tokyo Conference on the Environment and has also drastically cut back initiatives to develop alternative energy projects, acquisition of oil is a compelling objective.

It should not be a difficult policy decision: oil is always available on the international market because those lucky enough to have it cannot benefit from it unless they sell it. And, as more and more oil has been discovered, there appears to be no lack of desire to sell. We are unlikely to be without access to oil on regular commercial terms for the near future.

Also, given that it will probably cost more than $100 billion to seize Iraq (and its oil) and that the chief of the U.S. General Staff believes that upwards of 300,000 American soldiers will be required to hold it for perhaps ten years, seizing Iraqi oil, even if we just steal it, will certainly be far more expensive than buying it.

Moreover, Middle Eastern oil supplies the Far East and Europe rather than America. So why seek to control it? The main reasons are stability of price and assurance of supply. Should any one country dominate that major source, it could, at least theoretically, affect both supply and price. Were America, so the argument goes, so far only *sotto voce*, to control Middle Eastern oil, it could dominate the world market for the foreseeable future. It was for this reason that the US National Energy Policy Report of 2001 (the "Cheney Report") placed a high priority on control of Middle Eastern oil.

I find it difficult to credit the charge that those who have developed the Bush Doctrine are primarily interested in acquisition of Middle Eastern oil to enrich American companies. That seems too crass an objective. However, I have to admit that it is unfortunately true that some members of the administration have not been diffident in help given themselves, their friends and former companies. Halliburton, from which Vice President Cheney still receives between $100,000 and $1 million a year,[11] has been given the inside track on coordinating and (if Iraq blows up the facilities)[12] rebuilding the Iraqi oil industry.

Russian sources maintain (*The Guardian* October 6, 2002) that America will declare all previous oil concessions, including those of the Russians void and that "US companies will…take the greatest share of those existing contracts…Yes, if you could say it that way – an oil grab by Washington." In another context, plans and rumors on the oil industry would almost certainly be categorized as "smoking guns." Still, in and of itself oil is not sufficient, I believe, to account for the current policy.

It is not only oil, of course, that offers a major new market for American industry. If America launches the attack it has publicly announced, with thousands of missiles and bombs launched in the first days of the attack, the damage to roads, bridges, factories, water treatment plants, schools, hospitals, apartment buildings, etc. will be immense. Proposals for bids to rebuild have been circulating for months among a select group of American companies. Particularly those headed by close supporters of the Administration (Halliburton, Bechtel and Fluor) are already getting ready to bid for contracts that are expected to run into billions of dollars. And, radiating outward, large economic opportunities beckon. Writing in *The New Yorker* (March 17, 2003), Seymour Hersh told[13] of one bizarre episode involving Richard

N. Perle, chairman of the Defense Policy Board, and various American and Saudi financiers including the notorious arms merchant, Adnan Khashoggi, for what is expected to be a hundred million dollar contract in the security field.

If not oil and other economic opportunity, what else?

Much has been said about the ugliness of the Iraqi regime. It has gassed Kurdish dissidents, relocated Shi'a citizens whom it suspected of pro-Iranian feelings and performed ghastly deeds of torture, rape and murder. Even at its least lethal, it is not attractive. As I witnessed in Baghdad recently, people are careful about what they say because they believe that an army of informers and secret police keep watch on them. And the massive public displays of Saddam's personality cult conjures the image of Stalin or Mao and reminds many of East Germany under Ulbricht.

But, we have not let such ugliness interfere with our relations with many other regimes or even, in former times, with Saddam. Donald Rumsfeld was in Baghdad to conclude a deal on the very day in March 1984 when the United Nations issued its report on Iraqi use of poison gas; that was not an unlucky coincidence — Americans and the British had sold Iraq the means to make it. At the time of the Iraqi attack on the Kurdish village of Halabja, the first Bush administration was giving Iraq hundreds of millions of dollars worth of aid including help to manufacture chemical and biological weapons.[14] Nor was Iraq unique. We helped or looked the other way while other regimes have engaged in similar ugly activities. So, notions of civic decency cannot be a major reason for our displeasure.

If not fear, oil, commercial profit and anger at tyranny, not much remains. So, at last we come to what I have called "dark matter."

V

When astronomers similarly found that all they knew about the universe did not add up to the total they believed had to exist, they were driven to posit a new form of matter. It seemed on the very edge of scientific knowledge or even of logic: it was what they termed "dark matter." And dark matter, they have come to believe, is far more significant than all that we had previously observed. So, I have been driven to conclude, beyond what we all have been reading about and discussing, there is a hidden agenda, the political equivalent to dark matter, that dominates American policy toward Iraq.

In this hidden agenda, I find three elements that seem of particular importance: 1) a new strategic vision of American world dominance; 2) a messaniac thrust of Christian Fundamentalism and (3) a relationship between Christian Fundamentalism and Israeli Zionism. I begin with the new vision of American world dominance.

1) The administration's National Security Strategy[15] or as it is becoming known, "The Bush Doctrine," sets out a vision, as previous papers have done, of a generally hostile world to be made safe for democracy. Since America has "unparalleled military strength and great economic and political influence," so goes the statement, it has "the duty of protecting those values against their enemies…" These enemies are different from those of the past: "Enemies in the past needed great armies and great industrial capabilities to endanger America… Now shadowy networks of individuals can bring great chaos and suffering to our shores [because] Terrorists are organized to penetrate open societies and to turn the power of modern technologies against us." Everywhere we look, we find enemies and we must attack them wherever they are and deny them sanctuary anywhere before they can harm us. "America will act against such emerging threats before they are fully formed." That is, America will shift from its longtime policy of containment to preëmptive attack wherever it deems a threat to exist or be likely to emerge.[16]

This vision of America is very different from any previous concept. For most of its history, America regarded itself as a nation apart from the world, protected by its oceans from foreign turmoil. Between the British attack in 1812 and the Japanese attack in 1941, it had comfortably assumed that it did not need be to a fortress because enemies could not reach it. During the Second World War, little attention was paid to defense of the mainland; the battle was taken to Europe and the Far East.

During the Cold War, America built its major defenses abroad and sought to contain any threat far from its shores. It was this almost total inexperience with threats to its home territory that made the attacks on the World Trade Center and the Pentagon so stunning to the American public. Unlike most other peoples, Americans had never seen the hideous face of war.

It was to this perception that the Bush doctrine spoke and it was this experience that gave the Bush administration its popularity. Since few living Americans remembered the Japanese attack on Pearl Harbor 60 years before, the terrorist attack on New York and Washington on September 11, 2001 was a major turning point in American history.

In haste and panic, the Congress passed the USA Patriot Act. That act gave the government unprecedented powers of arrest and detention. In most cases the courts backed up the new assumption of authority. Abroad, the government also immediately attacked the principal haven of the terrorists, Afghanistan, capturing or killing not only them but also members of the Afghan government and army. Then it shifted its aim from terrorists to a country that, as recounted above, had no discernible links to terrorism or to the attack on America, Iraq. The doctrine makes clear that Iraq need not be, and probably will not be, unique: other nations such as Iran (which is thought to be developing a nuclear capability) and North Korea (which already has a nuclear weapons program) have been categorized as "the axis of evil." Still others are thought to be far more likely than Iraq to have terrorist affiliations. These certainly include Pakistan, now considered an ally but known to contain hundreds of schools, like those that turned out the Taliban soldiers, where thousands of young men aspire to be like the Taliban and al-Qaida guerrillas. Similar groups operate in the Philippines. Already in the Philippines at least 3,000 American soldiers are engaged. Nothing seems likely to prevent the implementation of a strategy, spelled out in the Bush Doctrine, that will take American troops all over the globe.

As I have spelled out in detail elsewhere, under the single rubric of "terrorist" are a variety of movements. Some are motivated by a thwarted desire for what America itself has long regarded as legitimate, the "self determination of peoples." Where such movements are repressed, governments have a vested interested in categorizing them as terrorist and so in winning our approval for repression. These include the Chinese in Tibet and Turkistan; the Russians in

Chechenya; the Indians in Kashmir and the Israelis in Palestine. If Americans accept the definitions of regimes that seek to repress their minorities, there can be almost no end to the "war on terrorism."

How did we embark on this road? While it is clear that the Bush Doctrine was given its legitimacy in American politics by the events of September 11, 2001, it did not spring fully blown from those events: rather, it was an adaptation of strategic planning that some of the key figures in the current Bush administration began to set out at least a decade earlier.

Already in 1992, Paul Wolfowitz (then and today a senior official of the Department of Defense) and Zalmay Khalilzad (who has played the key role in Afghanistan) drafted a "Defense Planning Guidance" document. Already in that document, they set out the notion that America's task was to prevent to any rival superpower from rising in any part of the world. Included in the list of potential dangerous powers were Russia, China, Japan and Germany. In a statement of principles dated June 3, 1997, Wolfowitz and Khalilzad were joined by Dick Cheney, Donald Rumsfeld, Jeb Bush and Elliott Abrams among others in urging a new strategy, based on American military power, to remake the world in line with American "global responsibilities."

The group kept in being and in September 2000 emphasized its goal of "maintaining global US pre-eminence" against all possible rivals. This theme was picked up by George W. Bush when, as a candidate, he identified China as a "strategic competitor" and "espionage threat to our country." The program laid out a twenty-year plan to acquire what Bush termed "full spectrum dominance."

What Bush's team had in mind, however, represented such a radical departure from American tradition that only in the atmosphere generated by the terrorist attack of September 11, 2001 could they have convinced Americans to implement it.

2) Who are the Americans who have so quickly become the political army led by the Bush administration and what motivates them? It is difficult for me to comprehend this hidden element because it falls completely outside of the parameters in which most Americans, and certainly I, have been trained to analyze international relations. For the first time in American affairs, our

policies are being formed by a small but determined group of leaders working with a highly developed ideological movement. Exactly how George Bush joined this group is still not completely clear. What is clear that it offered him a program to implement what he had already come to believe while still governor of Texas, that he has been "called" by God. As he told a friend,[17] "I believe God wants me to run for president."

Belief in a divine mission to reorder the world dates back in America to the early Puritan movement and is, of course, far older. It caused Pope Urban II to preach the Crusades, King Louis VIII to attack the flourishing but heretical civilization of Provence and St. Dominique to initiate the Inquisition. Ironically, as viewed by Christians, it was also the inspiration for Muhammad's proclamation of Islam.

Today, large numbers of Americans share a belief in the absolute rightness of their cause and therefore in the evil of the intent and actions of those who do not march to the same drum beat. Above all, this seems to typify the millions of Americans who belong to the Southern Baptist Convention, but it is by no means limited to them. Nearly half of all Americans, some 46%, described themselves in a recent Gallup poll[18] as evangelical or born-again Christians. Throughout the poorer parts of the world, movements like the Pentacostalists are among the most widely and rapidly growing. Nor is the influence of this group limited to foreign affairs. It finds expression also in such domestic issues is the teaching of science in schools, birth control, and the criminal justice system. These and other issues have provided a strong core group in American politics at the head of which President Bush has placed himself.

3) Motivated by a literal interpretation of the Bible, particularly of the Old Testament, this group has also reached out to embrace its birthplace, Israel. As former President Jimmy Carter pointed out,[19] such people "are greatly influenced by their commitment to Israel based on eschatological, or final days, theology."

The suggestion that Israel and its American Christian and Jewish supporters are in any way involved in the administration's policy making has drawn much-feared and sometimes-lethal charges of anti-Semitism.[20]

As Patrick J. Buchanan pointed out in The American Conservative (March 24, 2003) "a passionate attachment to Israel is a 'key tenet of neoconservatism.'"[21] In conclusion, it is important to note that Iraq is only the beginning.

March 17, 2003

1. Against the Palestinians. James Brooks on February 13, 2003 provided a summary of the information and sources and the effects of an unidentified toxic gas (www.antiwar.com). Jonathan Cook documented (http:///www.lawsociety.org/Press/Preleases/2002/sep/sep27e. html) the use of lethal concentrations of tear gas. Such gas was also used by the Egyptians, to considerable governmental anger, in Yemen in the 1960s. As the now open files of the International Committee of the Red Cross show, Israel used biological weapons (based on typhoid) first in the 1948-1949 war. See http://weekly.ahram.org.eg/2003/627;focus.htm for references. Many countries, including the United States and Russia, have developed and planned the use of chemical and biological weapons. As I have said, when I was in the American government, I was briefed on the American program because of work I was doing on the danger of the spread of weapons of mass destruction.
2. U.S. Government documents, assembled by the National Security Archives at George Washington University, show that "American companies were allowed to sell chemical precursors to the Iraqis. Washington in the 1980s licensed dozens of other firms to ship biologicals to Iraq – eadly viruses and toxins, the sort of stuff Washington is now demanding Iraq destroy." See Neill MacDonald on CBC News http://www.cbc.ca/news/iraq/issues_analysis/saddam_goodguy_030310.html
3. This has been a principal argument in numerous lectures and two books of Scott Ritter, the former U.S. Marine officer who was in charge of the inspections. Existing stocks of weapons and equipment to make them were almost totally destroyed, he maintains, by the 3,500 specialists who comprised UNSCOM.
4. In a now famous article in *The Washington Post* (October), Dana Milbank commented that for the Bush administration "facts are malleable," Among other examples he noted the President's assertion that Iraq "has a growing fleet of unmanned aircraft that could be used 'for missions targeting the United States.'" Bush was referring to crop duster aircraft which are, of course, light, slow aircraft with very short range. He also said that the International Atomic Energy Agency (IAEA) had reported that Iraq was "six months away from developing a [nuclear] weapon." No such report existed. Reacting to the article,

the White House spokesman said that on occasion the President was "imprecise." Paul Krugman noted (*The International Herald Tribune*, October 28, 2002) that Milbank "is now the target of a White House smear campaign."

5. Reported in *The New York Times* (October 24, 2002) with the comment that the Pentagon inner group "are intent on politicizing intelligence to fi t their hawkish views on Iraq." Reflecting the frustration of the Administration with the regular intelligence agencies, The Toronto Sun reported (October 10, 2002) that it was relying upon the Israeli intelligence Agency Mossad as its "primary source of decision-making information."

6. The debriefing, reported by Newsweek on February 24, 2003,is available http://casi. org. uk/info/unscom950822.pdf. Secretary Powell told the Security Council on February 5, 2003 that Iraq's "admission only came out after inspectors collected documentation as a result of the defection of Hussein Kamel, Saddam Hussein's late son-in-law." Hadley's comment was in *The Chicago Tribune* of February 16, 2003.

7. As Kenneth Rapoza revealed in *The Boston Globe* shortly after Powell's speech. The Israeli organization that published his paper is closely associated with the Washington Institute for Near East Policy, a pro-Israeli organization in which the Pentagon adviser Richard Perle is active.

8. As required by the Geneva Convention

9. As reported in *The Guardian* of March 7, 2003, U.S. Major Elizabeth Rouse, a pathologist, signed a homicide death certificate for one Afghan prisoner certifying that he died as a result of "blunt force injuries to lower extremities complicating coronary artery disease." Other prisoners told *The New York Times* (March 7, 2003) that they had been "kept naked, hooded and shackled and were deprived of sleep for days on end. Mr. Shah [one prisoner] said that American guards kicked him to stop him falling asleep." Others were refused medical attention or deprived of food and water for extended periods. Other techniques have already acquired a nickname, "torture light." Allegedly (*The Guardian* March 5, 2003) some people arrested even in Los Angeles have fl own out of the United States and turned over to the governments where torture is routine and unrestricted.

10. In his State of the Union address, President Bush said that "3,000 suspected terrorists have been arrested in many countries" while "many others have met a different fate" so that they "are no longer a problem to the United States."

11. Obligatory disclosure by all government officials noted in *The Guardian* (March 12, 2003). While Cheney's "deferred income" is legal, it gives the appearance of a conflict of interest since, obviously, current Halliburton employees will be treated by civil servants with a special deference because of their connection to the White House. Under Cheney's leadership, Halliburton did about $2.3 billion worth of business with the Federal Government.

12. *The [London] Times* reported on March 12, 2003 that the Kirkuk oil field has been mined and set to be detonated in case of American attack. This has been denied by Iraq.

13. Infuriated by the article, in which Hersh quoted Khashoggi accusing Perle and others of "peddling influence," Perle accused Hersh of being "the closest thing American journalism has to a terrorist" on a CNN program. (http://www.cnn.com/Transcripts/0303/09/le.00.html)

14. R. Jeffrey Smith in *Washington Post* reprinted in The International Herald Tribune (July 23, 1992) reported that the U.S. Commerce Department was investigating 34 cases of high-tech exports to Iraq including "bacteria and fungus cultures, computers and electronic instruments, chemical-process control equipment and missile navigation and communications gear." *The Guardian* (March 6, 2003) reported that at the same time, an English company with British government financing, built a £14 million chlorine plant known as Falluja 2 which was capable of making mustard gas and nerve agents.

15. Published in *The New York Times* (September 20,. 2002)

16. Offensive action, "the threat or use of force against the territorial integrity or political independence of any state" was treated as a war crime in the Nuremberg trials and is banned in Article 2 ¶ 4 of the UN Charter which, since it was ratified by the U.S. Senate, has the force of law in the United States. The sole permissible exception (Article 51) was response to a prior armed attack and then only under the authority of the Security Council.

17. Quoted in Jackson Lears's "How a War Became a Crusade," *The New York Times* (March 11, 2003).

18. Quoted in Nicholas D. Kristof in *The New York Times* (March 5, 2003).

19. "Just War – or a Just War" printed in *The New York Times* (March 9, 2003).

20. Most recently in the attack on Congressman James P. Moran, Jr.

21. He goes on to decry the use of the charge of anti-Semitism "to nullify public discourse by smearing and intimidating foes and censoring and blacklisting them and any who would publish them. Neocons say we attack them because they are Jewish. We do not. We attack them because their warmongering threatens our country, even as it finds a reliable echo in [Israeli Prime Minister] Ariel Sharon."

THE BAGHDAD MUSEUM:
A GREAT CULTURAL LEGACY AND PERHAPS A CASUALTY OF WAR.

ON APRIL 10, THE WORLD helplessly stood by as it witnessed the wanton destruction of Iraq's National Museum, no doubt one of the world's greatest repositories of cultural treasures. Only weeks before, I had walked its corridors, marvelling at the wealth of material on display. Standing alone in a corridor on the second floor of the Iraq Museum of Antiquities was a copy – fortunately the original is safely housed in the Louvre – of a stone stele depicting Hammurabi, the 18th century BC ruler of Babylon, receiving one of the first known code of laws from the sun god and god of justice, Shamas.

Shamas instructs Hammurabi "To cause justice to prevail in the land, to destroy the wicked and the evil, that the strong may not oppress the weak." Proudly, Hammurabi took as his title, "king of justice." The parallel with Abraham, said to have been born in Mesopotamia centuries later, receiving his laws from the Hebrew god Yahweh is too striking to miss.

As I walked through the museum a few days ago, I passed gigantic Assyrian wall carvings, some 15 meters long and about 5 meters tall, showing ceremonies in ancient Nineveh and Ashur. Giant human-headed, winged bulls that had once guarded the gates of the Assyrian capitals, loomed overhead. Buried for thousands of years, they blazoned forth as though carved only yesterday to proclaim the majesty of the greatest empire in the ancient world.

Scores of glass cases displayed thousands of tiny masterpieces of the earliest Mesopotamian craftsmen. In some cases were hundreds of stone cylinders, each the size of a child's finger. Painstakingly incised in reverse, they produced vivid images of griffons, sphinxes and other mythological beasts when rolled across wet clay. In other cases were some of the earliest known pieces of elaborate pottery, jewelry and statues from Ur, Babylon, Nineveh, Nimrud, Ashur and the score of cities scattered along the Tigris and Euphrates rivers. Still other cases contained scores of clay tablets on which the ancient Mesopotamians wrote contracts, letters, decrees that give us such a vivid picture of their civilizations.

I found in both Baghdad and in Washington is that the American assault on Iraq was expected to begin on or about March 20 with a furious air bombardment. The firepower of the assault would dwarf the London Blitz and perhaps even the destruction of Berlin in the Second World War. In addition to rockets fired from hundreds of aircraft, many of them launched from great heights and far away, American government spokesmen warned that the attack would include perhaps as many as 400 cruise missiles each day.

Fearing this, cultural leaders from around the world had petitioned the US Air Force targeteers to take all possible precautions to avoid the museum and other major cultural sites. They have pointed out that in the 1991 Gulf War, considerable damage was done to several major archaeological treasures. The great ziggurat of Ur, towering over the surrounding plain, was hit and the great vault of the Persian palace at Ctesiphon was cracked. In an attempt to protect the treasures of the Baghdad museum, parts of its collection were then dispersed to regional museums where some were destroyed or looted.

Basing their petitions on the 1954 Hague Convention on the Protection of Cultural Property in the Event of Armed Conflict, archaeologists and others urged that America had an obligation to do its utmost to avoid bombing or otherwise endangering cultural sites and institutions. Their petitions lost some of their force since America signed but did not ratify the convention.

With this in mind, I called on the museum director to ask him what precautions he had taken to protect his irreplaceable collection. In reply he simply raised his hands and eyebrows in a gesture of resignation, saying, "what can I do?"

He knew that even if the museum was not hit by a missile, and even if much of the collection was stored in underground vaults, it was still likely that in the confusion of the invasion, the museum would be looted. When law and order breaks down, and people are driven to desperation, some will certainly will certainly take the opportunity to seize what they can to sell for food or just to enrich themselves. Unless the time of the collapse of the Iraqi regime and the arrival of British and American troops were almost miraculously synchronized, there would be days or perhaps even weeks when no one would be able to stop the pillage.

This was the experience in the 1991 Gulf War. Then local looters, some acting in concert with international dealers and even with resident diplomats, took sledge hammers and chain saws to giant statues and wall carvings and simply grabbed what they could from the shattered glass cases of museum collections. An "antiquities mafia" sprang into existence, reaching from London and New York down to villages all over Iraq. Thousands of treasures flooded the markets of Europe and America, never again to be seen in the country's museums.

As I walked slowly from room to room, I wondered if I might be one of the last to see that legacy of the works of dozens of generations craftsmen and artists dating back thousands of years. Of all the terrible casualties of war, this would rank among the most costly.

In the short time that remained before the onslaught, I made a determined effort to try to save the collection. There was, of course, no way to stop the invasion or scale down the onslaught, so I tried to organize a scheme to remove the collection to a safe place. To this end, I approached the government of Jordan to ask if King Abdullah would agree to act as its custodian under the supervision of an international committee composed of the directors of the world's major museums. At the same time, I proposed to the W. P. Carey Foundation, on whose board I sit, to appropriate the money to have the collection packed and shipped.

The former prime minister of Jordan, who had been a student of mine, was sympathetic but reasonably pointed out that Abdullah would not consider such a move unless asked by the Iraqi government which, furious that they were being attacked, would say "if our buildings are to be blown up and we are to be killed, we will not make your attack easier by removing something you do not wish to destroy."

So I fell back on the last possibility: I offered to go back to Baghdad the first week of March to see if I could help organize and finance a move of everything into the museum cellars and the construction of sandbag walls around the huge pieces.

But it was too late. The attack began a few days later. And it would not have stopped the raging mob of looters. They were desperate and the rewards were too great.

As it turned out, during the attack, when they could have protected the museum, the American forces did not. They conspicuously guarded the ministry of petroleum but paid no attention to hospitals, schools and, above all, the museum. The failure to do so caused the chairman of President Bush's Advisory Committee on Cultural Property, Martin Sullivan, to declare on April 17, "The tragedy was foreseeable and preventable" and to resign his post.

For several days, gangs of men armed with axes, chainsaws, sledgehammers and guns rampaged through the museum, shattered the glass cases holding the objects I had seen, broke down or cut up those objects too heavy to carry and smashed their ways through the heavy doors of the cellar vaults. They were mainly after the commercially "high value" objects, but they also took the entire collection, some 80,000 pieces of the cuneiform "library" of ancient Mesopotamia. Almost worse, they ripped apart the records of the vast collection. While of no value to them, the records might have enabled UNESCO, as the UN Security Council had instructed it, to effect a worldwide ban on the sale of objects stolen by the looters. But without the records, such a ban will be difficult to enforce.

Attempts are now being made to repair what could have been saved: Italy has led with a grant of $400,000; such duplicates as other museums have of the records are being assembled and under the leadership of the British Museum experts are being gathered from the Louvre, the Metropolitan and the Berlin Museum. Universities and such organizations as the World Monuments Fund have mobilized to help. These efforts are commendable, but they are both too little and too late. In what has been lost is not just an Iraqi tragedy; it is a tragedy for us all.

April 20, 2003

Down, Down, Down in The Iraqi Quicksand

ADDING TO THE EXISTING despair and danger of the American position in Iraq, the country now seems to be on the brink of a religiously-driven civil war. The explosion in front of the shrine of the Imam Ali (cousin and son-in-law of the Prophet Muhammad and patron "saint" of the Shia sect of Islam) in the Shia religious center of Najaf on August 29 killed the most moderate and cooperative leader of Iraq's largest community. It not only galvanized anti-American activity but appears to have stunned the American authorities. It may later be seen to have been the first event of a civil/guerrilla/anti-foreign war, a veritable political "black hole."

Bad as the situation now is, it should come as no surprise: it was both predictable and predicted before the American invasion. Despite repeated warnings by knowledgeable scholars – and by government experts – the ideologically-driven "neoconservatives" then (and now) setting American policy convinced themselves that their "war of liberation" would be met by a smiling population bearing flowers and waving American flags. What actually happened is a litany of miscalculations and blunders.

The assumption of the Bush administration was that the Iraqi people hated Saddam Husain. It then lacked (and still lacks) any way to gauge how accurate that assumption was. What we do know is that, however much any people may hate or fear native despots, they rarely and then only temporarily welcome foreign meddlers. Nationalism is so strong an idea that it unites even bitter enemies against outsiders. The United States has been given many lessons to prove the truth of this statement. One particularly vivid lesson was in Somalia where the Americans ended up fighting almost the whole population of Mogadishu while trying to "liberate" them.

Also in Mogadishu, America should have learned that while acting solely on its own appeared to solve "command and control" military problems, it enormously increased political problems. The United States did not inform the

UN of its planned attempt to kidnap the Mogadishu warlord, but when its troops failed in their attempt and were in mortal danger, it turned to the UN for support. In Iraq today, the lesson of Mogadishu is being relearned. The Bush administration, having repeatedly heaped scorn on the UN and disdained "multilateralism," is now inviting UN cover and begging for troops from countries it hardly recognized a few months ago.

Meanwhile in Iraq, blunder has followed blunder. First was the confusion of "battle" with "war." It was always obvious that the US could overpower the Iraqi army. On the eve of the invasion, Iraq had only a rag-tag military force of dubious loyalty, poorly armed and disorganized. Some of the troops lacked even shoes. Iraq had no sophisticated air defense systems to defend its troops or cities. America's "shock and awe" military machine, created at a yearly cost equal to the combined military budgets of the rest of the world and thousands of times more than Iraq's pitiful little army, could have overwhelmed the army of any of the world's states with the possible exceptions of Russia and China. It literally obliterated the Iraqi army.

But, at a cost. Or rather at several costs, some of which are still to be calculated. Consider first the material cost. Estimates of what it will take to rebuild what was destroyed range to more than half a trillion dollars and to take years to accomplish. Less easy to calculate is the resentment of almost the whole population who had relatives among the tens of thousands wounded or killed. Virtually every independent observer has reported that even many of those who overtly cooperate with the occupation authorities covertly hate them.

These two facts – material costs and private fury – form the basis of a third problem: the standard of living of virtually all Iraqis has not just declined but even crashed. Clean drinking water is a luxury beyond the means of almost everyone; in the searing Iraqi summer where temperatures range above 45 degrees (115-130 degrees Fahrenheit), people who had become accustomed to air-conditioning now cannot even run fans. Garbage piles up and sewage clogs the waterways. Food is often hard to get and of poor quality.

In this environment, the American authorities, spurred on by the leading neoconservative and the architect of the Iraq war, Deputy Secretary of Defense Paul Wolfowitz, his proconsul, L. Paul Bremer III, and their principal Iraqi agent, Ahmad Chalabi, have mounted a sweeping campaign against those they identify as collaborators in the defunct Baath Party regime. In this campaign, thousands of Iraqis, not just policemen or soldiers but even medical practitioners, school teachers and university professors have lost their jobs and incomes.

Not surprisingly, nostalgia for the Baath regime is growing. From many sources, I hear words like these, "I didn't like Saddam, but I kept out of his way." "Then it was safe to walk on the streets." "I had clean drinking water." "I had a job." "Money was tight so I couldn't afford everything, of course, but that was the fault of the Americans. They kept us all locked up for ten years with their sanctions." "Oh, yes, it was much better then. Now look around. We live in the ruins."

Voices like these are apparently not heard even by the Americans in Baghdad. In truth, there is little contact between the Americans and the Iraqis. Fear has driven them apart.

The Iraqis fear that they will be taken for guerrillas and shot if they approach the Americans they see most often, the soldiers. The soldiers, naturally, tend to suspect that any Iraqi, even a child or a women, might be carrying a bomb or a kalashnikov. What are believed to be attacks but of which some may be just misunderstandings occur at least a dozen times a day. Usually many Iraqis are wounded or killed. Some are real attacks in which at least one American is killed every day. So fear feeds on itself.

It isn't only fear that keeps the Americans and Iraqis apart. In part, it is policy. The American occupation authority has allowed no Iraqi representation in the decision-making councils. True, 25 Iraqis are members of the "Iraq Governing Council," but, even though they were selected by the Americans, they have been given no authority. When needed, the Council members are brought to the American headquarters. Their inferior position is thus publicly and symbolically manifested. Local attempts at "grass roots" political organization have generally landed the participants in jail. American policy is to work "on" rather than "with" the Iraqis.

Policy is not the only reason the two groups are apart. Another reason is where and how the Americans live. The soldiers, of course, live in strictly segregated military camps. Everything about them is "extraterritorialized." Their food, water, soft drinks, tents, uniforms, equipment and entertainment all are brought in from abroad. This is both because that is the way the American army operates and also because it fears that anything acquired locally, even Coca Cola, might be poisoned.

The world the soldiers inhabit is not cozy. One observer, himself a senior military man, wrote that "The US troops here look like hobos, live like pigs and are still conducting combat actions." Many have expressed their fear that they will be in Iraq for months if not years. They appear to be increasingly depressed and angry and are writing home to tell relatives they feel misled or even betrayed.

The American civilians also live in a world apart. The most senior are accommodated in Baghdad's best hotel, Al-Rashid, surrounded by barbed wire and protected by tanks and military patrols. Relative to the general population, they live in what Kipling would have called "more-than-oriental splendor."

The UN mission was shunned by the Americans; it lived apart as a tolerated poor relation. And, on August 19, it was decimated by a huge car-bomb. Among the casualties were the UN special representative, Sergio Vieira de Mello, one of the most able peace "seekers" the UN had, and the deputy head of mission, Nadia Younes, a brave, spirited and intelligent woman who had just been appointed to be UN assistant secretary general in charge of the General Assembly. It will be difficult to replace people of this quality especially as any replacement will see himself as a target.

Sr. Vieira brought to his position 30 years of experience and was largely credited for the successful transition of East Timor from war to peace. He is known to have come to the conclusion that the problem of Iraq today is essentially sovereignty and that the American emphasis on "security" diverts or postpones achievement of peace and reconstruction. His analysis was not welcome in the office of L. Paul Bremer whom Sr. Vieira described (to Jonathan Steele of *The Guardian*) as "a true neo-con [servative] who does not care about getting international legitimacy."

Sr. Vieira's message will now be even harder to deliver. Whatever the long-term effect of his and Nadia Younes's deaths, they have already had short-term effects. Taking heed of the "message" the bomb signified, the World Bank withdrew its team. Several voluntary groups are pulling out. Among them is the International Red Cross which has long prided itself on its dedication and bravery in other crises.

Now comes the explosion on August 29 in front of the shrine in Najaf. Who did it? Why? What will be the result? These questions must be addressed.

Whoever did it would be foolish to "claim" responsibility. Creating chaos must have been a prime objective and it will be amplified by rumor. Rumors are already flying. Some Iraqis believe the attack is part of the American "war on Islam." From afar, American religious fundamentalists have given them chapter and verse for this suspicion. On the scene, American Marines have gotten involved in riots and fire fights at another Shia holy shrine in Karbala. Others in Iraq and elsewhere see the hand of the Israeli intelligence organization, Mossad. They point out that the Shiis are among the most formidable and determined of Israel's enemies. Still others focus on the "remnants" of the Baath regime – "a small group of bitter-enders" as L. Paul Bremer III called those who resist the American rule. After all, the Shia religious establishment regarded Saddam as a kafir (infidel) and Saddam regarded them as actual or potential traitors. Finally, in the religiously-charged atmosphere of Iraq, many Shiis will blame the Sunnis. In short, there is enough fuel to feed a number of fires.

Three things seem clear: first, the followers of the chief opponent of the Americans among the clerics, the young and aggressive Muqtada Sadr, who regarded Ayatollah Muhammad Bakr al-Hakim as a virtual American puppet, and who are not strangers to violence, are not probable suspects. For them to have attacked the shrine of their patron saint, Ali, is as unlikely as that the Catholic IRA would blow up St. Peter's at the Vatican.

The second is that the death of Ayatollah Muhammad deprives the Iraq Governing Council of its only moderating Shia voice and leaves Shaikh Muqtada Sadr the most important Shia leader. He now appears to have the potential to precipitate an Iraqi religious revolution on a scale similar to the one led by Ayatollah Ruhollah Khomeini in Iran in 1978.

The third is a further accentuation of the downward trend of America's position in Iraq. Under Saddam Husain, Iraq was a secular state, committed to modernization and posing no immediate (or probably long-term) danger to the United States. As we now know, it had no weapons of mass destruction, no serious capacity to damage its neighbors and no involvement with international terrorism. Such destructive tendencies as it exhibited could easily be and were (for us) painlessly contained. Today, as a consequence of American policy, most of these objectives have been lost.

Iraq is costing American tax payers roughly $5 billion a month just for "security." Hundreds of billions more will be needed to recreate a state America can afford to leave. There are reports that the anti-American Iraqi underground has now not only itself become a guerrilla (or what we today call a "terrorist") organization but is welcoming like-minded fighters from other lands. Religion, which was contained, admittedly in ugly and repressive ways, under Saddam is now becoming the justification and ideology of what could become a counter-crusade, a *jihad*. There still are no weapons of mass destruction, but as the American army is discovering, car bombs and bullets are no less lethal. If control of oil was a serious American objective, it is less available now than it was before. If chaos was the aim, the terrorists did an outstanding job.

Senator John McCain, who has just visited Iraq, apparently thinks that America should add another 20,000 or so troops. He should remember Vietnam where we added and added until we finally lost the war. The military route will almost certainly lead America into a wider, more complex and even less winnable series of conflicts.

However, no one in Washington seems to have thought of an "exit strategy." If America simply walks away, as it did in Somalia, the chaos it has created in Iraq seems likely to trigger domino-like crises throughout the area – Turkey will almost certainly invade Kurdistan; Iran will not be able to stand aloof because of its close affinities both with the Kurds in the north and the Shiis in the south; religious tensions – both Shii-Sunni and fundamentalist-establishment – which are already evident in the Gulf, will probably explode; the flow of oil will be endangered; moderate governments like Jordan and Lebanon will come under fire domestically and from abroad; in anger, fear or ambition, Israel will probably push further into the Arab world, thus creating new problems with Egypt, Syria and other Arab and Muslim states.

The current policy alternative appears almost as bad. Americans adopted the term "quagmire" to describe Vietnam. The US was never able there to create an southern alternative to Ho Chi Minh. For the mostly desert land of Iraq, quagmire is not the term of choice. But there the US is today similarly sinking into the Iraqi "quicksand." It is learning, once again – how many times do lessons have to be repeated – that thwarting nationalism is dangerous, creating governments is not a role for foreigners and rebuilding a shattered country is expensive. But, if the goal of the Bush administration's neoconservatives was permanent war, they, at least, should be pleased. They have now managed to turn Iraq into a seedbed of terrorism. Even they seemed shocked by what they have created.

As *New York Times* correspondent Dexter Filkins reported from Baghdad following the latest bombing, "There were no speeches calling for calm and few public appearances by anyone in charge. L. Paul Bremer III, the chief American administrator, was on vacation. Nobody seemed to know when exactly he would return. The American military command here said nothing." Shock and awe had given way to stunned silence.

Silence is something we cannot afford. Those who plan and execute disastrous policies often try to corner their critics by saying, "in retrospect, that was a mistake, but we are here now. No point in talking about the past. We must start from where we are."

So what to do? As an old policy planner for our government, I think there are several obvious moves:

1. Set a time for withdrawal. Were Britain and America to say that they promise to withdraw by a given date, some of the opposition to them would decline.

2. Take realistic steps to engage the Iraqis in planning their own future. Consultation has not been tried. It must be.

3. Stop playing games with the Iraq Governing Council. Genuine local figures, not American puppets, must be given some degree of authority quickly and then as quickly as possible be given more.

4. Decrease the presence of all foreign troops as much as possible and as quickly as possible.

5. Categorically affirm Iraqi ownership of its one significant national asset, oil. The US loses nothing by this since any future government of Iraq will share the goal of the Western powers: oil does not benefit Iraq unless it is sold and the only market is the West. But in nationalist terms, symbolism is the essence. It must be an Iraqi flag that flies over the fields.

Away from Iraq, there are two crucial moves; both are difficult. America should stop its "war" on Islam. When President Bush spoke of a "crusade," he opened a deep well of memory for Middle Easterners. The scurrilous attacks by American Christian fundamentalists on Islam and its prophet have done immense damage to the hopes for peace.

Last, most difficult and most crucial, is that the central issue of the Middle East, the relationship of Israel with the Arabs in general and the Palestinians in particular must be effectively addressed. As long as the Palestinian desire for self determination is thwarted, no Middle Eastern peace can be achieved. And, unless or until serious moves are made toward the creation of a nuclear-free Middle East, the temptation of Arab and Iranian governments to match Israel's nuclear arsenal will be irrestible.

Only if the Western powers seriously (and as justly as is now possible) address these issues can we hope for an acceptable degree of peace.

April 27, 2003

JANUARY 17, 2005

The American Conservative

EXIT STRATEGY

How to Leave Iraq

By William R. Polk

Graveyard of the British Empire

By Andrew J. Bacevich

Hitchens in the Himalayas

Taki: America's Fifth Column

The Phony Case Against France

A Time for Leaving

FROM CHILDHOOD, WE AMERICANS are deluged with slogans. We often select our breakfast food, our soap, and our toothpaste by jingles and catchphrases rather than by reading the labels. So we fall easily into accepting evocative expressions in place of analysis even when it comes to national security. Our parents were sold on the slogan that the First World War was the "war to end all wars," although the 20th century had more of them than any other in history. We went into Vietnam fearing the "domino effect," although the struggle there had little relationship to events in any other Asian country. We were rushed into the war in Iraq by the assertion that little, poor, remote Iraq was at the point of attacking mighty America, and now we are bogged down there allegedly by a ragtag faction of Ba'athist diehards.

Seldom do we hear hard-headed analysis of what is happening, what is possible, what the alternatives are, how much each will cost in lives, treasure, prestige, and security. When I was the member of the U.S. State Department's Policy Planning Council responsible for the Middle East, I had the duty to try to understand the reality in the problems we then faced, to comprehend the forces at work, and to identify what could be done. Now as a private citizen, I ask what is the reality of Iraq, what do we face there, and what can we do?

* * *

Leaving aside Kurdistan, where roughly a quarter of all Iraqis live, Iraq is a shattered country. Its infrastructure has been pulverized by the "shock and awe" of the American invasion. Few Iraqis today even have clean drinking water or can dispose of their waste. About 7 in 10 adult Iraqis are without employment. Factories are idle, and small shopkeepers have been squeezed out of business. Movement even within cities is difficult and dangerous. And the trend in each of these categories is downward. Iraq's society has been torn apart, and perhaps as many as 100,000 Iraqis have died. Virtually every Iraqi has a parent, child, spouse, cousin, friend, colleague, or neighbor – or perhaps all of these – among the dead. More than half of the dead were women and children. Putting Iraq's casualties in comparative American terms would equate to about one million American deaths. Dreadful hatreds have been generated.

Not all hatreds are on the Iraqi side. American soldiers, often not knowing why they are in Iraq but only that they are getting shot at in 50 to 100 attacks each day, are fearful. Against an indistinguishable enemy, who fades into the general population, their fear turns into general hatred. To GIs, the natives are "ragheads," just as in Vietnam they were "gooks." And they may be suicide bombers. Hatred of the enemy appeared in a film made by NBC News inside a mosque in Fallujah showing a Marine shooting a wounded Iraqi. It also appeared in the photographs of the torture of prisoners at the Abu Ghraib prison. Those scenes, in turn, helped to cement the image of the uniformed, indistinguishable foreign troops as the common enemy, whom the Iraqis are beginning to call the "crusaders."

Such graphic demonstrations of hatred and contempt also, of course, echo far beyond Iraq among the more than one billion Muslims throughout the world. They have tended to corrupt the greatest of America's national treasures, the nearly universal respect of mankind. As one former senior Army officer Andrew Bacevich said, "My sense is that such an impression has already taken hold in the Arab world." He is certainly right.

Thus, even when, as in the Fallujah battle, the insurgents were outnumbered at least 20:1, and it was obvious that they could not win against a phalanx of helicopters, gunships, fighter-bombers, tanks, and artillery, they fought to become martyrs for their cause and thus to inspire others to take up their mission. They lost the battle of Fallujah as they will lose every battle. But they have not lost the war. This is the reality with which America must deal.

* * *

Guerrilla warfare is not new. In fact, it is probably the oldest form of warfare. But in recent centuries, so much attention was given to formal warfare that most soldiers forgot about informal war. Although few guerrilla leaders have given us accounts of how they organized, got their supplies, fought, retreated, regrouped, and fought again, history provides a rich lode of information. We can study experiences dating from the 20th-century conflicts in Europe, Asia, and Africa, including the Irish struggle against the British, Tito's and the Greek

ELAS's struggles against the Germans in the Balkans, Mao Zedong's war against the Japanese and then against the forces of Chang Kai-shek in China, the Viet Minh's defeat of the French in Indo-China, the Algerian war of national liberation against the French, the Chechens' centuries-long war against the Russians and, of course, our Vietnam and Russia's Afghanistan.

The story they tell was well summarized by Mao Zedong when he described the guerrilla as a fish that must swim in the "sea" of the people. Absent popular support, Mao's sea, the guerrilla is at best an outlaw and, more likely and sooner, a corpse. But with the support of the people, he is elusive, nourished, and ultimately replaceable. Consequently, almost no matter what forces are brought against him, he – or at least his cause – has proven indefatigable. If we are ignorant of this history, we are doomed to repeat it.

Generation after generation of soldiers and strategists have done just that — repeated it. Often ignorant of history and of the reflections of their predecessors, they attempted to find techniques to defeat the guerrillas. The ultimate way was by killing them. Caesar's conquest of Gaul was essentially a war of extermination as was the British war against the Irish and the Tsarist and Communist Russians' war on the Chechens. Even genocide rarely succeeded because new generations arose to replace the dead.

If not all could be killed, at least their lands and other resources could be taken away from them and given to alien settlers. This was the gist of colonialism as practiced by the French in Algeria and the Russians in Central Asia. Since we regard neither genocide nor colonialism as politically correct today, experiments have been made with various other tactics. In Vietnam, America tried a variety of them, as did the Soviet Union in Afghanistan. Without ultimate success. Today, in Iraq and in occupied Palestine, Americans and Israelis are repeating these campaigns, focusing primarily on the application of overwhelming military power designed to dishearten the insurgents. In 40 years, the Israelis have not achieved security; the chances that the Americans will in five years appears unlikely.

Why is this so? The answer is essentially simple: people of all religions and races share a common desire to control their own lives. Our Declaration of Independence puts it eloquently for us, and President Woodrow Wilson summed it up neatly for others when he spoke of the quest for "the self-determination of peoples." Thwarted in this quest, some people – whom, if we approve of them, we call "freedom fighters" or, if not," fanatics" or "terrorists" – take up arms, as Americans did in our revolution. They are usually few in number, perhaps 15,000 or so in Iraq today and roughly the same in Algeria in the 1950s, but many more people who do not themselves actually fight support them.

Knowing that they cannot defeat the foreign enemy, the insurgents seek not so much to win battles as to wear him down, to inflict upon him what he will regard as unacceptable casualties and other costs, and to erode his political support. Thus, almost inevitably, the techniques of guerrilla warfare fade into terrorism.

We have mistakenly acted as though terrorism was a thing or a group against which one can fight. But terrorism is merely a tactic that can be used by anyone. Ancient Britons used it against the Romans, the Zionists against the British, the Algerians against the French, the French against the Nazis, the Chechens against the Russians, the Basques against the Spaniards, the Palestinians against the Israelis and so on. Terrorism is the traditional "weapon of the weak," who resort to it when all else fails.

At the beginning of the struggle against Saddam Hussein, the Bush administration charged that Iraq was a terrorist state acting in close collaboration with Osama bin Laden's al-Qaeda. In the emotional reaction to the attacks in New York and Washington, sloganeering drowned out intelligence. Saddam Hussein's regime was certainly evil, but Iraq was not a terrorist state. It had no significant relationship with any terrorist organization as the American, British, and Israeli intelligence agencies knew. In fact, Osama bin Laden, a religious fundamentalist, had offered to raise a military force to fight Saddam's secular government and denounced Saddam with the strongest condemnation a Muslim can utter, that he was a kafir, a godless person. Despite the findings of official American investigations, however, the rallying cries stick in our minds. Seven in 10 Americans still believe Saddam Hussein was working with Osama bin Laden in the September 11, 2001 attacks.

While that is wrong, Iraq has changed under American blows so that it is now a prime recruiting ground and justification for terrorism. As the commander of the 1st Marine Division, Maj. Gen. Richard Natonski, put it just before the attack on Fallujah, "After we take Fallujah, the terrorists will have no sanctuary, nowhere to hide." I remember similar words about the Vietcong. And within a day after the general said this, fighting broke out in a dozen Iraqi cities. The Russians could have told General Natonski that a decade after they did to the Chechen city of Grozny what his troops did to Fallujah, fighting continued. That is what we are now seeing in Iraq. This is the reality with which we must begin. So what can America do?

* * *

Today, there are no good options — only better or worse alternatives. Three appear possible:

The first option has been called "staying the course." In practice, that means continued fighting. France "stayed the course" in Algeria in the 1950s as America did in Vietnam in the 1960s and as the Israelis are now doing in occupied Palestine. It has never worked anywhere, in Algeria, the French employed over three times as many troops – nearly half a million – to fight roughly the same number of insurgents as America is now fighting in Iraq. They lost. America had half a million soldiers in Vietnam and gave up. After four decades of warfare against the Palestinians, the Israelis have achieved neither peace nor security.

Wars of national "self-determination" can last for generations or even centuries. Britain tried to beat down (or even exterminate) the Irish for nearly 900 years, from shortly after the 11th-century Norman invasion until 1921; the French fought the Algerians from 1831 until 1962; Imperial and Communist Russia fought the Chechens since about 1731. Putin's Russia is still at it. There was no light at the end of those tunnels.

At best, staying the course in Iraq can be only a temporary measure as eventually America will have to leave. But during the period in which it stays, say the next five years, my guess is that another 30,000 to 40,000 Iraqis will die or be killed while the U.S. armed forces will lose at least another 1,000 dead and 20,000 seriously wounded. The monetary cost will be hundreds of billions of dollars.

It is not only the casualties or treasure that count. What wars of "national liberation" demonstrate is that they also brutalize the participants who survive. Inevitably such wars are vicious. Both sides commit atrocities. In their campaigns to drive away those they regard as their oppressors, terrorists/freedom fighters seek to make their opponents conclude that staying is unacceptably expensive and, since they do not have the means to fight conventional wars, they often pick targets that will produce dramatic and painful results. Irish, Jews, Vietnamese, Tamils, Chechens, Basques, and others blew up hotels, cinemas, bus stations, and apartment houses, killing many innocent bystanders. The more spectacular, the bloodier, the better for their campaigns. So the Irgun blew up the King David Hotel in Jerusalem in 1946, the IRA a Brighton hotel in 1984, an Iraqi group the UN headquarters in Baghdad in 2003. Chechens blew up an apartment house in Moscow in 2003, while a Palestinian group blew up an Israeli-frequented hotel in Tuba, Egypt in 2004.

Faced with such challenges, the occupying power often reacts with massive attacks aimed at terrorists but inevitably kill many civilians. To get information from those it manages to capture, it also frequently engages in torture. Torture did not begin at the Abu Ghraib prison; it is endemic in guerrilla warfare. Two phrases from the Franco-Algerian war of the 1950s-60s tell it all: "torture is to guerrilla war what the machine gun was to trench warfare in the First World War" and "torture is the cancer of democracy." Guerrilla warfare and counterinsurgency inexorably corrupt the very causes for which soldiers and insuregents fight. Almost worse, even in exhausted "defeat" for the one and heady "victory" for the other, they leave behind a chaos that spawns warlords, gangsters, and thugs as is today so evident in Chechnya and Afghanistan.

The longer the fighting goes on, the worse the chaos. Viewing the devastation of Fallujah, one correspondent wrote, "Even the dogs have started to die, their corpses strewn among twisted metal and shattered concrete in a city that looks like it forgot to breathe... The city smelled like dust, ash — and death. "Viewing the same scene, the deputy commander of the 1st Marine Expeditionary Force said, "This is what we do... This is what we do well." This is not new or unique; it is classic. Recall the statement the Roman historian Tacitus attributed to the contemporary guerrilla leader of the Britons. The Romans, he said, "create a desolation and call it peace."

The second option is "Vietnamization." In Vietnam, America inherited from the French both a government and a large army. What was needed, the Nixon administration proclaimed, was to train the army, equip it, and then turn the war over to it. True, the army did not fight well nor did the government rule well, but they existed. In Iraq, America inherited neither a government nor an army. It is trying to create both. Not surprisingly, the results are disappointing. Most Iraqis regard the American-selected and American-created government as merely an American puppet. And the idea that America can fashion a local militia to accomplish what its powerful army cannot do is not policy but fantasy. An Iraqi army is unlikely to fight insurgents with whom soldiers sympathize and among whom they have relatives. Many have reportedly thrown off their new uniforms and joined the insurgents.

Much has been made also of the constitution we wrote for the Iraqis. It reads well, as did the one the British wrote for the Iraqis 80 years ago in 1924, but it is not anchored in the realities of Iraqi society. Absent the institutions that give life to a constitution, it will be simply a piece of paper as was the one the British provided. Representative government grows in the soil of the people or it doesn't grow at all. It cannot be mandated by foreign rulers.

Thus, the best America might gain from this option is a fig leaf to hide defeat; the worst, in a rapid collapse, would be humiliating evacuation, as in Vietnam.

The third option is to choose to get out rather than being forced. Time is a wasting asset; the longer the choice is put off, the harder it will be to make. The steps required to implement this policy need not be dramatic, but the process needs to be unambiguous. The initial steps could be merely verbal: America would have to declare unequivocally that it will give up its lock on the Iraqi economy, will cease to spend Iraqi revenues as it chooses, and will allow Iraqi oil production to be governed by market forces rather than by an American monopoly.

The second step, more difficult, is to make a truce and pull back its forces. If President Bush could be as courageous as Gen. Charles de Gaulle was in Algeria when he called for a "peace of the brave," fighting would quickly die down. This is not wishful thinking; it is what happened time after time in guerrilla wars.

Then, and only then, could Iraqis themselves set about creating a national consensus. It would probably not come through elections, although they might legitimize the process. We would probably not like the government that emerged, but we are already beyond being able to control that choice. What we should help and encourage is the essentially indigenous process of building civil institutions. Only as they emerge will some form of reasonably peaceful, reasonably free, reasonably decent government have a chance. This is the most sensitive and difficult part of the whole affair. It cannot be rushed, and we cannot do it for the Iraqis.

The danger during this period is twofold: on the one hand, Iraq, like Afghanistan, could shatter with local warlords seizing the pieces, or Iraq could split into a sort of eastern Balkans with Kurdish, Sunni Arab, and Shia Arab successor states. The one would certainly create mafia-style terrorism, while the other would promote mayhem as thousands of suddenly created refugees flee from now alien states. Further regional instability would be created, and possibly either Turkey or Iran or both would intervene, Turkey to suppress the Kurds and Iran to protect the Shi'ites. The results are unforeseeable but certainly ruinous.

On the other hand, in an attempt to avoid this disaster, we and our Iraqi protégés could, as we are now attempting, create a new Iraqi army. We should heed the lesson of Iraqi history. In the past, the British-created army destroyed moves toward civil society and probably would do so again, paving the way for the ghost of Saddam Hussein. In the period during and following American evacuation, Iraq would need a police force but not an army. A UN multinational peacekeeping force would be easier, cheaper, and safer. The balance between "security" and cohesion would be difficult to achieve and maintain, and we could be of only minimal help, but either extreme would be worse.

Meanwhile, a variety of service functions would have to be organized. Given a chance, Iraq could do them mostly by itself. With its vast potential in oil production, probably the greatest in the world, it could soon again become a rich country with a talented, well-educated population. Step by step, health care, clean water, sewage, roads, bridges, pipelines, electric grids, and housing could be provided by the Iraqis themselves, as they were in the past. When I visited Baghdad in February 2003, on the eve of the invasion, the Iraqis with whom I talked were proud that they had rebuilt what had been destroyed in the 1991 war. They can surely do so again. More important, in carrying out the rebuilding and reordering process, particularly at the grassroots level, Iraqis would begin to take control of their lives and start building the neighborhood institutions and consensus on which, if it is to grow at all, representative government will depend.

Economically, Iraq will also have to mend itself. Here the American role is primarily negative. We have imposed policies during our occupation that worked against the recovery of Iraqi industry and commerce. Abrogating these would spur development since any reasonably intelligent and self-interested government would emphasize getting Iraqi enterprises back into operation and employing Iraqi workers. That process could be speeded up through international loans, commercial agreements, and protective measures so that unemployment, now at socially catastrophic levels, would be diminished. Neighborhood participation in running social affairs and providing security are old traditions in Iraqi society and allowing or favoring their reinvigoration would promote the excellent side effect of grassroots political representation.

As fighting dies down, reasonable security is achieved, and popular institutions revive, the one million Iraqis now living abroad will be encouraged to return home. In the aggregate they are intelligent, highly trained, and well motivated and can make major contributions in all phases of Iraqi life. Oil production will play a key role. The income it generates can make possible great public works projects that will help to lure back Iraqi émigrés, employ Iraqi workers, encourage local entrepreneurs, and salvage the class of merchants and shopkeepers who traditionally provided security in Oriental cities. In its own best interest, the Iraqi government would empower the Iraq National Oil Company (INOC) to award concessions by bid to a variety of international companies to sell oil on the world market. This is obviously to the best interests not only of Iraq but also of the Western world.

Contracts for reconstruction paid for by Iraqi money would be awarded under bidding, as they traditionally were, but to prevent excessive corruption should perhaps initially be supervised by the World Bank. The World Bank would, of course, follow its regular procedures on its loans. Where other countries supplied aid, they would probably insist on (and could be given) preferential treatment in the award of contracts as is common practice everywhere.

In such a program, inevitably, there will be setbacks and shortfalls, but they can be partly filled by international organizations. The steps will not be easy; Iraqis will disagree over timing, personnel and rewards while giving the process a chance will require a rare degree of American political courage. But, and this is the crucial matter, any other course of action would be far worse for both America and Iraq. The safety and health of American society as well as Iraqi society requires that this policy be implemented intelligently, determinedly — and soon.

January 17, 2005

LESSONS OF IRAQ

ARE THERE ANY LESSONS TO BE LEARNED by the American venture into Iraq? The great German philosopher of history Georg Wilhelm Friedrich Hegel doubted our capacity to find out. "Peoples and governments," he wrote, "never have learned anything from history or acted on principles deduced from it." Writing about the Vietnam War, the neo-conservative American political scientist Samuel P. Huntington suggested that it would be best if policy makers "simply blot out of their mind any recollection of this one." It seems to me that they did. So, in at least some ways, the Iraq war has been proof of George Santayana's admonition that, having done so, we were doomed to repeat it. The urgent question today is, will the Iraq war itself be similarly blotted out and similarly repeated? The odds are with Professor Hegel.

Mr. Huntington's argument was based on the notion that Vietnam was unique since, as he saw it, imperialism and colonialism have "just about disappeared from world politics." That is, they were fading memories of a now irrelevant past. But is this true? Foreign domination has faded from our memory but not from the memories of many of the peoples of Asia and Africa. Focus on Iraq. Iraq became "independent" by treaty with Britain in 1922. Then it became "independent" by recognition of the League of Nations in 1932. But few Iraqis believe that it became really independent by either of these acts. Britain controlled the economy and maintained its military presence while it continued to rule Iraq behind a façade of governments it had appointed. It then reoccupied the country during World War II. After the war it ruled through a proxy until he was overthrown in 1958. So was 1958 the date of independence? On the surface yes, but below the surface American and British intelligence manipulated internal forces and neighboring states to influence or dominate governments; they helped to overthrow the revolutionary government of Abdul Karim Qasim and to install the Baath party which ultimately brought Saddam Husain to power. Knowing what they had done and fearing that they would do so again shaped much of the policy even of Saddam Husain.

By giving or withholding money, arms and vital battlefield intelligence, Britain and America influenced what Saddam thought he could do. So worried was he about his American connection that, before he decided to invade Kuwait, he called in the

U.S. ambassador to ask, in effect, if the invasion was ok with Washington. Only when he was assured in 1990 that the US had no policy on the frontiers with Kuwait by official testimony before Congress, by government press releases and by a face to-face meeting with our ambassador in Baghdad did he act. Either he misread the omens or we changed them. Our ambassador later said, incredibly, that we had not anticipated that he would take <u>all</u> of Kuwait. When he did, we invaded, destroyed much of his army and the Iraqi economy and imposed upon the country UN-authorized sanctions and unauthorized "no-fly" zones. Finally, in 2003 we invaded again, occupied the country and imposed upon it a government of our choice. Whatever the justification for any or all of these actions, they do not add up to independence. So even Iraqis who hated and feared Saddam always felt that they were living under a form of Western control. The simple fact is that the "memories" had not faded because they were based on current reality.

There are many things to be said about the American invasion and occupation of Iraq. I have written about most of them in my book, *Understanding Iraq*, which HarperCollins is publishing this month. But one thing stands out above all to me as a historian: we were (and I believe still are) ignorant of Iraqi history and culture. More pointedly, we had (and still have) no sense of how Iraqis saw their own past and their relationships with us. This ignorance has caused us, often inadvertently, to take actions that many or perhaps most Iraqis have read as imperialist. This has been true even of actions that we felt were generous, far-sighted and constructive. Take the provision of a constitution as an example.

Constitutions are surely "good." We treasure ours even when we do not always abide by it. We believe that other countries should have them because they are the bedrock of democracy. That sentiment was so widely held at the end of the First World War that the British made giving the Iraqis one a high priority. Experts were called in, phrases were debated, studies were made of the best then in operation, and finally, in 1924, a wonderful document emerged. It was greeted with great satisfaction but mainly by those who had given it, the British. Iraqis paid it little heed because it was not grounded in the realities of Iraqi society, practices or even hopes. Time after time, governments came into power that overturned or simply neglected every paragraph it contained.

So what did the American occupation government do? Was it aware of this history? Apparently not. It set about writing a new constitution. The emphasis was, of course, on "it," that is, the occupation authorities. They wrote the constitution without any Iraqi input and just handed it to their appointed interim government. That, to my mind, amounted to astonishing insensitivity. What was even more astonishing was that it somehow never occurred to the American lawyers who wrote it that it would become worthless, that is, illegal, when the interim administration was replaced by even a quasi- independent government. It was surely the shortest-lived constitution ever written.

If constitutions are necessary for democracies, elections are even more so. So, naturally, they too are good things. Iraq had to have one. Organizing and controlling it turned out to be a difficult task given what many Iraqis interpreted "our" election to mean: not to express a national consensus on democracy but to solidify our control over the country. Because at least some Iraqis were determined to get us out of their country, using guerrilla warfare tactics and terrorism against us and those Iraqis who supported us, we had to use our military forces to set parameters on the issues, the personnel and the form of this expression of freedom. As Jean-Jacques Rousseau long ago advocated, we decided to "force men to be free." The fact that, however unfree they were, the elections were held was hailed as a great victory for democracy. I remain unconvinced. I suspect that two fatal flaws will soon become evident: a heightening of the divisive tendencies already inherent in Iraqi society and a devaluation of the very concept of representative government.

Our policies on security are similarly subject to different interpretation. Where we have done most of what we have done in the name of security, our critics in Iraq have sought sovereignty. We believed that security had to come first. A close reading of history leads me to believe that the order is usually the reverse. When foreigners get out, insurgencies stop; they do not stop, no matter how massive the force used against them or how costly in blood and treasure the fighting is, until the foreigners leave. This surely is the lesson of Ireland, Çeçneya, Algeria, and even of our own Revolution. I predict it will be of Iraq too.

Believing that security comes first has led our government to concentrate on rebuilding an Iraqi army since doing so appeared to offer security at a bargain price. But, Iraqis remember the terrible costs to their society of the creation of armies. The one the British created, time after time subverted or overthrew civil governments. A new army, absent balancing civic institutions, which can grow only slowly and by internal developments, will surely again pave the way for a military dictatorship.

Related to, but to some extent external to, Iraq are other "lessons" we should ponder. What happened to Iraq showed other governments that they live at the sufferance of the United States. Iraq could not defend itself; nor can most other states. Those that can are those that have the ultimate weapon. Acquisition of even a few nuclear weapons provides "security" because the cost of attacking a power armed with them is too costly. African, Asian and even European observers believe that if Saddam Husain had waited until he had a nuclear weapon before attacking Kuwait, we would not have gone to war. North Korea today reinforces this assessment. There, we react with anger, economic sanctions and propaganda but not with military force.

However, the process of acquiring nuclear weapons is a time of deadly danger. So governments that decide to acquire them naturally try to move with the utmost secrecy and speed. They also usually seek to avoid provocations that might bring down upon them the wrath of the existing nuclear powers. That too is a lesson of Iraq: had Saddam not provided a provocation, we would probably not have gone to war. Indeed, we were supplying him with the components and equipment to make weapons of mass destruction right up to the time of our intervention. Surely, this "lesson" is in the minds of the Persians today as it was in the minds of the Russians, Chinese, Indians, Pakistanis and Israelis. The only alternative to this highly dangerous and ruinously costly drift in international affairs is mutual disarmament, but current American policies are rushing us, and the world, in exactly the opposite direction.

Finally, there is a grab-bag of other lessons again laid before us by Iraq: the first is that war is always unpredictable no matter how powerful the advantages one side seems to have at the beginning; the second is that they are always horrible. Not only are people killed or severely harmed, but whole societies, even of the victors, are brutalized. This was true of the British in Kenya, French in Algeria, Americans in the Philippines, Russians in Central Asia, and Chinese in Tibet. Finally, guerrilla wars are, at best, unwinnable – lasting as in Ireland for centuries and in Algeria for a century and a half. Çeçneya suffered massacre, deportation, rape and massive destruction for nearly four centuries and still is not "pacified." No one wins a guerrilla war; both sides lose. The only sensible policy is one that aims to stop them rather than to win them. Hegel and Santayana may be right, we may not learn, but certainly, Huntington is wrong in urging that we "blot" the lessons out of our minds.

March 26, 2005

DANIEL ELLSBERG: LEAK THE IRAN PLANS

HARPER'S

HARPER'S MAGAZINE/OCTOBER 2006 $6.95

THE WAY OUT OF WAR

A Blueprint for Leaving Iraq Now

By George S. McGovern and William R. Polk

THE BORDER IS WIDE

Guarding the Southern Flank of the American Dream

By Cecilia Ballí

TRIVIAL PURSUIT

The Fake Quest for an "Authentic Democrat"

By Kevin Baker

HAPPYLAND

The conclusion, by J. Robert Lennon

Also: Mike Davis and Tennessee Williams

THE WAY OUT OF WAR

A blueprint for leaving Iraq now*

STAYING IN IRAQ IS NOT an option. Many Americans who were among the most eager to invade Iraq now urge that we find a way out. These Americans include not only civilian "strategists" and other "hawks" but also senior military commanders and, perhaps most fervently, combat soldiers. Even some of those Iraqis regarded by our senior officials as the most-pro American are determined now to see American military personnel leave their country. Polls show that as few as 2 percent of Iraqis consider Americans to be liberators. This is the reality of the situation in Iraq. We must acknowledge the Iraqis' right to ask us to leave, and we should set a firm date by which to do so.

We suggest that phased withdrawal should begin on or before December 31, 2006, with the promise to make every effort to complete it by June 30, 2007.

Withdrawal is not only a political imperative but a strategic requirement. As many retired American military officers now admit, Iraq has become, since the invasion, the primary recruiting and training ground for terrorists. The longer American troops remain in Iraq, the more recruits will flood the ranks of those who oppose America not only in Iraq but elsewhere.

Withdrawal will not be without financial costs, which are unavoidable and will have to be paid sooner or later. But the decision to withdraw at least does not call for additional expenditures. On the contrary, it will effect massive savings. Current U.S. expenditures run at approximately $246 million each day, or more than $10 million an hour, with costs rising steadily each year. Although its figures do not include all expenditures, the Congressional Research Service listed direct costs at $77.3 billion in 2004, $87.3 billion in 2005, and $100.4 billion in fiscal year 2006. Even if troop withdrawals begin this year, total costs (including those in Afghanistan) are thought likely to rise by $371 billion during the withdrawal period. Economist Joseph Stiglitz and Linda Bilmes,

* (With former Senator George McGovern)

a former assistant secretary of commerce, have estimated that staying in Iraq another four years will cost us at least $1 trillion.

Let us be clear: there will be some damage. This is inevitable no matter what we do. At the end of every insurgency we have studied, there was a certain amount of chaos as the participants sought to establish a new civic order. This predictable turmoil has given rise to the argument, still being put forward by die-hard hawks, that Americans must, in President Bush's phrase, "stay the course." The argument is false. When a driver is on the wrong road and headed for an abyss, it is a bad idea to "stay the course." A nation afflicted with a failing and costly policy is not well served by those calling for more of the same, and it is a poor idea to think that we can accomplish in the future what we are failing to accomplish in the present. We are as powerless to prevent the turmoil that will ensue when we withdraw as we have been to stop the insurgency. But we will have removed a major cause of the insurgency once we have withdrawn. Moreover, there are ways in which we can be helpful to the Iraqis – and protect our own interests – by ameliorating the underlying conditions and smoothing the edges of conflict. The first of these would be a "bridging" effort between the occupation and complete independence.

To this end, we think that the Iraqi government would be wise to request the temporary services of an international stabilization force to police the country during and immediately after the period of American withdrawal. Such a force should itself have a firm date fixed for its removal. Our estimate is that Iraq would need this force for no more than two years after the American withdrawal is complete. During this period, the force could be slowly but steadily cut back in both personnel and deployment. Its purpose would be limited to activities aimed at enhancing public security. Consequently, the armament of this police force should be restricted. It would have no need for tanks or artillery or offensive aircraft but only light equipment. It would not attempt, as have American troops, to battle the insurgents. Indeed, after the withdrawal of American troops, as well as British regular troops and mercenary forces, the insurgency, which was aimed at achieving that objective, would almost immediately begin to lose public support. Insurgent gunmen would either put down their weapons or become publicly identified as outlaws.

We imagine that the Iraqi government, and the Iraqi people, would find the composition of such a force most acceptable if it were drawn from Arab or Muslim countries. Specifically, it should be possible under the aegis of the United Nations to obtain, say, five contingents of 3,000 men each from Morocco, Tunisia, and Egypt. Jordan and Syria might also be asked to contribute personnel. If additional troops were required, or if any of these governments were deemed unacceptable to Iraq or unwilling to serve, application could be made to such Muslim countries as Pakistan, Bangladesh, and Indonesia. Other countries might be included if the Iraqi government so wished.

It would benefit both Iraq and the United States if we were to pay for this force. Assuming that a ballpark figure would be $500 per man per day, and that 15,000 men would be required for two years, the overall cost would be $5.5 billion. That is approximately 3 percent of what it would cost to continue the war, with American troops, for the next two years. Not only would this represent a great monetary saving to us but it would spare countless American lives and would give Iraq the breathing space it needs to recover from the trauma of the occupation in a way that does not violate national and religious sensibilities.

The American subvention should be paid directly to the Iraqi government, which would then "hire" the police services it requires from other governments. The vast amount of equipment that the American military now has is Iraq, particularly transport and communications and lights arms, should be turned over to this new multinational force rather than shipped home or destroyed.

As the insurgency loses its national justification, other dangers will confront Iraq. One of these is "warlordism", as we have seen in Afghanistan, and other forms of large-scale crime. Some of this will almost certainly continue. But the breakdown of public order will never be remedied by American forces; it can only be addressed by a national police force willing to work with neighborhood, village, and tribal home guards. Ethnic and regional political divisions in Iraq have been exacerbated by the occupation, and they are unlikely to disappear once the occupation is over.

They are now so bitter as to preclude a unified organization, at least for the time being. It is therefore paramount that the national police force involve local leaders, so as to ensure that the home guards operate only within their own territory and with appropriate action. In part, this is why Iraq needs a "cooling off" period, with multinational security assistance, after the American withdrawal.

While the temporary international police forces completes its work, the creation of a permanent national police force is, and must be, an Iraqi task.

American interference would be, and has been, counterproductive. And it will take time. The creation and solidification of an Iraqi national police force will probably require, at a rough estimate, four to five years to become fully effective. We suggest that the American withdrawal package should include provision of $1 billion to help to Iraqi government create, train, and equip such a force, which is roughly the cost of four days of the present American occupation.

Neighborhood, village, and tribal home guards, which are found throughout Iraq, of course constitute a double-edged sword. Inevitably, they mirror the ethnic, religious, and political communities from which they are drawn. Insofar as they are restricted each to its own community, and are carefully monitored by a relatively open and benign government, they will enhance security; allowed to move outside their home areas, they will menace public order. Only a central government police and respected community leaders can possibly hope to control these militias. America has no useful role to play in these affairs, as experience has made perfectly clear.

It is not in the interests of Iraq to encourage the growth and heavy armament of a reconstituted Iraqi army. The civilian government of Iraq should be, and hopefully is, aware that previous Iraqi armies have frequently acted against Iraqi civic institutions. That is, Iraqi armies have not been source of defense but of disruption. We cannot prevent the reconstitution of an Iraqi army, but we should not, as we are currently doing, actually encourage this at a cost of billions to the American taxpayer. If at all possible, we should encourage Iraq to transfer what soldiers it has already recruited for its army into a national reconstruction corps modeled on the U.S. Army Corps of Engineers. The United States could assist in the creation and training of just such a reconstruction corps, which would undertake the rebuilding of infrastructure damaged by the war, with an allocation of, say, $500 million, or roughly the cost of two days of the current occupation.

Withdrawal of American forces must include immediate cessation of work on U.S. military bases. Nearly half of the more than 100 bases have already been closed down and turned over, at least formally, to the Iraqi government, but as many as fourteen, "enduring," bases for American troops in Iraq are under construction. The largest five are already massive, amounting to virtual cities. The Balad Air Base, forty miles north of Baghdad, has a miniature golf course, 2 PXs, a Pizza Hut, a Burger King, and a jail. Another, under construction at al-Asad, covers more than thirteen square miles. Although Secretary of Defense Donald Rumsfeld stated on December 23, 2005, that "at the moment there are no plans for permanent bases… It is a subject that has not even been discussed with the Iraqi government," his remarks are belied by action on the ground, where bases are growing in size and being given aspects of permanency. The most critical of these are remote military bases.

They should be stood down rapidly. Closing these bases is doubly important: for America, they are expensive and already redundant; for Iraqis, they both symbolize and personify a hated occupation. With them in place, no Iraqi government will ever feel truly independent. It is virtually certain that absent a deactivation of U.S. military bases, the insurgency will continue. The enormous American base at Baghdad International Airport, ironically named "Camp Victory," should be the last of the military bases to be closed, as it will be useful in the process of disengagement.

We should of course withdraw from the Green Zone, our vast, sprawling complex in the center of Baghdad. The United States has already spent or is currently spending $1.8 billion on its headquarters there, which contains, or will contain, some 600 housing units, a Marine barracks, and more than a dozen other buildings, as well as its own electrical, water, and sewage systems. The Green Zone should be turned over to the Iraqi government no later than December 31, 2007. By this time, the U.S. should have bought, rented, or built a "normal" embassy for a considerably reduced complement of personnel. Symbolically, it would be beneficial for the new building not to be in the Green Zone. Assuming that a reasonable part of the Green Zone's cost can be saved, there should be no additional cost to create a new American embassy for an appropriate number of not more than 500 American officials, as opposed to the 1,000 or so Americans who today staff the Green Zone. Insofar as is practical, the new building should not be designed as though it were a beleaguered fortress in enemy territory.

Withdrawal from these bases, and an end to further construction, should save American taxpayers billions of dollars over the coming two years. This is quite apart from the cost of the troops they would house.

America should immediately release all prisoners of war and close its detention centers.

Mercenaries, euphemistically known as "Personal Security Detail," are now provided by an industry of more than thirty "security" firms, comprising at least 25,000 armed men. These contribute a force larger than the British troop contingent in the "Coalition of the Willing" and operate outside the direct control – and with little interference from the military justice systems – of the British and American armies. They are, literally, the "loose cannons" of the Iraq war. They should be withdrawn rapidly and completely, as the Iraqis regard them as the very symbol of the occupation. Since the U.S. pays for them either directly or indirectly, all we need to do is stop payment.

Much work will be necessary to dig up and destroy land mines and other unexploded ordinance and, where possible, to clean up the depleted uranium used in artillery shells. These are dangerous tasks that require professional training, but they should be turned over wherever possible to Iraqi contractors. These contractors would employ Iraqi labor, which would help jump-start a troubled economy and be of immediate benefit to the millions of Iraqi who are now out of work. The United Nations has gained considerable knowledge about de-mining – from the Balkans, Afghanistan, and elsewhere – that could be shared with the Iraqis. Although cleanup will be costly, we cannot afford to leave this dangerous waste behind. One day's wartime expenditure, roughly $250 million, would pay for surveys of the damage and the development of a plan to deal with it. Once the extent of the problem is determined, a fund should be established to eradicate the danger completely.

These elements of the "withdrawal package" may be regarded as basic. Without them, Iraqi society will have little chance of recovering economically or governing itself with any effectiveness. Without them, American interests in the Middle East, and indeed throughout the world, will be severely jeopardized. These measures are, we repeat, inexpensive and represent an enormous savings over the cost of the current war effort. Building on them are further actions that would also help Iraq become a safe and habitable environment. To these "second tier" policies we now turn.

Property damage incurred during the invasion and occupation has been extreme. The World Bank has estimated that at least $25 billion will be required to repair the Iraqi infrastructure alone – this is quite apart from the damage done to private property. The reconstruction can be, and should be, done by Iraqis, as this would greatly benefit the Iraqi economy, but the United States will need to make a generous contribution to the effort if it is to be a success. Some of this aid should be in the form of grants; the remainder can be in the forms of loans. Funds should be paid directly to the Iraqi government, as it would be sound policy to increase the power and public acceptance of that government once American troops withdraw. The Iraqis will probably regard such grants or loans as reparations; some of the money will probably be misspent or siphoned off by cliques within the government. It would therefore benefit the Iraqi people if some form of oversight could be exercised over the funds, but this would tend to undercut the legitimacy and authority of their government, which itself will probably be reconstituted during or shortly after the American occupation ends. Proper use of aid funds has been a problem everywhere: America's own record during the occupation has been reprehensible, with massive waste, incompetence, and outright dishonesty now being investigated for criminal prosecution. No fledgling Iraqi government is likely to do better, but if reconstruction funds are portioned out to village, town, and city councils, the enhancement of such groups will go far toward the avowed American aim of strengthening democracy, given that Iraqis at the "grass roots" level would be taking charge of their own affairs.

We suggest that the United States allocate for the planning and organization of the reconstruction the sum of $1 billion, or roughly four days of current wartime expenditure. After a planning survey is completed, the American government will need to determine, in consultation with the Iraqi government (and presumably with the British government, our only true "partner" in the occupation), what it is willing to pay for reconstruction. We urge that the compensation be generous, as generosity will go a long way toward repairing the damage to the American reputation caused by this war.

Nearly as important as the rebuilding of damaged buildings and other infrastructure is the demolition of the ugly monuments of warfare. Work should be undertaken as soon as is feasible to dismantle and dispose of the miles of concrete blast walls and wire barriers erected around present American installations. Although the Iraqi people can probably be counted on to raze certain relics of the occupation on their own, we should nonetheless, in good faith, assist in this process. A mere two days' worth of the current war effort, $500 million, would employ a good many Iraqi demolition workers.

Another residue of war and occupation has been intrusion of military facilities on Iraqi cultural sites. Some American facilities have done enormous and irreparable damage. Astonishingly, one American camp was built on top of the Babylon archaeological site, where American troops flattened and compressed ancient ruins in order to create a helicopter pad and fueling stations. Soldiers filled sandbags with archaeological fragments and dug trenches through unexcavated areas while tanks crushed 2,600-year-old pavements. Babylon was not the only casualty. The 5,000-year-old site at Kish was also horribly damaged. We need to understand that Iraq, being a seedbed of Western civilization, is a virtual museum. It is hard to put a spade into the earth there without disturbing a part of our shared cultural heritage. We suggest that America set up a fund of, say, $750 million, or three days' cost of the war, to be administered by an ad-hoc committee drawn from the Iraqi National Museum of Antiquities or the State Board of Antiquities and Heritage, the British Museum, the World Monuments Fund, the Smithsonian Institution, and what is perhaps America's most prestigious archaeological organization, the Oriental Institute of the University of Chicago, to assist in the restoration of sites American troops have damaged. We should not wish to go down in history as yet another barbarian invader of land long referred to as the cradle of civilization.

Independent accounting of Iraqi funds is urgently required. The United Nations handed over to the American-run Coalition Provisional Authority (CPA) billions of dollars generated by the sale of Iraq petroleum with the understanding that these monies would be used to the benefit of the Iraqi people and would be accounted for by an independent auditor. The CPA delayed this audit month after month, and it was still not completed by the time the CPA ceased to exist. Any funds misused or misappropriated by U.S. officials should be repaid to the proper Iraqi authority. What that amount is we cannot predict at this time.

Although the funds turned over to the CPA by the U.N. constitute the largest amount in dispute, that is by no means the only case of possible misappropriation. Among several others reported, perhaps the most damaging to Iraq has been a project allocated to Halliburton's subsidiary Kellogg, Brown & Root as part of a $2.4 billion no-bid contract awarded in 2003. The $75.7 million project was meant to repair the junction of some fifteen pipelines linking the oil fields with terminals. Engineering studies indicated that as conceived the project was likely to fail, but KBR forged ahead and, allegedly, withheld news of the failure from the Iraqi Ministry of Petroleum until it had either spent or received all the money. Despite this, KBR was actually awarded a bonus by the Army Corps of Engineers, even though Defense Department auditors had found more than $200 million of KBR's charges to be questionable. There would seem to be more greed than prudence in the repeated awards to Halliburton in the run-up to the was, during the war itself, and in contracts to repair the war damage. Especially given that Vice President Dick Cheney was formerly CEO of Halliburton, The U.S. should make every effort to investigate this wrongdoing, prosecute and correct it, and depart from Iraq with clean hands.

The United States should not object to the Iraqi government voiding all contracts entered into for the exploration, development and marketing of oil during the American occupation. These contracts clearly should be renegotiated or thrown open to competitive international bids. The Iraqi government and public believe that because Iraqi oil has been sold at a discount of American companies, and because long-term "production-sharing agreements" are highly favorable to the concessionaires, an unfair advantage has been taken. Indeed, the form of concession set up at the urging of the CPA's consultants has been estimated to deprive Iraq of as much as $194 billion in revenues. To most Iraqis, and indeed to many foreigners, the move to turn over Iraq's oil reserves to American and British companies surely confirms that the real purpose of the invasion was to secure, for American use and profit, Iraq's lightweight and inexpensively produced oil.

It is to the long-term advantage of both Iraq and the United States, therefore, that all future dealing in oil, which, after all, is the single most important Iraqi national asset, be transparent and fair. Only then can the industry be reconstituted and allowed to run smoothly; only then will Iraq be able to contribute to its own well-being and to the world's energy needs. Once the attempt to create American-controlled monopolies is abandoned, we believe it should be possible for investment, even American investment, to take place in a rapid and orderly manner. We do not, therefore, anticipate a net cost connected with this reform.

Providing reparations to Iraqi civilians for lives and property lost is a necessity. The British have already begun to do so in the zone they occupy. According to Martin Hemming of the Ministry of Defence, British policy "has, from the outset of operations in Iraq, been to recognize the duty to provide compensation to Iraqis where this is required by the law…Between 1 June 2003 and 31 July 2006, 2,327 claims have been registered…" Although there is no precise legal precedent from past wars that would require America to act accordingly, American forces in Iraq have now provided one: individual military units are authorized to make "condolence payments" of up to $2,500. The United States could, and should, do even more to compensate Iraqi victims or theirs heirs. Such an action might be compared to the Marshall Plan, which so powerfully redounded to America's benefit throughout the world after the end of the Second World War. As we go forward, the following points should be considered.

The number of civilians killed or wounded during the invasion and occupation, particularly in the sieges of Fallujah, Tal Afar, and Najaf, is unknown. Estimates run from 30,000 to well over 100,000 killed, with many more wounded or incapacitated. Assuming the number of unjustified deaths to be 50,000, and the compensation per person to be $10,000, our outlay would run to only $500 million, or two days' cost of the war. The number seriously wounded or incapacitated might easily be 100,000. Taking the same figure as for death benefits, the total cost would be $1 billion, or four days' cost of the war. The dominant voice in this process should be that of Iraq itself, but in supplying the funds the United States could reasonably insist on the creation of a quasi-independent body, composed of both Iraqis and respected foreigners, perhaps operating under the umbrella of an internationally recognized organization such as the International Federation of Red Cross and Red Crescent Societies or the World Health Organization, to assess and distribute compensation.

In the meantime, a respected international body should be appointed to process the claims of, and pay compensation to, those Iraqis who have been tortured (as defined by the Geneva Conventions) or who have suffered long-term imprisonment. The Department of Defense admits that approximately 3,200 people have been held for longer than a year, and more than 700 for longer than two years, most of them without charge, a clear violation of the treasured American right of habeas corpus. The number actually subjected to torture remains unknown, but it is presumed to include a significant portion of those incarcerated. Unfortunately, there exists no consensus, legal or otherwise, on how victims of state-sponsored torture should be compensated, and so it is not currently possible to estimate the cost of such a program. Given that this is uncharted legal territory, we should probably explore it morally and politically to find a measure of justifiable compensation. The very act of assessing damages – perhaps somewhat along the lines of the South African Truth and Reconciliation Commission – would, in and of itself, be a part of the healing process.

America should also offer – not directly but through suitable international or nongovernmental organizations – a number of further financial inducements to Iraq's recovery. These might include fellowships for the training of lawyers, judges, journalists, social workers, and other civil-affairs workers. Two days' cost of the current war, or $500 million, would amply fund such an effort.

In addition, assistance to "grass roots" organizations and professional societies could help encourage the return to Iraq of the thousands of skilled men and women who left in the years following the first Gulf war. Relocation allowance and supplementary pay might be administered by the Iraqi engineers' union. Medical practitioners might receive grants through the medical association. Teachers might be courted by the teachers' union or the Ministry of Education. Assuming that some 10,000 skilled workers could be enticed to return for, say, an average of $50,000, this would represent a cost of the American taxpayer of $500 million. Roughly two days' cost of the war would be a very small price to pay to restore the health and vigor of Iraqi society and to improve America's reputation throughout the world.

We should also encourage the World Health Organization, UNICEF, and similarly established and proven nongovernmental organizations to help with the rebirth of an Iraqi public-health system by rebuilding hospitals and clinics.

One reason for turning to respected international organizations to supervise this program is that when the CPA undertook the task, funds were squandered.

At last count, some seventeen years ago, Iraq possessed an impressive health-care infrastructure: 1,055 health centers, 58 health centers with beds, 135 general hospitals, and 52 specialized hospitals. Many of these facilities were badly damaged by a decade of sanctions and by the recent warfare and looting. If we assume that fully half of Iraq's hospitals and health centers need to be rebuilt, the overall outlay can be estimated at $250 million, one day's cost of the current war. Equipment might cost a further $170 million. These figures, based on a study prepared for the United Nations Millennium Development Goals (UNMDG) project, throw into sharp relief the disappointing results of the American "effort:" one American firm, Parsons Corporation, has been investigated for having taken a generous "cost plus" contract to rebuild 142 clinics at a cost of $200 million; although the company put in for and collected all the money, only twenty clinics were built.

Estimating the cost of staffing these facilities is more complicated. Theoretically, Iraq has a highly professional, well-trained, reasonably large corps of health workers at all levels. Yet many of these people left the country in the years following the 1991 war. The Iraqi Health Ministry has estimated that about 3,000 registered doctors left Iraq during the first two years of the American occupation. Hopefully these workers will return to Iraq once the occupation and the insurgency have ended, but even if they do so, younger replacements for them need to be trained. The UNMDG study suggests that the training period for specialists is about eight years; for general practitioners, five years; and for various technicians and support personnel, three years. We suggest that a training program for a select number, say 200 general practitioners and 100 advanced specialists, be carried out under the auspices of the World Health Organization or Médecins Sans Frontières, especially given that some of this training will have to be done in Europe or America. Even if the estimated cost of building and equipping hospitals turned out to be five times too low, even if the American government had to cover the bulk of salaries and operating costs for the next four years, and even if additional hospitals had to be built to care for Iraqis wounded or made ill by the invasion and occupation, the total cost would still be under $5 billion. It is sobering to think that the maximum cost of rebuilding Iraq's public-health system would amount to less than what we spend on the occupation every twenty days.

The monetary cost of the basic set of programs outlined here is roughly \$7.25 billion. The cost of the "second tier" programs cannot be as accurately forecast, but the planning and implementation of these is likely to cost somewhere in the vicinity of \$10 billion. Seventeen and a quarter billion dollars is a lot of money, but assuming that these programs cut short the American occupation by only two years, they would save us at least \$200 billion. Much more valuable, though, are the savings to be measured in what otherwise are likely to be large numbers of shattered bodies and lost lives. Even if our estimates are unduly optimistic, and the actual costs turn out to be far higher, the course of action we recommend would be perhaps the best investment ever made by our country.

Finally, we as a nation should not forget the young Americans who fought this war, often for meager pay and with inadequate equipment. As of this writing, more than 2,600 of our soldiers have been killed, and a far greater number wounded or crippled. It is only proper that we be generous to those who return, and to the families of those who will not.

That said, we should find a way to express our condolences for the large number of Iraqis incarcerated, tortured, incapacitated, or killed in recent years. This may seem a difficult gesture to many Americans. It may strike some Americans as weak, or as a slur on our patriotism. Americans do not like to admit that they have done wrong. We take comfort in the notion that whatever the mistakes of the war and occupation, we have done Iraq a great service by ridding it of Saddam Hussein's dictatorship. Perhaps we have, but in the process many people's lives have been disrupted, damaged, or senselessly ended. A simple gesture of conciliation would go a long way toward shifting our relationship with Iraq from one of occupation to one of friendship. It would be a gesture without cost but of immense and everlasting value — and would do more to assuage the sense of hurt in the world than all of the actions above.

Published in the *Harpers Magazine* October 2006 issue

Address to the Progressive Caucus and the Out of Iraq Caucus of the U.S. House of Representatives on Friday, January 12, 2007.

CONGRESSWOMAN LYNN WOOLSEY, Congresswoman Barbara Lee and Congresswoman Maxine Waters, I address you particularly as chairwomen of the Progressive Caucus and the Out of Iraq Caucus. It gives me particular pleasure both as an American and as a historian to do so because the curious word "caucus" is deeply rooted in the American experience. One of the first practices that Captain John Smith observed when he met the Algonquians in 1607 was the way they got together to decide matters of high policy. As close as he could come to their pronunciation, their meeting was a caw-cawassough. The leaders of the Indians made no decisions without first holding a caw-cawassough or caucus. The practice was carried forward in later American history. It was in the "Caucus Club" of the Boston town meeting that Samuel Adams shaped American opinion in the years leading up to our Revolution. So I gratulate you for carrying forward one of the fundamental concepts of American government. I am honored to participate.

Today, I want to concentrate on three urgent issues.

The first issue is what should be done in and about Iraq.

I want to begin by paying tribute to the Baker-Hamilton Report. We need discussion and searching criticism of the enormous problem facing our country as a result of our invasion and occupation of Iraq. Secretary Baker and Congressman Hamilton have made a major contribution to this debate.

I find four good things about the Iraq Study Group report on Iraq: first, in it, two highly respected men, a Republican and a Democrat, made a clear statement that, for our own interests, we must get out of Iraq and must do so soon; second, they recognized that the occupation of Iraq is stretching U.S. military capacity beyond acceptable limits; third, they reminded us that Iraq is a part of the interconnected problems of the Middle East, each of which needs to be addressed; and fourth, they recognized that the war is moving our economy toward bankruptcy.

While Baker-Hamilton did not go into it, we can see that, taken together with massive tax cuts, we are mortgaging the future of our children to pay for the Iraq war and, in order to shield this reality from the public, we are borrowing vast amounts from foreign (mainly Chinese) lenders. As the foreign lenders have watched their loans fall in value as the dollar has slid from $0.80 to $1.34 to the Euro, they have lost an average of about 30%. Sooner or later, they will presumably stop lending or even call the notes. Either move could cause our currency to collapse.

The main failure of Baker-Hamilton is that, while it sets out what we wish would happen and where we wish we were, it fails to lay out concrete steps on how to get there.

In my time in government, I learned that a statement of policy was essentially inoperable unless it contained an analysis of the country or problem it sought to affect, a run-down of costs, a statement of determination to meet the proposed budget, a timetable with identified check points and a provision for contingencies. These are lacking in Baker-Hamilton. Baker-Hamilton sets out an understandable desire. But it is not a policy. It does not lay out a means to achieve what we want.

Baker-Hamilton calls for the governments of Iran and Syria to assist us in our quest for the solution to our problems in Iraq. Unfortunately this is naïve and almost certainly could not work. There are two reasons:

The first reason is that the leaders of these two states know from the (published) U.S. National Security Doctrine and from numerous statements by senior American officials, including the President, that for at least the last five or six years we have been considering attacking them and have denounced their governments repeatedly and in menacing terms. So why should they help pull our chestnuts out of the Iraqi fire if that would enable us to redeploy our combat forces elsewhere, meaning possibly – or even probably – against them.

The second reason is that we almost certainly exaggerate their ability to control or even sway events in Iraq. We have installed a government controlled by the Shiis who now, as we say in Texas, have the bit in their teeth. They share religion with Iran but have shown that they are determined to run their own show. While many are culturally oriented toward Iran, they regard themselves as Arab rather than Persian. They would have to be foolish to allow an Iranian government, even in the unlikely event that it wished to, to get them to do what they believe is not in their interest. It is even less likely that Syria could do much to shape events in Iraq.

Thus, in summary, I believe it is fair to say that Baker-Hamilton is not an operational plan. But there is another plan: what Senator McGovern and I have laid out in our book *Out of Iraq: A Practical Plan for Withdrawal from Iraq Now*. It is a coordinated, feasible program that is fully articulated with costs, timetable, estimates of success or failure and is based on comparative historical experiences in other guerrilla wars. It is a program that has been vetted by American, English and even Iraqi experts. We assert that Iraq is too serious a problem for America to be dealt with only with wishes and hopes. The American approach must be practical and hardheaded. That is what we offer.

<u>The second issue I want to address</u> is the group of questions or doubts that are frequently raised.

<u>Question number 1</u>: Will Iraq "implode" if we leave?

The honest answer is "possibly." We have not been able to prevent mayhem on the scale of a civil war with overwhelming military force. "Ah so," say critics of withdrawal. "Then we must stay."

To this assertion we have two answers.

The first answer derives from what happened in at least a dozen other insurgencies. That experience illustrates the fact that the usual object of insurgencies is to get rid of the "irritant," the foreigner/occupier. Whether or not we wish to admit it, all human beings, regardless of religion, nationality, race or political system are fundamentally territorial animals. None of us is willing to be ruled by foreigners.

Our own Revolution was triggered by the presence of British troops in Boston. Foreigners were the "fuel" that powered insurgency in IndoChina and Algeria (the French), Greece and Yugoslavia (the Germans), Afghanistan (first the Russians and now us), the Palestine Mandate, Cyprus, Kenya and elsewhere (the British), the Philippines (the Japanese and us) and Indonesia (the Dutch).

You may have seen the recent (December 2006) Department of the Army

Field Manual on Counterinsurgency prepared for Generals David Petraeus and James Amos. Their report is a well-written, detailed technical treatment and will almost certainly guide General Petraeus in his new role as our commander in Iraq. In reading it, however, I kept being reminded of Vietnam and the various programs put forward forty years ago to defeat the insurgency there. What the army (with its love of acronyms) then called "CORDS" is now known as "COIN." Both set out all sorts of techniques but dodged the central issue – nationalism. No matter how thorough the techniques, how massive the firepower or how numerous the foreign army, the natives are likely to continue fighting as long as the foreigners remain. But, observe what happens when the foreigners leave.

Then the 80 plus percent of the Iraqis who want us out will have accomplished their central objective. They will be independent. Most of them will then no longer be willing to sacrifice themselves to support the insurgents. This fundamental fact was laid out by that great practitioner of guerrilla warfare Mao Tse-tung in his manual on guerrilla warfare (*Yu Chi Chan*) in 1937. He said that the people were like "water." Without the support of the water, the combatants, whom he likened to "fish," cannot survive.

So we see in the insurgencies that took place in Algeria, Greece, Ireland (Eire), the Philippines and elsewhere, when the people feel that the main object has been accomplished, they stop supporting the fish. Then the remnants of the guerrilla forces are suppressed, with public approval by their own people. This is what President Éamon De Valera did in Ireland, President Tito did in Yugoslavia and President Ahmad Ben Bella did in Algeria. Foreigners could not do it but natives could and did.

Our second answer to the question of whether Iraq will not become even more chaotic when Americans leave is that our plan offers what we believe Iraqis will find to be an acceptable means to acquire an adequate – not perfect, mind you, but satisfactory – level of stability in the transition period. What we propose is a multinational, non-American "stability force" that would be employed by the Iraqis (not imposed on them), would have a sharply limited tenure (not be open-ended) and would be directed against the inevitable warlords who might otherwise loot the country (but not attempt to suppress the insurgency). A description of it, the means of recruitment, the cost, and the role are all laid out in our book, *Out of Iraq*.

Question number 2: Should we not wait until Iraq becomes "stable" before we leave?

The short answer is "no." If we do that, we will never leave or will leave under the same humiliating circumstances as we left Vietnam. What the history of insurgencies teaches is that stability cannot be achieved before sovereignty. The order must be reversed. Only when independence has been achieved – that is, when the fundamental nationalist objective has been achieved – will stability be assured.

Today, the Iraqis, both Shiis and Sunnis, Arabs and Kurds, recognize that Iraq is not independent. President Bush's speech Wednesday made this crystal clear. He merely confirmed what all our actions and statements show.

Question number 3: How can we help Iraq make the transition from occupation to independence?

To begin to answer that question, we must be realistic about where Iraq now is.

Start with public security. We promoted in the election we sponsored in 2005 the moves that are now tearing Iraq apart. The election contributed to sectarianism, indeed embodied it in the Iraqi government. Having let this terrible genii out of the bottle we cannot control it. Only the Iraqis are likely to be able to do that. Whether they will is an open question. Certainly, the current chaos will continue for a time following our withdrawal. Viewing the ugly manifestations of sectarian violence, some observers believe, and some even advocate, that Iraq be split into three parts. This would be a tragic outcome: it would uproot of hundreds of thousands of people, cause unimaginable misery, "balkanize" the country and create the precondition of further civil and perhaps international war. We should try as we leave Iraq to dissuade the Iraqis from such a policy and warn them of the consequences even for the sect we have made dominant. But if we are realistic and honest with ourselves, we will admit that we cannot prevent it no matter how many troops we put into the country.

It will become more likely the longer we stay.

Then consider unemployment. No society can survive as a coherent unity with an unemployment rate of nearly 50% so we have urged that instead of spending at least $2.2 billion (the published figure) to create a useless and dangerous new army, which in the past has been the seedbed of dictators, we should urge that the proto-army be converted into what Iraq really needs, something like our Corps of Engineers, that can build the infrastructure on top of which the Iraqi economy can be restarted and unemployment be diminished.

Help must be given to encourage the return to Iraq of its most precious asset, skilled men and women. Doctors, nurses, teachers, scientists, technicians of whom over a million are now living in exile. Most will come back only when they begin to see some hope for Iraq. But as a few come back, hope will grow. Then more will come, and they will begin to make an impact on the nature of the new Iraq. This will be a slow process but it is absolutely vital. We need to help it come about. We show how in *Out of Iraq*.

Assistance is also needed to strengthen the civic capacity of Iraqi society. This can be done in several ways – the encouragement of trades-unions and professional societies which will tend to balance government institutions, the training and facilitation of judges, lawyers, teachers, professors and various categories of nongovernmental workers and the creation of opportunities. We did this with great success following the Second World War II in Europe. We are good at this sort of work. Only if civic "grass roots" organizations prosper can Iraq move toward stability.

In Out of Iraq we have sketched out these and other measures that cumulatively could begin to put Iraq on a progressive path.

We point out that the whole program we urge would cost somewhere around $12-14 billion and would save American taxpayers at least $350 billion which we will waste if we stay another two years.

The third issue I want to address is composed of two warnings.

The first of these warnings is that we must beware of the danger of falling into half measures. In government affairs, the siren song is compromise. Compromise always sounds practical. Sometimes it even sounds statesmanlike.

And usually it also protects reputations whereas taking clear action may seem precipitous. Waiting to see what happens can rarely be faulted. So asking for more time seems sensible. A few thousand more troops, another 50 or so billion dollars…

That is what we did in Vietnam after the Tet Offensive. We "stayed the course" and refused to "cut and run." During those four years of waiting to see what would happen, an additional 21,000 young Americans lost their lives, that is almost as many as during the previous six years, scores of thousands of Vietnamese were killed and tens of billions of dollars were wasted. Then at the end we really did cut and run.

Today, we predict that if we do as President Bush asks, we will be saying to one another in a few months time – when another thousand or so American servicemen and women have been killed, five or ten thousand more are grievously wounded and end up in Veterans hospitals and we have wasted another 50 billion dollars – why didn't we just face reality in January.

The second warning is that Iraq may not be the last reckless gamble. I remember thinking after Vietnam that surely we had at least learned a terrible lesson. We did not. Have we at last learned in Iraq that military force does not work? It seems that, perhaps, the American people have learned the lesson, as they showed in the November elections, but it also appears from statements and actions by the Administration that it has not.

One of the leading Neoconservatives predicted that we would engage in permanent war. He welcomed it but said he hoped it would not last more than forty years. The maelstrom into which the Neoconservative policy would thrust us was horrifyingly described by George Orwell in 1984. When I read it many years ago, I thought it was just a good novel. But statements of the Bush administration and recent events give us compelling reasons to ponder Orwell's message. If we move toward the world he foresaw and the Neoconservatives propose, our whole civic culture would be destroyed, our lives would become impoverished – the cost of what is now called "the Long War" has been estimated at nearly twenty trillion dollars – and we would lose everything we believe we are struggling to preserve.

Is this just a fantasy? As an old Chinese proverb puts it, "every journey of ten thousand miles begins with a single step." Iraq was the first and Mr. Bush warns us that he would like to take more steps. In fact, he took another step in Somalia.

Somalia presents a curious story. It is even harder to make the case that it poses a threat to America than did Iraq. What most of us know about Somalia is from the movie "Black Hawk Down." In that literally explosive film, you will remember that our brave young men went in to beat the bad guys, the vicious warlords who were looting, raping and killing their own people. The film opens with a gruesome scene of the warlords doing these horrible things. The UN had a peacekeeping force there, but we didn't want it to do the job. So we mounted our own action. Our troops opened up with all our massive firepower. But then a curious thing happened: the whole population rose against our soldiers. We cut and ran, taunted by the very people we thought we were there to save. And then after we left what happened? The Somalis created their own movement to run the bad guys out of town. It was not the sort of movement of which we approve, a bunch of religious fundamentalists. They succeeded where we failed because they were, after all, Somalis, but now we have brought back the warlords, the very people we went into Somalia to suppress.

Events in Afghanistan sound a similar note. The Afghans are now so fed up with the warlords who control most of the country except downtown Kabul that they are welcoming back the Taliban religious fundamentalists.

As I have pointed out we have threatened Iran. The Iranians are intensely nationalistic. They believe that America intends to invade and "regime change" them. We are very worried about them acquiring nuclear weapons. We should be: nuclear weapons anywhere are a danger to people everywhere. But the current policy of threats will absolutely ensure that they will do all in their power to acquire them.

If you are not convinced, put yourself in their place and imagine what you would do if some superpower categorized us, as we have them, as a part of the "Axis of Evil." If you did not have means to defend yourself – and nuclear weapons are the final defense – you would certainly rush as fast as possible to get them. We would be foolish to think that the Iranians would do otherwise. The way to get them to stop is to work for regional arms control and drop our threats of preëmptive military action.

Having hit all these somber notes, I want to leave you with a good report:

I have managed to get my hands on a very secret document. It tells us that the government has decided to get out of Afghanistan. I will quote bits of it. "We will leave it to the Afghans themselves to create a government amidst the anarchy. To force a sovereign upon a reluctant people, as we now recognize, would be inconsistent with the policy and principles of our government. Moreover, the enormous expenditure required for the support of a large force in a false military position at a distance from our frontier arrests every measure we are taking for the improvement of the people and the country."

I said I wanted to end on a good note, but I must admit that there is one problem with the highly secret and sensitive dispatch I just read you. It was produced not in the administration of our 43rd president but in the time of our 10th president. The date was January 10, 1842 at the end of another Afghan war and the government that issued it was British.

PART III

PALESTINE

THE PALESTINE-ISRAELI TRAGEDY

PRESS ACCOUNTS AND TV IMAGES of events in the Middle East in recent days (in March and April of 2002) have been truly horrifying. And the worst has probably not yet appeared since the Israelis have prevented reporters from visiting many areas and, as you have probably seen, a group, including a CNN reporter who tried to observe, were attacked with stun grenades and shot at by Israeli soldiers. Although clearly marked and identified, another correspondent, one from The Boston Globe, was shot in an area "under full Israeli control." The evident callous disregard for life, reported by Israeli observers, killing unarmed civilians, shutting off water supply to whole cities, even preventing ambulances from retrieving women in childbirth and wounded women and children, is truly sickening. Wholesale arrests and executions of prisoners have been reported but cannot be confirmed or denied so far. One series of pictures detailing the arrest, binding and murder of a young civilian captive appeared on the internet. Considering the events and pondering how they came about, what they mean for the future and what can be done about them has impelled me to write the following notes. I begin with how they came about.

I

Minus the particular elements of horror in the current fighting, all this was predictable – and was predicted – nearly a century ago. Two short statements in the British record and two in the Zionist record tell almost enough to plot the whole story right up to today. First, the British:

When in 1917 the British Cabinet was debating the text of the Balfour Declaration which proposed the creation of a "national home" for the Jews in Palestine, Lord Kitchener dryly remarked that he was sure that the existing Arab population of Palestine "will not be content as hewers of wood and drawers of water" for the incoming Jewish settlers.

Lord Balfour (in whose name the Balfour Declaration, was issued) commented that "Whatever deference should be paid to the views of those...700,000 Arabs who now inhabit that ancient land, [we] do not propose, as I understand the matter, to consult them."

Why did the British interest themselves in the Zionist cause? Using the issue of Palestine, British policy focused on four targets:

First, to try to break the fighting spirit of the German army, British aircraft dropped millions of announcements to troops in Germany and Austria proclaiming that "the Allies are giving the land of Israel to the people of Israel... Remember! An Allied victory means the Jewish peoples return to Zion." Why the Jews and why in Yiddish, a language few German Jews used? It was because the British knew little of the German Jewish community and exagerated their influence in German industry, finance and intellectual life and, above all in the German army where they were thought to be a significant group, although very small and only recently allowed to join the officer corps. If they could be weaned away, the British thought, the German and Austrian armies might collapse; with them actively supporting Germany, it feared that the anticipated offensive of that year might succeed.

Second, believing that the new leaders of the Russian Revolution were nearly all Jewish, the British courted them with essentially the same promise. Their aim was to persuade the Russians not to make a separate peace with Germany. The British knew that the Russians were sick of the war and desperately wanted out; if they got out, the large German forces engaged there would be free to join the attack on the Western front.

In Russia, British policy was misdirected: while some of the leading Russian revolutionaries in 1917 were Jewish, at least the Communists among them regarded Zionism as a rival ideology. The Russians opted out of the war.

Third, with their economy choked by the U-boat blockade and their finances depleted, the British desperately sought American assistance. It was not forthcoming. In 1917, anti-British feeling was strong in America. The American press was full of attacks on British actions against neutral (especially American) shipping, and relations between the governments were often acrimonious. President Wilson's principal adviser, Colonel House, thought that, at best, the American government would not aid the Allies and might take an even stronger anti-British stand. The British were told, however, that the leaders of the American Jewish community might influence the American government and privately were in a position to make large credits available. As Prime Minister Lloyd George noted, "their aid in this respect would have a special value when the Allies had almost exhausted the gold and marketable securities available for American purchases" of food and war supplies. But, the British were told, American Jews were generally pro-German. As a part of the campaign to win them over, Lord Rothschild, to whom the Balfour Declaration was addressed, was encouraged to "bring this declaration to the knowledge of the Zionist Federation."

But, fourth, Britain was also an empire with millions of Muslim and Arab subjects. So, in the Middle East, publication of the Balfour Declaration was banned by military censorship. There, the British sought to undermine Germany's powerful ally, the Ottoman Empire by encouraging its Arab subjects to join the Allied side. The most famous of these overtures is an exchange of letters known as the "Hussein-McMahon Correspondence." On Palestine it was somewhat vague but other declarations, including the "Declaration to the Seven," promised "to recognize the complete and sovereign independence of the Arabs." Further, the British commander-in-chief, Lord Allenby, was instructed to declare that "the Allies were in honour bound to endeavour to reach a settlement in accordance with the wishes of the peoples." Lastly, and more or less in accordance with President Woodrow Wilson's call for the "self-determination of peoples," a joint Anglo-French declaration of November 7, 1918 affirmed a policy for "the establishment of national governments and administrations deriving their authority from the initiative and free choice of the indigenous populations…"

Obviously, the British were aware that these four policy objectives were in conflict with one another. Thus, as Lord Balfour wrote secretly to the Cabinet, "In short, so far as Palestine is concerned, the Powers have made no statement of fact which is not admittedly wrong, and no declaration of policy which, at least in letter, they have not always intended to violate."

So much for the initial British actions. I turn now to the early Jewish assessments and actions.

On the Jewish side, actions have been determined by the Zionist assessment of the Palestinians and what should be done about them. These assessments and decisions were clear from the beginning of the Zionist movement in the Nineteenth century.

One of the early fathers of Zionism, Israel Zangwill, coined a description of the Palestine issue that has permeated Zionism and Jewish thought ever since: Palestine was "The land without people for the people without land."

In fact, as the early Zionists knew, Palestine then contained somewhat more than 700,000 Arabic-speaking inhabitants, most of whom were small farmers living in villages. Given the technology of the time and the financial resources of the people, the country was fairly crowded. Yet, even now, otherwise reasonably informed people echo Zangwill's slogan. Just a few days ago, in the International Herald Tribune, a writer commented that to talk of Arab "Palestinians" was mere propaganda. That, generally, has been the line taken by Israeli governments. The non-Jews were newcomers, gypsies, nomads, Jordanians or other immigrants. Prime Minister Golda Meir went even further: "There is no such thing as a Palestinian people."

2) As soon as the Zionists had a good look at Palestine, they realized that the only way to make the land be "without people" was to drive out the inhabitants. Vladimir Jabotinsky, the father of "muscular Zionism" and the ideological mentor of Israeli prime ministers Begin, Shamir, Sharon and Natanyahu, told the 1936 British Royal Commission which was trying to find a way to satisfy both Jews and Arabs, that the Zionists would never be satisfied with a part of Palestine — "We cannot. We never can. Should we swear to you we would be satisfied, it would be a lie."

Although not personally a follower of Jabotinsky, Prime Minister Ben Gurion adopted his position. Prophesizing today's events, he said that "after we constitute a large force...we will cancel the partition of the country and we will expand through[out] the Land of Israel." In 1937, he wrote, "we must expel the Arabs and take their places." Israel, under his leadership, partly implemented that policy in the events leading up to the creation of the state in 1948 as Israeli government records, now published, clearly show. As Ben Gurion then bluntly put it, the Palestinian Arabs "have only one function left to them, to run away."

Against these British and Zionist policies, the Arabs of Palestine began resisting in 1921 and in growing intensity are still resisting. Lord Kitchner had been right: the Palestinians were not prepared be merely "hewers of wood and drawers of water" for the incoming Jewish settlers. Like other Asian and African peoples, they have fought for their land and their persons with every weapon they could find including the weapon of the weak, terrorism. In resorting to terrorism, they have adopted the course taken by the Çeçens, the Irish, the Basques, the Jews themselves and dozens of other ethnic groups.

Fighting for nationhood is a dangerous business. Imperial powers were strong; colonial peoples were weak, fragmented, ill-prepared and often unarmed. In the process we have seen unfold in Ireland, Russia, India, the Middle East, North Africa, South Africa and the Pacific, hundreds of thousands of people were killed or maimed; property destroyed; lives, blighted. So what, one must ask are the forces sufficient to drive these two peoples, the Jews and the Palestinians, to the current tragedy? First, the Jews.

II

The Jews have suffered generation after generation, from long before the Nazi onslaught, from western anti-semitism. Sometimes it was merely humiliating (as it often was in America in the 1930s); at other times, it penalized them (as the English did in that document most of us consider the first proclamation of civil rights, the Magna Carta); the Crusades, we should remember, began with attacks on European Jews; English, French, German and other European communities squeezed Jews and then expelled them as the Spain of Isabella and Ferdinand did in that memorable year, 1492. Russia set off a mass migration with its pogroms in the Nineteenth century. So what then happened to them?

With our eyes focused today on ugly aspects of Muslim fundamentalism, we should find it ironic that, before the creation of Israel, Jews often fled from Christian countries to the relatively tolerant and safe Muslim lands, as many Spanish Jews did when they were expelled from Christian Spain.

The well-attested historical fact, whether we like it or not, is that anti-Semitism is a Western disease. <u>Our</u> disease. Not an Arab or a Muslim disease.

Although the Oriental Jews did not suffer anything even remotely comparable to the Russian pogroms or the Nazi Holocaust, these events have become firmly fixed in the Israeli national myth and so shape the thought of all Israelis today. So strong is the sense of Israeli identity today that few of us know that in the Nineteenth century, the leaders of the European Jewish community had to create for the widely scattered Jewish communities – as other nationalist leaders were doing for ethnic groups in the Balkans and even Italy – both a "nation" and a sense of nationalism. *

From a Jewish perspective, anti-Semitism is a pervasive disease. As one of the early Zionists wrote, Jews "carry anti-Semitism on their backs wherever they go." Consequently, many Jews concluded that whether or not they are tolerated as they are in many lands or even assimilated as they were in pre-Nazi Germany, they would never be safe until they had their own country. That is a prudent conclusion. No one, I think, should wish to deny them this right.

Why did the Zionists pick Palestine for that country? The father of Zionism, Theodore Herzl, put it clearly – the different factions within the Jewish community could agree on no other place; had they taken up the offers they had from the British (for Uganda or Cyprus), the Japanese (for part of Manchuria), or parts of Australia, Argentina or Angola, Herzl feared, the Zionist movement would have shattered. Only Palestine exercised the sort of mystical attraction that could unite them. "Fo Palestine," as Chaim Weizmann soberly told a startled audience at the Council on Foreign Relations, "we have a covenant with God."

This, to an outsider, is doubly astonishing: first of all, Palestine is hardly the Garden of Eden. Even after nearly a century of extravagant investment, it is not high on the list of attractive real estate.

And, second, the Biblical "roots" of modern Jews are at best distant – comparable to the relationship of modern Americans to Roman Britain. Two thousand or so years is a very long time in human affairs. Moreover, just as most Americans are not descendants of English settlers but have been "Englished" by education, many of Jews are not Hebrew, not Semitic, but have been Judaized by religion. Many are descendants of Khazar, Berber, Arab and other converts to Judaism. They became Jews like my (English/Norman/Scots/French etc.) ancestors became Christians. Yet, even for them, or perhaps especially for them, Israel was so imbedded in myth and religion and so impacted by the terrible threat of anti-Semitism as to transcend all contrary facts.

* (After having written this essay, I read Tel Aviv University Professor Shlomo Sand's The Invention of the Jewish People, which discusses these themes over the long history of the Jewish people. The issue who is a Jew is still under debate in Israel.)

The "promised land" – which the British had promised to both Jews and Arabs – had to be their state. Israel could not be, as the British intended, just a "national home," an enclave in someone else's state. Only if they fully and completely owned and controlled it could it assuage their desperate need for a sanctuary.

III

At the time of the American intervention in the First World War, President Woodrow Wilson raised the issue of nationhood. He recognized the power of the concept of the "nation." In a world in which effective identity comes from membership in a nation and security comes from the embodiment of the nation in statehood, no other objective has been even remotely as desperately sought. Still today as in Wilson's time and before, dozens of ethnic groups have fought – and many died – for it. Wilson took the argument above political strategy to political morality: "self-determination of peoples" he saw as a fundamental right as well as a strategic imperative in the quest for peace. Much attention then focused on the Balkans but Wilson saw "self-determination" in broad terms: people everywhere should have that right.

Angrily observing the "old game of grab" in the Middle East, where Britain, France, Greece and Italy were cynically engaged in carving up the map, Wilson attempted to get the major powers at the Paris Peace Conference to appoint a committee of inquiry to find out what the inhabitants wanted. When neither Britain nor France would agree, he appointed an American committee (the "King Crane Commission") to go to the Middle East to ask essentially, "who do you say you are and what do you want to be?" By the time its report was ready, Wilson had left Paris, was stricken by the illness that later killed him and never read the Commission's report.

Finding that the British and French were reneging on their promises to allow "the establishment of national governments and administrations deriving their authority from the initiative and free choice of the indigenous populations…" the Arab delegation leader, Amir Faisal appealed (after Wilson's departure) to the head of the American delegation, my cousin, Frank Polk, to act as arbitrator. Frank Polk, who had to struggle constantly with the British and French even to be admitted to the key meetings of the Conference, demurred and urged the Arab delegates to seek other allies, particularly the Zionists. They should jointly put pressure on the British and French.

Meanwhile, the United States Senate had begun to take the stance against involvement in world affairs that would keep America out of the League of Nations and sweepingly repudiated almost everything for which President Wilson had stood. Among them, of course, was "self-determination of peoples." Again, an irony. It became the accepted wisdom of the "realist" school of international affairs experts that Wilson's program was either merely eyewash (at best) or (at worst) dangerous naïveté. This is not the place to argue the issue, but it seems to me that what was wrong with it was only that it was never really applied: it was listened to (and acted upon) by peoples struggling for national fulfillment but was stifled, wherever possible, by those who might have granted the right to hold peaceful plebiscites. For the discrepancy between assertion and fulfillment we (and others in many parts of the world, including the Israelis) are paying – and exacting – a heavy price.

Prevented from peacefully asserting their desire for nationhood, the Palestinians began in 1921 their struggle, first against the British colonial authorities (then termed the "Mandate Government of Palestine") and subsequently against incoming Jewish settlers.

The British reacted by reconsidering their promises and their actions. Under the chairmanship of Winston Churchill, then British Colonial Secretary, they announced that both Arab fears and Jewish hopes were exaggerated: the British intent was not "to create a wholly Jewish Palestine." Rather they proposed to create a bi-national state with each community to be represented by an "Agency" under the Mandate government. This, of course, satisfied neither Jews nor Arabs. The Arabs, unwisely as it turned out, rejected it and so lost the experience, limited though it would have been, of creating and working within national institutions. Meanwhile, the Jews, more wisely, accepted and turned their "agency" into a shadow government.

Both Jews and Arabs focused their attention on Jewish immigration. The Jews were still a small minority of the population. (They would not reach one-third until the end of the Second World War.) For them immigration numbers were the index of hope; for the Arabs, of fear. After an initial influx, immigration slowed in the late 1920s and in 1927 more Jews left than arrived. Then, from

1929, as economic conditions deteriorated in Europe, Jewish migration increased. With it came increased Arab fear and hostility. In that year, a number of Zionists organized a demonstration at the Wailing Wall where they raised the Zionist flag and sang the Zionist anthem. As in Sharon's election ploy in 2001, this touched off Muslim riots.

As they always did, the British appointed a commission to investigate. It reported that "The Arabs have come to see in the Jewish immigrant not only a menace to their livelihood but a possible overlord of the future..."

Embodying the findings of the commission in a Government "white paper," the British decided to halt immigration at least temporarily. The Arabs were elated, but the Zionists counterattacked politically in London. The British government backed down. Immigration would continue. Remarkably, the Prime Minister announced his policy of supporting the creation of the "national home" not in Parliament but in a letter to *The Times*.

Shocked by what they termed "the black letter," canceling the white paper, the Arabs attempted a nation-wide boycott. It was the first of their many failures of unified action.

What happened next was far from Palestine. In Germany. With Hitler's rise to power and the establishment of the Nazi regime, large numbers of Jews prudently decided to emigrate. With most other refuges, including the United States which was then highly restrictive, almost completely closed to them, many made their ways to Palestine. Between 1932 and 1936, the Jewish population of Palestine quadrupled.

In 1936, 137 Arab senior officials and judges foresaw the loss of their country and were angered that they were being forced to pay the price of European brutality. In a memorandum, they warned the government that "the Arab population of all classes, creeds and occupations is animated by a profound sense of injustice done to them...As a result, the Arabs have been driven into a state verging on despair..." That despair animated strikes, terrorist attacks and, soon, civil war.

The British reacted with tactics similar to those we are watching today: 20,000 British soldiers were rushed in, mass arrests were carried out, Arab leaders were interned in a concentration camp, houses of "suspects" or their relatives were blown up and whole villages were destroyed. The British refused outside mediation, but appointed another commission to investigate.

That Royal Commission concluded that "An irrepressible conflict has arisen between two national communities within the narrow bounds of one small country... In the Arab picture the Jews could only occupy the place they occupied in Arab Egypt or Arab Spain [something like the "national home" concept, a protected minority]. The Arabs would be as much outside the Jewish picture as the Canaanites in the old land of Israel. The National Home...cannot be half-national...This conflict was inherent in the situation from the outset... The conflict will go on, the gulf between Arabs and Jews will widen."

What to do?

The Royal Commission came up with the first of the many attempts to create peace by dividing the two communities: partition Palestine. To the British, that seemed as sensible as the saying, "half a loaf is better than no bread." To both the Arabs and the Jews, partition seemed subversion of their nationhood: Reluctantly after bitter internal dispute, the Zionists accepted, but the Arabs did not. Arab attacks on the British continued and, to counterbalance them, the British both exiled the prominent Arab leaders and armed 5,000 Jews. In short order, however, the Jews also began attacking the government and Arab targets. During 1938, there were over 5,000 "incidents of violence" including over a thousand by Arabs and Jews against the (British) government. A solution of some sort seemed imperative. A new commission was established to plan a partition. It decided that partition was virtually impossible: a Jewish state of sufficient size to be viable would have an Arab majority.

That dilemma, already evident in 1938, has been a nightmare for Zionists ever since. The reasons are simple: first, Israel was never intended by them to be a bi-national state; it was always meant to be a wholly Jewish state; second, even a minority of Arabs would grow faster than the Jews and ultimately might become a majority. This worry became a reality with even the remnant of the Arab community left in Israel after the creation of the state in 1948. Ultimately, an Arab minority would pose the dilemma, which in fact is evident today, that Israel would have to chose between being a multi-ethnic democracy or a quasi-theological apartheid state. As we shall see, expulsion of the Arabs was always, certainly by the middle of the 1930s, regarded by Jewish leaders as the most attractive option.

As both the Arab and Jewish communities continued their attacks on the British, the German army marched into Poland on September 1, 1939. In reaction to this wholly new and larger dimension of threat, some 21,000 Jews and 8,000 Arabs enlisted in various branches of the British army. Both communities, however, were ambivalent: both fought for the Allied cause but against the British in Palestine. Outside of Palestine, some of the Arab leaders, notably the mufti of Jerusalem flirted with the Axis which, with the help of Vichy France, briefly took an active role in Arab affairs and meanwhile, as the war receded, after the British victory at El Alamein in 1942, "Stern Gang" (LEHI) attacks on the British increased. In 1944 the Irgun declared a "revolt" and attempted to assassinate the British High Commissioner. Then the LEHI did murder a British minister of state in Cairo.

As the war in Europe ended, the United States, for the first time, joined the British in seeking a solution to the dilemma of Palestine. But, this time, the focus was not on Palestine or its people but on Europe: what would happen to the survivors of the holocaust? The Jewish Agency did not wait for the answer but immediately began a widespread campaign of terror, blowing up bridges, buildings, railway stations and kidnapping British personnel. In reprisal, the British published intercepted telegrams showing that this time it was not just the renegade terrorist groups, Irgun Zvai Leumi and Stern, that carried out the attacks but the Jewish shadow government. The British then arrested and interned about 700 Jews and seized huge stockpiles of arms and explosives. In reprisal, the Irgun belew up the King David hotel in which the British administration and high command were located.

All this was, practically speaking, a side show: the irresistible demand was to help the displaced Jews of Europe. And with no one else willing to give them sanctuary, the American government demanded that Palestine be opened to them, and the British, anxious to get out of the mess they had created, acquiesced. A new committee, this time nominally a United Nations group, UNSCOP, drew up another partition plan but one with "economic union." The best UNSCOP could come up with showed the dilemma: the Arab state would have an Arab population of 725,000 and a Jewish population of 10,000 while the Jewish state would have 498,000 Jews and 407,000 Arabs. Jerusalem was to be internationalized and would contain 100,000 Jews and 105,000 Arabs.

The Jewish state was estimated to have revenues about three times that of the Arab state.

Needless-to-say, neither community was happy with this proposal. The Zionists took some comfort from the elevation of their status from a "national home" to statehood even if their state was not to a very large one. The Arabs were adamantly opposed. Curiously, in retrospect, the Russians approved the "aspirations of the Jews to establish their own state" which, Andrei Gromyko caustically pointed out at the United Nations, was due to the "fact that no western European state has been able to ensure the defense of the elementary rights of the Jewish people."

It should also be admitted that it never occurred to UNSCOP, the Americans or the British that those who had caused the problem should pay for it: no one suggested that an "Israel" should be created in Germany. And, as determined as the Americans were that Israel be created, no American politician suggested that Americans would be willing to donate some part of our land. It is difficult to avoid the charge that our altruism was cheap at the price: we were quite content to let someone else pick up the tab for Western anti-Semitism.

Meanwhile, in Palestine the rival communities prepared for war.

IV

Before the Zionists could deal with the Arab inhabitants, they had to force the British to leave Palestine. They could not be sure that the British would, in fact, leave or that something like the UNSCOP deal would be implemented. So they began to recruit the Jews who had served in various Allied armies during the war and quickly were able to add to the existing armed forces of Haganah, Palmah, Irgun and Stern men who had been trained to break codes and intercept communications (two of the most crucial abilities in which they have excelled ever since), fly aircraft, make or adapt equipment they looted from British stores or purchased in Europe. Most important, they had to increase the "critical mass" of Jews on the ground. The numbers were all against them as the UNSCOP plan made plain. To build up the Jewish population, they organized the so-called "secret roads" (*Ha'apala*) program that brought tens of thousands of immigrants into the country. And they kept up their attack on the British who, belatedly, were trying to keep the lid on the pot they had set upon the fire.

To push the British out was primarily the work of terrorist groups inspired by Vladimir Jabotinsky and led by Menachem Begin. Begin, who was born in Brest-Litovsk and educated in Poland had entered "violent politics" in the Polish Zionist youth organization, Betar, and came to Palestine with a Polish army contingent. There he joined and soon became the leader of the Irgun which had been founded in 1929 and reorganized in 1937. Having murdered a British minister of state, his associates went on to murder the United Nations representative, Count Folke Bernadotte, and various others. Because of them, the period between 1945 and the establishment of the State of Israel in May 1948 was one of the most violent times of "peace" ever recorded. I know first hand because I spent two months there in late 1946 and early 1947. Almost every night, machine-gun fire mingled with the explosion of bombs; streets were reduced to narrow pathways through thickets of barbed wire. Heavily armed British troops of the parachute division were everywhere. As in all such confrontations, the cost was enormous: never mind the killed and wounded, the British could not afford the upkeep of their army. They had to get out. May 15, 1948 was their deadline.

Evacuation, of course, took time. So the British began to withdraw in 1947. As area by area they pulled back, the Zionist armed-force-in-being, the Haganah, was ready to move in, flanked and helped by the terrorist organizations. Their targets shifted from the British to the Palestinians. When the Palestinians attempted to assert their control over the villages and towns, or to defend themselves, they were overwhelmed with "aggressive defense." As the Israeli historian, Benny Morris, quotes Israeli sources, leaders of the Haganah determined "to reply [to any challenge] with a decisive blow, destruction of the place or chasing out the inhabitants and taking their place." Words like "levelling," "uprooting," "evicting," "destroying" figure in all the Israeli records. Some are even more frank: The Haganah Intelligence Service recommended, Morris quoted from the Israeli government archives, "The village [of Sukreir] should be destroyed completely and some males from the same village should be murdered." Shortly thereafter, Haganah took the Arab village of Deir Yassin. There the Irgun and LEHI, working together, massacred the entire population and widely publicized its action to promote terror among other villages and thus to encourage their inhabitants to abandon their homes and lands. Through this and other programs, such as "Operation Broom," hundreds of thousands of Arab villagers and townsmen were literally "swept" out of the land.

(As an aside, I should mention that to write that Israel had deliberately sought to expel the Palestinians, when I was working on my first book on Palestine in 1955, was certain to get one charged with anti-Semitism. That was then a less public but almost as damaging a charge as to be called a Communist. Now, as I say, it is freely admitted in Israel although still taboo in America.)

V

The Arabs endured nothing so dramatic as the Holocaust and nothing so cohesive as anti-Semitism. While they are Semites, cousins of the Jews, unlike the Jews, they have generally lived in communities of their own people. What they began to experience, generations ago, was a very different form of suppression: imperialism. During centuries of rule by others, all Arabs including the Palestinians generally lost the capacity, even the memory, of conducting their own affairs. And this has left scars that affect even the most sophisticated today.

The predominant memory of those who lived in Palestine was the neighborhood of villages. If asked what his "nation" was, a villager customarily would give the name of his village. It was the village that gave him identity. Indeed, identification of man with land was almost mystical. The terrace walls of one's father, grandfather and great grandfather, the fields in which one played as a child and in which one's ancestors were buried, the localities where saints have been venerated and besought, all these gave rise to emotions virtually impossible for Western industrial (and virtually nomadic) man to fathom. Before their diaspora, villagers built their genealogies physically into the layout of their neighborhoods. Placement of dwellings corresponded to family "trees." Consequently, they had not only the sort of feeling most of us have about our homes, temporary as they are to many of us, but a more intense, more permanent, more "living" sense of relationship to the earth. Even in the cities, people recreated their villages as autonomous neighborhoods. Over the years, I have talked with scores of individuals who have described for me rooms, houses, gardens, orchards, streets as vividly as though they were seeing them at that moment. And, in retrospect and in the mind's eye, these scenes have taken on the extra, all-pervasive emotional dimension, a melancholy longing, that only loss can bring. The idea that these people did not love their land or were wandering gypsies for whom any place is as good as another is not only nonsense, but is, itself an ugly variety of disparagement, an anti-Semitism against Arabs comparable to the anti-Semitism experienced by Jews.

This extraordinary, to the Western mind, commitment to a piece of earth, in part, explains why when the refugees had to "camp out" in the surrounding countries (Lebanon, Syria, Jordan) or the miserable ghetto of Gaza; even when they found jobs and houses elsewhere, the Palestinians never felt "at home" but always dreamed of Palestine. For them, "Palestine" took on a mystical meaning akin to that professed by the early Zionists: it was not just a land of milk and honey. It was a mythic land, a land of the heart.

In their diaspora, the Palestinians were encouraged in this feeling by the surrounding Arab states. This has been a source of derision as viewed by outside observers. Why did Saudi Arabia, so rich, so empty, not simply take in the Palestinians? Or Syria, Lebanon or Egypt? They are, after all, fellow Arabs.

The answers are both simple and complex. The simple answers are that when most of the Palestinians became refugees in 1948-1949, the surrounding states were particularly poor, with large numbers of unemployed people. Their weak economies were nearly drowned with landless farmers. That was what most of the Palestinians had become, landless farmers. Every economic study, every proposed aid program during most of the last half century has recognized this fundamental point.

Beyond economic considerations were political impulses. The governments of the neighboring Arab states that had grown out of a generation or more of Western domination were weak, often corrupt and rarely represented any sort of national consensus. Vaingloriously, they had declared themselves responsible for the protection of their Palestinian "brothers." When tested in the 1948-1949 war, they failed miserably. Indeed, their performance was ludicrous. Some of the troops were not even fully armed, many had only parts of their uniforms. At least one Iraqi unit marched into the fray with most of the soldiers barefoot. One by one, they were roundly defeated by the better armed, more numerous and unified Jewish forces. Like other governments, even in sophisticated Europe, they tried to deny the magnitude of their defeats: the cheap solution was to proclaim that the Palestinian diaspora was just temporary.

For their own reasons, the refugees accepted this dissimulation. They were as reluctant to give up their dream of returning as the Zionists had been to give up their far more abstract vision of "return." More practically and immediately, they were reluctant to settle in the places to which they had fled. Many were Christian and did not wish to become permanent residents of Islamic states. They wanted, above all, to go home: emotionally, even after years, exile was a temporary condition. As memories were embellished, no current reality could compare with the vision of what had been. The "promised land" became not just an abstract ideal but a nearly concrete vision.

And, as time passed, the Arab "hosts" exploited the refugees for cheap labor while keeping them at arms length. They, in turn, criticized their hosts. A noted Palestinian wrote, "In the face of the enemy the Arabs were not a state, but petty states; groups, not a nation…[with the result that] nothing remained except the offal and bones."

These and other words stung and were, often imprudently, repeated so that the governments and peoples of other Arab states came almost to hate the Palestinians: their very existence was a reminder of their own shame of weakness and failure. As I have documented elsewhere, shame is perhaps the most powerful emotion in Arab culture and to ease, if not completely to avoid, it became the political imperative of the Arab regimes. This was to be accomplished by living with the fiction that the war was not really over, that the refugees, huddled in makeshift camps in Lebanon, Syria, Jordan and Egyptian-controlled Gaza, living on $27 a year per person worth of food, clothing and shelter, were there only temporarily. The United Nations fell in with this fiction by passing a face-saving resolution affirming the refugees' right to return.

Few were fooled even when they wanted to be. One after another the Arab regimes were overthrown by men who promised to restore Arab dignity. Most were simply opportunists, but a few made serious attempts at reform. Foremost among them, of course, was Gamal Abdul Nasser of Egypt. Nasser was no intellectual giant and certainly no democrat, but he did understand that if his country was deal with the shame of Arab poliltics, it had to advance, to come out of the shade of imperialism into the sunlight of independence. To do that it had to deal with the domestic causes of its backwardness. So, as he felt his way into power, Nasser embarked upon a program of land reform, educational enrichment and industrialization. None of these worked satisfactorily. Certainly none brought Egypt to Israel's standard.

Why is that? Given their apparent numerical superiority, their relatively vast size and the inflow of wealth from oil, why have the Arab states performed so poorly in comparison to the Israelis? This is not merely a rhetorical question: it is significant in explaining the kind of war the Palestinians are now fighting against the Israelis and the kind of war the Israelis are now fighting against the Palestinians. It therefore deserves careful examination.

Begin with land: a look at the map shows how huge the Arab world is in comparison to Israel. Then deduct from the map the essentially unusable portions where there is no water. Egypt, for example, then ceases to be the size of Texas and New Mexico and becomes much smaller than tiny West Virginia; Jordan declines from Indiana to even smaller Rhode Island; Iraq ceases to be the size of California and becomes also the size of West Virginia; and Saudi Arabia, the territorial giant, as big as Alaska and California combined, dwindles to Maryland.

Land is, of course, only the foundation: except for oil-related activity, which has pumped into the area enormous amounts of money, there are few natural resources with which to build much on the land. Such industry as has been created is small-scale, mostly uneconomic, heavily dependent upon subsidies.

Like industry, technical skills are still few, new and mostly not of "world class." My favorite statistic comes from Iraq: when I first went there in 1952, Iraq had 5 mechanical engineers. That figure can be paralleled at various levels of the society of the several Arab countries. While student enrollments have risen, on average, about ten or twelve times since the end of the Second World War, quality has generally declined or at least not kept pace. What is most interesting, I find, is among the general work force. There we find something analogous to land utilization: without going into great detail, my studies indicate an "effective" component, that is a group oriented toward modern technology, of less than 5% of the total. Thus, Egypt, for example, with a population or 60 or so million, would have something on the order of a million and a quarter of what I have called "new men." Similar discounts can be made for the population of other countries. Relatively speaking enormous strides have been made there and elsewhere, as they have been in India, Pakistan, Iran and other "emerging" countries, but the results are still meager.

Naturally, or at least politically, the governments of the other Arabic-speaking countries in the Middle East have focused their energies on their own citizens. "The Arabs," despite attempts to create a sense of pan-Arab nationalism, are really quite distinct and separate peoples. There is less that unites the Palestinians to the Saudi Arabians, for example, than gives me a sense of fellow feeling with Australians or South Africans. We both speak more or less mutually intelligible dialects of a mother language, and watch the same movies, but our way of life is quite distinct, and our sense of loyalty is engaged in different directions for different purposes. Probably few Americans feel closer to Australia than to Mexico or Poland. So the Saudis, Iraqis, Egyptians, Kuwaitis and Lebanese, were engaged with their own, separate, affairs.

For years, most Palestinians sat in enforced idleness under ragged tents or in huts made out of battered tin drums in camps and waited. Divided religiously, socially and geographically, they had no national institutions or recognized national leaders. This was their time in the wilderness. The refugee mentality, as Moses found, dies slowly. It was not until the late 1960s, after a generation had grown up in their diaspora, that they, like the Hebrews in the parable of Abraham, coalesced into something like a nation.

The contrast with Israel could hardly be more dramatic: even for those Jews who did not initially benefit from exposure to the advanced, technological society of Europe (as many of the so-called "Oriental Jews" did not), Israel has created a very sophisticated milieu. This is evident at every turn: Israel is a modern industrial state with an income far higher than any other Middle Eastern state. It not only has more engineers, physicists, chemists, doctors and technicians but can even field a larger army than any of its neighbors. It is culturally a European country physically present in the Middle East. Its universities are world class, its industry is highly developed (was even able, with help from South Africa and France, to manufacture nuclear bombs as early as 1960), and its land was manured with that best of all fertilizers, money. Israel has received from the United States grants totaling approximately $100 billion ($100,000,000,000) or an endowment roughly $33,000 for every Israeli man, woman and child. America not only opened its purse but its universities, its industries, its government contracts and its heart to Israel.

Nothing, of course, like any of these things happened to the Palestinians — or indeed to any other underdeveloped nation. This is not to argue that these things should not have happened to the Israelis, but the fact that they happened the way that they did goes some way to explain the disparity of the capacities of the two communities.

VI

This disparity was made evident in the wars fought between the Arabs and Israel in 1956, 1967 and 1973. It is not necessary or useful to go into detail on these: in each case, the Arabs were outclassed and defeated decisively. Israel had capacities simply of a different order – always a generation ahead of even the most "advanced" of the Arabs. Not only did it have sophisticated command and control techniques, including ground control for aircraft, but it could increase its army from a standing force of no more than 50,000 to 300,000 in about 48 hours. I once was taken by the Israeli government to visit a tank brigade south of Tel Aviv that was maintained by only 200-300 men but could be put into action with 3,000 men in a few hours. And the Israeli army was supplied and also backed up – with arms occasionally as in 1973 being delivered to the battlefield – by the United States.

Even when Israel and the United States disagreed, the American government backed Israel to the hilt. The first test came in the so-called Lavon Affair ("Operation Susannah") when members of the Israeli intelligence force in 1954 burned down an American government building in Alexandria to attempt to break American-Egyptian relations. (The Israeli government decorated the attackers in 2005.) This event was quickly hushed up. The acid test came in the Israeli attempt to sink the United States Naval ship, Liberty, in 1967. It was the first time since Pearl Harbor that an American naval ship was attacked in peacetme. The story illustrates several aspects of Israeli policy and Israeli-American relations but is still little known. It was so tightly restricted at the time that although I was working in President Johnson's office in the White House, I did not learn of it until much later. Indeed, the key intelligence materials including intercept tapes were kept secret for the next 35 years.

What happened was this: The American government had been concerned with the build-up of Soviet armaments in Egypt and sent the electronics surveillance ship, Liberty, and several Air Force C-130 and Navy EC-121M aircraft to monitor radio traffic in the Eastern Mediterranean. Based primarily on U.S. National Security Agency (NSA) records, supplemented by CIA, DOD and other American papers and Israeli government papers, James Bamford recounts (in *Body of Secrets*, New York: Doubleday, 2001, 185 ff) what happened.

Shortly after Israel attacked Egyptian forces in the Sinai, it cut off and took prisoner a large number of Egyptian troops. At El Arish, just 13 miles from the Liberty, the Israeli army began killing their prisoners, whose hands were bound behind their backs, and discussed doing so on the radio. As Bamford wrote, "the Liberty had suddenly trespassed into a private horror." Egyptian soldiers were not the only casualties: a convoy of UN Indian peacekeeping soldiers was attacked and a number of the soldiers were killed and UN headquarters in Gaza, flying the UN flag, was "blasted" by Israeli tanks. Bamford quotes confirming evidence from the Israeli military historian Aryeh Yitzhaki. A number of other instances of such killings were later confirmed. Bamford believes that the Israelis were afraid that the Liberty had intercepted evidence of these acts and determined to destroy the evidence by sinking the Liberty.

The Israelis first observed the Liberty during the morning of June 8 from an air force Noratlas NORD 2501. The ship was identified at Israeli naval headquarters not only from naval reference books but by seeing its name painted in large letters on both sides of the hull with a huge American flag flying on the mast. All morning, the Liberty was under constant observation, being circled according to the deck officer, thirteen times. It was the only ship in the area. At 12:05 three motor torpedo boats and a number of Mirage IIIC jet fighters set out to attack it: in the first run, the aircraft killed a number of the crew and shot out most of the radio gear. However, the ship got in a "mayday" distress call to the USN Sixth Fleet. The EC-121 high overhead recorded one of the Israeli pilots saying, "Great, wonderful, she's burning." Israeli ground control headquarters asked, "Menachem, is he screwing her?" He was, indeed: "A later analysis would show 821 separate hits on the hull and superstructure... [and proclaim that] it would take a squadron of fifteen or more planes to do such damage..." Then the serious slaughter began with napalm and thousand-pound bombs. The captain managed to hoist the largest American flag, a so-called "holiday ensign," just before the three torpedo boats attacked with cannon and five torpedoes. (Fortunately, only one torpedo hit.) The boats then systematically destroyed the life rafts and life boats still aboard and those that had been launched in the sea. As one sailor later said, "It was obvious that no one was meant to survive this assault." Another said, "If you jumped overboard, the way these people were attacking us, we knew they would shoot us in the water."

At 3:28 PM (local time), the aircraft carriers USS Saratoga and America scrambled aircraft and National Security Council director Walt Rostow advised President Johnson of the attack. As Bamford recounts, "According to NSA documents classified top secret/umbra [a code classification beyond Top Secret]…[NSA Deputy Director Louis] Tordella was told that some senior officials in Washington wanted above all to protect Israel from embarrassment… that consideration was then being given to sink[ing] the Liberty in order that newspaper men would be unable to photograph her and thus inflame public opinion against the Israelis."

Meanwhile the US naval attaché in Tel Aviv was summoned to Israeli Defense Force Headquarters and there was told that Israel had attacked the Liberty "in error." "Shortly thereafter," wrote Bamford, "a total news ban was ordered by the Pentagon." At 5:29 PM (at the site of the Liberty) Johnson instructed the Joint Chiefs of Staff to recall the fighter protection "while the Liberty still lay smoldering, sinking, fearful of another attack, without aid, and with its decks covered with the dead, the dying and the wounded."

The aftermath was that 32 crewmen were already dead and two more would shortly die; 171 others were wounded; with his navigational equipment shot out and having little power, Commander William McGonagle worked his ship out to sea. Over sixteen hours later, near Crete, two American destroyers finally arrived. When the ship reached Malta on June 14, "A total news blackout was imposed. Crewmembers were threatened with courts-martial and jail time if they ever breathed a word of the episode to anyone – including family members and even fellow crewmembers."

Two years later, after crew members obtained legal counsel, Israel paid $20,000 each to the wounded and $100,000 each to the families of the dead. The ship commander was awarded the Congressional Medal of Honor, but

Johnson would not personally present it or allow it to be given at the customary White House ceremony; it was given McGonagle more or less secretly at the Washington Navy Yard.

Other than the drama and the pain, what is the long-term import of this incident? If I were an Israeli policy planner, as I have been an American policy planner, I would discount all future American protests and warnings. After all, if the US Government did not react strongly to an attack on one of its ships with the killing of uniformed sailors, would it react forcefully to lesser provocations? Apparently, that message has not been lost on Prime Minister Sharon today. I am not privy to what is going on between the American and Israeli governments, but judging from what I have seen of diplomatic negotiations, I would guess that the Bush administration has told Sharon he had better finish the job in Palestine quickly so as not to embarrass the Americans. That guess appears confirmed by the rather leisurely timetable of the trip to Israel of the Secretary of State. The headline in the *International Herald Tribune* reads "Defying U.S., Sharon vows to press ahead; Bush repeats demand."

A third episode occurred later: Jonathan Pollard is an American of Jewish faith who was employed by Israeli intelligence as a spy, as the Government of Israel acknowledge on May 11, 1998, to pass documents to it. When he learned that he was about to be arrested by the FBI, he fled to the Israeli embassy. He was never tried but entered a plea bargain under which he was imprisoned. Allegedly, for the whole story has never been completely revealed, the documents he passed to Israel contained information on American agents operating in the Soviet Union and the means by which America could track Soviet missile submarines. Israel then allegedly traded that information to the Soviet Union in return for special consideration of Jews; the CIA "assets" disappeared and presumably the Russians reorganized their submarine fleet. The result thus was, in effect, a replay of the espionage of Kim Philby. Indeed, what the Israelis did with Pollard's thefts was probably more damaging to American security than what Philby managed to do on his own.

It is, of course, true that Israelis by and large believe themselves justified in their acts although there is a significant and growing number who question at least the form of their actions. At some point, however, even the most hawkish will have to ask themselves what the reaction abroad would be if they were not

Jewish. Certainly what they are now doing in the occupied territories would have brought crowds of protesters into the streets of every major city in the world if the actions had been taken by South Africans, the British, the French or the Americans. Sooner or later the reservoir of good will – or guilt over western treatment of the Jews which is, after all, a sort of reverse anti-Semitism – will dissipate and Israel will be treated as a "normal" state among states. The Palestinians have long proclaimed their dispute as one "of oppressed people against a strong, colonialistic, oppressive state." In other words, a Jewish David has become the Israeli Goliath. If others begin to see a transformation of this kind, sympathy for "David" will not be so easily accorded "Goliath."

VII

I turn now to the Palestinians. As I mentioned above, during the generation that the Palestinian refugees passed in their diaspora, the years from 1949 to roughly 1968, their lives and their attitudes were profoundly changed. That was the period in which the younger, more aggressive men and women decided to take up arms to assert their rights to Palestine and to nationhood. As General Yahosafat Harkabi, former chief of Israeli military intelligence, wrote (in "The Position of the Palestinians in the Israel-Arab Conflict and their National Covenant," 1968), life in the camps helped bring about a new group identity; curiously but understandably, in that environment the refugees were influenced by the Zionist example. Those who became the new leaders made "efforts to mould a Palestinian people although it had no territory. In this also the Jews, as a people without territory and government, served as an example." Life in the camps had radicalized the refugees and convinced them, as Harkabi wrote, to adopt a "war of national liberation…[which] will take on the form of guerrilla warfare." As Harkabi and others (including I) have pointed out, the failure of the Arab states in the 1967 war threw the issue of Palestine back into the hands of the Palestinians.

Just as the Zionists have never renounced their claim to all of Zion – from the sea to the Euphrates – so the Palestinians in their 1968 National Covenant (Article 2) claimed all of what was included in the original mandate of Palestine and specified that all Jews who were living permanently there before 1917 will be considered Palestinians. Others would have to leave. Most important, the

Covenant argued that (Article 9) "Armed struggle is the only way to liberate Palestine [and]...to exercise its right of self-determination in it and sovereignty over it."

To attempt to accomplish these objectives, groups of Palestinians formed a bewildering array of semi-secret groups of widely differing political and paramilitary attributes. I cannot here analyze them; some were led by "crazies" or psychopaths like Abu Nidal. Others like Issam Sartawi, whom I negotiated with in Jordan in 1970, were sincere patriots. But, most of the groups they commanded were tiny off-shoots or splinters. Some lasted only a short time. The main group that emerged was FATAH which was led by the Gaza engineer, Yassar Arafat.

Arafat today is clearly a spent force and his entourage is widely believed to be corrupt and increasingly unpopular among the Palestinians, but in his earlier days he was a dynamic and persuasive leader. He almost single-handedly created FATAH despite opposition from most of the Arab governments. In fact, Arafat had to flee Egypt in 1954, but Syria gave it some initial support. Its model was the Algerian FLN. The Algerians with never more than 13,000 militants had won a war, not battles, but a war against 485,000 French troops, a million European settlers and about 2 million of their own pro-French fellow countrymen. Also influential was the Irish Republican Army which, with even fewer resources, was battling the British. Like them, FATAH focused its activities on publications or propaganda and on actions by "freedom fighters" or Fedayeen. Its central thesis was that the armed struggle would create a Palestinian revolution out of which would emerge the Palestinian nation.

While the Palestinians sought to pattern themselves on other national groups, they had to adapt to two different problems: on the one hand, Jews were accorded a special status throughout the Western world. Those who had marched and demonstrated against South African and Rhodesian whites and French colons in Algeria did not protest Israeli actions, even when, like the French in Algeria, they were torturing or murdering prisoners and harrassing civilians with racial taunts, cutting off water and sewage facilities and confiscating land. On the other hand, whereas the British were clearly alien in Ireland as the French were in Algeria, the Israelis were operating in Israel. So the Palestinians, particularly the more violent of the groups, had to act against the

Israelis outside Israel. That meant hijackings, murders and bombings in places where non-Israelis lived and worked and so made the world community regard them as pariahs. That is a view they have never overcome. It accounts, I think, for much of the indifference toward the fate of the Palestinians in the current tragic war.

However, in the aftermath of the Camp David accords of 1978, only FATAH remained a candidate to embody the Palestine Authority.

VIII

From 1921, commission after commission, arbitrator after arbitrator, agent after agent has been searching for some means of ending the tragic and seemingly unending conflict. I have been involved in some of them and did, successfully, in 1970 negotiate one ceasefire.

Almost everything has been tried – dividing the waters of the River Jordan (so the states would not clash over that vital resource, the American "Johnston plan"), aid programs to create a labor shortage (so the refugees could be absorbed, the American "Lilenthal Plan"), state-to-state negotiations (so as to by-pass the Palestinians, the Carter-Begin-Sadat "Camp David Negotiation"), redrawing frontiers (various British, United Nations and American plans), honoring the principle of the right of return while making it unattractive (the American "Johnson plan").

Almost, that is, except for the one thing that the Israelis realized from the beginning was central to Zionism and the Palestinians now realize is central to their future: the embodiment of the nation in a state. Unless or until this issue is faced and resolved, I do not think there is any significant hope for peace.

Instead, Israel has moved determinedly toward what it believes will bring it security. It has done so with two policies: the first is the settler policy or as the Israelis have described it, "creating facts." This policy has resulted in the planting of scores of Jewish settlements interlaced with roadways and checkpoints on the occupied West Bank. In his first year in office, Sharon oversaw the building of 34 new settlements in the West Bank.

While this policy is a direct violation of international law and in defiance of a number of United Nations resolutions, it has created not only a physical presence that would be difficult to dismantle but also a political position that would be virtually suicidal for any Israeli leader to oppose. Recall that when the French found it impossible to end the Algerian war unless they withdrew, it was only the enormous prestige of De Gaulle that made withdrawal possible. I see no comparable statesmen on the Israeli scene today and no motivation so strong as that which impelled the French action.

The second policy is the application of force. Israel is not alone in trying this policy. The Russians have fought the Çeçens for over two centuries; the British have been fighting the Irish since the time of Henry VIII; India has been holding down Kashmir since 1947; we fought and killed large numbers of Muslim Filipinos before the First World War. Israel has fought the Palestinians for over seventy years.

None of these was successful. None brought security, much less peace.

What did work, where it was applied, was recognition of what Woodrow Wilson urged, "self-determination of peoples." Examples are, sadly, not many but are significant. When Britain allowed the Republic of Ireland to come into existence, it became an ally; when Britain allowed India to become free, it became a leader of the Commonwealth; when France recognized Algeria, it became a major trading partner. Americans might remember that after the scars of our Revolution and other attempts at bullying America had healed, America ultimately became, as Prime Minister Tony Blair loves to repeat, Britain's closest friend.

Scars of the current Israeli attack on the Palestinians are certainly going to take a long time to heal; they will not heal as long as they are picked off with senseless, racially ugly, violent actions. Healing will require both time and separation. But, steps can be taken soon that will, at least, move in the right direction. Progress will certainly be slow; there will be set-backs; but, surprisingly, I think that the Israelis and Palestinians will ultimately come to recognize elements of kinship, shared definitions of a better life and, perhaps, some sense of mutual interest. Of course, much that has now been destroyed must be rebuilt and much more added to that to make Palestine a viable state. That is the easy part; it is the rebuilding of hope, trust and respect that are hard.

This is vague, very long-term and far from the horror of the events of today. The only virtue it has is that any other course of action will lead to war-withoutend that will brutalize, still further, both the Palestinians and the Israelis and cause misery beyond reckoning. Those who care about humanity cannot espouse such a course.

April 7, 2002

PART IV
IRAN

THE DANGER OF WAR WITH IRAN

This essay is amended to avoid repetition with my book on Iran and other articles in this volume. However, I reference sources in detail because many of the items I discuss are still either controversial or little known.

FROM 2002 ONWARD, WORRIED about the possibility of an American and/or Israeli attack on Iran, with disastrous consequences for Iran, of course,[1] but also for nearly all the rest of the world[2] and certainly including America, I wrote a number of analyses. I put these in the context of Iranian history and Iranian-American relations in my book *Understanding Iran*.

For a while, it appeared that I was like the little boy who cried wolf. But, as in the story, the "wolf" was real. The prospect of war, my "wolf," was a clear and present danger although like the wolf in the fable, the immediacy of the danger was not always apparent. But, for much of the these years, about half of the American navy was positioned along Iran's frontier; hundreds of cruise missiles were aimed at its nuclear sites, factories, military camps and cities; hundreds of aircraft were on alert at bases surrounding Iran in Qatar, Iraq, Turkey, Uzbekistan, Kyrgyzstan, Afghanistan and the Indian Ocean; other USAF aircraft were primed to deliver bombs directly from the continental United States; amphibious assault ships, equipped with helicopters and fast hovercraft, had been sent to the Gulf in 2007 to be ready to "insert" troops within hours of a decision to attack; covert agents and special forces were meanwhile deployed inside Iran;[3] drone aircraft, gathering intelligence and "also employed as a tool for intimidation" had been overflying Iran since 2004;[4] and the Bush administration was issuing a stream of warnings that "all options were on the table."[5]

To realize what those options amounted to, popularly known as "shock and awe," harken to USAF General (Rtd.) Thomas McInerney in "Target Iran"[6] on April 26, 2006 in the neoconservative The Weekly Standard. His description is so detailed that it appears to have come from Pentagon planning documents and was certainly read by the Iranians. He writes:

"A military option against Iran's nuclear facilities is feasible...What would an effective military response look like? It would consist of a powerful air campaign led by 60 stealth aircraft (B-2s, F117s, F-22s) and more than 400 non-stealth strike aircraft, including B-52s, B-1s, F-15s, F-16s, Tornados, and F-18s. Roughly 150 refueling tankers and other support aircraft would be deployed, along with 100 unmanned aerial vehicles for intelligence, surveillance, and reconnaissance, and 500 cruise missiles. In other words, overwhelming force would be used..[to] hit more than 1,500 aim points. Among the weapons would be the new 28,000-pound bunker busters, 5,000-pound bunker penetrators, 2000-pound bunker busters, 1000-pound general purpose [GP] bombs, and 500-pound GP bombs. A B-2 bomber, to give one example, can drop 80 of these 500-pound bombs independently targeted at 80 different aim points. This force would give the coalition an enormous destructive capability... [and would] allow the initial attacks to be completed in 36 to 48 hours. The destruction of Iran's military force structure would create the opportunity for regime change as well..."

Casualties would be enormous and much of the modern infrastructure of the country would be destroyed. However, the consensus is that even such a massive strike would not accomplish its supposed objective, to deter Iran from acquiring a nuclear capability. As I will point out later in this essay, it would have precisely the opposite effect: it would make absolutely certain the acquisition of nuclear weapons by whatever government emerged from the catastrophe.

Of course, as in the fable of the little boy and the wolf, the wolf might not come: having troops and equipment "at the ready" does not necessarily mean that they will be used. But history shows us that it does make their use more likely. The choice gives rise to the common military expression, "use it or lose it." Moreover, the official US military objective in the Middle East, established by Defense Secretary Donald Rumsfeld, certified by Vice President Dick Cheney and approved, indeed amplified, by President Bush, was the overthrow of the Iranian government. "Regime change" has been a persistent theme since the 1990s of American neoconservative advisers to the White House, the Defense Department and the CIA as well as of the more visible and often clamorous neoconservative commentators in the media and of the pontificating and often vociferous neoconservative strategists in a number of "think tanks."

It was not just Americans who were talking about and preparing to attack Iran: year after year an attack on Iran was perhaps the most common subject in Israeli political discussion, in the Israeli media and in Israeli diplomatic and lobbying encounters with American officials and legislators. Moreover, the Israeli military was at the ready: America had supplied Israel with fighter-bombers (the F-16i and the F15i) with sufficient range to reach at least some Iranian sites and with the munitions (the GBU-28 and the more powerful GBU-39 "bunker-buster" bombs) designed for just the sort of attack planned against Iran.[7]

In June 2002, the Israelis tested the performance of 100 of their F-16i and F-15i aircraft in a well-publicized mock attack carried out over the Mediterranean Sea.[8] What this war game made clear was that while the American-supplied aircraft had the range to reach at least one site, other necessary aircraft (including rescue helicopters) did not and would have to be refueled in the air or at stopovers.[9]

Meanwhile, since Israeli and American intelligence had identified more than 1,200 suspected nuclear and other military sites,[10] it was clear that a single Israeli strike even with 100 aircraft would not suffice. Either multiple raids, more aircraft or nuclear weapons would be required to accomplish the mission the Israelis had set for themselves. They nevertheless have continued to assert their determination and ability to carry out an assault if the United States does not bring the presumed Iranian nuclear-weapon program to a halt.

These events, massing of forces and repeated statements convinced me that the danger of war during 2008 constituted an unacceptable risk to America. Along with a number – but not a very great number – of others, I hammered away at consequences of this drift into war in every forum I could reach.

Subsequently, in November 2008, the US National Intelligence Council dropped its own bombshell. In a National Intelligence Estimate (NIE), the 16 federal intelligence agencies declared "with high confidence" – that is, as the publication explains, "the judgments are based on high-quality information [making] it possible to render a solid judgment" – that Iran had halted its nuclear weapons program four years before: "We judge with high confidence," the NIE continued, "that in fall 2003, Tehran halted its nuclear weapons program...and we judge with high confidence that Iran will not be technically capable of producing and reprocessing enough plutonium for a weapon before about 2015."[11]

Fortunately, perhaps because the NIE showed that the Bush administration's frequently asserted justification for an attack on Iran was unsubstantiated, President Bush apparently came to agree in the final weeks of his administration that the danger posed by an attack was unacceptable. He decided not to authorize American military action. He also turned down an Israeli request for a "green light" to raid Iran.[12] His decision was approved by NATO leaders including French President Sarkozy who said "an attack would be 'a catastrophe' [and] must be prevented."[13]

President Bush could order the USAF and the US Navy not to attack Iran, but, of course, he could not absolutely prevent the Israelis from carrying out an air raid. His administration, as I have pointed out, had given them the required equipment, and they repeatedly asserted their determination to use it in precisely the situation President Bush had created, refusal by America to do what the Israeli government demanded, to destroy Iran's capability to move toward nuclear weapons. What the Israeli Air Force lacked was a route, a flight path.

At this point, as Victorian novelists liked to say, "the plot thickened." Or it may have since there is so far (and may never be) concrete evidence. But based on snippets of information and reasoning, it seems to be at least possible that an undisclosed aspect of the August 2008 crisis over Georgia may have involved an Israeli attempt to solve the dilemma of a flight path. Unlike Israel which has no common boarder with Iran and is at the extreme limit of Israeli aircraft range, Georgia is right next door. If Israeli aircraft could be based there, they could relatively easily hit any site in Iran. Farfetched? As the Israeli blog, ynet news.com, reported on August 10, 2008, "The fighting which broke over the weekend between Russia and Georgia has brought Israel's intense involvement in the region into the limelight. This involvement includes the sale of advanced weapons to Georgia." (At the same time, Israel has also been selling its aircraft technology to Russia to enhance the performance of Russian fighter bombers.) How, if at all, this complex set of moves fits into the Iran story is, as I say, obscure. If it was part of a plan, the plan was not then effected. Unless or until we learn more, all one can say is that it is certainly intriguing.

Another intriguing episode was the September 6, 2008 Israeli attack on an alleged nuclear site in Syria.[14] The most logical explanation I can find for the attack, based on my own observations of RAF and USAF probes during the Cold war, some of which I watched on radar on the Black Sea in 1963, was to get the Syrians to "light up" their radar air defenses. That is what we were doing in the Crimea and elsewhere to establish a potential flight plan into the Soviet Union. This ploy would have been useful to the Israelis only if they wanted to develop the option of overflying Syria.

Overflying Syria, however, would not get Israeli aircraft to Iran. They would still have to overfly American-controlled Iraqi airspace. Would they be allowed to do so? It is inconceivable that if planes of the Israeli Air Force appeared over Iraq on a mission against Iran the USAF would attempt to shoot them down. [15] Consequently, both the Bush and Obama administrations have made only ambiguous statements advising caution and expressing sympathy, but not flat prohibitions or threats to cut military supply or other largess if Israel attacked. In short, as one commentator put it, America was "sending mixed signals."[16]

In their attack on the Iraqi nuclear installation Oisraq in 1981, the Israelis overflew Jordan and Saudi Arabia. They could presumably use the same route today if the Syrian route proved too dangerous. But, to avoid Iraqi airspace, they would have to swing far to the south, overflying Kuwait, and this might require the use of tanker aircraft in which they are thought to be deficient. The other route, over Turkey, would, similarly, be technically difficult and would probably be opposed by the Turks who maintain strategically important relationships with Iran.

Recognizing these problems, the Israelis have positioned missile-armed submarines in Indian Ocean waters known as the Arabian Sea and, perhaps, in the Gulf.

In short, it would be difficult but not impossible for Israel to attack Iran.

II

The presumed danger, to which the Bush administration was reacting and which the Israelis are today stridently proclaiming, is that Iran is on the brink of acquiring a nuclear weapon. Is this true? The November 2008 NIE said no, but it also admitted "we do not know whether it (Iran) currently intends to develop nuclear weapons." The Israelis believe they do.

These assertions pose three further questions: what would make Iran seek nuclear weapons? And, if it acquires them, how great a danger would they pose? And, finally, if the potential acquisition by Iran of a nuclear weapon capability is a great danger, what can be done about it? These are surely among the most important questions that the Obama administration must address.

I will address these questions in this paper, but first a general comment on nuclear weapons as we have witnessed them in the last half century of their existence: no state has actually fired nuclear weapons (although Israel nearly did in 1973); nuclear powers treated them as deterrents. Nor has any state shared its weapons with non-governmental groups such as terrorists. And, finally, acquisition involves testing which requires a large, remote and safe area. That is what prevented the Germans from acquiring weapons in World War II and drove the Israelis into an alliance with the South African apartheid regime. Testing, given today's technology, would be extremely difficult and impossible to hide.

I turn first to why might the Iranians wish to acquire a nuclear weapon.

To understand a possible motive for Iran to acquire a nuclear weapon capability requires some insight into Iranian interpretation of American-Iranian relations.

Beginning with the way "the other fellow" sees an issue is not how we Americans usually address a problem. We usually start at the other end: in this case, what the Iranians have done against America, what they are believed or are alleged to be doing and what they might do. So I take that first.

Foremost among American grievances is that the Iranian regime, in violation of international law and diplomatic custom, sanctioned the seizure in 1979 of the United States embassy in Tehran and the taking as hostages of most of its staff. The "hostage crisis" was probably the most important and certainly was the most emotional issue in that year's presidential election.[17] The charge has been made that on behalf of Ronald Reagan, William J. Casey, later head of the CIA, arranged that the hostages not be released before the election, thus denying Carter the political boost their release would have given his candidacy. If this is true, it would have put the Iranian regime in position to blackmail the Reagan administration. It is certain that after winning the election, the Reagan administration, seconded by Israel, secretly began dealing with Iran on more favorable terms in the so-called Iran-Contra affair.[18] So to some extent Iran faded from the American hate list. There were subsequent ugly events, including the terrorist car bomb attack on the American embassy annex in Beirut on October 23, 1983 that killed 241 American servicemen, which was partly blamed on Iranian influence, but there were no direct government-togovernment clashes.

Americans by and large have forgotten or, if they remember, wish to put aside their own actions against Iran. The Iranians have not forgotten and have repeatedly brought them forward. In brief summary, the actions they mention are, first, the American overthrow of the first democratically elected government of Iran. That happened in 1953 in a coup that was suggested by the British Secret Intelligence Service (MI-6) to then Secretary of State John Foster Dulles and was carried out by the CIA under its senior Middle Eastern affairs officer, Kermit Roosevelt.[19] The coup resulted in the re-imposition of Muhammad Reza Shah whose repressive policies led ultimately to the Iranian Revolution of 1979.

The second action was American military assistance to Iraq in its war against Iran. The US directly or indirectly supplied weapons, including cluster bombs, anthrax stocks and equipment to manufacture poison gas, as well as satellite intelligence to the Iraqis under Saddam Husain. These donations assisted the Iraqis in killing hundreds of thousands of Iranians.[20] In addition, America actually fought Iranian armed forces, sinking most of the Iranian navy. Economically, America also took the leadership in imposing a quasi-blockade that caused great suffering in Iran. Then, shortly after a visit by Donald Rumsfeld to Baghdad, the United States removed Iraq from the "terrorist list" and added Iran.

The third action to which the Iranian regime has pointed was the shooting down, in Iranian air space, on July 3, 1988 of an Iran Air civilian Airbus, thus killing 290 passengers, including 66 children, and the crew. The US government agreed to pay $61.8 million in damages but refused to apologize and awarded the captain of the Cruiser USS Vincennes that fired the missile a medal.

Despite these episodes, the Iranians both as individuals and as a government showed notable friendship for America and support for its policies. In the aftermath of the September 11, 2001 attacks in New York and Washington, 60,000 Iranians observed a minute of silence in bustling Tehran and many thousands of others held candlelight vigils.[21] The Iranian government assisted the United States in its campaign against the Taliban and in the establishment of American-designated Afghan government[22] and has employed about 20,000 troops and police, sustaining almost as many casualties as America suffered in Iraq, trying to interdict the drug trade.[23] The Iranians also deported large numbers of suspected al-Qaida operatives and forced or won-over Afghan regional strong men to the American side.[24] In these actions, Iran made major contributions to the achievement of America's major objectives in its Afghan campaign.

Despite the opposition of their own "hawks," successive Iranian government have made conciliatory gestures.[25] For example in May 2003 then-President Muhammad Khatami offered to open negotiations for a "grand bargain;"[26] Prime Minister Ahmadinejad, although wary and at least verbally hostile, made a comparable offer in May 2006 and has just repeated it to President Obama. On April 7, 2009, he said he welcomed "honest" talks which he explained meant concrete actions rather than just words.[27]

Contrariwise, the Bush administration repeatedly rebuffed Iranian gestures, ignored Iranian offers to negotiate differences[28] and damned the Iranian leadership. President Bush categorized Iran in his January 2002 State of the Union address as a part of the "Axis of Evil." That terminology set the style of American-Iranian relations during the Bush administration as I have set out above. What it also did was to force upon Iran's leadership two "lessons:"

The first lesson derived from the contrast between the American treatment of Iraq, which did not have a nuclear weapon, and North Korea which did: Iraq was effectively destroyed as an independent state and its government overturned while North Korea was offered an aid program. Iranian officials could hardly miss the point: not having a bomb put them in mortal danger. Many Iranians thought they were next on the list.[29]

The second moral was almost as important: it was that once a country actually gets a bomb, it is safe. No country will attack a country that, in retaliation, can inflict "unacceptable" damage. North Korea was the proof of that.

Moreover, the history of the nuclear age shows that once a country gets the bomb, it is quickly accepted by the other nuclear powers as a "member of the club."[30] India is a recent proof of this: although it secretly acquired the weapon and did not join the Nuclear Non-Proliferation Treaty (as Iran did), the Bush administration said, in effect, "we will make an exception – as we have done for Israel, which also has not joined Nuclear Non-Proliferation Treaty – and share with you our nuclear technology."[31]

So what is it likely that Iran will do about these "lessons." Put another way, what do we know or what can we infer from what we know?

III

While serving as a Member of the Policy Planning Council, during which I spent a great deal of time trying to figure out what dozens of other governments were trying to do, I learned that our ability to accomplish that task is severely limited. We spent many billions of dollars on diplomatic encounters, intelligence gathering from friends and agents, interception and decoding of radio traffic, collecting satellite imagery and even more recondite means, to get the raw data. But information collection was only the beginning of the problem. The data had to be interpreted so that "appreciations" could be made of the current events and projections could be made into the future.

In recent years, Americans have evolved two methods of accomplishing these tasks. Both are flawed; indeed, both have occasionally misled us into danger. The first of these is the adaptation mathematicians have made of the German Army General Staff *kriegspiel*, the "war-game." Essentially the war-game sets out to show how the opponent will respond to an escalating series of "moves." It assumes that he will be guided by a balance sheet of potential profit and loss. If he does not add them up accurately (as the mathematicians taught us to say) he has "miscalculated." Gaming thus views the foreigner as a sort of accountant – culturally disembodied, mathematically precise and governed by logic. In short, we posit in him precisely those qualities that do not shape our actions. So when we apply the lessons to "grand strategy" in our culturally diverse world, the results of the war-game are nearly always misleading.

In the aftermath of the Cuban Missile Crisis (during which I was a member of the "Crisis Management Committee") I was ordered to participate in a sort of replay of that crisis; it was a war-game designed to press the events into nuclear conflict but not quite to nuclear war. My colleagues on "Red Team" were some of America's most senior military, intelligence and foreign affairs officers and we drew upon the most sensitive information available in the American government about the Soviet government. We focused on an escalating crisis at the end of which we were informed that "Blue Team" had obliterated a Russian city. How should we respond? Do nothing, retaliate by "taking out" an American city or go to general war?

After careful consideration, we opted for general war, firing all our missiles to attempt to wipe out all American retaliatory capability and even the country.

The "umpire," Thomas Schelling, an MIT mathematician and author of *The Strategy of Conflict*, called a halt to the game, saying that we had "misplayed," and called a general meeting in the War Room of the Pentagon the next morning for what would have been in real life literally a postmortem. Schelling opened by saying that if we were right, which of course we were not, America would have to give up the theory of deterrence. Why had we acted in this irresponsible way?

In response, we showed that Red Team went to general war because it had to. If the leader of Red Team had done nothing, he almost certainly would have been regarded as a traitor and overthrown by his own military commanders; had he played tit-for-tat, obliterating, say, Dallas, what could an American president have done? He also could not "turn the other cheek." He would have had to reply. In turn, Russia would have had to react. And so on. Thus, despite the catastrophe it meant for both nations, neither government could have found a place or time to halt the fateful process. In short, whatever the "interest of state" (which clearly called for avoiding war even if in humiliation), the "interest of government" compelled actions that were not shaped by the same category of "logic." No previous war-game had predicted this outcome. Indeed, the dozens or hundreds "played" over the past decade, had all predicted, as did Schelling, exactly the opposite: the Russians would back off in the face of threat. The game we played was designed to show that they would also back off even after an attack.

We did not then know how very close we had come to total world annihilation in the real-life Cuban Missile Crisis and how much had depended on sheer luck[32] – and on the bravery or foolhardiness of Nikita Khrushchev.[33]

To supplement or correct the war-game, America has evolved a second means of evaluating the present and predicting the future. This is the "National Intelligence Estimate" (NIE) like the one on Iranian nuclear capacities and intent of November 2008. An NIE represents the considered opinion of the most knowledgeable (or at least best informed) senior officials of the US government who are presumed to speak without fear or favor. I have myself requested several NIEs and have been allowed to sit through the preparation of a number of others. NIEs are the common way that major problems are examined and predictions are made on how they will evolve.

The flaw in the NIE is perhaps lesser than that in the war-game, but it is nonetheless serious. It depends upon assembling "facts." That is, the staff that prepares the draft takes the vast input of statements, acts and capabilities of the adversary and from them makes an "appreciation" describing what the adversary is doing and drawing from it the inference of what he is likely to do. What is often deficient in this approach is that no assemblage of facts can ever be complete. Even more important is that it cannot account for all the "non-facts," the emotions, religious beliefs, fears, memories and even ignorance of the opponent.

The draft thus prepared is then put before a designated group of senior officials, drawn from all over the Executive Branch, to be discussed and brought to a consensus. The consensus may or may not be right: what seemed to the National Intelligence Council in 2005 was the opposite of what seemed right in 2008.

So let me suggest an alternative. It relies in part on what the war-game and the NIE require, as much information as can be assembled, but it then goes in a slightly different direction: it involves putting oneself on "the other side of the table." That is, it requires that one try to look at the issues the way the opponent does. Let me take the issue before us and pretend to play the role in the Iranian government that I actually performed in the Kennedy administration. As an Iranian policy planner, how would "I" see events and trends and what would "I" advise?

I am here attempting to accomplish two purposes: first, in my diplomatic and business experience, I have found that it is always enlightening to put oneself "on the other side of the table," to try to understand what the other person sees, what he is thinking and what he wants. Then, second, with as much of a sense of how the other person one sees the issue, one can evaluate whether or not there is a basis for a "deal" and if so what it costs, how likely it is to be successful and what the alternatives are.

I begin with what my hypothetical Iranian policy planner – "I" – thinks America (under the Bush administration) has been aiming to do:

IV

Reading in the press what President Bush, Vice President Cheney and other administration officials were saying, "I" (the Iranian Policy Planner) would begin by assuming that they are planning to attack Iran, abort its nuclear program and "regime change" it.[34] The policy of the Bush administration is more extreme but continues elements of the Clinton administration policy;[35] so I believe it is likely to continue into the Obama administration.

My job as the regime's policy planner is to figure out how to make invading Iran less attractive, and so less likely, and to offer an alternative that America will accept and that Iran's rulers can afford to approve. My first step is to ask Iran's intelligence analysts what the risks are. In American terms, this is equivalent to asking for a NIE. I believe that the Iranian equivalent to the National Intelligence Council would probably respond with this:

"The first danger is espionage. That is, the United States could attempt through covert action to bring about a coup d'état.[36] It did this in 1953 when the CIA and the British MI6 overthrew the government of Prime Minister Mosaddegh. Could it do so now? The odds are against it because the Iranian regime has both purged the regular army of the kind of officers who in 1953 supported the monarchy and has stationed among all army and air force units mullas who monitor officers and men; it also has offset the regular army with the Revolutionary Guard. Moreover, with members of the ulama living in every community throughout the country, it would be very difficult for any significant group of Iranians to assist foreigners, as the senior army leaders and some political dissidents did in the 1953 coup.

"Even without mullahs watching them, the Security Services believe that the bulk of the Iranian people are with the regime at least on the issue of national defense. True, there are dissident groups among the minorities – the Kurds in the northwest, the Arabs in the southwest and the Baluchis in the southeast – but these dissident groups are small, uncoordinated, distant from strategic centers and unpopular with the bulk of the Iranian population. They can commit occasional terrorist acts, as each has done – for example, murdering a Revolutionary Guard officer and blowing up a cultural center in Shiraz[37] – but those acts will only increase popular antipathy to them.

"The only truly Iranian dissident group was the Mojahedine Khalk and they were effectively destroyed or chased out of Iran from 1982. They have no significant following in the country and blackened their name by their association with Saddam Husain during his attack on Iran. The Americans initially aided and abetted their terrorist attacks on Iran,[38] but subsequently the Americans bombed their bases in Iraq in 2003.[39] Our friend and ally in Iraq, Prime Minister Nuri al-Maliki, has ruled that they cannot use Iraq as a staging ground for attacks on Iran.

"Even with the support of some people in minority communities, American "Special Operations Forces" constitute no serious threat to our regime. They can be provocative, occasionally kidnap or kill a few of our officers or commit sabotage, but these are only pin-pricks.

"The U.S. Air Force has consistently violated Iranian airspace with unmanned drones in recent years.[40] What our radar and ground observers told us has been confirmed even in the western press. Their intrusions are insulting but not a serious problem. In any event, even if we shoot down the drones, we cannot prevent satellite photography; however, we can hide whatever we wish to prevent being photographed by simply roofing our facilities as we did at our IR-40 Nuclear Research Reactor.[41]

"More serious is the risk of air attacks. The American Air Force appears eager to stage such attacks. They have publicly stated that they can destroy our armed forces, our industry and indeed our whole country. Perhaps the closest they came to acting was in April 2007 when we had a minor confrontation with the British in the waters off the Shatt al-Arab. The Americans offered to act, but British refused the offer.[42] At about the same time, judging that the Americans were on the edge of military action, the head of the International Atomic Energy Agency warned against "new crazies who say 'let's go and bomb Iran.'"[43] He did not name American Vice President Dick Cheney, but just a few days before Mr. Cheney had issued threats to Iran on the deck of an American aircraft carrier just off our coast.[44] At the present time, we do not have the capacity to stop a massive or sneak air attack, but we are getting advanced anti-aircraft rockets (SA-20 and later models) from the Russians. We probably could not stop the USAF but we might be able to stop the Israelis.

"We have had a curious relationship with the Israelis. They were close allies of the Shah, as we learned when the students who had seized the American embassy pieced together shredded secret documents, but we have traded with them and, during the Reagan administration, have even purchased military equipment from them. More recently, they have repeatedly threatened to do to us what they did in their attack on the Iraq on June 7, 1981. They demonstrated recently over the eastern Mediterranean that they could attack us. We could not now stop them. Perhaps we could after we get more anti-aircraft missiles. But, unless they used nuclear weapons, they could not defeat us. To attack us, they would have to refuel in the air or at American bases in Iraq. Before he left office, President Bush told them they could not do this; the cost to America of allowing Israel to attack us would be high.

"Moreover, since Israel and Iran do not share a frontier, Israeli aircraft would have to overfly Turkey – and we don't think the Turks would allow this – or Syria[45] and Iraq. The Syrians would not be able to stop them and we doubt that any American administration would or even could prevent them from overflying Iraq. No American president could afford to order the USAF to shoot down Israeli aircraft flying against Iran.

"So we have taken such precautions as we can, by burying many of our installations at least 70 feet (21 meters) underground (much as America and Russia did their nuclear facilities and missiles); so we think an attacker would have to use nuclear weapons.[46]

"The use of nuclear weapons against us would be catastrophic for us and also for the Israelis, but Israel has the means and has been training for a nuclear attack on Iran at least since 2007.[47] It is the world's fifth largest nuclear weapons power with what the US Defense Intelligence Agency publically estimates to be 60 to 80 bombs.[48] Two of its 'Dolphin-class' submarines, each armed with 24 US-made Harpoon missiles, perhaps nuclear tipped, patrol off our southern and western coasts, well within range of every town in Iran.[49] Other Israeli missiles could be fired from Israel itself; they would be disturbing but not decisive unless they were nuclear armed.

"Israel is thus Iran's greatest danger, but it is only the tip of our security problem: Iran is surrounded by nuclear powers – India, Pakistan, China and Russia in addition to Israel. We now have relatively favorable relations with these powers, but conditions could change. The Russians, particularly, might be prepared to drop their (somewhat tepid) support of us in exchange for the Americans pulling NATO back and/or dropping their plan to install missiles in Central Europe. Of more immediate concern, the United States maintains nuclear weapons and delivery systems in bases in Qatar, Iraq, Turkey, Uzbekistan and Afghanistan; America has the capacity to deliver bombs directly from the continental United States; and its huge fleet in the Persian Gulf varies between 2 and 6 carrier battle groups with hundreds of aircraft and cruise missiles, each of which can be tipped with nuclear weapons already present on the ships.[50] The Americans have threatened time after time to use them[51] and have even developed a special bomb, which they have apparently also given Israel, that US Secretary of Defense Donald Rumsfeld called a 'robust nuclear earth penetrator.'

"If nuclear weapons were used, probably tens or hundreds of thousands of our citizens would be killed immediately;[52] the bombs would also throw up perhaps one million cubic meters of radioactive soil with unimaginable consequences for us but also for people all around the world. Consequently, we think this would be such a catastrophe that sane governments would not do it. Now that the Bush administration is gone, we think the danger has somewhat lessened. But, the danger remains. Particularly from Israel."

This is what I imagine an Iranian intelligence analyst would tell his government.

V

Based on this analysis, Iran's policy planner would be expected to recommend what his government should do. Imagining myself in that role, I believe he would say something like this:

"Looking at the Axis of Evil sequence and hearing the cacophony of American threats, I urge that Iran get a nuclear device as quickly as possible. That, after all, was the successful policy of Russia, China, India, Pakistan and Israel. Indeed, as a leading student of strategy at the Hebrew University recently said, 'Had the Iranians not tried to build nuclear weapons, they would be crazy.'

"But, the acquisition process – that is, when other governments believe a country is working on getting a bomb but does not yet have one – is a time of great danger. How to get through this period of danger is the major challenge. There are several components in the answer:

"Clearly we must make a military strike on Iran unattractive. Iran's first defense is its people. Although the government may be unpopular with many Iranians, they are as unlikely to aid a foreign invader as the anti-Castro Cubans were during the American attacks on Cuba at the Bay of Pigs in 1961 and the anti-Saddam Iraqis were during the 2003 American invasion. Iran is better prepared and in a position to inflict more damage on an invader than either the Cubans or the Iraqis. The Cubans were few in number and the Iraqis had no organized fallback force after its army cracked. The Iranian regime must assume that a campaign of "shock and awe" would destroy its regular armed forces, but Iran has a potent fallback force. The 150,000 Revolutionary Guards and even more numerous Sazman-e Basijs (who showed their fanatical bravery during the Iraq-Iran War) are trained and equipped for guerrilla warfare. We should make it clear that they would inflict large and continuing casualties on any invader. Iran is large and has several times the population of Iraq so the cost of invading or trying to occupy it would be many times that of Iraq. We must be sure that the United States realizes this.

"In addition to this land-based guerrilla potential, Iran learned from the Iraq-Iran war, when America sank its larger ships, to go for small boats. Iran has nearly a thousand high-speed boats scattered among more than 700 little ports along the Persian Gulf. They could be used in Kamikaze type attacks with missiles and bombs and would certainly do great damage to attacking forces.[53]

Again, we need to be sure that all outsiders realize the consequences of an attack.

"Iran has developed and built missiles of which at least the Shihab-3 has a range of about a thousand miles (1,600 kilometers) and so could reach Israel. We must make it clear that if attacked we will use them against Israel. Iran also has large numbers of smaller missiles that could be used to destroy oil facilities and sink ships along the Gulf. In response to an attack, Iran like any other state would naturally use all its means of defense or counter-attack. The states in the Gulf should be made to realize the cost to them of any attack on us.

"Additionally, unlike remote and isolated North Korea, Iran has trading partners, friends and allies abroad. Both China and India rely heavily on Iranian energy exports. An attack on us, they should be reminded, would derail their own development programs. Other countries – indeed the whole Islamic world – would view an American and even more an Israeli – attack on Iran, as an attack on Islam. Iran's national religion, Shia Islam, has millions of adherents in Afghanistan, Pakistan, India, Indonesia, Lebanon, Syria, Saudi Arabia, the United Arab Emirates and Bahrain. Our enemies will try to accentuate the Shia-Sunni split, but we must portray the attack as one on the religion as a whole. An attack by America and/or Israel would also conjure memories, even more widely shared, of imperialist "gunboat diplomacy." Africans and Asians are already sensitive to this issue and we can draw on their anger. Finally, America's European allies would not support the attack. We need to keep the issue before them. Americans are well aware of these facts. Iranians must doubt that the American people would support a ruinously expensive war particularly in the midst of their enormous financial difficulties; America would have to be mad to add Iran to its problems. The logic of our position should be self-evident.

"From these short-range considerations, Iran needs a longer-range policy that has two features: first, it should aim at a result that would give it safety, prosperity and, above all, dignity. The simplest answer to this objective would be acquisition of a nuclear weapon. Once that was achieved, Iran would automatically be made a member of "the club" of nuclear powers. However, we must not lose sight of the fact that acquisition of a nuclear weapon is only a means, and not necessarily the best means, to accomplishing our objectives. It is expensive in terms of money, industrial capacity and talent. Once acquired, a nuclear arsenal is expensive to maintain and control. Moreover, having a weapon does not get us further toward the development of our country. Look at Pakistan. And we learned from the regime of the Shah that excessive expenditure on the military weakens a country. But, it is fool-proof: if we have a weapon we will not be attacked.

"If our leaders decide to weaponize, we must protect ourselves during the dangerous acquisition phase. Doing so will require shrewd tactics and subtle action. It will also require – and must aim to acquire – time to bring the various elements together.

"There are well-tested models for handling this dangerous process. The United States, Russia, Israel, China, India, Pakistan and North Korea each rushed through the acquisition phase as rapidly and as secretly as possible. Iran cannot hope to achieve the same degree of secrecy, but it has a means to overcome excessive surveillance or interference. The model for that action was provided by China and Vietnam, and if done with care, it can be effective. In essence, it simply alternates offers to negotiate with moves to build the still-legal nuclear manufacturing capacity.[54] We Iranians add an element to the Chinese and Vietnamese model. It is the traditional Shia protective mode of dissimulation (*taqiyyah*). Such a tactic would give Iran the option at any time of agreeing to nuclear restraint or, if our conditions are not met or we find that danger increased to an intolerable level, of moving ahead to acquire a weapon. Alternating the two activities, what Mao called 'talk talk fight fight' thus for Iran would become 'offer to talk, offer to talk, spin centrifuges, spin centrifuges.'

"Such a policy requires subtlety and close attention to the temper of the United States and Israel. Pushing too hard or fast could precipitate an attack.

"We may not have a free choice in these matters. Israel may attack us whatever we do and even whatever the cost to Israel itself. After all, governments do not always act on rational intelligence assessments and are often driven by anger, fear or ideology. Consequently, 'I' must affirm that the most certain way to deter attack is to acquire at least one nuclear weapon and the means to deliver it. That is what Russia, China, India, Pakistan and Israel have done. The means to deliver a weapon, the Shihab-3 missile, has been in hand for five or six years.[55] The bomb itself is not in hand. And getting it will be both dangerous, as I have said, and costly in intellectual resources and money.

"Therefore, if security can be achieved in ways that also contribute to the wealth of the country, they would be obviously preferable. So, we should explore the alternatives."

VI

Now reverting to my own position as an American and drawing on considerable experience in planning policy, negotiating difficult problems (including helping to end the Algerian war as head of the US government Algerian Task Force and negotiating a ceasefire in the "Suez War" at the request of Israeli Prime Minister Golda Meir), I suggest that the answer to the question I posed above is that there is the possibility of a "deal" that would prevent war and thus work to American and world interests.

As I see the major elements of such a deal, they include, in order of precedence, the following:

1. The United States must renounce its assertion in the "National Security Paper of the United States" of its right and intention to preëmptively attack any country "at the time, place, and in the manner of our choosing."[56] As long as this remains a valid statement of American policy, the Iranian government would be foolish not to seek a nuclear weapon. As the former head of the U.S. National Security Agency, Lt. General William Odon, wrote, "...President George W. Bush's threat of regime change has only driven Iran and North Korea to accelerate their efforts"[57] to acquire nuclear weapons and as Charles Ferguson added, "a U.S. attack would undoubtedly convince Iran's leaders to take that momentous step."[58] An attack would not only guarantee that Iran would acquire a weapon, but would set off a race among other powers to acquire them.

2. The second step is to help to organize and become a signatory to an internationally guaranteed statement recognizing Iran's sovereign independence and certifying that no other state will attack it. As even senior American generals and other officials have pointed out, "Iran cannot accept long term restraints on its fuel-cycle activity as part of a settlement without a security guarantee."[59]

3. Such guarantees have often been made among states, but in and of themselves they have rarely prevented war. So the third step would be to create a nuclear-free Middle East. This and other steps could be taken in a phased manner. It could begin with a decision by the US to stand down its own enormous naval and air forces on Iran's frontier.

4. More complex, of course, is what to do about the neighboring already

nu-clear-armed states. The means to accomplish this part of the objective will require international negotiation of a high order. But the essential element is clear: "imbalance" is what has successively motivated other powers to acquire nuclear weapons. Russia had to have the bomb because America had it; China, because of Russia, India and Pakistan, because of one another. So Iran will not definitively give up its ambition unless other states do too. We must recognize that this is virtually a universal truth: it was clearly stated by the then head of the Indian nuclear program to justify his nation's acquisition of the bomb. He said, essentially, that there can't be one standard for the Europeans who were the original members of the Nuclear Non-Proliferation Treaty and another for the Asians who were late comers. But cutting back and then abolishing nuclear weapons inventories is in everyone's interest. This now appears to be the policy of the Obama administration. It is the correct policy since nuclear weapons anywhere are a danger to people everywhere.

5. Would Israel join in such an effort? Now, it will certainly say "no," but Israel has logical reasons to reconsider this decision because, whether or not Iran decides to get a nuclear weapon, other countries in the area eventually – and probably soon – will. So while, arguably, nuclear weapons were a source of security for Israel in the past its nuclear arsenal is now becoming a source of insecurity. It will be extremely difficult to convince Israel of this point, but the logic will become clearer as time passes, and there are incentives that can be offered to encourage this move.

Within a nuclear-weapon-free Middle East, Iran and other countries could, of course, benefit from the intellectual, industrial and energy-saving aspects of nuclear technology and, within a balanced approach to getting rid of these horrible weapons, Iran would not find it humiliating to take up the various proposals[60] to have other powers monitor its activities and safeguard its fuel.

The Iranian government, like the Israeli government, will be reluctant to join such an effort. Its "hawks'" like the Israeli "hawks" will argue that having a bomb is a surer means to deter enemies. The issue will be hard fought domestically in both countries. Both must be persuaded that "giving up the gun" is virtually necessary for survival.

Here consider Iran: I assert that all indications are that Iranians are tired of living under the gun and want peace and security; they want their government to meet their desires for a richer, fuller life. If security guarantees are supplemented with more open international trade, for example enabling Iran to join the WTO (which the United States has blocked), to have better access to capital for investment, and to get the advanced technology required to improve oil extraction and to liquefy natural gas, the Iranian government will have achieved a true "victory." If the Iranian government fails to move in this direction, it almost certainly will become increasingly unpopular particularly among the rising generation. It is for this reason, I believe that, despite the opposition of Iran's own "hawks,"[61] President Ahmadinejad wrote to President Obama on January 29, 2009.

Perhaps even more to the point, the Iranian government is now cooperating with the United States and other nations in the Organization for the Prohibition of Chemical Weapons. While not so dramatic as nuclear weapons, chemical weapons have been used frequently and have killed about as many people as died in the American nuclear attacks on Japan. Moves to get rid of them offer at least a pattern that could be adapted to the nuclear threat.

Suspicions remain deep, memories on both sides remain painful, but with care trust can be built and wounds healed.

VII

Now I turn to the Israeli role in these events. Here the end of the "never cry wolf" story seems apt. You will remember that everyone tired of the little boy's warnings so when the wolf really did come, no one reacted with sufficient speed and vigor. The "little boy," the bystander, was eaten by the "wolf," the war. What is the danger before us? Some of us, and certainly I, believe what the Israelis say, that it is immediate and real.[62]

In its pronouncements, the incoming new Israeli government has said that it intends to short-circuit any moves toward resolution of the crisis that do not definitively destroy the potential for Iran to acquire nuclear weapons. It has repeatedly said that it has the means and the determination to take action. "In an interview with Jeffrey Goldberg of *The Atlantic*, incoming Israeli Prime Minister Benjamin Netanyahu claimed to have told President Barack Obama that either America stops Iran or Israel will...So once again, in spite of President

Obama's best efforts, the military option was put back on the table and the atmosphere for dealing with Iran was turned into 'Do as we say – or else...' The message of Israeli hawks has been that it can only afford to give diplomacy 'a few months...otherwise Israel will take military action."[63]

Several events in the last few weeks and even days appear to translated these words into visible preparation for military action. "'The message to Iran is that the threat is not just words,' one senior defence official told *The Times*... .'We would not make the threat [against Iran] without the force to back it. There has been a recent move, a number of on-the-ground preparations, that indicate Israel's willing to act,' said another official from Israel's intelligence community."[64]

To evaluate how clear and present this danger is, we must now look at it in the Israeli context as we have Iran's statements and likely actions in the Iranian context.

The Israeli attack on a convoy in the Sudan which was believed to be carrying arms to Gaza gives, I suggest, an example of the mindset of each of the Israeli governments in recent years. Asked about the Israeli operation, "Outgoing Israeli Prime Minister Ehud Olmert would not confirm the attack but stressed that Israel would act 'whenever it can' against its enemies, and said: 'Who dares wins – and we dared.'"[65] Dozens of other examples could be brought forward. As Roane Carey points out in a recent article,[66] the fundamental Israeli strategic principle has always been that "no neighboring state or combination of states can ever be allowed to achieve anything faintly approaching military parity, because if they do, they will try to destroy the Jewish state..." Thus, Israel must maintain what Vladimir Jabotinsky, the patron saint of Likud and a succession of Israeli prime ministers, called "the iron wall."

The policy of overwhelming force that permeates Israeli strategy today arose in the Palestine Mandate vis-à-vis the Palestinians. Jabotinsky was a "realist." He never expected the Palestinians would just lie down in the face of Zionist ambition or welcome the immigrants with open arms. He did not analyze so much as proclaim, but to him it was inconceivable that "tillers of the soil" would peacefully acquiesce in losing their lands nor would the Palestinians, no matter how divided and backward, give up their country. The only way to effect the Zionist program was force. And, Jabotinsky realized, the application of force could not stop at the borders of the Mandate. As he told the British Royal Commission of 1936, "even the whole of Palestine may prove too small for that humanitarian purpose we need. A corner of Palestine, a 'canton,' how can we promise to be satisfied with it. We cannot. We never can. Should we swear to you we should be satisfied, it would be a lie."

Those Zionists in the 1920s and 1930s who disagreed[67] thought, or said they thought, that the Palestinians would simply sell their lands to the Jewish National Fund and move to other lands. The Palestinians, they maintained, were merely squatters without legal rights. To justify their contention, the Israelis referred to the 1858 Ottoman land code. In that code, the Turks had superimposed upon traditional and customary rights to land a legal system designed to increase tax revenues. Under it, anyone, usually an absentee or even someone from another country, who could guarantee tax payments and could reach an agreement with the sometimes corrupt Ottoman authorities, could acquire a form of legal "ownership." It was this system which the British rulers of the Palestine Mandate inherited and enforced. So in the early days of the Mandate, the Zionist organization was able to buy blocs of land from people who in many cases had never set foot upon it. (One of the first large sales was by a Lebanese merchant family.)

The peasant cultivators were then forced to leave, or were hired as day laborers on, what had been for time out of mind of man "their" lands. Naturally, this created great bitterness on the part of the Palestinians but was regarded as morally and legally right by the Zionists. As this system spread, Zionist holdings reached 180,000 hectares (444,600 acres) on the eve of the 1948 war. This was a tiny portion of what Israel would have needed to survive so driving out the Arab population[68] became a major objective of the war effort. Nearly a million people including whole villages of farmers thus became refugees. Jabotinsky's acolytes played a significant part in this activity but they were joined by those who had professed the belief that Israel could be created by peaceful amalgamation.

After their victory in 1949, the new Israeli government made some concessions to those Palestinians who remained – for example the granting of limited Israeli citizenship and some civil rights – but both internally and vis-à-vis neighbors, it followed, as Jabotinsky had realized, that the Israeli state could exist only if it maintained an overwhelming military power. This reliance on "the Iron Wall" explained Israeli policy and performance in the series of wars that followed 1948.[69]

Thus, today, rather than being an aberration, the Israeli policy on Iran grows out of this fundamental system first applied to the Palestinians and then to other Arab states. The integral nature of the Israeli approach to Israel, to the occupied areas of Palestine, to the neighboring states was stated, perhaps in its most extreme form, by the new Israeli Foreign Minister, Avigdor Libermann, who favors denationalization of Arab citizens of Israel and probably their expulsion from Israel, but it is not different in content from the beliefs and statements of the early Zionists even to the British government at the time of the formulation of the Balfour Doctrine. The apex of this policy has been Israel's refusal to allow the formation of a Palestinian state, its continued acquisition of Palestinian land and its reliance on military force and ultimately on nuclear weapons.

So interwoven are these policies that it will prove nearly impossible to deal successfully with any one without dealing with them all. So far, at least, the Obama administration has shown an understandable reluctance to grab this thorny nettle. But it is true, if not entirely obvious, that there is no conceivable solution to the problem of the "Middle East" whether defined in terms of Arab-Israel affairs or of a broader area now including Iran that fails to address the totality of the issue.

So where does this leave us? To speculate, it seems to me that the Israelis are on the edge of a cliff: if they move ahead in their plan to attack Iran, as they say they will, regardless of whatever restraints are applied or cautionary words voiced by the Obama administration[70] or others, I believe they will create a catastrophe not only for Iran but also others. Their action will precipitate at minimum a guerrilla war of more serious dimensions in Lebanon, in Jordan and Gaza, possibly revolution in some of the surrounding states, particularly in Egypt and perhaps in Saudi Arabia. Growing hatred of Israel throughout much ofz Asia, Africa and even Europe. Severe worldwide economic dislocations. Indeed, I believe that it will later be seen to have marked the beginning of the end for Israel itself.

April 19, 2009

1. *The Guardian*, February 13, 2006, Ewen MacAskill. "Consequences of a War," Up until April 2006, the White House was planning to use nuclear weapons in the attack but was dissuaded by Chairman of the Joint Chiefs of Staff General Peter Pace, USMC, according to Seymour Hersh in *The New Yorker*, July 10 and 17, 2009. Consider the result of what the Bush administration decision would have meant: As former Secretary of Defense Robert McNamara pointed out ("Apocalypse Soon," *Foreign Policy*, May/June 2005), a "small" (one megaton) nuclear weapon today is roughly 70 times as powerful as the weapon that killed 280,000 people in Hiroshima. He commented that to drop a nuclear weapon on a "nonnuclear enemy would be militarily unnecessary, morally repugnant, and politically indefensible." It would thus have severely damaged America's world leadership and probably convinced a number of other countries that they would need nuclear weapons to protect themselves from the United States; so it would have ratcheted up the world nuclear arms race to a new level of danger.
2. I have laid out the economic consequences in a number of papers. In summary, they would remove at least temporarily upwards of 25% of the world's energy, certainly causing severe dislocations (since the kind of oil produced in various other areas would require extensive modification by refineries that do not have the capacity to do so), and would almost certainly cause a panic in which energy costs would soar. It would obviously make working out of the current depression even more difficult.
3. In 2007, President Bush requested $400 million to "destabilize" Iran's government; and, as Seymour Hersh reported in *The New Yorker* of July 7 & 14, 2009, "Clandestine operations against Iran are not new. United States Special Operations Forces have been conducting cross-border operations from southern Iraq, with Presidential authorization, since last year."
4. *International Herald Tribune*, February 13, 2005 Dafna Linzer, "U.S. Uses Drones to Probe Iran for Arms."
5. Most notably, of course, President George W. Bush's "State of the Union" address of January 2003.
6. *The Weekly Standard*, April 26, 2006.
7. The Israeli newspaper Haaretz, September 11 and 14, 2008.
8. *International Herald Tribune*, June 21-22, 2008, Michael Gordon and Eric Schmitt, "An Israeli dry run for raid against Iran?" More than 100 F-16 and F-15 participated over the eastern Mediterranean and Greece, flying the exact range of flight to the principal target, 1,400 km.
9. The F-16i and F-15i may have the range, but most Israeli aircraft would have to be refueled. Andrew Brookes, in the March 2007 World Today (Royal Institute of International Affairs).
10. *The Sunday Times*, September 2, 2007: Sarah Baxter, "Pentagon 'Three-Day Blitz' plan for Iran."
11. Issued by the Office of the Director of National Intelligence. The report contradicted some aspects of a May 2005 NIE on Iran's nuclear program. The fact that the NIE was

published, an unusual action, seemed to indicate a growing worry by the intelligence agencies that America was sliding toward war with Iran and an attempt to make such a move impossible by showing that it was unjustified.

12. As Jonathan Steel reported on September 27, 2008 in *The Guardian*, "Israel asked US for green light to bomb nuclear sites in Iran." "Israel gave serious thought this spring to launching a military strike on Iran's nuclear sites but was told by President George W. Bush that he would not support it..."
13. Daniel Levy, "Talking Point Memo" (*Salon*), September 11, 2008.
14. Norman Dombey, "At Al Kibar," *London Review of Books*, June 19, 2008, pointed out that the reactor, if it existed, had "no fuel, and no prospect of getting any..."
15. I think this is self-evident given the power of the Israeli lobby throughout America, but it is also exemplified by one historical episode. The U.S. Navy did not intervene even to protect a US Navy ship, the USS Liberty, from Israeli aircraft and ships that were endeavoring to sink it. This was during the 1967 war. For a graphic account see James Bamford, Body of Secrets (New York: Doubleday, 2001), 200 ff.
16. *The Nation*, April 13, 2009, Roane Carey, "US must Stop Mixed Signals on Iran."
17. Captain Gary Sick USN (Rtd.), who was the NSC officer most closely involved, has written a chronology of the events in *All Fall Down: America's Fateful Encounter with Iran* (New York: Random House and London: I.B. Tauris, 1985). Mark Bowden later interviewed a number of the militants and describes their activities and motivations in "Among the Hostage Takers," *The Atlantic Monthly* (December 2004). I also deal with this episode in my forthcoming *Understanding Iran* (New York and London: Macmillan, 2009).
18. Gary Sick, October *Surprise: America's Hostages in Iran and the Election of Ronald Reagan* (New York: Random House, 1991).
19. The official, still classified, history written by Donald M. Wilber, *The Overthrow of Premier Mossadeq of Iran, November 1952-August 1953*. Mr. Wilbur's account, which was intended as a text book on how to overthrow governments to train CIA officers, was turned over to *The New York Times* in 2000.
20. William R. Polk, *Understanding Iraq* (New York: HarperCollins, 2005 & 2006), 131-132.
21. The BBC, Gordon Corea, "Uncovering Iran."
22. *The New York Review of Books*, January 15, 2009, Max Rodenbeck, "The Iran Mystery Case."
23. "*International Herald Tribune*, December 1, 2006, Antonio Maria Costa, "The New Golden Triangle, "Iran has deployed almost 20,000 antinarcotic police and border guards along its 1,845 kilometer border with Afghanistan and Pakistan – the world's most active opium smuggling route. Twenty-eight mountain passes have been blocked by huge concrete structures. Hundreds of kilometers of trenches – four meters wide and four meters deep – have been dug to stop drug caravans eluding patrols. Towers and barbed wire stretch as far as the eyes can see."
24. Flynt Leverett and Hillary Mann Leverett, "Opportunity Knocked," *National Interest*

Online, July 23, 2008.

25. *International Herald Tribune*, December 7, 2007, Flynt Leverett and Hillary Mann Leverett, "Bush's real lie about Iran: despite recent claims otherwise, the White House has rebuffed negotiations with Iran at every turn..."
26. *Financial Times*, March 17, 2004, Guy Dinmore, "US stalls over Iran talks offer." The Bush administration was furious and complained to the Swiss Foreign Ministry that its ambassador in Tehran had exceeded his authority by even transmitting the offer.
27. *Associated Press*, April 8, 2009, printed in *The New York Times*.
28. *International Herald Tribune*, August 18, 2006, "from news reports" "Twenty-two former high-ranking military officers and retired diplomats urged President George W. Bush on Thursday to open discussions immediately..." *The New York Times* correspondent Nicholas D. Kristof headed his column on January 22, 2007, "Hang up! Tehran is calling."
29. *The Guardian*, January 29, 2009, Julian Borger, "Soft-spoken line from Washington may terrify Tehran." "While mixed messages emanated from the Bush administration, only one was clearly received in Tehran – that Iran was next on the Axis of Evil list after Iraq...The lesson of the Iraq invasion for the Iranian leadership was that Saddam lost his job and then his life not because he might have had weapons of mass destruction but because he had none. North Korea, the third member of the axis, which had nuclear bombs, was treated with much greater respect."
30. *The London Review of Books*, June 22, 2006, Brian Jones "Nuclear Blindness."
31. *International Herald Tribune*, September 12, 2008, Former President Jimmy Carter, "India deal puts world at risk" and October 3, 2008, Peter Baker, "Congress approves U.S. nuclear trade with India."
32. As former Secretary of Defense Robert McNamara found ("Apocalypse Soon," *Foreign Policy*, May/June 2005) years later the commanders of the four Soviet nuclear submarines then trailing the American fleet had authorization to fire their nuclear armed torpedoes without recourse to Moscow. Being out of touch with their headquarters, they continued to patrol for four days after Khrushchev announced the withdrawal and the crisis had ended.
33. He was not overthrown, but after his death he was "down-graded" and not buried at the Kremlin Wall as were other Soviet leaders.
34. *Asia Times*, May 6, 2008, Gareth Porter, "Yes, the Pentagon did want to hit Iran." "Three weeks after the September 11, 2001 terror attacks, former US defense secretary Donald Rumsfeld established an official military objective of not only removing the Saddam Hussein regime by force but overturning the regime in Iran, as well as in Syria and four other countries in the Middle East..."
35. Iran's President Ali Akbar Hashemi-Rafsanjani told *Time* on May 24, 1993 that there had been no real change from the [first] Bush to the Clinton administration. The US Navy continued to maintain a massive presence in the Persian Gulf, where the previous Bush administration had sunk about half of the Iranian navy. President Muhammad Khatami

called for a "dialogue with the American people" on a US TV interview in 1998, and Iranian Foreign Minister Kharrazi met with US Secretary of State Madeleine Albright at the UN in September, but these encounters did not notably change our relationships.

36. *The New Yorker*, July 7 & 14, 2008, Seymour Hersh "Preparing the Battlefield": "Late last year, Congress agreed to a request from President Bush to fund a major escalation of covert operations against Iran, according to current and former military, intelligence, and congressional sources." For them he sought up to $400 million which he described in a Presidential Finding "designed to destabilize the country's religious leadership." US "Special Operations Forces have been conducting cross-border operations from southern Iraq, with Presidential authorization, since last year. These have included seizing members of Al Quds, the commando arm of the Iranian Revolutionary Guard, and taking them to Iraq for interrogation, and the pursuit of 'high-value targets' in President Bush's war on terror, who may be captured or killed." Funding was approved. "...a secret military task force, [is] now operating in Iran, that is under the control of JSOC [Joint Special Operations Command]." Then just before the end of his term, the *International Herald Tribune* of January 12, 2009 President Bush "embraced more intensive covert operations aimed at Iran...to undermine under systems, computer system and other networks on which Iran relies."

37. *The New Yorker*, July 7 & 14, 2008, Seymour Hersh, "Preparing the Battlefield," "Earlier this year, a militant Ahwazi group claimed to have assassinated a Revolutionary Guard colonel, and the Iranian government acknowledged that an explosion in a cultural center in Shiraz, in the southern part of the country, which killed at least twelve people and injured more than two hundred, had been a terrorist act and not, as it earlier insisted, an accident. It could not be learned whether there had been American involvement in any specific incident in Iran, but, according to [Colonel Sam] Gardiner, the Iranians have begun publicly blaming the U.S., Great Britain, and, more recently, the C.I.A. for some incidents."

38. Ibid. They have "received arms and intelligence, directly or indirectly from the United States."

39. *The New York Times*, April 17, 2003, Douglas Jehl, "U.S. bombed bases of Iranian rebels in Iraq." The Mojahedin-e Khalq maintained bases with several thousand fighters with tanks and artillery on Iranian border from which they have made cross-border attacks and have killed "scores of soldiers." They have been supported by the House of Representatives International Relations Committee's subcommittee on the Middle East. The attack "almost certainly represented an end to the group as a fighting force, after the years in which it operated freely from Iraq with support from Saddam Hussein."

40. *International Herald Tribune*, February 13, 2005, Dafna Linzer "U.S. Uses Drones to Probe Iran for Arms," "The Bush administration has been flying surveillance drones over Iran for nearly a year to seek evidence of nuclear weapons programs and detect weaknesses in air defense, according to three U.S. officials with detailed knowledge of the secret effort...The aerial espionage is standard in military preparations for an

eventual air attack and is also employed as a tool for intimidation."

41. *Report of the Director General to the Board of the IAEA*, February 19, 2009.
42. *The Guardian*, April 7, 2007, Ewen MacAskill, Julian Border, Michael Howard and John Hooper, "Americans offered 'aggressive patrols' in Iranian airspace. The British "said the US could calm the situation by staying out of it...[and]At the request of the British, the two US carrier groups, totally 40 ships plus aircraft, modified their exercises to make them less confrontational."
43. Reuters, June 1, 2007.
44. *The New York Times*, May 12, 2007, David E. Sanger, "Cheney, on Carrier, Sends Warning to Iran."
45. *U.S. News and World Report*, March 12, 2008.
46. *The Sunday Times*, January 7, 2007.
47. *The Sunday Times*, January 7, 2007: "...if things go according to plan, a pilot will first launch a conventional laser-guided bomb to blow a shaft down through layers of hardened concrete. Other pilots will then be ready to drop low-yield one kiloton nuclear weapons into the hole."
48. *The Guardian*, July 29, 2008, George Monbiot, "We lie and bluster about our nukes – and then wag our fingers at Iran,"
49. *The Independent*, May 1, 2004, James C. Moore, Why Shouldn't Iran Have Nuclear Weapons?"
50. *The Guardian*, May 4, 2006, Tariq Ali, "Why has the US Manufactured a Crisis Over Iran?"
51. *The New Yorker*, July 10 and 17, Seymour Hersh, "Last Stand." "In late April [2006 the chairman of the Joint Chiefs of Staff Marine General Peter] Pace achieved a major victory when the White House dropped its insistence that the plan for a bombing campaign include the possible use of a nuclear device...'Bush and Cheney were dead serious about the nuclear planning,' the former senior intelligence official told me. 'And Pace stood up to them."
52. *The Guardian*, February 13, 2006, Ewen MacAskill. "Consequences of a War," by Professor Paul Rogers and published by the Oxford Research Group.
53. *The New Yorker*, July 10 & 17, Seymour Hersh, "Last Stand." American Naval Intelligence found that "Iran has more than seven hundred undeclared dock and port facilities along its Persian Gulf coast." The Japanese Kamikazes killed about 5,000 Americans.
54. *International Herald Tribune*, December 2, 2005, Richard Bernstein: "Mao's fight talk' strategy is a winning one for Iran." Mao Zedong's fight talk strategy. Offer to talk, then resume work on nuclear process. "There is no very good military option on Iran... there is no feasible alternative to negotiations [but that] is the reason Iran in the end will probably become a nuclear weapons power."
55. *The New York Times*, July 8, 2003, Nazila Fathi, "Iran Confirms Test of Missile That is Able to Hit Israel."
56. "Department of Defense, "The National Defense Strategy of the United States of America,"

March 2005. Another version came out the following year. It was savaged by William Pfaff who wrote (*International Herald Tribune*, March 20, 2006) that "Intellectual poverty is the most striking quality of the Bush administration's new National Security statement, issued on Thursday, Its overall incoherence, its clichés and stereotyped phraseology...reveals the administration's foreign policy as a lumpy stew of discredited neoconservative ideas with some neo-Kissingerian geopolitics now mixed in." The June 2008 version, signed by then and now Secretary of Defense Robert Gates, was cosmetically improved, but the assertion of the right to act preëmptively remained. New emphasis was added to "non-state" and "rogue-state" warfare.

57. "The Nuclear Option," *Foreign Policy,* May/June 2007

58. *International Herald Tribune*, February 15, 2006. "Been there, botched that"

59. *The New Yorker*, July 10 & 17, 2006, Seymour Hersh, "Last Stand," quoting Major Generals Paul Eaton and Charles Swannack, Jr.

60. For example, the proposal of William Luers, Thomas Pickering and Jim Walsh, "A solution for the US-Iran Nuclear Standoff," in the March 20, 2008 *New York Review of Books*. "We propose that Iran's efforts to produce enriched uranium and other related nuclear activities be conducted on a multilateral basis, that is to say jointly managed and operated on Iranian soil by a consortium including Iran and other governments." And their subsequent article in the February 12, 2009 issue of the same journal.

61. *The Guardian*, January 29, 2009: The chairman of "the Guardian Council," Ayatollah Ahmad Janati, denounced attempts to rapprochement with the US.

62. *The Los Angeles Times*, April 16, 2009, Paul Richter, "Gates warns against Israeli strike on Iran's nuclear facilities." Israeli President Shimon Peres told Israel's Kol Hai Radio on April 12 that Israel would attack Iran if it did not stop work on its nuclear program; "'We'll strike him', Peres said in the interview." The new prime minister, Benjamin Netanyahu called the Iranian program an "existential threat."

63. *Alternet*, April 13, 2009, Trita Parsi, *Huffington Post*, "Israel is Bluffing: Constant War Threats Against Iran Are Empty, But Still Dangerous." "Netanyahu's tough talk undermines the Obama administration's prospects for diplomacy...it fuels Iranian insecurity and closes the window for diplomacy."

64. *The Times*, April 18, 2009, Sheera Frenkel, "Israel stands ready to bomb Iran's nuclear sites."

65. *Energy Compass*, XX, #16, April 17, 2009, Paul Sampson, "Will Israel Hit Iran?"

66. *The Nation*, April 13, 2009, Roane Carey, "US Must Stop Mixed Signals on Iran." Carey further says that "The new Israeli prime minister, Likud Party hawk Benjamin Netanyahu, has warned President Barack Obama that if Washington does not quickly find a way to shut down Iran's nuclear program, Israel will."

67. Jabotinsky resigned from the Zionist executive in 1923 in opposition to the relatively

moderate methods and policies of Chaim Weizmann. In 1935, he founded the Irgun Z'vai Le'umi which became the basis for the Herut after 1948.

68. This was denied for many years, but has been fully documented by various Israeli scholars including Benny Morris in *The Birth of the Palestinian Refugee Problem, 1947-1949* (Cambridge: Cambridge University Press, 1987), his *The Birth of the Palestinian Refugee Problem Revisited* (Cambridge: Cambridge University Press, 2004) and his "Revisiting the Palestinian exodus of 1948" in Eugene L. Rogan and Avi Shlaim (eds.), *The War for Palestine* (Cambridge: Cambridge University Press, 2001). Also see Ilan Pappe, *The Ethnic Cleansing of Palestine* (Oxford: Oneworld Publications, 2006). A much earlier account, before the Israeli records were available is in the book I wrote with David Stamler and Edmund Asfour, *Backdrop to Tragedy* (Boston: The Beacon Press, 1957) when to say what Messrs. Morris, Shlaim and Pappe now say was regarded as proof of anti-Semitism.

69. Avi Shlaim, *The Iron Wall: Israel and the Arab World* (London: Penguin, 2000).

70. Such as those of Secretary of Defense Robert Gates to Marines at the Marine University at Quantico Naval Base. *Los Angeles Times*, April 16, 2009.

PART V

ATTEMPTS TO UNDERSTAND

Bulletin of the Atomic Scientists

A JOURNAL OF SCIENCE AND PUBLIC AFFAIRS

JANUARY 1967 • 85 CENTS

RABINOWITCH: New Year's Thoughts

MORGENTHAU: A New U.S. Foreign Policy

POLK: The Middle East

KAHIN & LEWIS: Escalation and East Asia

THE MIDDLE EAST: ANALYZING SOCIAL CHANGE

This article was published in the *Bulletin of the Atomic Scientists*. A different article on the same theme was published in *Foreign Affairs*. They present a political conceptual scheme to analyze economic and social change to help bridge the gap between theory, reporting and formulation of policy.

THE US GOVERNMENT NOW maintains teams of observers, reporters, and social engineers in nearly all of the countries of the underdeveloped world. These men and women accumulate vast amounts of data on virtually all aspects of the countries in which they are living. A significant proportion of these data are then transmitted to Washington where they are made available in raw form to a large number of officials and are used as background material in the projection of intelligence estimates, development studies and policy papers.

Highly specific questions are routinely posed from Washington to the representatives in the field. Occasionally a "circular" will go out asking for additional information on such categories as youth activities, internal security, and scientific development. But in general, reporters are left largely to their own devices.

Because no reporting can ever completely satisfy its recipients, Washington officials try whenever possible – that is, in practice, whenever funds are available —to visit all of the areas in which they are particularly interested. Conversely, observers are often brought back to Washington for consultation.

In my experience, however, at no point in this process is information forced to yield a coherent pattern. Some experiments have been made, particularly by the State Department Bureau of Intelligence and Research, to develop an essay form which allows for analysis of the political dynamics of selected countries. To this extent, the bureaucratic hurdle, by no means the least of the many hurdles, has been passed, but there still remains the problem of how officers in the field can devote their time economically to produce information which is susceptible to coherent analysis. Lacking a usable matrix, reporters can only guess whether or not they are missing the significant while reporting the obvious, or the urgent.

At this point the onus falls largely on the academic community. Most of the reporting officers to whom I have spoken, as well as the analytical and policy officers in Washington, found little stimulus in most of the material produced by American political scientists, whom they accuse of having retreated into scholasticism. They appear to be analyzing in more and more detail refinements of a nomenclature which bears less and less relationship to the world with which government officials are dealing.

Similarly, while economists may ask policy-oriented questions, the answers rarely yield information of political importance and occasionally yield political misinformation. An example is the concept of gross national product (GNP). Most economists appear to be interested solely in whether the GNP is increasing or decreasing. If GNP – particularly the GNP per capita – is rising, then a certain political corollary is drawn: since things are improving, the people will not use violence to bring about political change.

This concept has, however, proven so unworkable in the past as to discredit, at least in part, the economist's view of social change in the mind of the political reporter. For example, between 1952 and 1958, Iraq not only had a major overall increase in GNP but a considerable increase of GNP per capita. Yet, the more rapid the rise of GNP per capita, the more explosive and unstable the political situation became. This trend culminated in the 1958 revolution. A second, contrasting example is the UAR (Egypt). Between 1955 and 1960, the GNP of the UAR per capita hardly changed at all. Yet during this period the UAR was politically stable.

One result of this lack of congruence between theoretical patterns of analysis and the real world is that it is fashionable for official reporters to ignore them entirely. This is, incidentally, true not only of American concepts. Soviet recognition of the inappropriateness of their own class-based Marxian analysis of the modernization movement was borne out recently in a lecture given by A.I. Kesekev, Candidate of Historical Science and Member of the Afro-Asian Institute, who commented that "One difference between their (the Arabs') socialism and the Soviet Socialism is that they do not all recognize Marxism-

Leninism. Another is that some of their socialist parties represent many classes, not just the proletariat."

A SCHEME FOR POLITICAL ANALYSIS

To attempt to bridge this gap between theory and reporting, I would like to set out one relatively simple conceptual scheme for the political analysis of social change. If this scheme has utility, it is primarily in enabling reporters to concentrate their efforts on relatively few points of high political leverage in a given society. Its application is probably confined to developing societies and may not be relevant in many of those. It is extrapolated primarily from my observations in Iran, Turkey, Iraq, Egypt, Algeria, and Morocco.

In common practice today there are two general categories of social analyses. One category relates primarily to horizontal divisions between classes; the other category relates to groups of people within a given society.

Let me suggest a visual schema for the first:

By drawing three horizontal lines, with linear projections to indicate population size in each class, one can get a profile of American society, for example, which shows the tremendous preponderance of the middle class. The factors which make up this class differentiation can be grouped psychologically, economically, politically, and in other ways coherently and satisfactorily.

This model does not work well in complex societies such as that of Lebanon because within each "horizontal" class, there are significant divisions among ethnic and religious groups. Of course, these divisions can be projected onto the "horizontal" model by inserting vertical lines to separate the Maronites, for example, from the Druze. But, in practice, this model becomes too cumbersome to use. Consequently, most political analyses of such a society concentrate on groups. When, however, reasonably rapid social change begins to take place, one finds a considerable intermingling of the social groups and the development of some coherence of class, occupational, and geographical interests. For this reason, a political analysis of even such a small complex society as Lebanon can be extraordinarily difficult.

The overwhelming number of cases in the underdeveloped countries, however, are not as complex as Lebanon. Most of the countries have a clearly defined dominant social layer. Many political scientists conceive of this group as an "elite." That can be a useful concept, but it leaves out much that is economically and politically crucial. Here I will argue that the key political differentiation is between the "traditional" element of the society and what I have called the "new men." The new men are those who possess the skill, the discipline, the orientation, and the motivation to modernize society. However much they may differ among themselves in terms of income, education, and ability, they are even more sharply differentiated from the traditional element of society.

IN EGYPT

For example, Egypt today is a country of approximately 28 million people. Of these about 25 million are Sunni Muslim and 3 million are Coptic Christians. The vast majority of the population, between 60 and 75 per cent, are dependent upon agriculture either directly or indirectly as a means of subsistence. The GNP of Egypt is $3.5 billion. The GNP per capita is approximately $120. The rise of GNP per capita has been extremely small in the past. Indeed, it has been largely offset by the rapid (3 per cent) rise of the population. In the last two or three years the rise of the GNP per capita has been between 2 and 3 per cent. In previous years, there was no statistical rise at all. Meanwhile, expectations have risen, and continue to rise, sharply. Yet, the regime remains stable.

Obviously, what this calls for is some categorization – disaggregation – of information. The schema which appears to make the most sense to me is one which divides the society into six compartments: 3 horizontal divisions into classes and a vertical lines to separate the traditional from the modern component.

Rough approximation of Egyptian society from 1945 to c. 1960

Upper modernizing	?	Upper traditional	1% (-)
Middle modernizing	?	Middle traditional	10%
Lower modernizing	0	Lower traditional	85%

As shown in the graph, perhaps 85 per cent of the Egyptian population was in the traditional lower class. In this period, there was no discernable political differentiation between the rural and urban extensions. Indeed, the urban component of the traditional lower class formed itself into "villages" within cities while rural villages developed urban extensions. The people in this social category took part in relatively few functions of urban life and remained isolated from urban political movements. Moreover, they were only schematically a "group" but were actually fragmented into thousands of village communities and millions of kinship clusters. Thus, despite, extreme dissatisfaction – often verging on desperation – as reported in Egypt between the end of World War II and the coup d'état of 1952, they were capable only of occasional outbursts of violence but never of organized militancy.

The middle box on the right (traditional) side of the schema was composed of merchants, people educated in traditional subjects such as Islamic law and Arabic literature, owners of medium-sized plots of land, and others who, while educated, did not earn their livings through modern technology and/or were not oriented toward a modern society. Like the traditional lower class, the middle class traditional society was both urban and rural based. In Egypt, its members number, at a guess, about 10 per cent of the population.

The top box on the traditional side has dwindled considerably in Egypt since land reform was instituted in 1952. Prior to land reform there were approximately 5,000 "proprietors" of land in units of over 100 acres. However, a number of these proprietors were not separate individuals since a single person might be proprietor over several pieces of land. So, if one accepts this arbitrary definition of the landed component of the upper class (100 acres of irrigated land in 1945 would yield approximately $12,500 of rent) and discounts for duplications, the traditional Egyptian upper class may be estimated at somewhat less – probably considerably less – than one per cent of the population. At a maximum, they probably numbered roughly a quarter of a million people or perhaps 40-50 thousand families.

Historically, Egypt has made several attempts to create a modern component of its traditional society. The first, the most dramatic and rapid, was from approximately 1820 to 1840; the second, which was less consciously undertaken or concentrated, took place from approximately 1900 to the beginning of World War II; and the third, now in process, began shortly after the 1952 coup d'état.

In the first period, the great Turkish governor of Egypt, Mehmet Ali Pasha, attempted to create in Egypt a movement of modernization somewhat similar to the Meiji of Japan. Power, Mehmet Ali realized, meant more than having uniformed soldiers and modern guns; it meant also having the means to clothe and feed soldiers, to make and supply guns, and to organize and control the soldiers. Such a program required building factories, training people to run them, and acquiring the financial power to pay for them.

In his attempt to modernize Egyptian society, Mehmet Ali dispossessed traditional land owners, destroyed the medieval guild system, crushed the Mamluk aristocracy, largely replaced the traditional handicraft industry, altered the agricultural crop system, and sent large numbers of students, technicians, and potential industrial workers to Europe for training. By 1841, he had created a modern, disciplined military force of nearly 200,000 men, a relatively large textile industry, dockyards and arsenals sufficient to supply his growing navy and about 30,000 industrial workers.

Whether Egypt would have become the Middle Eastern version of Japan we do not know because in 1849 Great Britain invaded and forced Mehmet Ali's regime to give up tariff barriers, its domestic commercial monopoly, and reduce its army. Modernization stopped, but Egypt did not return to exactly the pattern that had existed before Mehmet Ali: the guilds did not return; the Mamluks were all dead; and the land was divided among new proprietors.

Although it failed, Mehmet Ali's experiment is of more than antiquarian interest for two reasons. First, it shows that once the intense drive of modernization stops, the new and the traditional are apt to meld into a new pattern as the new acquires some of the vested interests of the old, and the new elements gradually develop on the modernizing side of the schema. Thus the arbitrary, analytical division of new and traditional society can be seen to be historically fluid; indeed from a cultural point of view, it may be the movement z categories which is of most interest. Second, even an abortive thrust toward modernization can lay the groundwork for subsequent development by destroying or modifying the old structure of power so that it cannot be reimposed.

I jump to the modern period: Three basic policies can be noted in Egypt since the monarchy was overthrown in 1952 which have tended to transplant people from the right (traditional) side of the schema into the left (modernizing) side.

The first of these was an attempt to redistribute rural income through land reform. This policy stripped away the financial power of the traditional upper class which was the principal rival of Nasser's new regime. Redistribution of the confiscated land was also a step toward raising the standard of living of the traditional lower class to the point where some elements of it would become amenable to modernization.

The Egyptian government early recognized that this land distribution alone did not reform the peasants. Even with more land and more income, they clung to their traditional ways. Seeing this, the regime undertook a second program to create a new sort of Egyptian peasant. This was the essence of the "Liberation Province" scheme. There a "new man" was marked off from the traditional Egyptian peasant by a standardized uniform in place of the traditional gown, by a much higher caloric intake of food and by a salary four times the average. In addition, the workers were ordered to put their children into boarding schools, in some ways similar to the practice in Israeli *kibbutzim*, to foster a more modern upbringing. Moreover, like the rest of Egypt, Liberation Province was to become a mixed rural and industrial economy with factories interspersed throughout the agricultural area.

The third thrust of Egyptian Policy has been toward industrialization. Repeatedly and consistently American and other advisors have warned the Egyptian government that it was making a costly economic mistake in promoting industry rather than agriculture in its development scheme. It was pointed out to the Egyptian government that Egyptian infant industry could never compete on the world market and that the building of such monuments as the Helwan Steel Factory was a frivolous if prestigious waste of critically short Egyptian resources. What Egypt needed, in the opinion of foreign advisors, was to concentrate on exportable agricultural commodities which would increase foreign exchange earning.

The Egyptian government has consistently refused to follow Western advice and has devoted an overwhelming proportion of its resources to industrialization. Undoubtedly, from an economic point of view, Western advice was sound. However, the Egyptian government's actions have responded to political criteria: they needed not only to weaken the remnants of the old regime but to build a constituency for their regime. In their attempts to do this, through land reform and the Liberation Province scheme, they were disappointed. It was clear that the transformation of the peasant was going to be a long and frustrating process. Industrialization appeared to be a more rapid means to build that constituency since industrial workers necessarily are on the left side of the dividing line. Not until they became a large and secure group could the regime be powerful and secure. A detailed analysis of the Egyptian development plan will show conclusively its political intent.

CREATING "NEW MEN"

In addition to creating niches in the modern sector, the regime had to create the "new men" to fill them. Essentially, Egypt has used two methods of accomplishing this transition.

The first, education, is slow and costly, but ultimately the most productive. In 1945, approximately 900,000 Egyptians attended school. By 1960, this number had been more than trebled, and by 1970 it will reach nearly six million. Technical education was virtually a creation of the 1952 revolution. By 1961, nearly 40,000 Egyptians had graduated from Egyptian universities in the natural sciences and technology and nearly 120,000 were then in training in vocational schools.

The army traditionally stood apart from society. The rulers, both foreign and domestic, feared the military so it was not until nearly the end of the nineteenth century that native Egyptians were able to rise to senior ranks and it was not until the eve of World War II that the military academy was opened to young men of the lower middle class. Among the first cadets was the future president and leader of the coup d'état, Gamal Abdul Nasser.

Armies alone among state institutions have long tended to be organized along nationalist, modern lines without commitments to the past; unlike the civil service, the commercial community or academics, they had a defined code, a clear line of command, communications, mobility, force, and, ultimately, will. What happened in Egypt is duplicated in many "evolving" societies. The more efficient the army became, the less committed the officer corps was to the traditional rulers and their state.

In Egypt today the army regards itself not only as a defense force but as a school to impart modern skills, a hospital to cure the ills of society by turning out healthier men and a training ground to impart a sense of discipline. Each year, approximately 20,000 Egyptian are inducted into the army for three-year enlistments. From 1957 to 1961, about 130,000 Egyptians passed out of the armed forces into civilian life. When one considers that larger scale, modern Egyptian industry in 1961 employed roughly a quarter of a million workers, the impact of this output of ex-soldiers can be appreciated.

It appears relatively certain that few of the soldiers have returned to the traditional society. The reason is simple: they are possessed of rudimentary technical training, a sense of discipline, and indoctrination in nationalism and certainly a far higher standard of health than those who have not shared their army experience. All of these are rare and prized possessions in a backward, poor but rapidly evolving and industrializing society. Even more basic is the effect of simple instruction in health: when a man knows what the bilharzia worm disease does to the human body, he can no longerbe a Nile peasant. The army can thus be seen to be a primary agent in the creation of "new men" who fit in the lower left hand box of the schema.

The creation of the other two boxes on the modernizing side of the column is almost a mechanical process consequent to the development of the lower left side. Former noncommissioned officers and those with industrial experience have become the foremen and the technicians who mobilize the industrial labor force. Officers are increasingly relied upon to manage the government, commercial, and industrial bureaucracies. They thus become a new bureaucratic middle class.

Finally, the upper left hand box in our scheme is composed of the senior administrators, technicians, bureaucrats, and officials. In many ways, this group has already acquired the accoutrements of political and social power that formerly pertained to the traditional upper class. Such men as the directors of the Suez Canal Authority and the Petroleum Authority, the senior officials in the presidency, governors of provinces, and the director of the steel factory have relatively great affluence and power. At the pinnacle of this column is Nasser himself.

Rough approximation of Egyptian society from c. 1965

Upper modernizing 0.5%	Upper traditional 0.5%
Middle modernizing 1%	Middle traditional 8-9%
Lower modernizing 2-3%	Lower traditional 80%±

An analysis of Egyptian politics over the last ten years and a projection of plans for the coming decade would indicate that the primary policy of the Egyptian government is to shift the Egyptian population into the modernizing column. That is to transform as many as possible and as rapidly as possible the traditional society into "new men." To accomplish this primarily political purpose, the developmental policies of the Egyptian government appear consistent and coherent.

The question of whether or not the Egyptian government can afford to sustain this program is a crucial one. Much, of course, depends upon the extent of foreign aid Egypt can command. In general, however, at the current rate of expenditure and the current levels of foreign aid, the momentum can be sustained only if the foreign debt can be rolled over virtually continuously. At some point, major changes either in the allocations or in the revenues will have to be made. Thus, predictable economic, particularly foreign exchange, crises may drive the Egyptian regime either toward a more radical policy or toward a slow down; alternatively, a major crisis could bring about a change of regime. Since a successful modernizing regime must be aware of these challenges, it will seek to protect itself by rushing the creation of its constituency, its "new men."

Prior to the 1952 coup, when the traditional upper and traditional middle class were dominant in Egypt, a precipitous change in their income might have been reflected in serious political disturbance. Today that is no longer the case. Since 1952, the income of upper and middle traditional classes has fallen as their political power has declined. While most still live well by any standards, they no longer hold a commanding position in the Egyptian economy. Conversely, a precipitous downward change in the income in any one of the three modernizing classes, might today produce considerable political unrest since today they control the economy, the press, the security forces and the bureaucracy. These changes are not reflected in statistics on GNP or even GNP per capita, but they are crucial to an understanding of Egyptian politics.

Somewhat over 80 per cent of the Egyptian population remains in the traditional lower class. While this group does enjoy somewhat better health today than half a century ago, and does have some access to schooling which it did not have until recently, its per capita income has always hovered near subsistence. Today, as it has always been, this group is politically irrelevant except as a quarry from which to mine "new men."

What of these "new men?" We don't yet know in detail, but it is clear that the real income of all three modern classes has risen sharply since 1952. These groups have been the principal beneficiaries of economic growth and reallocation. Indeed, virtually all of the new men are the children of the revolution. To date, at least, while the performance of the regime has been deficient economically, it has been quite able to satisfy those who count politically.

IN ALGERIA

Applying this scheme to Algeria produces results which are quite different from those we see in the analysis of the economy and the society by more traditional methods.

The GNP of Algeria has fallen from $2.9 billion to $1.9 billion in the period from 1960 to 1963. Thus, there has been a precipitous statistical fall in GNP per capita.

It is also evident that a very large section of the population, most of the traditional lower class, has not benefited in any way by the revolution. The traditional upper and middle class, composed of approximately one-third Europeans and two-thirds Algerians, has been the loser. Large numbers have emigrated and many have had their properties confiscated.

The principal gainers have been the new men who have emerged from the revolution. These people fall into four main groups: the army, the industrial labor force, the modern agriculturists and the bureaucracy. They have benefited directly from the turmoil of the revolution by acquiring rent-free housing in the major cities, primarily in apartments which were vacated by the French, and by moving into positions in the economy and government structure which were formerly French preserves. Moreover, in other ways, the government has sought to cater to their needs and desires so that they have become the privileged elite of Algerian society. Thus, while it is evident that the Algerian economy has suffered greatly in the war and mass emigration, it appears that the political position of the regime is strong and probably growing stronger.

From this analysis in Algeria, as in Egypt, follow certain deductions about American policy. Since the achievement of independence in Algeria, the US government has been of major assistance in providing wheat under Public Law 480. But the government regards this donation both with suspicion – as institutionalizing Algerian dependence upon the United States – and as essentially irrelevant to its core objectives. True, American wheat enables the Algerian regime to feed the traditional, mainly rural, lower class, but it does not enhance the regime's program of modernization. Both the Algerian and the Egyptian government, moreover, wrongly believe the West wishes to keep the underdeveloped world backward, rural and poor. More astutely, the Soviet Union and China have offered assistance in the area that the Algerian government believes to be vital to its political survival: industry. As the Egyptians, so the Algerians, believe that their future depends upon the growth and satisfaction of the aspirations of "the new men."

TRADITIONAL SOCIETIES IN TRANSITION

When one views from the perspective here announced the vulnerabilities of traditional regimes whose societies are in transition become clear. For example, take Iraq to see what might be beginning in Morocco, Libya, Saudi Arabia, and perhaps Iran.

In Iraq, political power was exercised by men in the upper right hand box of the diagram, but it was the consistent policy of the government to develop resources in the three left hand boxes. Its development authority sent thousands of Iraqi students abroad for advanced, modern training and fostered an industrial economy which could employ them. These "new men" alone could manage the new economy. Consequently, the regime enriched and empowered them. Parallel to the civilians, it created a modern military establishment. The fact that this establishment was primarily trained and equipped by the United States rather than the Soviet Union, although regarded by the American government as a major source of political stability, was largely irrelevant. In fact the source of the equipment and training made little difference in domestic Iraqi politics.

As real economic, social, military, and other forms of power shifted increasingly to the technically able men of modern component of society, the traditional government came to rely increasingly upon instruments of repression to keep itself in power. Ultimately, even the instruments of repression had to be manned by the "new men" as they came increasingly to reply upon modern tools and techniques and, perhaps inevitably, they used these tools and techniques against the old political order.

Is this a likely development in Morocco, Libya, Saudi Arabia, and Iran?

Iran is perhaps the most fully described society in which this problem arises. Beginning with the 1905 Constitutional Revolution, modernizing elements in Iran have attempted to create for themselves a political position. Time after time, outside forces have intervened to check their progress. Yet the government of the Shah is now embarked upon an even more rapid enhancement of the economic and social position of the "new men." Iran is rapidly becoming a complex, industrial society. Its factories, banks, transportation and communication facilities, and its security forces all must be staffed by the "new men." Some 14,000 Iranian students are abroad studying today and in Iran, as in Iraq, the development authority has been rapidly creating a new structure of economic and social power.

The most recent of the Shah's reforms, additionally, has tended to destroy the economic and political power of the traditional landed aristocracy. Thus, in two ways, the Shah has embarked on a program which has weakened both absolutely and relatively the power of that component of society, the traditional element, with which royalty is generally associated.

In Morocco, similarly, political power is now exercised by the upper right hand box. In Morocco, however, the labor organization (Union Marocaine du Travail), the strongest on the African continent and one of the major labor organization in the world, has set about carefully and deliberately to create a shadow government. The labor organization has had for some years a program of providing scholarships for study abroad to promising Young Moroccans in all phases of modern training. The Moroccan government has, itself, accentuated the same sort of program. The net result is a major shift of the focus of power in all but political manifestations from the right hand side of our ledger to the left.

The central problem of the coming decade in both Iran and Morocco is probably the method of a transfer of elements of political power from the upper right hand box to the upper two left boxes. Ultimately, if this is not done gradually and constructively, a dislocation of political power by more violent means is probable.

In both Libya and Saudi Arabia, much the same pattern of development is taking place but is at an earlier stage. In both of these countries the military is potentially the key. With the lesson of Egypt and Iraq before them, however, the astute leaders of Libya and Saudi Arabia have managed to balance the growth of modern military establishments with "white" armies which are drawn from the traditional society and are presumably loyal to the ruler.

Judged in terms of the criteria established by our conceptualization, the situation in Libya is a great deal more fragile, as the traditional power elite is extremely small while the relatively more modern traditional middle class is numerous and is opposed on geographical and urban-rural bases to the traditional power elite. In Saudi Arabia, on the other hand, there is no major urban bourgeoisie as yet, and the traditional power elite – roughly the royal family with hangers-on – is extraordinarily numerous. So numerous are the progeny of King Ibn Saud as to constitute virtually a class in this society in its own right. Moreover, each member of the royal family is a condottiere with armed retainers so that the royal family represents, as a whole, a very real military as well as economic power in the country.

The experience of these countries suggest two further points. The first is that it is the pattern of development rather than the size of the groups involved which is politically significant. The enormous leverage gained by the "new men" as new forms of power are created is startling. The men who began the Egyptian, Iraqi, and Algerian revolutions numbered only a few score.

The second observation is that representative government is a necessary ingredient of political stability. From an amoral point of view, however, those whose interests are represented in the government need not be "the people", or even the literate people but must at minimum include those without whom the power of the society cannot be wielded. The key problem of politics will be the creation of such a degree of satisfaction and identification as to prevent revolution. It is only when the government refuses the principle of accommodation that revolution is virtually certain.

US OBJECTIVES IN THE MIDDLE EAST

A problem posed by this form of analysis concerns the proper role for American foreign policy. This problem has two aspects: first is predicting the effect of the now evident social and political change on American interests abroad; second is the efficacy with which America can and should influence the course of social change through its AID program, technical assistance, and cultural exchange.

Egypt is relatively further along in this process of change than any of the other countries now under discussion. There one can already perceive the development of vested interests in the modernizing category of society. This was not evident until perhaps a year or two ago. Prior to that time, the tiny ruling elite, essentially Nasser and his small group of colleagues, was able to act virtually at its whim or its interpretation at least of the goals of its "new men." Now the new upper class has begun to enjoy the fruits of the revolution and is not anxious to have funds allocated to external adventures. Moreover as individuals within the new upper class have to come to be identified professionally with such projects as the Suez Canal, the steel mill, of other facets of the modern economy, emotional vested interests have been created so that the bureaucrats of the government fight for the allocation of resources for their projects just as pressure groups within American society fight for the allocation of government resources here. Both of these factors have tended gradually but perceptibly to narrow the freedom of action of the UAR government.

Similarly, the "new men" have demanded a larger share of representation in at least the formal aspects of political power. The Egyptian government has felt obliged to cater to this sentiment with the creation of a parliament, the Arab Socialist Union, and the Liberation Rally in its decade of power. Today, there exists a parliament which worked rather hard for its existence, and for the first time, the Prime Minister is himself a product of the new Egypt.

When one silhouettes this development against the conception of American objectives in the Middle East, he will perceive that the middle-term future is more with us than against us. The United States wants a stable and prosperous Egypt, for example, which is not open to external subversion or aggression and which is concentrating its energies on domestic Egyptian affairs. As the society develops vested interests and as the government is less able to embark on dangerous foreign policies, US interests throughout the Middle East will be served.

Iran and Morocco, however, offer more of a challenge to American policy. Only if new elements are peacefully included in the structure of power, will US interests be protected. This is true for two reasons: the people who now make up the "new men" of Iranian and Moroccan society are committed to popular participation in rule with which would fit well with American domestic conceptions; and the structure of the society they represent is developing vested interests which will force their states toward a relatively stable, peaceful, and constructive approach to world affairs.

It has been difficult in the past to project such ideas as these within the government because the analysis of social change in Iran, for example, has indicated there was simply no choice between the Shah and the Communist Party, no middle ground or station on the way to chaos and communist domination. Without arguing whether or not this was true in the past, the above analysis suggests that it certainly will not be true in the future. The corollary to be drawn from this is that American interests will be served if the governments of Iran and Morocco allow a greater involvement by the "new men" in political power.

The second question which arises is how the United States can and should influence the course of economic and social development. In the past, it has been difficult for American policy planners and practitioners of American military assistance and AID programs abroad to make their programs add up to a coherent underpinning of world stability and order. If creation of stability and orders is the true purpose, and it certainly appears to have been, then such programs as we have embarked upon in Iraq in 1952 are clearly inimical to American interests. Similar programs have been undertaken in Libya, Ethiopia, Morocco, Saudi Arabia, Jordan, and Iran. This analysis would suggest that when power is exercised by the traditional elite, then AID programs and military assistance are bound enormously to increase the strain on the existing political structure and to accentuate the danger of revolution. When, however, political power is exercised by a modernizing elite, such programs will facilitate the growth of stability and order by increasing the component of society which supports the government order.

Thus, an AID program which increases military capability, industrial potential, and educational opportunity in Libya will have almost diametrically opposite results from one which does the same in Egypt.

In no country of the underdeveloped world can a government exist which does not at least pay lip service to a program of rapid economic and social development. It is noteworthy that even the Imam of Yemen felt obliged to send a student mission abroad. This suggests, therefore, that the proper role of American advisors is to facilitate both development of those programs which will less severely and less rapidly disrupt the organization of society, while encouraging the orderly transference of power as the society develops. The one without the other is bound to produce a revolutionary situation; both together may produce an orderly and stable development.

Such delicate political and economic programs can be carried out in practice only with a far greater degree of coordination and cooperation between the various agencies of the American government than today exists. They also would require a sort of social and political inquiry upon which the government is not now embarked. And finally they involve a coherence of policy planning which is now only in its early stages of development.

A first step in the process of developing this greater degree of understanding, coordination, and implementation of American policy may be accomplished by the development of a usable scheme of analysis such as the one I have here presented.

January 1967, *Bulletin of the Atomic Scientists*

HUMPTY DUMPTY SAT ON A WALL
HUMPTY DUMPTY HAD A GREAT FALL
ALL THE KING'S HOURSES AND ALL THE KING'S MEN
COULDN'T PUT HUMPTY TOGETHER AGAIN

THIS RHYME THAT WE ALL learned as children has many interpretations – the defeat of a king, the explosion of a cannon, the overturn of a siege tower and even the downfall of President Richard Nixon. Over the years, many people have found the verses memorable because, although apparently simple, they jog us to think about important truths. That is probably why they have endured and are reinterpreted in light of contemporary affairs, age after age.

For our times, I suggest that "Humpty Dumpty" points to something so taken for granted that we often overlook it. I have been guilty of this. In my writings on the consequence of wars in Afghanistan, Iraq and Somalia, I have emphasized the costs in terms of human bodies, constructions and money. These were the obvious things and the things for which we have numbers. They were horrifying enough in themselves. Just getting hold of the magnitude of the costs eludes most of us for most of the time. So recognizing them is important. But, as I look back over what I have written, I find that I have not emphasized enough what Humpty Dumpty can teach us.

Consider decoding the rhyme like this: Humpty Dumpty is our "social contract." The social contract is the basis for a healthy, functioning society. Yet it is fragile. Sometimes written out in constitutions, laws and treaties, the way we manage to live relatively peacefully next to one another is often just an implied consensus. In some societies, it is referred to as "the way."

Historically, the idea of a social contract probably grew out of kinship. Our remote ancestors, who lived in small clans, were able to get along with one another because they were fathers and children or brothers and sisters. Few were more remote from one another than first cousins. Then, when about 5,000 years ago clans grew into villages and towns grew into cities, the idea of kinship was transformed into neighborhood. One was supposed to treat his neighbor as a sort of kinsman rather than a foreigner — which often meant "enemy". Over the last few thousand years, society after society has struggled with the challenge of making this notion effective.

Where they succeeded, they created what the rhyme pictures as a sort of smooth, round egg, sitting up on the wall, not part of the rough and tumble, the push and shove, the give and take, of our daily lives but a presence that in some abstract way facilitates our daily lives. As long as it exists and we accept it, we do not need massive and intrusive military force to keep us from killing one another. We mostly continue to do what we do and refrain from what we should not do because we accept "Humpty Dumpty."

But, if Humpty Dumpty is knocked off his perch, we lose our implicit agreement on what is right and proper. This is more or less what the Seventeenth century philosophers thought of as returning to the "state of nature." It evoked the great English philosopher Thomas Hobbes' memorable phrase in which he saw men outside the social contract as being in a state of war "of every man, against every man."

Hobbes thought keeping order required force but, as we have seen in the attempts to impose order in Baghdad, even overwhelming military force fails. We stationed a large part of the American army in Baghdad without bringing back stability. Indeed, the very act of attempting to impose order often has precisely the opposite effect. The "trigger" of the American Revolution was probably the attempt of the British to impose order in Boston by military force. Today in Afghanistan a similar process seems to be at work as it surely was in Somalia. In Afghanistan, "all the king's horses and all the king's men" are of no avail.

There is another message we can wring out of the rhyme: if "Humpty's" fall is not long-term, that is, not really mortal, then "he" can probably be resurrected by those who live under his spell. Thus, the people of New Orleans and Haiti, while they suffered catastrophes could fairly soon return to living with one another on reasonably satisfactory terms. The descent into chaos was momentary and the effects, while horrifying, were self-correcting. If, on the contrary, the social contract is broken and remains broken for a long period of time, relations of groups of people, particularly if they are easily identified by racial or religious differences, become so infected as to be virtually irreparable.

That is a danger America would be wise to avoid. By shattering the social contract, even if in our eyes it is not attractive, we run the risk of leaving in our wake anarchy over which we have no control and which will be a breeding ground for the very forces we thought we were taming. Then the costs to society, both ours and theirs, will be virtually unending.

We would be wise to ponder the message of Humpty Dumpty.

June 28, 2010

Encounters with Ibn Khaldun

AMONG THE SCHOLARS OF the Islamic Middle Ages, by far the most original and thought-provoking was the great Fourteenth century Andalusian/North African Arab historian Abdur-Rahman Ibn Khaldun who has been described as the "father" of modern social science, and one of the first modern historians. In the attention he paid to ways in which small social groups coalesce and interact, he was a harbinger of the French Annales historical school; the English historian Eric Hobsbawm remarked, "I take my stand with that great and neglected philosopher of history..." and sees his analysis analogous to Marx's emphasis on the social and economic basis of events; and Arnold Toynbee lauded his study of history as "undoubtedly the greatest work of its kind that has ever yet been created by any mind in any time or place." But, despite the brilliance of his analysis and the influence he had on a few Western historians, he remains surprisingly little known outside of the circles of Orientalists. Even there what he had to say has been little utilized or appreciated. The reasons are partly mechanical and partly cultural.

The fundamental reason is that Ibn Khaldun not only wrote in medieval Arabic, which itself is relatively complex, but drew upon a cultural tradition that is rich, difficult of access and involuted. Few western historians could follow the allusions he makes to pre-Islamic Arabic poetry, the religion of Islam as it had evolved by the Fourteenth century or the politics of the rise and fall of the Islamic dynasties. Contrariwise, while Arabists have, from time to time translated his *Muqaddimah* or Introduction to History, they have rarely been concerned with his ideas. In the Oxford University program of Oriental Studies, for example, the man recognized as the world's foremost Arabist, Professor Sir Hamilton Gibb, gave a series of courses on Ibn Khaldun without once mentioning his ideas on society, culture or history; like most Orientalists, Gibb used Ibn Khaldun's writings as exercises in grammar and syntax, arguing that before one could seriously address his ideas, the student had to be able fully to comprehend not only the text, itself difficult enough, but also the wide-ranging allusions. His point was well taken, indeed it was Orientalist dogma, and few scholars even attempted to sally beyond the formidable cultural barrier.

The second reason for the lack of appreciation of Ibn Khaldun was that he was analyzing a society which seemed to most western historians irrelevant or merely quaint. To dispute this patronizing view is consequential, I believe, precisely because at first glance, it appears to be true. After all, Ibn Khaldun lived in and wrote about a world which is triply alien to modern Western experience — he was a medieval Muslim reacting to a tribal society.

Today, very few of us have any direct relationship with any of those attributes. Most of the Asian and African vestiges of the medieval world have long since been swept away by the flood tide of modernization; Islam today is staging a resurgence but most observers, concentrating on its "fundamentalist" or extremist (*al-mutatarrafah*) wing, see it as a movement that is far from the cosmopolitan, intellectual religion known to Ibn Khaldun — as far, one might say of Christianity, as Pat Robertson is from St. Francis of Assisi; and finally, there is that curious word, tribalism.

Few "mainstream" historians have knowledge of the nomads who roamed and ruled the areas known to medieval geographers as "the Third Zone," the vast semiarid sweep of lands that runs from the Atlantic along the North African coast through the Middle East into Central Asia and on to the Pacific. Today, nomads are an endangered species who have nothing to do with the "important," that is European and American, areas of the world.

This is, of course, a shallow view of history. Even if we examine only European history, we see that nomads swept into the continent from inner Asia on their newly domesticated horses about 4,000 to 5,000 years ago to create the "ancient" world. Then, over the next two millennia, wave after wave of tribal peoples — Celts, Avars, Lombards, Goths, Visigoths, Franks, Huns and hundreds of others whose names are now forgotten — overturned the classical world, destroyed the Roman empire, gravely wounded its eastern Christian successor, Byzantium, set the pattern for medieval society and laid the basis for the modern nations of Europe.

Among other civilizations, nomads also played formative roles. The early Chinese state (the Shang dynasty) grew out of and in reaction to its nomadic neighbors; the nomadic challenge, one of the major themes of Ibn Khaldun, is perhaps the most visible thread running through the tapestry of Chinese history from the Shang right down to the Jürchen tribesmen or Manchus who founded the Qing dynasty that ruled China until 1912. In India, the ancient Dravidian civilization which is known to us from one of its Indus River sites as "Harappan" was destroyed by Indo-European-speaking nomadic Aryans whose heritage shapes modern Indian language, religion and society. A similar invasion by Semitic nomads overthrew its great contemporary, the Sumerian civilization of Mesopotamia, and, somewhat later, other groups of foot-loose warriors overwhelmed Middle Kingdom Egypt. Then, of course, there are the Arabs, Berbers and Turks who dominated western Asia, North Africa and some of south Europe during the Middle Ages and with whom Ibn Khaldun was concerned.

Even when historians overcome their parochialism, most retain what might be termed a "peripheral" perspective. That is, when they venture into Asia, they only skirt its edges. Arabists, Turcologists and Iranianists deal with West Asia; Indianists, with South Asia; and Sinologists and Japanologists, with East Asia. Very few have attempted to find how, when and by whom the shores of Asia were linked or even what experiences they shared. It is particularly about this much neglected aspect of the human record, the restless nomadic societies, that Ibn Khaldun has much to tell us. But there is more: in his time and for centuries hereafter, "history," as conceived not only in Africa and Asia but also in Europe, was little more than a chronicle of the doing of kings. Ibn Khaldun was a pioneer in the search for a broader and more concrete view of the evolving pattern of human affairs. In this sense, he is not only "modern" but "universal."

Born in Tunis in 1332, Abdur-Rahman Ibn Khaldun came from an Andalusian Arab family which, about a century before his birth, had emigrated to North

Africa as the Christian *Reconquista* began to menace Seville. In Tunis and elsewhere, the young Ibn Khaldun acquired a classical Arabic education, indeed, more or less the Orientalist syllabus taught at Oxford, with emphasis on the Qur'an, the Traditions, poetry, philosophical and historical writings and the literary language.

His first job consisted of the routine task of inscribing invocations on official documents. His career might have been stuck there, but Ibn Khaldun, presumably unauthorized, began to read the documents and to ponder their contents. The contrast between the dull chore he was expected to do and what he thought he might be able to do was so unsettling that he ran away to the more cosmopolitan city of Fez to join the intellectually exciting circles of that city's new rulers.

In Fez, Ibn Khaldun continued his studies and then served for a while as secretary to the ruler. Falling under suspicion, possibly for opposing the ruler's expansionist policy against Tunis, he was put into prison for nearly two years. His life might have ended there since prison life was not healthy and prisoners had an unfortunate proclivity to fatal "accidents," but youth was on his side and, fortuitously, it was the prince, not he, who sickened and died. In the Muslim principalities as in the city-states of contemporary Italy, rulers rarely bequeathed secure regimes, and as he emerged from his cell Ibn Khaldun watched the collapse of the ruling establishment. The events he witnessed were his first glimpse into the decline and fall of dynasties, a theme that was later to figure prominently in his analysis of history.

The man who became ruler of Morocco in 1359 carried Ibn Khaldun from the dungeon to the palace. But, once again he fell afoul of intrigue, and, deciding that this time he could not count on the ruler's ill-health to get him out of prison, he determined to get away while he could. Since conditions were unfavorable in other directions, he went north to the land of his ancestors, *al-Andalus* (Muslim Spain), to live for two years in Granada whose ruler he had met while that man had himself been in exile in Morocco. It must have seemed to Ibn Khaldun that everywhere he turned, there was turmoil; no ruler and no regime seemed secure; not surprisingly, he came to see that change itself was central in the historical process.

When he had returned from Spain to North Africa in 1364, Ibn Khaldun was again drawn into government and again was thrown into prison when yet another new ruler of Fez was overthrown. Narrowly escaping execution, he was lucky to be sent on a mission to effect a truce among the nomadic tribes then living around the oasis of Biskra, southeast of Algiers. Reading between the lines, one suspects that the assignment may have been a sort of internal exile of the kind familiar to us today as Third World successful rebels pack off defeated rivals and inconvenient supporters to be ambassadors or military attachés abroad.

The experience at Biskra, which Ibn Khaldun probably at the time regarded as a derailment of his career, was formative of what was to become perhaps his most important insight into history, the interaction of civilized (urban) and wild (nomadic) peoples.

Again a sojourn in urban North Africa proved disquieting, and again Ibn Khaldun tried to escape to Spain. But, by then, he was too well known to pass inconspicuously, and, at the request of the ruler of Fez, he was arrested in 1375 and extradited to Morocco. Luckily for him, the ship taking him back to face punishment or death was blown off course and landed him in an outlying province whose ruler gave him sanctuary. Sanctuary was a right to be freely claimed but it came at the price of service to the benefactor. By then known to have been successful in dealing with the troublesome nomadic tribes, he was once more sent on a mission to the desert, this time to Berbers living in the hinterland of Oran. It was there, camped out in a little village, stringing together the impressions of his already remarkable, varied and turbulent exposure to urban life in North Africa and Spain and what he had observed among the nomads, that he began to write his "Introduction to History," the *Muqaddimah*.

The portion of the Islamic world then known to Ibn Khaldun was composed of scores of Lilliputian city-states ruled by families whose fortunes rose and fell with startling speed. One would not do violence to the contemporary reality to compare them (as indeed he did) to a Moroccan market where little assemblies gathered around stallkeepers, jugglers, *gulla-gulla* men, snake charmers and other mountebanks. Sometimes the onlookers and hawkers jostled one another, but each performer had his own space. As one set up his act, others were closing theirs; separated by the twists and turns of the streets and the blind alleys they rarely clashed and, despite their diversity, they evinced an overarching unity: all belonged to the market. So it was among the North African village-, town- and city-states of the Fourteenth century where Ibn Khaldun wandered from one performance to another, entertained by each actor, each *king, amir, dey or pasha*. He probably felt as much "at home" in any one of the little states as in another. ("Patriotism" was a concept for which an Arabic word would not be coined for another four centuries.) As he moved from place to place, he knew that hospitality was incumbent upon hosts and that gratitude was expected from guests, but these were conventionally accepted to be finite both in time and amplitude. In practice, they depended on self-interest. Both patron and dependent were opportunistic. So Ibn Khaldun was welcomed when he was useful, sent away when he was inconvenient and imprisoned when he might be dangerous.

The experience of living in city after city was occasionally hazardous, but it was certainly exciting. Ibn Khaldun approvingly quotes Aristotle on the Greek belief that life in all of its dimensions could be led only in a city. In his *Muqaddimah*, he uses the closest term available in Arabic for a city man, *madani*, to translate Aristotle's term "a dweller in a *polis*" – a phrase which often is translated into English as a "political animal." But *madani* in medieval Arabic does not mean just "city man." Rather, it means something more profound, a "man of *the* City," that is, *the* city of the Prophet Muhammad where the Islamic community was born. So it takes something of the sense of "the heavenly city" of the medieval Christians.

Heavenly or not, the city had negative aspects. First, as he had painfully experienced, its pleasures sometimes came at the cost of loss of freedom. Thus, whereas contemporary Europeans had coined the expression *Stadtluft macht frei* ("city air makes [men] free"), Ibn Khaldun observed that even the wild men of the desert soon lost their freedom when they migrated into urban centers. More significant as his concept of politics began to take shape, he came to see that city life also exhausted and corrupted its inhabitants.

It was in his virtual exile in the little Algerian village, far from any library, that Ibn Khaldun began to put all these experiences, observations and reflections into the book we know. For him, it was a time of tremendous excitement with "words and ideas pouring into my head like milk into a churn…" As he put his pen to paper, the "milk" began to divide before his eyes into two major themes, the impermanence of urban societies and the wild power of the nomads, and from his observations and reading he began to discern a process: ruling families (*dawlahs*) often arose from non-urban origins, seized power, consolidated their rule and then, becoming corrupted or weakened by urban life, declined in vigor and, in turn, in his choice of a colorful phrase from the Classical poetry, "dismounted to their encampment."

Ibn Khaldun's choice of the phrase from pre-Islamic Arabic poetry brings to the fore another aspect of his thought and writing. As educated men of his time were, he was steeped in the canon of Arabic literature. His choice of words, his allusions and even the process of his analysis can hardly be understood apart from this fact, and that is what makes translating his work so difficult: words conjure images that are usually alien to the western reader. Under the hand of a master, and Ibn Khaldun took great pride in his literary skill, the text appears at two levels. Beneath the obvious meanings, key words become "triggers" that fire concrete and vivid images in the mind of the educated reader. To miss these allusions, which are often drawn from the Classical poetry and are drilled into the consciousness (and unconscious) of pupils and students by years of memorizing texts, is to bowdlerize his thought. It is largely the awesome challenge of crossing that barrier, as I have said, that has rendered him so difficult of access to Western historians.

For example, Ibn Khaldun presaged the Enlightment philosophers by positing a "natural" condition for humans, but whereas Hobbes, Locke and Rousseau were influenced by explorers who were discovering primitive peoples, and their imagery takes off from this concept of a "state of nature," Ibn Khaldun, whose "primitives" (the bedouin nomads) were at hand, uses a very different image.

He probes mankind's original condition), using a word (*fitrah*) that when applied to bread means "unleavened." At the pre-social stage, morally at least, man was unformed "dough." As the Qur'an puts it, God took a neutral position: He "placed in [the soul both] what is wrong for it and what is right for it." After being "leavened" by contact with other men, what any man becomes is mostly a function of his upbringing. In the Islamic tradition, nurture triumphs over nature: it is the leavening process that forms him. "Man is the son of his customs and his habits, not of his nature and constitution." He writes. Often, he suggests, this comes down in part to how a person earns his living and, by extension, to the kind of society in which he lives. Some forms of society turn the "dough" into people who are loyal, brave and virtuous. These are the poorer (mainly nomadic) societies; in richer (settled) societies where life is easy and temptations are strong, men become corrupted by materialism or "acceptance of the [physical] world."

Ibn Khaldun was aware that the task he had set himself was easy to misunderstand or to understand only superficially. As he wrote,

"The art of history is among the arts that…people bandy among themselves… Both the learned and the ignorant consider themselves alike in understanding it since, on the surface, it consists of little more than accounts of battles and dynasties with happenings from past centuries [presented by means of] colorful expressions and proverbs. Audiences are entertained with it…But, [to get at] its deeper meaning [history requires] vision, ascertaining concrete facts, repeated examination of the causes of reality, since the origins [of contemporary situations] are but faint tracings, and [it also requires] theoretical knowledge of the "howness" (*al-kaifiyah*) of events, since their ways are deep. For this reason history [must be considered] a branch of philosophy…"

In an unconscious echo of Ibn Khaldun, the great French historian Marc Bloch also spoke of history as "a knowledge of…tracks…which some phenomenon, in itself inaccessible, has left behind." Indeed, Bloch also picked up a theme which I have emphasized in speaking of the impact of imagery and the choice of words on Ibn Khaldun's thought: "each science has its appropriate aesthetics of language. Human actions are essentially very delicate phenomena [and] Properly to translate them into words and, hence, to fathom them rightly (for can anyone perfectly understand what he does not know how to express?), great delicacy of language and precise shadings of verbal tone are necessary." For Ibn Khaldun, this "delicacy of language and precise shadings of verbal tone" is the heritage of the great poetry of the pre-Islamic nomadic culture. It is the imagery there set forth and constantly repeated in the corpus of the education to which all Arabic speakers were then (and still today are) schooled that set not only the "verbal tone" but the very matrix of his historical thought.

Ibn Khaldun has often been compared to Giambattista Vico, Thomas Hobbes, Niccolò Machiavelli and Edward Gibbon; I have made those comparisons myself. But it would be a mistake to fall into easy analogies or to judge him by how well his ideas "fit" our heritage, our thoughts or our philosophy. We are willing to listen to the Chinese Sun Tzu or the Indian Kautilya when they sound like our Machiavelli, and so are "relevant," but their categories of thought derive from very different backgrounds. Thus, the great Chou dynasty Chinese historian Sima Qian is read, not for his view of the human parade, but merely for his recounting of events. To really appreciate such writers, we must make the not inconsiderable effort to comprehend the context in which they wrote.

So too, I suggest, we must take Ibn Khaldun for what he was, a man who grew in a tradition which, while very different from ours, was coherent, long-lasting and rich in experience and to which he reacted with penetrating and provocative insights. His aim was to help his colleagues and successors understand that culture. If, in addition, he offers us "general" — by which, if we are honest, we mean "relevant to the Western experience" — insights, as Eric Hobshawn, Arnold Toynbee and others have found he did, so much the better, but that was not his intent and should not be the criterion by which we judge him. So, while he may be compared in some ways to Vico, for example, the Italian world in which Vico lived three hundred years later set different questions to which Vico gave different answers.

For Ibn Khaldun L.P. Hartley's aphorism "the past is another country" was literally true. Not only was it alien to our European heritage, but his North

Africa was also beyond the frontiers of the great Islamic centers of civilization — Umayyad Spain and its various successors, Fatimid Egypt and its Mamluk successors and the Abbasid East and its Turkish successors. It was in those areas that most of what Muslim scholars had thought of as "history" took place. In Ibn Khaldun's time, seven centuries since the time of the Prophet Muhammad, a rich literary, religious, legal and scholastic culture had grown and spread. But, communication with the great centers was sporadic. North Africa was a backwater, regarded by the people of the cosmopolitan areas much as Englishmen used to regard Australia. So, although as scholars everywhere do, he stakes out his claim as a discoverer, he says, as though reacting to the anticipated challenge that he is a rustic, far from the mainstream of contemporary sophisticated thought,

"I am not aware of any discussion along these lines by anyone, but I do not know whether [my predecessors] simply overlooked [these insights] and the thought did not occur to them or [whether] perhaps their writings on these matters and their deep studies of them simply did not reach us. After all, academic fields are numerous and there have been many sages among the various nations, and much more has not reached us than has."

Where, he asks in confirmation of this, is the vast trove of learning of ancient nations? Lost to his times and place, he realizes, are the rich lodes of thought of the Persians, the Chaldaeans, the Assyrians, the Babylonians and the Ancient Egyptians. Luckily, some Greek philosophical writings came to the Arabs (and he alludes to Aristotle's *Politics* with respect), but the little he saw was mostly in a corrupted form. Lamenting how little was available, he resignedly quotes the Qur'an, "And you were given but little knowledge."

Little knowledge was, indeed, then the norm at least where Ibn Khaldun lived. His contemporaries were uninformed about all but the most recent and the most nearby events. Worse, what little they heard was exaggerated or given bogus interpretations. Ibn Khaldun lived (as Iris Murdoch later and with less reason wrote of our times) "in a fantasy world, a world of illusion. The great task in life is to find reality." For North Africans in his time, this was a daunting task as they had no news gathering organizations (as to some extent the Church bureaucracy then was in Europe); consequently, he had to provide rather more information than a modern historian would think necessary and often had to give it on very slim authority and in the face of both the authority of accepted tradition and the tradition of accepting authority.

So rational, at times, was he that we are brought up short when we hear him talk, for example, about astrology. That he believed in the preternatural should not surprise us since even the men we so much admire in the European Renaissance held similar beliefs. Ibn Khaldun was no less rational than, for example, Isaac Newton. But, while not denying the reality of a hidden world containing *jinn* and other marvelous creatures and accessed by soothsayers, necromancers and astrologers, he sought more perceptible causes than they provided for human events. For them, he wanted his readers, as he wrote, to "throw off from your hands the fetters [of silly stories] and ground yourself firmly on [a knowledge of political] affairs." Whereas today historians routinely tone down or even dismiss medieval accounts, because we have the means, Ibn Khaldun could not easily do so because he did not have the sources of information.

Such books as were available to him dealt not with contemporary affairs and certainly not with his area but with the "important" period of early Islam. Early Islam was taken to be the stable center of the Islamic world, but that stability was little more than a memory, virtually in fact, a myth, already many centuries old. This presented a special and difficult problem for Ibn Khaldun. While he was virtually obligated to respect the traditional authorities, he had to break free of them. The means he chose was simple: arguing that the texts then available had been corrupted. While the "heroes among the [Islamic] historians," he wrote, "dug out for themselves the reports of events, assembled them and wrote them down on the pages of books and stored them away, subsequent writers padded them out with the spurious nonsense, with which they concerned themselves, or [even] invented and with fanciful tales and discredited reports." Compounding the problem of sloppy or mendacious authors was their audience: not only are "error and imagination are close kindred and mingled with [real] information but gullibility is a basic trait of all mankind."

To counter this weakness, Ibn Khaldun could not resort, as later European scholars did to "diplomatics" or the study of the authenticity of documents since he had no access to the originals. Rather, he had to develop a system by which all inherited information could be evaluated. That is what he did in his *Muqaddimah*.

The *Muqaddimah* is not a long book, at least weighed in the scales of a Gibbon. A modern Arabic printed edition runs to about 450 pages. The most complete translation into English, together with notes, runs to roughly three times that many pages. By modern tastes, it often rambles into areas not central to the main theme so it has occasionally been abridged.

The *Muqaddimah* opens with the assertion that human beings necessarily gather together. Then alluding (without attribution) to Aristotle, Ibn Khaldun comes as close as Arabic could to his statement that "man is a creature of his small society." (As I have noted, he translated Aristotle's man of a *polis as madani*, warning the reader that he is treating it as a technical term, with a meaning different from the usual Arabic sense in the same way that North Africans today adopt the French word for "country," *pays*, to mean "village" or "township.") While every man must join society, the way he does so leads Ibn Khaldun into a discussion of "human civilization in general" and the setting out of his preliminary ideas. Perhaps both because he lived on the edge of "marginal" land and because the study of geography fascinated him, as it has most historians, Ibn Khaldun begins with considerations of the physical bases of collective life. He then veers off, from our standpoint, into discussions of the effect of natural and occult forces on individuals.

In his second section, he zeros in on nomadic society and lays out what he sees as its major political and military characteristics. Contrasting bedouin society, in section three, he discusses governance of settled areas and here asserts his conclusion that dynasties like individuals have finite life spans. In the fourth section, he turns to an analysis of society and rule in settled areas. Then in sections five and six, he describes and analyzes the way people make their living and the organization of knowledge, craftsmanship, science and culture. His account of history, *per se*, he gives in other books.

❧ ❧ ❧

Medieval and modern Muslim scholars have always sought historical knowledge, but usually in a static and limited way: they were usually not so much interested in history as the account of a process as in a picture of a particular moment, the time of the Prophet Muhammad. To know what Muhammad had done and said (the *Sunna*) was considered to be crucial to the definition of an acceptable moral life. This was not just the assertion of scholars; rather, it was what government required since, by amplifying and clarifying the Qur'an, history helped to separate the legal from the criminal. Consequently, Muslim historians did not have to justify themselves, as Western historians often try to do, by alleging a benefit from their research in achieving an understanding of the present or in helping to predict the future; the exact record of early Islam was universally taken to be the lodestone needed to guide the present.

We might compare the *Sunna* to the thoughts and actions of the framers of our Constitution. For Muslim jurists, however, the task of getting at the record was more difficult than for modern scholars of Constitutional Law. This was true because practically nothing was written about the Prophet and his Companions until long after their deaths; what remained was only a loose body of orally transmitted traditions (*Hadith*) which were subject to the vagaries of memory. Worse, because these traditions acquired so important a contemporary political and legal role, they were vulnerable to misinterpretation, exaggeration or forgery.

Muslim scholars were well aware of these weaknesses and in their attempt to separate the true from the spurious they developed a technique of evaluation known as "wounding and verification" (*al-Jarh wa't-tacadil*) which grew into a major field of Islamic scholarship. At the center of this process was the examination of "chain of transmission" (*isnad*) — the list of people through whose memory each *hadith* was said to have been handed down. The access, reputation, position, etc. of the transmitters were what counted; if the *isnad* was taken to be sound, the substance was more or less blindly accepted, particularly if it fit with contemporary beliefs or desires.

Ibn Khaldun found this canonical form of verification insufficient for the very different task upon which he embarked, not bringing into focus one short span of history but trying to understand the process of change, but even if he had wished to rely upon the traditional means of ascertaining truth, he could not because, apart from the first Islamic century in Arabia, what modern historians think of as primary sources hardly existed; he had no archives, libraries, runs of periodicals or other sources which modern historians take for granted. He had only what we call secondary sources, the accounts of other historians. And much of what they said he found simply ridiculous. So he had to supplement or replace the traditional ad hominem method of inquiry with other criteria which he calls "fundamental principles" (*usul*). In this effort, he was far ahead of his time and for it he may justly be ranked as one of the earliest and most important students of society.

He also took a stand on another aspect of Islamic scholarship, the question of free will versus determination. As a devout Muslim, Ibn Khaldun believed that God is omnipotent but that He does not ordinarily intervene in human affairs; thus there is a wide margin of freedom for human action. God, he wrote in his invocation, "raised us like plants from the Earth as living creatures and arranged us by races and nations on it, appointing us to use it for our benefit by generations." That is, God set out the parameters of our lives. It followed that man could understand how he was to live within those parameters. Man cannot reach up the hierarchy of knowledge to understand the prime cause, but he can, if grounded in "comprehensive science," go far enough to acquire what he needs to understand the events of his times.

While morally rudderless, men are endowed by God with certain "inspirations" (*al-wahi*) or instincts. The most important for the study of history, Ibn Khaldun asserted, were an intense attachment to immediate kinsmen (*an-na^{c}rah*), a desperate desire to avoid shame (*al-ghadadah*) and aggressiveness (*al-^{c}adwan*). The interaction of these innate characteristics draw men inexorably to their folk since in associating closely with kinsmen to whom they feel an intense attachment, men strive or fight to protect them and to enrich their lives and are naturally anxious to avoid conduct that would bring shame upon them.

These concepts are embodied in classical Arabic poetry in which Ibn Khaldun had been immersed since early childhood. Central to them was shame whose importance in Arabic culture it is difficult to exaggerate. Pre-Islamic poetry is full of references to the desire to avoid the stain of dishonor and, when it was incurred, to the absolute imperative to "wash" it away by vengeance. Even today in Saudi Arabia, for example, when a person commits a crime for which he is to be punished, it is shame more than punishment that he fears; and, when he commits a crime that brings shame upon his immediate kinsmen, it is they, more than the police, he seeks to escape.

Ibn Khaldun's view of aggressiveness as another one of man's proclivities or instincts is one of the most striking features of the pre-Islamic poetical canon; Ibn Khaldun sees it as a part of man's animal nature. However, he observes that it is not uniform in mankind, being let free among the nomads (who produced the great traditional poetry) and tamed by settled life; even in settled life, curbing it requires law and government while among bedouin aggression is directed by kinship — fighting is prohibited among close kindred and turned outward against strangers.

In addition to implanting in human nature basic proclivities, God also subjected man to change. Instead of creating a world at rest — as the Qur'an tells us that Heaven will be — He ordained ceaseless transformation. Man cannot achieve mastery and just settle down to enjoy the fruits of victory. Rather, he is both beset by and is himself the cause of perpetual change. Not only does each human go through a personal process of mutation as he grows from infancy to manhood and ages toward death, but whole societies alter themselves internally, growing and dying like individuals, and fluctuating in their capacities vis-à-vis one another. "With the passing of eras and [even] with the flow of days…their sandals do not tread a single path." Change is the one constant. This was the reality Ibn Khaldun had witnessed and the stimulus to which he reacted. His theories were aimed to answer the question, "How does this turmoil happen in practice?"

Turmoil, he asserts, is a process which does not end with the victory of the strong. As a group rises, it predictably and inevitably loses momentum and upon reaching its apex begins to fall, losing its capacity to defend itself. Then it becomes the target for others who are themselves on the rise. Thus, history is characterized by patterns that are neither linear nor cyclical (as many Western philosophers of history have asserted) but oscillating in a wave-like pattern. This pattern does not depend upon chance events, and, over the long run, no society can avoid decline and fall although wise policies will lengthen its natural span.

So Ibn Khaldun turns to an examination of the actors in this drama. Who they are and where they come from are questions virtually answered for him by his choice of words and his literary allusions. Like most Arabs, he divided mankind into two categories: sedentary (*hadar*) and nomadic (*badu*) societies. He regards both forms of social organization as natural or appropriate, each to its particular ecology: the one cultivates vegetables and foodgrains, because that is what the relatively benign climate in its part of the Earth allows, or, settles in villages, towns and cities to engage in commerce and crafts, while the other, living in more desolate areas, has to depend upon animals.

Between the settled and the nomadic way of life he sees a stark and fundamental contrast: the settled people are able to aspire to the arts and crafts because they are well fed while the nomads, always hungry, existing barely above the level of starvation, "are the least tamed of all people, living almost like wild animals." In the desert and steppe, only the savage, untamed, self-reliant and mutually supporting survive.

Nomadism, being so wild, so primitive, so animal-like, is, he believed, the oldest form of social organization. We now know this is not true since nomadism is, obviously, dependent upon the domesticated or at least "managed" animals that became available only some thousands of years more recently than humans began to practice rudimentary agriculture. And, far from being "primitive," nomadism requires quite sophisticated techniques.

His essential point remains: life in the harsh conditions of the desert inevitably fails to satisfy the nomads' desires. Driven by hunger, particularly in the frequent periods of drought-caused starvation, or by lust, "each one of them stretches out his hand to acquire his needs, taking them from him who then possesses them." Even when nomads prevail, however, they cannot bring what they have seized from settled peoples to the desert. As they acquire more than they can carry, they must stop being nomads. In the Classical poetry, there is even a word for settling, *qantara*, which means, literally, to acquire a "heavy weight."

Himself a city man, Ibn Khaldun is ambivalent toward the nomads. They are savage or uncivilized but because uncorrupted by the evils of opulence, they are "nearer to the Good" than settled peoples. The desert peoples he came to see as a sort of reservoir from which, carried out on floods of invasion, become human silt to manure the depleted settled societies. In their timing and power their forays are virtually acts of nature.

Inspired by Ibn Khaldun, Western scholars have assigned natural causes for the nomadic invasions. One theory held that they were caused by "desiccation," but there is no evidence of a major climate deterioration during the last two thousand years. However, for Ibn Khaldun's neighborhood there is evidence of long-term human destruction of the environment and much recent evidence of over-grazing by animals. But the more compelling evidence for nomadic invasions points toward political and military causes. These are the causes on which Ibn Khaldun concentrated.

For extended periods, Asian and African nomadic societies have lived in a sort of dynamic equilibrium. Governed by a barren ecology, a "tribe" could not herd animals, travel or fight as a group because the available water and grazing resources were insufficient to support large concentrations; the tribe which might number in the thousands was, therefore, a nominal concept. The effective unit was the much smaller part we call a clan. Normally, this group, for which the Arabs have many names and which existed in all ancient and primitive societies including those of our ancestors, was composed of progeny of a single patriarch, usually numbering not more than 50 to 100 people. Bound together by close kinship and by common interest, they were constantly engaged in hostilities with other clans within their own and other tribes. Thus, while tribes were potentially powerful "armies," they were rendered impotent by the fact that their constituent clans were always at one another's throats.

Occasionally, this equilibrium was disrupted. While climate was not *the* cause, it must have played a role. Periodic cycles of comparative wetness and dryness are now documented, and these may have also promoted fluctuations in population. In wet periods, more children would survive and with the return of dry years, hunger would give rise to desperation. Pre-Islamic Arabic poetry is full of references to "the blackened faces of starvation." Other causes probably include the spread of the domesticated animals, particularly the horse (first) and (later) the camel, that gave nomads greater mobility, the decline of military power among the neighboring settled peoples, the rise of charismatic figures among the nomads — men like Attila, Chingis, Timur — or the arrival of a religious movement.

Focused on the Arabs, Ibn Khaldun produces a vivid turn of phrase to explain what happened with the annunciation of Islam — "turning their faces in the same direction and causing internal dissension to go away." Islam at least temporarily stopped tribal warfare by treating all believers as "brothers" (*ikhwan*); that is, as members of the Islamic "clan" whose members could not fight among themselves; their hostilities could be vented only outwardly. So, as each pagan clan joined the Islamic community, its aggressive energies, which were certainly not diminished and indeed were given a new form of encouragement, were turned against non-members. Peripheral, still pagan, groups were thus caught between their traditional rivals, the still-pagan clans who were their near neighbors, and the increasingly numerous forces of the Islamic "super-clan." Unless they rushed to "submit," the meaning of the word islam, the pagans were crushed. And, as each group joined, the pressure on the remaining non-members increased still further. Islam spread like wildfire across Arabia.

Pouring out of Arabia, the Arabs first raided and then seized much of the Byzantine empire, conquered Sassanian Persia and within a century had marched deep into Central Asia and across North Africa and through Spain to reach into central France. Ibn Khaldun quotes with approval the *hadith* that says "God sent no prophet except under the protection of his folk." Islam tolerates no prophets unarmed. By adapting the dynamics of nomadic society's clan to his mission, Muhammad had virtually created his own community and ensured its worldly success. He was certainly the prophet armed.

But, as Ibn Khaldun realized, once the conquering nomads had settled down in cities, religion produced quite a different effect: then, instead of justifying and encouraging aggression, it made itself felt through laws and other restraints which tended to rob the previously self-reliant, proud and violent men of those very qualities. In this part of his analysis he can be compared to Edward Gibbon who, looking at Rome, deplored the day when "the last remains of the military spirit were buried in the cloister."

Ibn Khaldun, as I have pointed out, believed that nomads had a single objective, to leave the harshness of desert life to acquire the good things of life from the settled people. But, for some nomadic incursions, I believe he was wrong. Unfortunately, we have little information on any nomads' motivations *before* they arrived among settled peoples, but for some, particularly on the frontiers of China, we know enough to at least consider another model in addition to aggression — flight.

The Chinese records, which were not available to Ibn Khaldun, support this model. From at least the Chou dynasty, agrarian and urban China expanded onto traditional grazing areas, and various of the "Warring States" built enormous walls to interdict tribal migrations. Periodically, Chinese forces invaded tribal lands, driving some nomads into the territories of their neighbors; they did this in the south and the west also, but the results were most dramatic in the north. During the Ch'in dynasty, about 220-200 B.C., the Chinese began to push the powerful Hsiung-nu confederation northward, and, as it retreated, it shoved other nomads before it, and they displaced still others and so on right across Asia. In this original example of the "domino theory," one of the groups they evicted, whom the Chinese call the Yüeh-chih, fell upon and routed a people we know as Scythians.

This migration of the "Scythians" (the word which we take to be the name of a particular people simply means "nomads") was but one of many unrecorded convulsions. An earlier one must have been the cause of the "Scythian" attack on Assyria in the Seventh century B.C. which Herodotus describes in similar terms, saying that he was told that the Scythians were *fleeing* from other nomads, known as the "Massagetae, whose country lies far to the eastward beyond the

Araxes [river]."

In the course of their flight westward across Asia, the Yüeh-chih, like hundreds of tribes and clans of Indo-Europeans, Aryans, Celts, Goths, Avars, Huns, Iranians, Medes and other less well known groups, became conquerors. As the Yüeh-chih reached Central Asia, they entered the belt of Hellenistic city-states which Alexander the Great had left behind in Bactria, and having overrun them, they went on to found the Kushan Empire in India.

We do not know much about the Huns, the Avars, the various Celt peoples, the Vandals, the Goths and others before they fell upon the Romans and Byzantines, but it seems likely (as Edward Gibbon thought) that their pre-history was also one of flight from forces "from the frozen regions of the north." For thousands of years, deep in Central Asia, far from historians, stampede after stampede had been set in motion by forces then unknown. Indeed, in the Middle Ages, when Europeans heard the Turkish name for the Mongol nomads who then threatened them, *Tatar*, they ascribed their origin to "Tartarus," a Greek name for the Underworld and changed their name to *Tartar*.

Other than fear and greed, Ibn Khaldun finds another force at work on nomadic society; it is this force for which he is best known. From his reading of bedouin Arabic poetry and from his two periods of residence with tribes in what is today Algeria, Ibn Khaldun distilled the concept of *ᶜasabiyah*. The basic meaning of the word, used of a rope, is "twisted tightly;" in the poetic tradition he would have heard the phrase, "he drew the folk close together" (*ᶜasaba'l-qawm*). For him the concept comes to mean "that emotional attachment to a group which causes men to overcome their selfish aims to act in the collective interest." He sees *ᶜasabiyah* as the dynamic that gives cohesion and power to societies and argues that the absence of it is the cause of social disintegration. It is, for him, the prime bedouin virtue because, without it, man could not survive in the desert. Writing in an age that knew little of propaganda or even of ideology, he asserted that *ᶜasabiyah* could not be inculcated or "manufactured." It comes about naturally among men who belong to a single lineage "since the absolute attachment to one's immediate group of relatives is the most important of the emotions that God put into the hearts of his creatures." He is not interested in genealogy to assert nobility but only to illuminate "ties of the womb." That is, to establish that kinship is politically and militarily effective.

So as he sees it, tightly twisted together into intensely loyal fighting clans, always hungry, driven by fear of those pressing from still deeper in the wilderness or more numerous, anxious for the plunder of the cities and united by a charismatic leader or a religious mission, the nomads plunge into the settled areas.

When they arrive among settled peoples, nomads gain access to *material* civilization. At that point, they soon realize that "dominion is a noble calling, full of delights, in which one wraps oneself in all of the worldly excellences, bodily pleasures and personal proclivities." And, being savage, unused to rule, powerful and greedy, they plunder the conquered and fight among themselves for the spoil "because of the tyranny and aggressiveness in [man's] animal nature." When this anarchy becomes intolerable, they turn to a strong man to restore order. This man, being recognized (whether legitimately or fraudulently) for his noble lineage, assumes the position of monarch, a position that did not exist in egalitarian nomadic society; so he is forced to formulate a radically different concept of dominion. This he bases on his immediate family. He pushes aside many of his former partisans, replacing them with new and unrelated supporters and *their* followers and so on in a pyramid of power. Monarchy thus becomes independent of, indeed antithetical to the *ᶜasabiyah* that brought it to power; so the new elite no longer shares the profits of conquest with those upon whom they no longer depend.

Thus are set in motion tendencies that will lead to the ruin of the new regime. Soon the vices of the city—excessive indulgence in food, drink and promiscuity—spread. The decline in public morals is important in Ibn Khaldun's analysis not so much because of its violation of religious laws as for its political effect. When the society becomes libertine "each one is ignorant of his son since sperm is mixed in the wombs." As "purity of lineage is lost...its fruit, *ᶜasabiyah*, is wasted and thrown away."

Thus, because of the action of the new rulers and the tendencies of their old partisans, the clock begins to tick. It is only a matter of time before the virtues of the desert are forgotten and the atrophying state falls before new conquerors. Generally, Ibn Khaldun believes, this process of decline and fall takes three generations.

Because the first generation retains the desert characteristics, its roughness and its lack of domestication, its harshness of life, its self-sacrifice, nobility and the sharing of glory, the valor of *ᶜasabiyah* continues to be preserved…

"Then in the second generation, in dominion, its circumstances change from bedouin life to settled life, from privation to ease and luxury, from the sharing of glory to the monopolization of it and from standing tall to crouching subservience; thus the pattern of *ᶜasabiyah* is somewhat fractured as [people] become used to gentleness and submission. Yet much remains to them from what they recall of the first generation…"

"As for the third generation, they forget the era of nomadism and roughness as though it had never existed, and they lose [the taste for] the sweetness of power and *ᶜasabiyah*…and [instead of being its valiant warriors] they become a burden on the dynasty…"

If the state is a large one, it will fall apart from the outlying provinces first, so that the home province will remain in the hands of the dynasty longer. But, like the tides, the forces of history cannot be denied and in an ever recurring rhythm will flow and ebb beyond the control of any man or dynasty.

Ibn Khaldun invites comparison to several later historians but the one who, to my mind, bears the closest relationship is Edward Gibbon who lived 400 years later and never heard of Ibn Khaldun. When Gibbon addresses the question of why the Islamic empires declined, he unconsciously echoes Ibn Khaldun:

"When the Arabian conquerors had spread themselves over the East, and were mingled with the servile crowds of Persia, Syria, and Egypt, they insensibly lost the freeborn and martial virtues of the desert."

Or, in speaking of the conquest of China by the nomadic Mongols, he writes that "The Mogul army was dissolved in a vast and populous country; and their emperors adopted with pleasure a political system which gives to the prince the solid substance of despotism...One hundred and forty years after the death of Zingis [Chingis], his degenerate race, the dynasty of the Yuen, was expelled..."

Gibbon also speculated on what the power of the thrust of nomadism might have accomplished had it been maintained. That is, although he did not imagine the concept, had what Ibn Khaldun called *ᶜasabiyah* remained vigorous: after the Arab conquest of Spain and the South and west of France in the 8th century,

"A victorious line of march had been prolonged above a thousand miles from the rock of Gibraltar to the banks of the Loire; the repetition of an equal space would have carried the Saracens to the confines of Poland and the Highlands of Scotland; the Rhine is not more impassable than the Nile or Euphrates, and the Arabian fleet might have sailed without a naval combat into the mouth of the Thames. Perhaps the interpretation of the Koran would now be taught in the schools of Oxford and her pulpits might demonstrate to a circumcised people the sanctity and truth of Mohammed."

Much is made of the inspiration Gibbon received from the ruins of Rome but the inspiration (and reward) of Ibn Khaldun's life was less romantic and more political. He had a sort of ring-side seat on some of the great events of his time. While in Spain, still in his early thirties, he participated in a remarkable diplomatic mission. It was to the by-then Christian city of Seville where Pedro I ("the Cruel") offered to take him into his service. Crossing the religious frontier was then common in Spain where the relatively backward Christian rulers often called on the superior technical and managerial skills of Muslims. Pedro had compelling reasons to reach abroad for trustworthy assistants since his court was riven by hatreds and ambitions among his five illegitimate half-brothers whose mother had been murdered by Pedro's mother. As king of Castile, he was also in bitter conflict with the king of Aragon, Pedro IV, and at daggers drawn with the king of France whose daughter he had married, spurned and then put into prison. As a neutral foreigner, Ibn Khaldun would have been a valuable addition to the ruler's entourage, but, wisely, he declined Pedro's offer.

It is an indication of the richness of his life experience that Ibn Khaldun was thus to meet and exchange ideas with a Christian king in the West and, after spending nearly twenty years in Egypt as a judge, professor at the Azhar University and confidant of the ruler, and then 68 years old, he was to be lowered by rope from the walls of Damascus in 1400 to meet and spend weeks with the great Central Asian Chagatai Turkish conqueror Timur — known to us in corruption of his Persian nickname, *Timur-i Lang*, ("Timur the Lame") as Tamerlane.

Like many later scholars who have aspired to enlighten statesmen, Ibn Khaldun thought that Timur wanted to ponder his brilliant insights and grand conceptions whereas the wily old soldier appears to have sought him out only to learn the best roads to take on a campaign he planned to conquer Morocco.

Perhaps that is the real lesson he has left us. *Sic transit ambitio mens.*

On Violence

Working paper for the Fellows of the
Adlai Stevenson Institute of International Affairs.

"Why has government been instituted at all?" Alexander Hamilton in Federalist Paper 15 replies to his rhetorical question that it is, "Because the passions of men will not conform to the dictates of reason and justice, without constraint."

Since those words were written, the "passions of men" have been searched as never before in human history. Indeed, in the last three generations whole new fields of inquiry have been created. Some of these appear likely to offer us insights into issues which were previously the subject only of the speculations, prejudices, and – passions – of the great philosophers.

I

The first of these fields is psychiatry. To Sigmund Freud, above all others, may be credited its development. As his ideas gradually coalesced, several stand out as major contributions. The first is that in each individual adult both infantile and primitive natures coexist. Freud once compared the human personality with a truly Eternal City: new structures were continually being created but old structures were never destroyed. Consequently, regardless of how "rational" or "adult" an individual may appear, he retains both primitive and infantile impulses.

The range of human impulses fall, Freud gradually came to think, into two categories which he called "life impulse" and the "death impulse." Under these two headings, he categorized the whole range of human activity. Popularly known for his emphasis on sex – it must not be forgotten that he grew up in a "Victorian" atmosphere in Vienna – he is perhaps most valuable to us for his insights into violence and unhappiness.

Freud reacted to the horrors of the First World War with sharp pessimism.

During the course of his long experience with therapy, he came to believe that it was not possible to extirpate the violent and destructive aspects of the nature of man. Rather he emphasized the notion of balance as fundamental to mental health. In his conceptions of the id, the ego and the superego, one is reminded of the Enlightenment philosophers' conception of the balance of powers within government. The fit is not quite exact but is suggestive: proper government of the individual as of the state lies not in the destruction of one branch or the other but in the balancing of their forces. The id, like a general assembly, parliament or congress, is immediately responsive to the body. The ego, like the executive branch, gives shape and individuality, and the superego, like a supreme court, exercises judgment and restraint. "Government" could not safely or effectively function in default of any component.

But the individual, like the body politic, finds tranquility or happiness elusive. Writing in *Civilization and Its Discontents*, Freud argues that "Life, as we find it, is too hard for us; brings too many pains, disappointments, and impossible tasks... One feels inclined to say that the intention that man should be 'happy' is not included in the plan of 'creation.'" He then asserts that, even if man lived in a perpetual Garden of Eden, he would not be happy because "We can derive intense enjoyment only from a contrast and very little from a state of things." Our problem arises, he finds, not only in individual man but in civilization per se. "... what we call our civilization is largely responsible for our misery..." But by civilization, Freud did not mean so narrow a concept as is raised by such issues as race, industrialization or property. He specifically denies, in *Why War*, the Marxian contention that the abolition of property will result in a lessening of man's inhumanity to man. "Aggressiveness was not created by property. It reigned almost unlimited in primitive times, when property was still very scanty, and it already shows itself in the nursery almost before property has given up its primal anal from; it forms the basis of every relation of affection and love among people (with a single exception, perhaps, of a mother's relation to her male child)."

Two of Freud's principal collaborators and followers, Alfred Adler and Carl Jung, turned away in horror from his conception of human nature. Adler suggests that Freud was unduly influenced by the admittedly sick individuals of his psychoanalytic practice to find in all men a violent, sordid and unredeemable nature. To the contrary, Adler found what he called the "social interest" to be intrinsic. As Adler's own philosophy of life evolved, partly under the influence of socialism, his conception of man's quest for what he called "superiority" altered. Superiority gradually was transmuted from a sexually based quest for dominance into a desire for personal unfolding, for perfection and for the well-being of mankind. Carl Jung, likewise revolted by Freud's conception of man, found salvation for man on a more mystical plane.

Despite its very great insights into the nature of human problems, psychoanalysis is generally, and rightly, modest in its claims of success in handling these problems.[1] Increasingly, evidence has accumulated that major brain problems are physiological in origin and appear only partially susceptible to non-physiological treatment. Freud himself was pessimistic about the ability of his therapy to affect many of the problems he had identified and realized that many aspects of man's nature are left beyond the range of analysis.

II

Thus, parallel to, but largely uninfluenced by, the growth of psychoanalysis has been the elaboration of the field of neurology. In a general way, the human brain was recognized as the seat of intelligence or "mind" at least as early as Classical Greek times. Over the centuries, areas of the brain were thought of as related to or even as governors of various bodily functions. As autopsies were performed on wounded or deformed men after their deaths, correlations were made between brain, speech and limb. Yet, like psychiatry, the scientific field of neurology is barely three generations old.

Particularly in this generation, tremendous strides have been made in the "mapping" of the brain. Applied first to animals and later to humans, electrical, chemical stimuli and surgical transformations of the brain, area by area, have led to the beginnings of understanding of this enormously complex piece of machinery.

Insofar as the problem of violence is concerned, brain research is concentrated on the hypothalamus. In general terms, the hypothalamus is the physical counterpart of Freud's intellectual construct, the id. It is the part of the brain that is most immediately responsive to the needs of the body and most urgently demanding of their satisfaction. Also like the id, it performs essential functions. It deals with metabolism, sex, aggression, control of heartbeat, surface temperature, etc.

Experimenting primarily with cats and rodents, scientists have discovered that by exciting, chemically or electrically, certain regions of the hypothalamus, they can induce rage, fear, sleep and various muscular movements. Conversely, either through surgery or by chemical means, they can calm down or altogether eradicate the same emotions and actions. Because its functions are fundament to life itself, the hypothalamus is regarded as the most "primitive" part of the brain. But it does not act completely alone: the hypothalamus is partly under the control of the middle brain or cerebellum and of the cortex which may be roughly equated to Freud's superego. Further research has, however, indicated that while the brain may be usefully divided, by areas, into the many functions it performs, these functions and the physical components themselves tend to be closely interrelated. At certain times in its life, the brain can correct for malfunctions in one part by a growth of activity in another. At all times, tampering with the function of any given area produces side effects in others.

The mechanic of "memory" is still unclear. The latest theories hold that memory may be a function of "vibrations" or patterns of electrical charge rather than a static "impression." That is, memory may be a process, like ripples on the water, rather than a print or cut like a phonograph groove. Scientists differ as to whether the brain, at birth, is "an unfilled vessel" or whether it is, to some indiscernible extent, pre-programmed. At minimum, whether or not men inherit already developed traits, it appears that the structure of the brain influences man toward certain tendencies by means of its capacities or inadequacies. At maximum, it may be, as Freud and others have suggested that we enter this world partly or largely programmed by "instincts" which have evolved or have been emphasized by natural selection over the long history of human evolution.

It becomes useful, consequently, to consider the form of "programming" to which the human experience has subjected man and which may color our contemporary actions.

III

Archaeological evidence, small and scattered though it is, gives us roughly the following picture. Man appears to have emerged as a separate species roughly 80,000 generations or roughly two million years ago. At that time, our ancestors were not much larger than the pygmies of today and probably emerged from the forest not because they were more successful than the other primates but rather because they were less. There is much disagreement and little evidence, but it seems to me likely that they must have been driven from the relative comfort and security of the forests into the greater danger and privation of the open savanna.

At that time, Africa teemed not only with the wild life familiar to us today but with various giant forms of animals. Pigs as large as water buffalo, sheep with a horn spread of seven feet, various forms of giant bear and the saber tooth tiger among other dangerous beasts were early man's neighbors. Their simple, chipped stone tools would not have enabled men to kill these giant animals. The little evidence we have suggests that they were not hunters but scavengers for what little meat they ate; from their teeth, we know they lived mainly on vegetable matter.

It appears that the major transformation of early man into a hunter rather than a gatherer was incredibly long and laborious. Indeed, it was to be well over a million years before men acquired effective weapons for hunting. An even longer time was to pass before men mastered fire with which to render meat, which often must have been rotten by the time they got it, digestible. Fire also was the best way to keep wild animals at bay. Other weapons probably followed slowly. Men do not appear to have acquired the use of the spear until perhaps 20,000 generations ago. Use of the bow and arrow was very much later and it was not until perhaps 1,000 generations ago that men became truly proficient hunters.

Men did have certain advantages. As intellectuals, we like to think of these as featuring the ability to communicate, but there appears more solid evidence to emphasize man's ability to walk upright (which freed his hands to make tools, to carry food and use weapons), his ability to sweat (which enabled him to move about freely in the middle of the African noon while most animals slept in the shade) and the configuration of his teeth and stomach (which enabled him to eat virtually all forms of food stuffs). None-the-less early man was weak, slow – our cousins the chimpanzees can run faster – unarmed and ill-equipped for survival.

Inferring from scanty evidence, most anthropologists believe that the life of early man was, as Thomas Hobbes has told us, "nasty, poor, brutish and short". Presumably very few individuals lived to be more than forty and all must have been, for much of their lives, hungry and frightened. Thus, it seems to me logical that we must account for certain peculiarly human traits – particularly related to violence – in the context of our ancestors' weakness. To these I will return but here, to speculate, I think we can infer from the universal fear of man in the animal kingdom that a key reason for man's survival was his ferocity. Terror, the weapon of the weak, may have been the main – almost the only – arrow in his quiver.

That arrow, of course, was as easily turned on other men as on animals. Probably for most of our evolutionary experience, we could handle this danger by running away from one another. But sometime around 500 generations ago, running away became more difficult. That was the time when groups of previously nomadic people began to invest in the land rather than merely living off of it. The "agricultural revolution," the beginning of settled life was thus, from an evolutionary point of view, only yesterday. And it is from that period that we may date the attempt of men to live together in supra-clan aggregations of several hundred individuals. Another 200 or so generations were to pass before, in larger towns and cities of thousands of social, economically and culturally differentiated people, who no longer remembered the ties of kinship, that people had to learn to control their conduct vis-à-vis one another through elaborate codes or laws and to create civil and religious institutions. This experience, dating back to pre-Babylonian times, constitutes perhaps less than ½ of 1% of man's total historical experience.

The frustrating thing is that we can know little more about the other 99-½ % of man's experience. Sophisticated attempts are constantly being made to interpret marks on bones, placement of holes in the ground, scraps of debris, but the picture is not only incomplete but often contradictory. So to try to illuminate, some anthropologists draw analogies with existing or recent "primitive" groups, such as the Kurelu of central New Guinea. Such analogies are suggestive, but also flawed. In perhaps vital but certainly unclear ways, modern primitive peoples are different from our ancestors. Put simply, our ancestors "evolved," whereas the ancestors of today's "primitives" did not. We do not know why. Therefore, the analogy, while useful in provoking our analytic insights, must be used with caution.

IV

This frustration has given emphasis to the new field of inquiry into animal behavior known as ethology. The great name in ethology is Konrad Lorenz whose book On Aggression is the 'classic' of the field. Bitterly opposed to his conceptions is the English anthropologist Ashley Montagu. Essentially their massively-illustrated argument boils down to two contentions: is there any utility to our attempt to understand the nature of man in knowing the way various animals behave toward one another? And, is man controlled or influenced by "instinct?" Lorenz says yes to both. Montagu gives a guarded and limited "maybe" to the first but asserts flatly that man has no instincts.[2] It is indeed, Montagu believes, the lack of instincts which make men different from animals.

As Freud did with his opponents and detractors in his *History of the Psychoanalytic Movement*, Lorenz has set out his position clearly and polemically. We study animals' bodies, Lorenz points out, to help us learn about human biology; so why not study their habits to help us learn about our adaptation to environment. "The fact that the behavior not only of animals but of human beings as well," he wrote, "is to a large extent determined by nervous mechanisms evolved in the phylogeny of the specie, in other words, by 'instinct,' was certainly no surprise to any biologically-thinking scientist. It was treated as a matter of course, which, in fact, it is."

To deny these impulses or instincts and to believe, as the behaviorists do, that man is infinitely pliable and "can be turned into angelically ideal citizens" is foolish, he states. "If there is anything more dangerous than founding public policy on a lie, it is living in a fool's paradise."

Less based on scientific research but even more popular than Lorenz's writings have been those of Desmond Morris (*The Naked Ape and The Human Zoo*) and Robert Ardrey (*The Territorial Imperative and African Genesis*). Their "muscular" view of human evolution has stimulated a lively debate which Ashley Montagu carried on in his *Man and Aggression*. For him, there was nothing intrinsic in human violence. But, beyond rhetoric, there was little hard evidence in any of these books. That was what Jane Goodall, and those inspired by her work sought to provide in studies of the chimpanzees in East Africa. The supposition is that these, our closest non-human relatives, live and interact in ways that may have a direct relevance to the experience of early man. And, by extension, what we can observe in them enables us to reëxamine ourselves for conceptions and, equally important, for the absence of traits we can see more clearly in other animals. Desmond Morris' book, *The Human Zoo*, develops this theme.

Essentially, what we get from the ethological literature is an emphasis on factors making for survival of each species. Put simply, the task of the individual members of each species, as Darwin tells us, is to stay alive. Survival put a high premium on aggressiveness. In nature, the best defense has always been a good offense. The process of natural selection has favored opportunists who were flexible and who constantly and energetically sought their individual advantage. Territoriality, dominance or "pecking order", adaptability to changing circumstances, and social cooperation make for greater likelihood of survival. But, it must be admitted that individual survival can be in competition with group or even species survival: driven by starvation, animals and even human beings may eat their young. If done often, the species could die out, but done only in rare occasions of extreme need, cannibalism or infanticide – such as we know in human societies over the ages – would enable the adults to survive to breed again.

While arguably, such violence has a survival value in extreme situations, it is obvious that both animals and humans are inhibited from practicing it. Clearly, no species which has the capacity to destroy itself will prosper or, even, survive, as Konrad Lorenz argues in his book *On Aggression*, unless it develops strong intraspecific inhibitions against the use of violence. That is an important point, but what may be even more significant is that inhibitions against violence are not so necessary, and therefore not so likely to be emphasized, in those species which lack the innate capacity – fangs, claws or bulk – to destroy themselves.

This points up what I find to be the most significant finding in Lorenz's studies. Not having bodily weapons, or, until recently (from a genetic point of view), efficient extracorporeal weapons, our ancestors did not develop intraspecific inhibitions common to dangerous beasts. These and other insights have given us much food for thought in analyzing both human development and our contemporary dilemma.

V

To evaluate this issue, we must put it into the overall context of human development and contemporary society. To put it baldly, what moves us and what restrains us? From my observation, reading and research, I find six basic human "impulses". I do not call them "instincts" for I cannot find justification for their biological existence. I refer not to the sort of "instinctual behavior" related to the conditioning of the body or such actions as birds' building of nests but rather to what might be thought of as social-action propensities. My list is the following:

1) The preservation of life. Under this heading, I group various drives and actions associated with hunger, thirst, and self-defense. While, under most circumstances, we may regard this as the basic human impulse, an impulse upon which the preservation of the species as well as the individual is dedicated and one which would justify the right of self-defense, there is evidence that in certain circumstances this impulse either is weakened or totally loses its guidance. Under these circumstances, as I will point out, the individual either commits suicide or simply gives up his life.

2) The continuation of life. This propensity is shared by nearly all creatures and accounts for reproduction.

3) More narrowly shared among all living creatures is the propensity to associate with others. As Aristotle told us, man is a social animal. Indeed, he is probably the most social of all animals. Our preoccupation with the social aspects of animal life has given rise to one of the richest parts of the English language, venery.[3] And there is a practical aspect: only those animals which have a strongly developed social sense have been effectively domesticated by man.

4) "Territoriality" is the identification of an individual with a particular area. Not all animals appear to have such a sense of identification but it is exceptionally strong in man. The almost mystical association of the peasant for his land extends in subtle ways throughout our thought and experience. Its abstract manifestation, nationalism, is the most powerful idea of our times.

5) The need to attempt to control destiny takes on a wide variety of forms. One of the most basic of the differentiations between man and beast is man's consciousness of death and his attempts to ward it off or transform it into a continuation of life. There are subtle indications of this urge in burial sites dating from at least the earliest homo sapiens. Preoccupation with death and his struggle for immortality is certainly the prime motivation behind the development of religion. Closely linked with religion but usually differentiated from it are political impulses. The agricultural revolution, some 500 generations ago, allowed humans the capability of struggling coherently with nature. Whether this impulse pre-dates the agricultural revolution or not, it is clear that it is of fundamental importance in our own times. Man appears at his most human when he is at his least passive.

6) The sixth and most complex human propensity, I find to be curiosity. At its most simple, we see in our fellow primates a desire, almost a hunger, to know what things taste like, what is under them, what will happen if... In man, this sense is developed far more aggressively and widely than in animals. As Dr. D.E. Berlyne has pointed out[4] "Few human impulses are more inexorable than the urge to escape from monotony and boredom to some new form of stimulation... An active striving to encounter new experiences, and to assimilate and understand them when encountered, underlies a huge variety of activities highly esteemed by society, from those of the scientists, the artists and the philosopher to those of the polar explorer and a connoisseur of wines. 'The instinct of curiosity', says McDougall, 'is at the base of many of man's most splendid achievements, for rooted in it are his speculative or scientific tendencies.'" To curiosity we have brought systemization, history and a refinement or gradation of pleasures to produce science, art, learning in all of their manifestations.

It is possible, in extreme situations, where men are deprived of one or more of these needs – often even when physical existence is not threatened and bodily functions not impaired – to show the breakdown of the human personality. Perhaps the most obvious and certainly the best documented are concentration and slave labor camps. There, when people are deprived of "community," men are occasionally driven to suicide and often become incapable of performing effectively. A loss of territorial identification, even in the relatively luxurious surroundings of the American slum, appears seriously to dislocate the individual. The loss of control over one's destiny, as experienced by such administered populations as the American Indians, leads to lassitude or fatalism. Yet, there is evidence from the concentration camp experience that even in conditions of horrifying deprivation, when the body was wasting away, colleagues were rivals for food, sex was denied, all reality of and even symbols of, territory or "home" were lost, and the future was thought to be totally beyond one's control or even influence, "curiosity" enabled some to survive.[5] Curiosity is so powerful an impulse among humans that I pin some hope for finding – and wishing to find – a way through the terrifying maze of the contemporary age.

VI

Throughout history men have experienced and used violence. There appears ample evidence that, unlike other animals, men are caught in a terrifying dilemma which is posed by our ability to project ourselves into the feelings of a sufferer. From this projection, we develop both altruism, a feeling unknown to animals, and what appears to be a ghoulish delight in the sufferings of others. Unlike the baboon which simply abandons the sick and the aged, we care and try to help. This is humanity at its best and for which we have coined the term "humane." But, there is a dark side to our ability to project ourselves. The inventive genius lavished upon instruments of torture, the popularity of scenes of execution, the delight with which men have found new ways of inflicting pain on their fellows are both striking and ubiquitous.

As mentioned above, man emerged as a separate species devoid of the organic tools for lethal damage. He did not develop extracorporeal weapons until late in his evolution. Consequently, unlike the wolf, which usually cannot bite the bowed neck of his opponent, we have little inhibition against the use of our fists, feet or puny teeth against our fellows. Even if our acquisition of weapons has begun to help us to acquire inhibitions, for which there is very little evidence, our astonishing technological capabilities have allowed us to harm others at ever increasing distances; this enables us to avoid seeing or feeling suffering in others. Consequently, the man who would never consider dousing a child with gasoline to burn him to death can easily be persuaded to drop a napalm bomb on a village. Distance enabled American and English aviators to kill hundreds of thousands of Germans, Japanese (and Allied prisoners) in Dresden, Hamburg, Hiroshima, Nagasaki and Tokyo. We react to this by forgiving the distant inflictor of pain and blaming the nearby. It is the ability of the torturer to look at the victim, talk with him, reach out and touch him, which makes such actions as deliberately burning prisoners with ignited phosphorus from an incendiary bomb in Buchenwald appear so horrible to us.

A catalogue of man's inhumanity to man certainly makes dreary and probably unprofitable reading except to bring out two points: in the first place, violence is spread so generally through political systems, religions, cultures, climates, historical circumstances and ages as to dispel forever the contention that it is unusual, the product of a few sick minds in disturbed times or the result of any particular system of human organization. Violence is, indeed, so commonplace as to be banal. At some times, men have engaged in it with openness and obvious delight; at others, they have relegated it to a place of shame. But no group, anywhere, even amongst those we think of as living in the near utopias of the South Sea Islands, have done much to remove it from the human heart. The most pacific of men, indeed, appear to be those who have struggled most strenuously against the violence in their hearts. Gandhi, as we have learned from Erik Erikson's perceptive biography, *Gandhi's Truth: On the Origins of Militant Nonviolence*, offers a startling example.

In the second place, while it is fashionable among contemporary social scientists to ascribe to violence such labels as "instrumental" (purposeful) or "expressive" (that which merely, even aimlessly, highlights unhappiness with underlying causes), it is clear that there are at least two other general categories of violence: the first is the violence which is triggered by a sudden event or released by chemical or other means and the second is the violence in which men have everywhere indulged to gratify what appears to be a particularly human attribute, the enjoyment of pain and suffering in others.

The first category certainly includes crimes of passion. It is a fact that homicide, for example, is most often committed on the spur of the moment by men and women with no previous criminal experience. Many instances of violence, obviously, are associated with alcohol and some with drugs. Others, such as wartime massacres, are associated with intense fear or mob intoxication. The Song My massacre in Vietnam is not so unusual as we might like to think.

Dozens of others have been reported in wars and civil upheavals. "Our boys" have been joined by Turks and Armenians, Greeks, Jews, Indonesians, Germans, Russians, Tanzanians, Congolese, French, Chinese and others in recent years. Britain had several Song My's in India and a massive, domestic one in Scotland after the Battle of Culloden.

Violence for enjoyment is not just a feature of the Nazi concentration camp. Great ingenuity and hard work have everywhere and at all times been expended on instruments of torture and war. And people enjoyed the results. Burnings of witches, beheadings of criminals, drawings and quarterings of traitors, floggings through the streets, etc. were quite popular entertainments until recently in even so civilized a country as England. Ritualized warfare among primitive tribes, where we are told display was more important than killing, appears to have involved the best available technological means of inflicting pain on the adversary. The widespread – virtually world-wide until recently – practice of cannibalism, which is rare in all mammals but man, and is not often to be explained by near starvation, appears usually to have been accomplished by particularly ingenious methods of humiliating and inflicting pain on the victims. In many reported incidents not only was the victim forced to prepare his own cooking pot but, slowly killed piecemeal, even to taste the stew. In short, man's fascination with pain has far exceeded any rational purpose – even in the spread of terror – involved in its use.[6]

Even when not motivated by personal hatred or fury, men everywhere have made themselves ready instruments of those who wish to use violence on others. The Nazi concentration camps were not run simply by a few sadists but rather were large, efficient bureaucratic organizations. So were – or are – the Soviet labor camps. Interviewed torturers in Greece and Algeria have not appeared, on the surface at least, to be demented monsters but common, decent, "family men" doing a job, complaining the while about long hours, low pay and the high cost of living. As the psychoanalysts warn us, even those of us who are revolted by such horror and brutality reveal in our dreams and fantasies desires which vie with the worst we know who actually carry them out.

VII

The question also arises what could be the purpose of violence. There are, of course, several categories of answers. Let us take them one by one.

First, we must recognize that a number of rulers and even some philosophers have espoused violence. Dictators and conquerors have often found it useful: throughout history, great conquerors employed it as a routine tactic. Timur Khan ("Tamerlane") had pyramids of skulls built outside cities that resisted him and, in our own time, Hitler and not just such special forces as the SS but even the regular German army engaged in attacks and reprisals intended to incapacitate possible adversaries. It was not just the state, but also philosophers who justified violence. Georges Sorel observed that force is so intrinsic an element of the state that it can be opposed only by organized violence. He may be said to have been the link between Marx and Mussolini. Where organization, such as the general strike Sorel favored, was judged not possible, anarchists proposed that individuals should act against state power and those who yield it.

It was not just "wild men" who justified violence. Even the cultivated Enlightenment philosophers and the American Founding fathers proclaimed that violence, embodied in the right of revolution, was the final shield against tyranny. It was to protect the citizens from the state that our right to right to own and bear arms is enshrined in the Constitution. Otherwise, the Founding Fathers believed, our basic rights to Life, Liberty and the Pursuit of Happiness would be unprotected from inherently tyrannical government. In Jefferson's words, "the tree of liberty must be periodically watered with the blood of tyrants."

More recently, Fanon (who may be said to stand in the same relation to Mao as Sorel stood to Marx) glorifies an extension of this notion for the downtrodden. Violence, Fanon holds, is the way in which the oppressed not only can destroy their oppressors but can create or heal themselves. For Fanon, himself a psychoanalyst and a black, violence takes on a self-liberating function. By acting out a violent drama *The Wretched of the Earth* could engage in a sort of group therapy. Faced with such challenges, other state "security" organs or private groups of vigilantes deployed to defend public order or private interests.

A wholly different justification or violence is posited by philosophers and psychiatrists who believe that closely, perhaps inextricably, linked to man's aggressive tendencies is his source of energy, creativity, and indeed affection. Were man to lose these other facets of what has made him uniquely human, uniquely civilized, uniquely creative.

VIII

Obviously, not everyone agreed. Whether justified or not, violence was disruptive. So most societies made attempts to suppress it or at least to moderate and channel it. Societies everywhere "weeded out" their most dangerous members. In ancient Arabia, for example, pathological killers were driven out of their clans because of the fear of vengeance which their actions would bring down on other tribal members. Where settled life made it possible, the particularly violent were usually incarcerated. And capital "punishment" was common. Even those whose violence was sanctioned by political authority, such as torturers and executioners, were frequently set apart from "normal" society.

Organized suppression of violence by police, counterinsurgent organization and armies of occupation have been repeatedly proven to be of limited effectiveness. Unless the general community is governed by a social contract under which individuals and groups agree to live contiguous to one another, coercive action can work only in what amounts to genocide. Short of genocide, suppression of violence appears effective only as an arm of community action. Then, in Mao's metaphor, the violent are like fish deprived of their water. But where, as in Sicily, Vietnam or in dissocialized slums, the organizations of the state are often more target than shield.

Thus, manifested in various forms, as unwritten norms of conduct and formal codes of law, the cultural-political consensus upon which society rests provides networks of ritual and form which are certainly the strongest and most effective safeguards against unauthorized, large scale violence. The great Eighteenth century English upholder of civil order, Edmund Burke saw "manners" as a vital ingredient of civilized life.

Where no overarching authority exists, vengeance and the fear of retaliation, both intranational, in such tribal societies as the Arabs and international in our world of nations, provide, in the delicate balance of terror, a limited but always tenuous security. Statistics from America and other countries suggest an inverse relationship between severity of punishment, or even certainty of punishment, are inversely related to recidivism.

Attempts have been made to preemptively control violence through chemical and other means. A news dispatch from Nebraska reported in July 1970 that between 5 and 10 percent of the 62,000 children in the Omaha school district were being given "behavior modification" drugs to improve classroom deportment. Experiments are on-going. *Time* reported on March 30, 1970 that researchers at Princeton University were experimenting with suppressing "murderous behavior" in rats by injecting methyl atropine into their brains. The scientists found that they could turn killers into "instant pacifists."

Finally, some, including Institute Fellow Novell Morris, believe that repetitively violent offenders must simply be removed from society, and that society has the right to do so. Penal colonies – the French in Devil's Island and the British in Australia, the Caribbean and North America – are well known. Some American prisons are, in effect, domestic Devil's Islands, with prisoners incarcerated no attempt at redemption and no provision for return to society.

IX

Another means of handling violence is by "venting" hostility through other outlets. External warfare has long been recognized as a cure for internal strife. At usually less cost, domestic scapegoats have often been found. Deviant religious groups such as the Cathars in France, the Muslims in Spain, the Mormons in America and the Jews in Russia provided easy targets as did racial groups like the blacks in America and Aboriginals in Australia.

More benign are violent sports. "Danger as a way of life" has become increasingly popular in recent years. And, even more important, such extreme sports can be "enjoyed" vicariously. The circuses of ancient Rome and the bull fights of modern Spain are examples. "The Tenth Victim" provides an imaginative 21st Century suggestion: people with murderous tendencies could be licensed to hunt one another provided they do not involve the rest of us except as spectators.

Drugs, liquor and sex in easy access may afford safe, even if not socially acceptable, outlets. It is also possible to sublimate, displace or limit the extent of violence through various ritual means. For example, the Indians or the American Great Plains practiced a "touching" war in which the enemy was not killed but merely touched or deprived of his weapons. Various kinds of international competitions, including the Olympic games, are variations on the same theme. Lorenz and others think we should invent and practice ever more varied peaceful competitions as a substitute for war.

Of course, it is not clear whether such activities are substitutes or stimuli for violence. Do they allow a sort of masturbation of violent propensities or the encouragement of the belief that violent action is socially acceptable? The jury is out. My own hunch is that, at least, they trivialize violence. In television, the portrayal of violence is graphic, almost microscopic, and ever present. But the dangerous aspect of the portrayal of violence lies not in these features but in the fact that it appears to be without consequence. The viewer, often a child, hears the gun go off and sees the victim fall, but with no conception of pain. Perhaps Aldous Huxley's notion in *Brave New World* of the "feely" could turn violence spectacles into morality plays if the viewer not only saw the shot, the stab or the blow, but also felt the pain.

X

The fourth means of handling the problem of violence is to avoid violence-prone situations: particularly eradicating racial and class injustice and minimizing jealous envy. This is primarily a domestic issue and has been the thrust of such programs as President Johnson's "Great Society" and the citizen-led civil rights movement. There is reason to hope that the trends set in motion by such efforts will diminish the anger that gives rise to much of our violence.

Internationally, there is great danger. We often overlook the fact that our generation has inherited the legacy of Nineteenth century colonialism. The severe dislocations of that era and the often desperate attempts to create some alternative form of order have given rise to a number of violence-prone situations. In some of these, as we have seen, the declining colonial powers are engaged against natives using the only available tactics, terrorism and guerrilla warfare. As the French patron saint of counterinsurgency, Colonel Roger Trinquier, has told us, there is only one way to fight a guerrilla war: as the guerrilla does. Terror, he wrote in *La Guerre Moderne*, is to guerrilla war what the machine gun is to conventional war. Torture is not only necessary but morally justified. France tried to apply his tactics in Algeria where, after years of "dirty" war, the recognition of the terrible cost to France – the corruption of a whole generation of Frenchmen and the infection of the French body politic with the cancer of torture – played a crucial role in the French decision to get out of Algeria. Knowing at first hand the terrifying costs of this struggle, Gandhi stressed Satyagraha as the surer path to an acceptable future for India.

XI

In addition to the various means of suppressing, containing, venting and avoiding violent-prone situations, there is the long-term goal of increasing our compassion and humane attitudes toward one another. Herein, of course, lies the long-term hope of mankind. It is here, I suggest, that we must build upon man's sense of "curiosity." Individually and separately, we must seek to refine the humane aspects of our lives. Here, we tread upon unknown ground. While there are "humanities" programs in all of our educational systems, they appear to do little to increase a humane feeling in us. Those of us who have struggled with the problem of violence are sure to find, as we examine our own experiences, some overwhelming personal sense of injury and pain of others.

Often these experiences can be gained vicariously and they may be cumulative. Certain great examples of literature, notably recently Alexander Solzhenitsyn's novel, *The Cancer Ward*, great pieces of art, Daumier's paintings and the drawings of the horrors of war and Picasso's "Guernica," appreciation of music and exposure to the pain and suffering which is lamentably so common a feature of the lives of the blind, the deaf, the deformed, the mentally defective and the ill, all create in us not only a sense of compassion but also a desire to build a better world. It is, in large part, that desire which alone will enable us to take concrete steps to handle the problem of violence. But, there are no sure roads so we must experiment and allow for wide diversity. So far we have done far too little; it is clear that we need to spend more time and attention in finding these ways than we have in the past. It is also clear that much of what we have done has traduced many of the basic human impulses toward decency and kindness. We must seek to identify both the positive and negative steps with more precision so that we may choose our way haltingly through the dangerous mine field that presents itself to us in the latter part of the 20th Century.

XII

However we seek to control violence, we must reckon that we are on the short end of a very long lever. "Man" is about 80,000 generations old. For perhaps 99% of his experience violence must have occasioned little disapproval. Only in the last 500 generations, since the agricultural revolution, have men attempted to cope with the problem of how to live with large numbers of their fellows in an ordered society.

The history of those 500 generations is so full of wars, massacres, crime, torture and hatred – much of it elaborately and laboriously justified – as to make us realize both how much a struggle it has been to achieve the little peace we have and how easily we lapse into acceptable inhumanity.

Only in the last three generations have we begun to dig deeply into the causes of the problem in living together. And only a very small proportion of our time of even those three generations has been spent in trying to inculcate a humane approach to our life together. Indeed, it is arguable that a large part of what we have done, even in modern, apparently sophisticated and knowledgeable society, has directly counteracted the development of humane attitudes.

Examples abound. We place high value and strong emphasis on technology, bureaucracy and consumption. The individual becomes linked with the machine, either real or bureaucratic, and his goals become facets of this linkage. That these have played a part in removing a sense of "texture" from life is, it seems to me, undeniable. We have removed, from our presence those who do not fit the "machine", or are inefficient, our aged, our sick, our ugly and our handicapped. Whatever else they have done, these changes in life style have tended to lower our standards of compassion. There is great evidence that Americans have taken to heart the injunction to be our brothers' keeper but equal evidence that we have sharply limited our definition of brothers. Having surpassed Darwin's nature by the use of our brains to create our environment, we find ourselves in the grip of at least as fierce a struggle for survival. The definition of the "fittest" has changed but "natural selection" is as remorseless and even more rapid than before.

There is much to be gained, I believe, in exposure such as some great literature and cinema can provide and have provided us. Erich Maria Remarque's

All Quiet on the Western Front, Ingmar Bergman's *Shame* and Constantinos Costa-Gavras's Z should be used today, as the Greeks used their morality plays to humanize their people. Aleksandr Solzhenitsyn's *The First Circle* and Ken Kesey's *One Flew Over the Cuckoo's Nest,* are great texts for our times on the inhumanity of bureaucracy and the struggle for humanity against impersonal power. How few of our students read them!

Nothing, of course, can take the place of the individual assumption of civic responsibilities and in this there is much to be hopeful about America. We are an involved and engaged society. Perhaps most of our problems stem primarily from the fact that we do everything on a grander scale, with more dedication and energy and with more perceptible results than ever before. Against the good we are doing and the care we give one another, we also glorify violence more effectively, stimulate one another to violence more pervasively, undercut basic needs more massively than ever before. With urban renewal, with overcrowding of the cities, with lessening of a sense of control over destiny, with the diminution of social satisfactions and with an increase of economic frustration by advertising envy we tend to dehumanize life. It is but a step from this to denigrating life. And but one more to despoil it.

In conclusion, I would stress that we cannot afford either enervating pessimism or numbing naïveté. The dangers of violence are clear and present but with a realistic view of the problems and prospects, and within a reasonable view of the future, human curiosity may lead us to livable adaptations even as the process stimulated by curiosity offers a reason for survival.

Sept 10, 1970

1. S. Freud: *History of the Psychoanalytic Movement* (New York: Collier Books, 1963), 83.

2. *The Human Revolution* (New York: Bantam, 1967), 114.

3. J. Lipton, *An Exultation of Larks or The Venereal Game* (New York: Grossman, 1968).

4. *The British Journal of Psychology,* Vol. XLI, 1950-51, Cambridge, 1951, 68.

5. V. Fankl: *From Death Camp to Existentialism,* a Psychiatrist's Path to a New Therapy (Boston: Beacon Press, 1959) and B. Bettelheim: "Individual and Mass Behavior in Extreme Situations", *Journal of Abnormal and Social Psychology,* Vol. 38, 1943.

6. See the excellent book by Institute Fellow Anthony Storr: *Human Aggression* (New York: Bantam Books, 1970), 101, 103.

PART VI

VISIT TO THE SOVIET UNION

Visit to the Soviet Union in 1972

Report to the Fellows of the Adlai Stevenson Institute of International Affairs

I HAVE JUST RETURNED from two weeks in the Soviet Union where I was a guest of the Academy of Sciences. During my stay, I lectured at and met with senior officials of four of the Academy's principal institutes dealing with international affairs. I certainly make no pretense of any expertise on the Soviet Union, as a result of my two weeks stay, but because the American Embassy and American journalists resident in Moscow indicated that I had been given a most unusual, indeed virtually unique, opportunity to exchange ideas with some of the leaders of the Soviet Union and to learn how they approach international relations, I will share with you what I learned.

The Academy of Sciences is responsible for virtually all research work undertaken in the Soviet Union. It is a self-perpetuating body which comes directly under the Soviet Presidium, but its members appear to have at least equal access to and familiarity with the Communist Party structure. A number of the members of the Academy are advisors to the Party's Central Committee.

The Academy functions primarily through research institutes in the natural sciences, the social sciences and the humanities. The director of each institute, I was told, is elected by the Academy to serve for five years. He is restricted in his scope of operation by a council elected within the Institute. This council is composed of approximately 40 members. The head of each research section is elected by his colleagues. I will tick off, one by one, what I observed or was told. I begin with the Institute of Africa.

The Institute of Africa was founded in 1959. The director of the Institute is Dr. Solodovnikod who is a Corresponding Member (not a full member) of the Academy. The deputy director is Dr. Igor Petrovich Beliaev, an economist, who like a number of the senior members of the research institutes in the social sciences was a Pravda correspondent. Dr Beliaev has had extensive experience in Egypt and was in close contact with President Nasser. He and Dr. Evgeni Maximovich Primakov of the Institute of World Economy and International

Affairs are close friends, associates and accompanied Nasser during his frequent trips to the Soviet Union. Dr. Beliaev was also a former chief of Afro-Asian affairs for Pravda in Moscow. In addition to his duties at the Institute of Africa, Beliaev is head of a coordinating committee founded in 1971, made up of members of several of the institutes, on the current crisis in the Middle East.

The Institute of Africa has 200 staff members engaged in research. The members are scattered through some 15 to 17 sections, (Dr. Beliaev added two additional sections to the first 15 during our conversation). These are: 1) Egypt-Libya-Sudan; 2) Arab North Africa; 3)South and Colonial Africa; 4) Independent Africa; 5) Nigeria; 6) Soviet-African political relations; 7) Soviet-African economic relations; 8) Theoretical and general economic studies including development; 9) Mathematical methods of forecast; 10) The "socialist" countries (Guinea, Mali, Somalia, Ghana, Tanzania); 11) Economic-geographical studies; 12) Information department; 13) Publishing; 14) Public relations including relations with like bodies throughout the world; 15) History up to the period of the national liberation movements; 16) Ideology; and (17) Political organizations.

Dr. Beliaev pointed out that these divisions were largely a matter of administrative convenience since the work of any one man might fall in several sections but they roughly accord to the content of his study. He also pointed out that there is considerable overlap between the work done by researchers in his Institute and that in other Institutes. This, he said, was purposeful. The Academy planned that, with this overlap, useful insights could be drawn from slightly different perspectives by men enlivened and invigorated by colleagues working in different organizations. Thus, the approach to Egypt within the Institute of Oriental Studies would tend to be influenced by cultural factors while that in the Institute of World Economy and International Affairs would be influenced more by strategic-geopolitical notions. Researchers in the African Institute would be affected by "area" considerations. (I replied that the latter is the more common organization in American universities, while those in the Institute of World Economy and International Affairs, as the name suggests, would be more wideranging.)

When I raised the question of the use of Institute members as government advisers, Beliaev made the same disclaimer as others were to do, that the Institute does not directly or systematically work for the government. He said, however, that there is considerable casual or particular use of Institute members as government advisers. Researchers do not, however, he said, take on government assignments; they are free of all obligations except those determined collegially within the Institute as laid down in general terms by the Academy. Thus, he summarized, the party and the government use the individual scholars but not the Institute as a source of research.

It was not altogether clear to me, in my conversations with the members, in this Institute or others what the real product is. This Institute (like all the Institutes I visited with the sole exception of the Institute of Oriental Studies) had relatively few publications to its credit given the size of its staff. It would appear, a priori, that the task of the Institute is at least in part more than that mentioned by Dr. Beliaev: viz. to undertake a systematic review of all generally available materials on an important area of the world from the perspective of Communist Party ideology and Soviet government needs. What form these studies ultimately take or what their audience they reach was not, of course, evident to me.

Thus, I found aspects of the African Institute similar to area research programs in Western universities. In the area studies programs in the University of Chicago, for example, the various centers did not work for the government but some individual members accepted contracts for their research and/or supplied their studies to various government offices. Organizationally, there was perhaps somewhat more administrative rigidity and careful definition of areas of interest than in any major American university. On the other hand, there appeared to be somewhat less interrelationship with the government, at least on a formal basis, than in such government supported or "spun off" organizations as the US Air Force-funded Rand Corporation. There was a notable lack, for example, of safes where confidential papers might be stored. There was no security apparatus evident and once I had been identified, I was able to move freely about the rooms and among the offices of the Institute. However, I did notice that the doors to all offices were normally closed and the staff did not seem to move casually from place to place.

I might say, parenthetically, that all of the information I am presenting here was delivered freely and voluntarily by the named representatives of the various institutes. Each seemed anxious to brief me fully on the activities of the institutes and to exchange comparable information on various operations. However, there was a notable lack of willingness to receive either American Embassy officials or American journalists in any of the institutes. An Embassy official did manage to get himself invited to one of my lectures, and I was allowed to bring along Hedrick Smith, the resident correspondent of the *New York Times*. I was pointedly told later, however, that without my intervention neither one of them could have ever hoped to set foot in the Institute.

The Institute of Oriental Studies is a very much older organization than the others. In a different form, it was founded in the Nineteenth century and is located on Armenian Street in Moscow which gives a hint to its origins.

I was briefed on its activities by Dr. Roman Achramovich whose specialty is Persian and Pashto on its structure and activities.

The Institute is very large, with 500 or more researchers plus secretarial assistants and staff. Some of the members also teach part-time at the University of Moscow.

Like the other institutes, it is divided both regionally and functionally. In addition to separate departments of literature and languages and separate functional departments dealing with such special problems as modernization, sociology, East-West relations and financial and credit problems, it has eight major area divisions. These are the Near and Middle East (Turkey, Iran and Afghanistan) ; 2) the Arab countries (headed by Dr. Levidev and Dr. Lev Kotlov) ; 3) Pakistan ; 4) South Asia (India, Ceylon, Nepal) ; 5) Southeast Asia ; 6) Korea, Mongolia, Vietnam ; 7) China (which is also separately covered in the Institute of Far Eastern Studies which I did not visit) ; and (8) Japan.

The Institute has no students, but does have 100 post graduates who are at work on their candidate's degree (M.A. or Ph.D.).

In addition to a branch in Leningrad, five separate similar but somewhat smaller institutes exist in Baku, Tashkent, Ervian, Tiflis, and Dushanbeh. Their work is coordinated by a Union-wide committee. Moreover, there are two Oriental Studies faculties in universities. In all, I was told that there are perhaps 1,000 researchers in the Soviet Union working on Asian studies.

The Institute publishes between 100 and 120 books yearly and jointly with the Africa Institute, two journals: *People of Asia and Africa* and a monthly called *Asia and Africa Today*.

It has its own Library but relies heavily upon the Lenin Library in Moscow.

The Arabic section of the Institute has approximately 20 researchers plus 20 Arabists in other departments. Approximately 2/3rds of these deal with contemporary affairs. A division on Hebrew studies and modern Israel was organized, I was told, in 1971 but is still quite small. Most of the work on history, literature and art is done in the Leningrad branch.

The budget of this institute, Dr. Achramovich told me, is an item on the overall State budget and is approximately 1.5 million rubles. The salary scale is very low by American standards. A senior researcher receives approximately 300 rubles a month. If, however, he has a doctorate degree he receives 400 rubles a month. If he is the head of a section, he receives an extra 100 rubles. If he teaches at a university, he gets an extra ½ salary. Researchers at the Institute, Achramovich said, receive a smaller salary than university faculty members as their work load is considerably less. The average researcher spends only two days a week in his office and is given great freedom to pursue his own research interests at his home or in a library. Each research member has a year-long study plan and is apparently given some sort of incentive pay for fulfilling it. This is particularly the case when he produces a publishable manuscript.

The Institute of the U.S.A. was founded in 1968. It does not now include studies on Canada. The head of the Institute, who has figured much in the international press lately, is Dr. Gregori Arkadiovich Arbatov. The Deputy Director is Vitili Vladimirovich Zhurkin who gave the most of the following information. Two other senior members of the Institute to whom I owe thanks for the following information are Vladimir Petrovich Filatov and Alexandr Konstantin Koslov.

The Institute now has 200 members including 100 research staff and 40 postgraduates. Like all the other institutes, it awards advanced degrees, but to date it has had only five or six graduates. I infer from this that most of its work is highly contemporary and closely involved with government activities. It does not seem to be as self-perpetuating as the other institutes; most of its younger members come to it from the Moscow University School of the International Relations.

The Institute publishes a monthly magazine with a circulation slightly above 30,000 and has, to date, published 8 or 9 books. Its emphases are on economy, social affairs and the policy of the U.S. government in both domestic and foreign affairs. The senior members come from diverse backgrounds including the Foreign Office, the universities and journalism.

Its main purpose, I was told, is to study and help to develop US-USSR ties. To this end, it has more frequently than the other institutes invited visitors from other countries, most from the United States, but also from Great Britain and particularly from the Institute of Strategic Studies.

Its philosophical commitment, as summarized by Dr. Zhurkin, is a direct antithesis of the often discussed theory of "convergence." While it is true, he said, that the requirements of any industrial-urban society have made Soviet and American society comparable in certain ways, these are primarily superficial. Beneath the surface, our societies remain and should remain profoundly different. We not only adhere to a different contemporary ideology but develop from exceptionally different historical and cultural backgrounds. It has been a profound mistake, he says, to underestimate the importance of this difference. Our task, he said, is not to seek to minimize it but rather to seek to understand it and to develop a sense of mutual respect. Each society, he said, can learn from the other but our generally clumsy attempts, in the past, to suborn or force one another to be like ourselves are not only sterile but highly dangerous.

I remarked that convergence has been rather hotly debated in America. That he may have stressed it too much was one of the attacks made on Walt Rostow when President Kennedy wanted him to be chairman of the Policy Planning Council. American conservatives were in accord with Zhurkin in the first half of his comment – that we are very different – even though many or perhaps most of them do not follow him into advocating mutual respect.

He sighed and replied, "Yes, I know. That is perhaps our most difficult problem."

I asked how much reliance was placed by this Institute on defectors of marginal groups. Little or none, he replied – rather too quickly, I thought.

I probed further. Specifically, I pointed to the famous English defector Kim Philby and asked how much his advice was sought on the nature of Western society. The reply here as elsewhere whenever Philby's or other defectors' names came up during my visit was wholly negative. While that reply might well have been expected, it was backed up by an explanation that gave it some verisimilitude. Philby was not a reliable guide, I was told. He was a particular case whose life had always been "apart." The attempt was rather to find people in the mainstream of Western life whose opinions and whose very lifestyle could be regarded as more representative and therefore more insightful.

Despite this statement, I was disturbed there as elsewhere during my visit by the parade of American scholars' names who are apparently closely read and listened to by Soviet academicians. These include such "Cold Warriors" as Herman Kahn, Thomas Schelling, Albert Wohlstetter and Morton Kaplan, but do not include people who I believe most American scholars or politicians would regards as more representative of the genius or culture of American society. Works by the "big bomb" scholars are avidly read and contemporary literature on theoretical and mathematical approaches to international affairs are closely followed. For example, I was asked if Oscar Morgenstern had already published his study on zero sum games, but not whether Senator Fulbright's hearings on the American Constitution had received much attention. I suggested that the Institute had skewed the emphasis, and we agreed to discuss it over vodka and caviar which, since it was my birthday, was immediately forthcoming!

The Institute of World Economy and International Affairs is, I was told, one of the largest and most advanced institutes in the Soviet Union. It is a "complex, economic, political, social research institute with many branches. So impressive has it been that the others are copying us."

The Institute's main focus is on the "capitalist world." Its departments are devoted to studies of the economy of the capitalist world; economic correlations (which I was told meant comparative studies); problems of development; international affairs (a large division); special country studies; an information department dealing with current intelligence from the popular press, biography, bibliography, etc. The Institute, uniquely I believe, has a computer but the directors told me that they have been so disturbed by problems of data retrieval and storage of information as not to rely too heavily on it.

The Institute maintains a large degree of overlap with other research institutes. For example, it also has a large department dealing with the United States. That it is growing rapidly is demonstrated by the fact that it is planning to move over the course of the next couple of years to a large suburban building of over 30 stories.

"Our main philosophical motivation" said the Deputy Director, Dr. Evgeni Maximovich Primakov, "is to preserve the system of political pluralism." The Institute promotes this, he said, not only by undertaking general research on major international issues but also by studies of specific crisis situations of which the Middle East is now regarded as the most dangerous and demanding. These various research projects are handled by the several divisions.

The Department of International Affairs, headed by Colonel Vasily Mikhailovich Kulish, is problem oriented. It is one of the largest in the Institute. Colonel Kulish is an extraordinarily interesting man. One of the youngest assistant division commanders in World War II, he retired from the Soviet Army six years ago to pursue his studies. He now has the titles of professor and doctor in addition to his military designation. A large and jovial man, he spent six months visiting almost every major American research institute.

(As an aside, I emphasize this point as visits between our universities and research organizations has generally been on a one-way basis. Few Americans come here. I was the first American to visit the Soviet counterparts of Chicago's area studies programs. But many Russian scholars go – and frequently – to Europe and America. In part the problem is money. Relative to the several institutes of the Academy, the typical American area studies center is poor. My trip, for example, could not have been paid for by Chicago's Center for Middle Eastern Studies. There is a second problem: language. Like most of the senior research members I met, Kulish is reasonably fluent in English. So during my visit I was able to lecture in English to a large and obviously understanding audience, but no American university could have coped with a visitor speaking in Russian about politics or economics.

Since I returned from the Soviet Union, I received a call from Dr. Vitili

Zhurkin, Deputy Director of the Institute of the U.S.A. to say that he is in this country for two months. This makes a point which seems to me well worth considering, Soviet scholars both through their greater linguistic facility and because of a plenitude of travel and research funds, as well as other factors, clearly keep in much closer contact with us than we do with them. It is obviously very much more difficult for an American scholar to travel freely in the Soviet Union than for a Soviet scholar to travel here. However, it appears that research activities are so highly concentrated in Moscow and Leningrad that it should be relatively easier for one of us to see virtually everybody concerned with international affairs there than it is for a Soviet scholar to visit all of the research institutes here.)

The Institute's "Division on Theory and Methodology" is headed by Professor Vladimir Israel Gantman. Within this division, there is a small, two-year-old section dealing with mathematical approaches to international affairs. Its staff is made up of two young research assistants without foreign office experience. Their task, Professor Gantman told me, is to attempt to probe the possible utility of a composite (Western and Marxist) approach to mathematical prediction in the field of foreign affairs. The rest of the division, considerably larger, is non-mathematical and more traditional in form.

Separate divisions deal with "area" programs. The "Division of the United States" is headed by Dr. Yuri Melnikov while the "Division on European Affairs," headed by Dr. Daniel Melnikov (no relation) contains specialists on each country. The "Division on the Far East and China" is headed by Dimitri Vasiliavich Petrov. The "Division on Military Affairs" is headed by Colonel Kulish (in addition to his chairmanship of the Department of International Affairs). The United Nations division is headed by Dr. Gregory Morozov. Other senior men associated with this or the Institute of the U.S.A. in ways that were not clearly defined are the son of Foreign Minister Gromyko, the nephew of Anastas Mikoyan and a former son-in-law of Stalin.

The Institute of World Economy and International Affairs is contemplating the establishment of a branch in Leningrad but now works exclusively in Moscow.

❧ ❧ ❧

I found the response to my four lectures extraordinarily gratifying. Not only was the attendance large and the attention close but I was kept, in two cases, for over two and a half hours of questions and discussion after my presentation. I found each position firmly and cogently argued but I never encountered blind dogmatism. There was in intense professional concern with each academic discipline as well as a concern with the substance of the discussion.

But as Russians must find of American visitors or those they encounter on their trips to America, I found a particular and, to my mind, distorted view of our separate academic communities. I found theirs, and presume they find ours, to be very much Cold War oriented. The scholars whose opinions were particularly closely followed were those who had a vogue in the late 1950's and early 1960's.

The academic fad in the Soviet Union today is politico-military war gaming, the work of people like MIT's Thomas Schelling. I have long been a persistent critic of this approach to international affairs. By emphasizing so heavily as it does conflict, by an almost total neglect of social and cultural diversity and by a failure to differentiate "interest of state" from "interest of government," I find war gaming dangerously misleading. Obviously, what I had to say was very disturbing and caused a sharp but polite and attentive debate. I illustrated my argument with reference to the war game played in the Pentagon after the Cuban Missile Crisis; some of the members of the audience had apparently played roles similar to mine in the actual Crisis so the exchange was extremely pointed and informed. I brought the house down, so to speak, when I said that I had been the political expert on "Red Team" in the Pentagon war game!

On a more serious note, I think that my visit showed how very important, perhaps in times of extreme stress even vital, that we learn how one another thinks, how we find out about each other and how we inform our peoples and governments. My criticism of the Soviet aspect of these ventures is the lack of Russian attention to the culture of American society in comparison to attention given to the writings of our "big bomb" writers. This particularly surprised me because the Russians made such a strong attempt to expose me to their ballet, their symphony, their folk music and were clearly worried that I was likely to think of the Soviet Union solely in terms of missile sites and labor camps.

Since it is obvious that the research institutes of the Soviet Academy are a "chosen instrument" to assist in establishing ties between our countries, it would be beneficial, in my judgment, if we would undertake a concerted effort to make certain that this is a two-way street.

March 20, 1972

Visit to a Central Asian Collective Farm

DURING MY TWO WEEK VISIT in the Soviet Union as a guest of the Academy of Sciences, I was allowed to visit a *kolkhoz* just outside of Tashkent on March 8. This particular *kolkhoz*, Ahunbabaev, in the village of Bektamir, was founded in 1930 and named after the first President of Uzbekistan. The visit was arranged by Professor Vladimir Israel Gantman, of the Institute of World Economy and International Affairs, who acted as my guide in Central Asia.

The day was grey and chilly as we drove into the *kolkhoz*. A small party of the senior members led by Ruzmatov Mir Aziz Aka, its president, met us. A solid, self assured man of perhaps fifty-five years of age, Mr. Aka described himself as a mechanic-engineer. He had been the President of this *kolkhoz*, he informed us, for fifteen years. Leading us into his office, a rather bare, high ceilinged room enveloping a large conference table, he took his seat, one felt as though at a committee meeting, behind his massive desk. After a few words of welcome, he suggested that I ask questions and he would answer. He spoke in Russian, the second language of Uzbekistan and one he had learned as a youth, and I in English. Our words were translated by a young scholar from the Institute of World Economy and International Affairs.

This *kolkhoz*, Mr. Aka informed me, was founded in 1930 on land which, prior to the great collectivization, had been private. So successful had its founders' efforts been that it now has eight "daughter" communal farms. Throughout our discussion, my mind kept running back to my visit to an Israeli *kibbutz* in 1946; there were striking parallels but also notable differences. The two differences that were particularly evident were that the Russian collective, unlike the Israeli collective, was not militarized since it was not under challenge from those it had displaced and the Russian collective was markedly poorer than the Israeli since it did not draw on foreign governmental and private contributions.

Restricting my questions just to the kolkhoz which we were visiting, Mr. Aka answered that it had 700 families, comprising 4,800 people of whom 800 worked and 600 lived on pensions. I was amused that Mr. Ata gave a sort of sociological insight in the population: Statistically, on average, he said, "each worker has 4-1/2 children." The total area it occupies is 1,900 hectares or 4,693 acres. I was surprised at how large it was.

Each *kolkhoz* member works on the common land several days a week, the exact number being dependent upon a work plan which is agreed by all and dependent upon the season. In addition, each family has 0.15 hectares or a little over a third of an acre as its private plot on which it grows vegetables and other produce which it can use to supplement its diet but which it is also allowed to sell.

The work force is divided into 15 "brigades," one for each piece of land of approximately 100-150 hectares. Each brigade has its own work plan and calls for something like 180 days per year for each man and 150 days a year for each woman.

The work of the brigades is internally competitive. Their quotas are set by the kolkhoz itself rather than by the State although each *kolkhoz* undertakes, by the contract in advance, to supply a given unit of output to State sales agencies.

The main crop of this *kolkhoz* is cotton but it also produces 200 hectares each of rice and jute and a smaller area of sugar beets.

Ahunbabaev Kolkhoz contains no industry but owns all the equipment required to mechanize 75% of its work including five bulldozers, 20 tractors and sundry other farm equipment. It does not, however, have machine shops to repair its equipment or carpenter shops to build furniture and buildings.

Mr. Ata suggested that I narrow my questions to a single unit. So, arbitrarily, I asked about the 7th brigade.

That unit, Mr. Aka told me, pulling out a small black notebook from his pocket and flipping through to the right page, is composed of 30 workers who farm 100 hectares of land. During 1971, he said, it cultivated cotton on 80 hectares returning 3,200 kilograms per hectare which, Mr. Aka said proudly, was up from 800 kilograms per hectare some 40 years ago. The 7th brigade also grows jute on 20 hectares, averaging 20,500 kilograms of raw material per hectare or 5000 kilograms of pure fiber.

Divided amongst the members of the 7th brigade, is 4.5 hectares of land for tomatoes and other vegetables. Each worker within the brigade privately owns one cow, two calves, five sheep, eight pigs and any amount of poultry.

Needless-to-say, I had no way to check these figures which he read off from his little notebook, but I confess they sounded a bit theoretical or abstract to me. Perhaps he had been through this series of questions before.

A member of the 7th brigade receives an monthly salary of 160-170 rubles or approximately the salary of a junior research member at the Institute of World Economy and International Affairs, said my translator with some astonishment. Upon retirement, the pension depends upon previous jobs, but the worker is paid approximately 70% of the average of his old income. In addition to the salary, each member earns from the private land and supplements his diet to an extent worth perhaps 800 to 900 rubles a year. On this amount, he pays no taxes.

Little work is done during the winter on the *kolkhoz* land but the workers are kept busy in cattle breeding, etc. and do not work as part-time laborers in Tashkent. During the working season, the workers eat in brigade "cottages" out in the fields, which Mr. Ata said are equipped even with small libraries and television sets. Normally, the workers and their families live in individual apartments. All of them receive medical attention and schooling free.

Distributed among the workers on the collective farm are approximately 80 automobiles and 200 motorcycles which are privately owned. The *kolkhoz* plan calls for each family to own its own automobile by 1980. Today, President Aka said proudly, each family owns a television set, a radio and has a gas equipped kitchen.

When I asked how and for what amount of money the farmers had purchased these goods, Mr. Ata replied that the *kolkhoz* has six consumer goods shops but that individual members of the *kolkhoz* are free to buy goods in the neighboring city of Tashkent. Prices in Tashkent appeared to be, in the standard sample I later examined, uniform with those in Moscow, but the shops seemed somewhat more fully stocked in Tashkent than in Moscow. Where consumer goods are in short supply, availability is a probably a more crucial factor than price.

The kolkhoz has its own construction brigade but also has formed an alliance with other collective farms to undertake special building tasks. This appears to be the one remnant of the previous system, replaced in 1958, which pooled the most expensive and technologically oriented equipment on which the separate collective farms could draw. Since 1958, however, there are no independent "tractor" stations. All such equipment is now owned individually by each *kolkhoz*. Mr. Ata did not comment on this, but I understand from other sources that the reason for the change was that the collectives could not count on getting what they needed when they needed it; so their production suffered.

To join a *kolkhoz*, I was told, an individual or a family applies to the Chairman's Board. Once the Chairman approves the application, he brings it before a general meeting which must approve each application. Must an applicant be an Uzbek? I asked. Not by any means, he replied. The members, today, he rather proudly went on, include nine nationalities. Must he be a Communist? I asked. No, he shook his head. In the whole collective farm, only 93 of the members are members of the Communist Party. Well, given Communist ideology, I persisted, what happens to membership privileges upon the member's death? Property can be passed to heirs, Mr. Ata nodded. And this, he said, includes the private plot of land. Property other than the land can be sold to the farm.

To withdraw from the collective farm, a member must apply for and be allowed by the General Assembly to leave. Then he can sell his property to anyone he wishes. At that time, he severs all relationships and forfeits all rights in the collective farm.

Shortly after I left Ahunbabaev Kolkhoz, I asked to have a look at shops and a public market in Tashkent and Samarkand. Obviously, my information and observations were spotty and based on very limited exposure, but for what they may be worth, here they are.

First, the public markets. This is a form of economic activity which I gather does not exist in the northern, Europe-oriented parts of the Soviet Union. To a limited extent, I felt as though I were in Iran or Afghanistan. People looked the same in dress and some of the goods were familiar. But that was virtually the end of the similarities. In the first place, the markets were nearly empty. There was none of the bustle, noise or life one would see just a few miles to the south in Kunduz or Mazar-i Sharif. To give them their due, however, the Uzbekistan markets were cleaner than those in Afghanistan. The most striking difference, however, was that all prices were fixed and high. Individual farmers stood behind shelves or counters on which they displayed the produce of their tiny garden plots. Honey, pickles, nuts and dried fruit were the most common items for sale. It was the season of pomegranates and these were tremendously inviting. Overall, there were really not enough goods to make a fair comparison but I found most of the items to be comparable in price to the farmers' market in Los Angeles. Here, it was obviously availability rather than price that attracted buyers.

A question which constantly interested me was the extent of free enterprise within the Soviet system. Was each man, I asked, free to sell or not sell his goods. Oh yes, I was told by Professor Gantman, provided that he sold the goods for a fixed price. A small private joke developed between us. Professor Gantman would emphasize that the prices were "stable". There was no haggling, no gouging and no dumping. These were obviously of considerable importance and probably were emphasized by the long years of scarcity following the revolution. I could not escape the feeling that whatever stability existed was purchased by such state control as to make the goods very scarce. That was, to me, very impressive. To Professor Gantman, it was less so. It seemed normal to him but surprising to me that newspaper venders in their small kiosks, for example, were State employees. Men making deep fried pancakes filled with chicken and other delicacies, the equivalent of the tamale man in southern Texas, was also a State employee. This was totally different from what was normal not only in America but just across the Oxus river in Afghan villages just to the south of us.

I was really not able to do a thorough job of looking into department stores and shops either in Moscow or Leningrad or in Central Asia. But, I could not help noticing that the few I went into had some of the characteristics of a Potemkin village. Leningrad and Central Asia shops made a pretense of building a façade by exhibiting windows full of goods. Often, however, when one entered a shop, he found the shelves virtually bare. To test this, I would occasionally ask for an item I had seen in a grocery shop window – a bottle of preserved fruit, for example – only to be told that there was none.

In Tashkent, Professor Gantman and I did an elaborate, if brief, survey of consumer goods in two shops. I found that a black and white television set which at a typical "discount store" in America would cost on the order of $125 to $175 was nearly 400 rubles. Officially, the ruble is worth slightly more than $1. What that meant was that a television set cost approximately 10 working weeks for a member of the Ahunbabaev Kolkhoz. Some other items appeared to be approximately the same price as their European or American counterparts.

Cameras, for some reason that I could not fathom, fell in this category.

Professor Gantman and I had a running and discursive conversation – really more a jesting argument than a conversation – on these matters. Two things emerged rather sharply.

On the one hand, Soviet intellectuals, particularly those with a European or American exposure, like Gantman, feel defensive and sensitive on the relative backwardness, shabbiness and expense of Soviet consumer goods. I was repeatedly asked, not only by him but by almost every person I got to know in the Academy, whether I had found a meal, a hotel room, the clothing of the people I saw, etc. adequate. When I tried, as a good guest, to say something good about each item, I was sadly but firmly told "No, it is not good but it is better than it was and perhaps already adequate."

On the other hand, there was a clear awareness of the importance of State policy in dictating the availability and the price of consumer goods. One is immediately struck by the lack of advertising on the streets, in the newspaper and in the shop windows. Long lines form outside of a shop when it acquires even a small quantity of luxury items. That reminded me of my time in Oxford in the early 1950s. In Russia, what counted as "luxury" was perhaps not so august. The importation of a few pottery pieces, for example, in one shop caused a near stampede.

But not only are Russians appetites not whetted with advertising, various barriers are introduced to make the task of shopping unattractive. Bureaucracy is Kafkaesque. It is frustrating and difficult to attempt to do almost anything. From the point of view of the consumer, this makes even the most backward of the African countries appear advanced. However, one senses that this was probably true even under the Tzarist regime and is apparently stodily accepted by the population. At the same time, there is a healthy adjustment in the form of a grey market which enables people, at a price, to get extra services and to drain down their surplus income. The Russians call this "on the left hand". Here, as everywhere, corruption often takes the form of a peaceable and reasonably satisfactory means of adjustment.

In many conversations, on the faces of shoppers and in the very existence of long lines of would be purchasers, one sees evidence of the hunger for goods. People certainly appeared to hanker after many of the things of the West and secretly to relish the glamor of what is assumed to be a rich capitalist way of life.

At the same time, in the rather rarefied atmosphere in which I traveled, I found a sense of calm assurance, a lack of fanatacism but a fundamental dedication to the Communist system. Wherever possible, this was underpinned by a tendency to emphasize the ugly qualities of Western life, violence, social disruption, petty materialism, greed, etc.

In short, the differences between the Soviet and American ways of life, despite superficial similarities brought about by industrialization and modernization of our societies, remain and possibly even are growing. It is a parlor game to pick away at points of detail in each, but the fundamental reality is that each represents a system which works, generally I suspect with the acquiescence if not warm support of its people. The difficult task, I came away feeling was for the Russians and us to learn to understand, tolerate and perhaps even moderately enjoy our differences. We are as unlikely, I believe, to fundamentally alter their way of life as they to fundamentally alter ours. Convergence, it seems to me, is a dangerous myth; pluralism, a safer and much more interesting alternative.

Bearing in mind that these are superficial impressions from a two weeks visit, I offer them as the result of a rather unusual opportunity afforded me as a result of the lectures I gave at the Academy.

March 30, 1972

PART VII

VISIT TO CHINA

THE WORLD OF THE FUTURE

VISITORS TO CHINA HAVE adapted an old joke to explain their reactions. Hong Kong, they say, is for pessimists but Shanghai is for optimists; put another way, Hong Kong is now regarded as a city of the 20th century but Shanghai is the city of the 21st century. To a person, visitors report being stunned by the dynamism of Shanghai. Along the river front, one can still see the remains of the city of a century ago, much as the British, French and Japanese left it. The buildings, then so grand that they caught the imagination of visitors, now appear squat and even dingy while all around them rise huge skyscrapers. Starting with its population of about 16 million people, every statistic spells explosive growth. But, even modern Shanghai is now being put in the shadow by what used to be its kitchen-garden, its suburb, Pudong.

Hardly a decade old, Pudong is separated from old Shanghai by the Huangpu River. It is still in the process of being built on a triangular peninsula of about 570 square kilometers fronting on the sea and is the permanent home to nearly 3 million people.

To learn more about what is happening in Pudong, I accompanied a group from the Arizona State University's W. P. Carey School of Business to call on Du Jiahao, the governor of Pudong and a member of the Standing Committee of the Shanghai Committee of the Chinese Communist Party.

Getting to Pudong from Shanghai is not easy. Despite the construction of super highways and tunnels, lines of the most modern and expensive automobiles form a solid chain of traffic in both directions. At least one and a half million people move in both directions each day.

As one emerges from the tunnel under the river, he finds himself suddenly amidst buildings that dwarf even those of Shanghai itself. Few are as much as five years old.

Futuristic is perhaps the most apt word to describe the architecture. But since the government owns the land, it was possible to situate the new buildings in park land without concern, as in western cities, for price. Pudong regards itself as a "National Garden Town" and proudly proclaims that it has 108.8 million square meters of open land or an average of 19.6 meters per person. Most of this open space is beautifully planted with flowers, bushes and trees.

The Chinese government has made Pudong the symbol of its drive to modernize and "open-up." The extent to which it has succeeded is shown in two numbers: the first is that evaluating its production as though it were a separate country gives a yearly income of $18.1 billion. The second statistic is that whereas in 1990, it accounted for 8% of the income of Shanghai, today, despite the explosive growth also of Shanghai, it accounts for 24% and expects to hit 33% within a decade. That is, whereas a high rate of growth for most economies is about 4% to 5%, Pudong has grown at a yearly average since 1990 of 19.6%.

When the Government set out to make Pudong the model of what it wanted the new China to be, it hired some of the outstanding architectural firms of the world to design the buildings and parks. Naturally, each architect set out to build a monument. So the buildings became fantasies cast in concrete. One now under construction as a financial center is expected to be the world's tallest. The museum of science and industry was described by one observer as a futuristic space station, seeming not to rest on the ground but to hover over it. By building high rises, the planners left room for gardens below. And since the government owns all the land, it had no incentive, as in Western cities, to jam buildings together. So the impression of "monumentality" is heightened by the variation between fl at gardens and soaring towers.

Clearly a major purpose of the project has been to attract foreign investors. A major target group has been the overseas Chinese who over the last two centuries have moved to Indonesia, Formosa (Taipei) and North and South America. They are being shown rather than told that the future is here in China rather than in the places to which they or their ancestors went during the long times of trouble – the Boxer Rebellion, the Japanese invasion, the Civil War and the Cultural Revolution. All these are now in the process of being forgotten in the golden rush toward the future that Pudong symbolizes.

The overseas Chinese are not the only people being lured to Pudong. The international community is growing rapidly and is catered to by specialized schools for each major language group – English, German and French primary and secondary schools are available at European rates while Chinese language schools are free. A major new hospital complex is being developed in conjunction with the Harvard University Medical School. Sports facilities are about as good as they can get. And almost every fashion and retail company of note in the world has been encouraged to set up outlets.

But, of course, what really counts, Pudong Governor Du Jiahao told us yesterday is the move into the area of major international business organizations. To facilitate this and to keep a balance in production and living arrangements, Pudong has been divided into four areas including a free trade zone of nearly ten square kilometers which is projected to be the major transit point for trade in the Asia Pacific zone and for the vast Chinese market. The financial district has already attracted 71 of the world's major banks and other financial organizations and houses a stock exchange, a commodities exchange and a real estate exchange. The "Hitech Park" attracted $6.5 billion worth of foreign investment during the last few years. And, lest the area become solely a white collar area, a 20 square kilometer manufacturing zone, which last year produced $12.5 billion worth of goods and a housing development for the workers and staff, has been set up.

At the end of the Pudong triangle is the new international airport which is already one of the world's busiest, rivaling Chicago's O'Hare, New York's JFK and London's Heathrow. Far more than any of these, the airport appears as a huge park with hundreds of acres of roses, fruit trees, shrubs and lawns. And it is tied to the city by a $1 billion bullet train that moves at an astonishing 400 kilometers an hour and so puts downtown Shanghai just minutes away. In addition three metros are under construction. Private cars are limited to try to cut down on the already paralyzing traffic jams while buses regularly tour the area. But, addicted to bicycles, the Chinese still peddle to work in Pudong as everywhere else.

Perhaps most impressive of all, and a living symbol of the new China, the governor of this vast project quietly announced that he wants to go back to school himself to learn the skills he believes he needs to make the project work better. The Chinese respect for education is a tradition that remains strong among even the most striking signs of revolutionary change.

May 24, 2004

THE TOURIST'S DREAM

"HERE IN LIJIANG," Said Mayor He Zixing, "we believe we have the tourist's dream. This is an undiscovered place. It is not even in most guide books. But look around you. It is what remains of the Buddhist Western Paradise, a little piece of heaven on earth."

Lijiang is truly reality copying art: the town thinks of itself as Shangri-la from James Hilton's novel *Lost Horizons*. And Lijiang has good reason. For centuries, it was isolated from its Chinese, Burmese, Vietnamese and Tibetan neighbors. Towering more than 5,596 meters over its lush valleys are the glacier-covered Jade Dragon Snow mountains and nearby is one of the world's most spectacular river gorges, "Leaping Tiger," where rushing waters tumble down 3,600 meters toward the Yangtze river. Many of the most beautiful sites where springs and streams have cut ponds into the mountains are occupied by Buddhist monasteries and antique villages. Everywhere, the countryside is ablaze in the springtime with over 50 varieties of wild azaleas – some with trunks up to 40 centimeters in diameter – and rhododendrons, 5 species of camellias and 4 species of peony; they flourish amid dwarf pines, flowering crabapple and over 400 other varieties of trees and shrubs.

Although far to the south in China's Yunnan province, Lijiang is given a mild climate by being 2,400 meters above sea level. Rarely are the days hot, almost never is there snow in the valley and the evenings are only bracingly cool. Rainfall is plentiful, but most days are sunny and dry. High along the mountains there is a nearly perpetual mist that accounts for the luxurious plant life. Flowing through the valley is the Jinsha river which is noted for the gold mixed into its sands. If one stands on one of the many hills or mountains, he peers down onto countless terraces, marching like stair-steps down the valley walls. Each the product of thousands of manhours of labor, the terraces are constantly tended and planted with rice paddies.

The area around Lijiang was discovered and inhabited already millions of years ago in Paleolithic times and proudly preserves its own skeleton of a remote ancestor, the "Lijiang Man." The first historical records date to the period of China's "Warring States" – roughly contemporary with Classical Greece – but Lijiang was only sporadically affected by the march of events in Chinese history.. In recent centuries, it was a separate kingdom whose wang (king) showed his independence by building a replica here of the Chinese emperor's palace at Beijing. The palace, which was destroyed by the "Red Guards" during the decade-long cultural revolution (1966-1976), has recently been lovingly restored to its former gaudy grandure.

All around the palace is "Old Town," which has been designated a UNESCO World Heritage Site. Its nearly four square kilometers are laced with rushing canals, spanned by stone bridges and occasional precarious wooden plank walkways. Cobblestone lanes weave past hundreds of tiny shops and scores of restaurants, tea houses and inns. Washed by the Yu river, a tributary of the Yangtze, Old Town is impeccably clean. Street-sweepers must number in the hundreds; many are armed with what amount to long tweezers with which they search out the occasional scraps of paper. Automobiles, motorbikes and even bicycles are banned. Yet it is a functioning town with about 5,000 inhabitants and is far from the pollution that mars so much of modern China.

Unlike many old Chinese cities, Lijiang was not walled. The probable reason is that it was protected by its isolation, but, like many things Chinese, this sober explanation is embroidered by a legend rooted in the written Chinese language. The early city was made largely of wood, for which the Chinese character resembles a snow flake 木. When this character was combined with the character for city wall, a square, the resulting meaning was to be "besieged" 困. The citizens apparently thought it best not to tempt the gods!

Hit by a terrible earthquake in 1996, much of the new city was destroyed. The drama of the event brought international attention on a scale never before experienced. That started a rush toward modernization that figures most startlingly in the tourist industry. Ten years ago, according to Mayor He, Lijiang had only one more or less modern hotel; today, there are over 100. Tourists now arrive at the modern airport 24 kilometers outside the city. Last year, they numbered nearly four million, of whom about 8 in each 10 were Chinese. The others were mainly Japanese. The number of Europeans and Americans who have "discovered" Lijiang is tiny. Walking around Old Town, sitting in tea houses and restaurants and attending a brilliant concert of Naxi and Chinese music, I saw less than a dozen.

The town population contains some 26 of China's 56 nationalities. Although China's record of treatment of minorities has occasioned much criticism, the "minority peoples" as they are called here have the unique privilege of having more than one child for each couple. Most of them aggressively keep their national customs and continue to wear their native dress. Because of their value to the promotion of tourism, the provincial government encourages them by subsidizing music and dance performances in the town's many entertainment centers.

Probably the most interesting of Lijiang's nationalities are the Naxi (pronounced Nakh-si). Who the Naxi are, where they came from and much about their past are still unknown. A gentle, friendly people, they number today less than 300,000 and would, undoubtedly, have long since disappeared into the ethnic maw of China had they and their distinctive culture not been protected by China's vast distances. Lijiang is 3,780 kilometers from Beijing and 600 kilometers from the more accessible provincial capital, Kunming. Even more important, all around the town and its valley are high mountain barriers.

Naxi follow a religion known as Dongba. Dongba has neither priesthood, temples nor elaborate doctrine. Its followers believe in a pantheism in which all natural objects and forces are held to have "spirits." Thus, the Naxi venerate nature in all its variegated forms. Their ancient culture was recorded in pictographs which had no relationship to Chinese characters. A surprisingly well-preserved but nearly dead literature can today be interpreted only by Dongba shamans. In government schools, the modern inhabitants still study their language along side of the dominant Han Chinese language, Mandarin.

The Naxi are the anthropologist's dream. Their society claims to be matriarchal. Young women become free at age 13 to *mi rou huo* (experiment with love) and at 16 begin to take lovers but do not marry. Since their children do not know who their fathers are, they are cared for by their mothers' brothers.

The Naxi have a particularly strong musical tradition which gives rise in Lijiang to the Dongba Ensemble. Its performers, wearing traditional dress, are as captivating for their faces and antique instruments as for what they sing and play. Like many Chinese of his age, the conductor, Xuan Ke, is a victim of the Cultural Revolution. After years in prison where he underwent "re-education," he reconstructed his orchestra, strictly devoted to classical Chinese music and now performed by a vanishing generation of men in their late 70s and 80s. The ensemble, like much of traditional China hovers on the brink of modernization. How long it – and Shangrila – can survive is in doubt.

June 3, 2004

PART VIII

AMERICA

American Religious Fundamentalism

WITH PERHAPS AS MANY AS 50 million Americans describing themselves as Religious Fundamentalists, and allegedly almost half again as many calling themselves Evangelical Christians, I decided that I should try to understand better the beliefs by which they profess to live. Like most Americans, I had some exposure to Sunday School Christianity while I was growing up but never made a determined effort to study the Bible in the same "academic" way that, being concerned with Middle Eastern history, I studied the Qur'an. So I have recently tried to fill in this gap in my education. Here, I will share with you some preliminary findings.

The first thing that struck me was how extraordinarily different were the Old and New Testaments. I think that any outside observer, unless he was told differently before he began to read them, would conclude that they were the texts of separate religions. It is not only that the Old Testament portrays itself as the Holy Book of a single people, the Israelites, whereas the New Testament does not so constrict itself, but that the philosophy of the two appears contradictory.

Attempting to highlight this gap, some commentators have said that the God of the Old Testament, Yahweh, is a judge who is intent on warning his people and threatening them with punishments (Leviticus 26/14-46, Deuteronomy 28/15 ff) whereas the God of the New Testament lays down moral precepts and focuses not on "justice" but on love.

It is, incidentally, the Old Testament that is echoed in the Qur'an; the God portrayed there, Allah, is the stern judge of the Old Testament and some of the most vivid passages of the Qur'an speak of the punishments meted out to those who associated (Arabic: *sharaka/shirk*) other gods with The God (the literal meaning of Allah) or who killed or drove away the prophets (including Moses, Jesus and various Arabs) sent to them by God.

Apart from the philosophical aspects of the differences between the Old and New Testaments, we know that in the early days of the codification of

Christianity, there was a profound split between those who were more influenced by the Judaic traditions embodied in the Old Testament, notably Paul/Saul, and those who opposed them and who, to some degree, were influenced by Hellenism and emphasized the New Testament.

The most famous today of non- or anti-Judaizers are the people about whom we know (very little) from a collection of documents found in the Egyptian desert at Nag Hamadi. The people who wrote them were purged and mostly exterminated, but periodically over the centuries other groups took up aspects of their beliefs, almost certainly unaware of the original group but driven by their readings of the teachings of Jesus. Overall, however, it was the Judaizing tendency that predominated and survived. It was the Judaizing tradition that grew into both the Medieval Catholic church and, paradoxically, was adopted by most of the Protestant breakaway sects. Indeed, most of these groups became even more "Judaizing" than the Catholics; they sought to strip away the "accretions" of theologians, most of them of course Catholic, to "purify" their beliefs and to get back to the origins of what they assumed God intended. The followers of Luther and Calvin in Europe and the Puritans and Pilgrims in the New World were the more famous of these groups in Seventeenth century England and America, but there was a profusion of others that split away from these and other dissident sects and established themselves in America in the Eighteenth and Nineteenth centuries.

During his visit to America in 1831, Alexis de Tocqueville was astonished by the diversity of Protestant sects, each of which he observed, "adores the Deity in its own peculiar manner …there is no country in the world where the Christian religion retains a greater influence over the souls of men than in America…it must be regarded as the first of their political institutions." As he traveled round America during his nine-month visit, Tocqueville found that "Although the desire of acquiring the good things of this world is the prevailing passion of the American people… Here and there in the midst of American society you meet with men full of a fanatical and almost wild spiritualism [and] From time to time strange sects arise which endeavor to strike out extraordinary paths to eternal happiness. Religious insanity is very common in the United States."

Tocqueville would have been even more impressed by today's America with people pouring into megachurches or glued to their television sets to give televangelists audience ratings beyond rock stars...but certainly never forgetting the task of "acquiring the good things of this world" each for himself.

So what can we say about these groups in American society? Begin with the Puritans. Their most striking endeavor was their attempt to institutionalize their reading of the Bible into a set of laws, customs and government and to force others to live by their code in their theocratic virtual state, the Massachusetts Bay Colony. They attempted to avoid all compromise and to enforce rigidly the commandments of the Old Testament while paying relatively little attention to the New Testament admonitions on love, tolerance and generosity. They took to heart the injunction (Leviticus 25/18): "ye shall do my statutes, and keep my judgments, and do them..." That is, the believed that they had to enforce everything ordained in the Bible. Since they truly believed that it was the literal word of God, they could not pick and choose among its commandments. Each was obligatory. Yet, no matter how hard they tried, they were unable to carry all the Biblical injunctions into force. And when the first generation of "true believers" passed away, their children and grandchildren heaved a collective sigh of relief and set about dismantling the theocracy of their fathers.

It seems to me that their failure highlights the dilemma of contemporary Fundamentalists as well: just as the conflict between the letter of the commandments and the mores of Seventeenth century Anglo-American society – one is tempted to say the universal tendencies of human nature – precluded strict adherence initially and ultimately forced a willful if unspoken revision of Biblical injunctions, it is evident that modern Fundamentalists feel the need to pick and chose among commandments, obeying some and neglecting others. I think most would be shocked by the idea that they should actually shape their lives by the ordinances of the Old Testament. Let me illustrate:

<u>Punishment:</u> A number of ritual crimes are to be punished by stoning to death. Blasphemy is one. Does anyone among American Christians, no matter how strict, today advocate stoning a person to death? If asked, I imagine that most of our fellow citizen would think of this as the ultimate proof of the barbarism of those other Fundamentalists, the Muslims. Yet, there it is, undeniably set forth in the Bible as God's order. (Leviticus 25/14, 16 & 23)

<u>Apostasy:</u> Allowing one's children to stray from the path of true religion

(that is Judaism as defined in the Old Testament) by going over to other faiths, draws the death penalty. So Jews who convert to Christianity and Christians who become Jews are to be condemned. Conversion to Islam, Hinduism or Buddhism is literally unthinkable! What kind of punishment could match that crime? Does anyone in America today wish to carry out this sentence? The same injunction carries over to Islam, and Muslim Fundamentalists believe it must be effected; American Christian missionaries have always been horrified by this aspect of Islam, but it is also firmly rooted in Christianity. (Leviticus 20/2).

Ritual: Violations of ritual strictures should result in exile from the nation or community. For example, as set forth in the quaint Elizabethan English of the King James Bible, when a man "hath discovered her fountain, and she hath uncovered the fountain of her blood..." (Leviticus 20/18) – that is. engaging in sex while the woman has her menstrual period – results in the two people being driven into exile. Even without sex, her "flowers" (her menstrual discharge) contaminate everything on which she sits (Leviticus 15/16).

Conception: Women are sullied, ritually, for seven days after having "conceived seed." (Leviticus 12/2) And after giving birth to a boy child for 33 days but after a girl for only 14 days (Leviticus 12/4-5).

Working on the Sabbath draws the death penalty (Exodus 35/2). In the first case that came before the Massachusetts Bay Colony's courts on kidnapping Africans into slavery, the charge against the slavers was not kidnap per se but kidnapping on the Sabbath, a more serious (because Biblical) charge. Do Fundamentalists today wish to enforce this order? It does not appear so.

Lesser crimes: for them, a judge can order up to 40 lashes. Again, this is seen as one of the uglier aspects of Islamic theocracy. I certainly find it so. But, let us admit that it was a common form of punishment both in England and America until recently. Do Christian Fundamentalists feel bound to reinstitute it here? It is clearly obligatory by the words of the Bible. (Deuteronomy 25/2-3)

Crimes against deportment: Cursing one's father or mother, engaging in homosexuality (Leviticus 18/22 and 20/13), and loose conduct by the daughter of a high priest (Leviticus 21/9) draw the death penalty. The latter also by burning. Possibly some members of the Christian Far Right would not object to punishment but even they would have trouble with burning..

Social crimes: For example, adultery draws the death penalty (Leviticus 20/10). According to all the studies I know, Americans are in mortal danger!

Incest: At least one form of incest draws the ultimate punishment of being burned to death (Leviticus 20/10). Other degrees draw the death penalty (Leviticus 20/11-12), but not necessarily at the stake. I think most Americans, including Fundamentalists, would today think of burning at the stake as a ghastly memory of the Catholic Inquisition. They are right, but it was practiced by Protestants too. A horrifying response. Yes, but there is a good deal of evidence that incest is far more common even today than anyone would like to admit. And, devastating to families as it undoubtedly is, there are circumstances when the Bible permits it: to ensure the continuation of a lineage, daughters are allowed to trick their fathers into getting them pregnant by getting them drunk and seducing them. (Genesis 19/31-36)

Virginity: when a young woman gets married, she is to be tested. To prove that she is a virgin, her "tokens of virginity," blood on the sheet on the nuptial bed, should be exhibited to the community. (Deuteronomy 22/17). I have never seen this mandatory test performed in America or Europe, but it is still common in the Islamic world as it was in the West until quite recently.

If the woman fails this test, "Then they shall bring out the damsel to the door of her father's house, and the men of her city shall stone her with stones that she die." (Deuteronomy 22/13-21) She faces a similar fate if during her engagement she lies with another man: "Then ye shall bring them both out unto the gate of that city, and ye shall stone them with stones that they die." (Deuteronomy 22/23-24) That would certainly interest the police almost anywhere today.

The current campaign to get young people to abstain from sex before marriage is certainly encouraged in the Bible. Here the Old Testament and contemporary social mores are somewhat in accord. But, what happens to a young woman who lapses from this standard is rather different. Today, if she conceives, her baby may be discretely put out to adoption while her parent or parents probably register disapproval. Their reaction should be quite otherwise according to the Bible. By its orders, she should be stoned to death.

Birth out of wedlock: An illegitimate child is ritually unclean and beyond the pale surrounding the community although the nature of his birth is hardly his fault. "A bastard shall not enter into the congregation of the Lord; even to his tenth generation shall he not enter into the congregation of the lord." (Deuteronomy 23/2). Given the nature of American frontier society and the immigration into the country of a large portion of our citizenry in circumstances that were not conducive to marriage sacraments, few of us could "enter into the congregation of the lord" today.

Aggression among the citizenry: capital punishment is mandated for killing a person. (No distinction between homicide and murder is drawn in Leviticus 25/17 or Exodus 21/12.) Lesser crimes, presumably arising from fist fights, are to be punished "Breach for breach, eye for eye, tooth for tooth, hand for hand, foot for foot...burning for burning, wound for wound, stripe for stripe...life for life." (Leviticus 25/19-20; Exodus 21/23-25) If a woman intervenes in a fight, even to try to save her husband, and grabs the "secrets" of the other man, her hand is to be cut off. (Deuteronomy 25/12)

Breaking and entering: If a thief is caught in the act and killed, "there is no blood [to be] shed for him." Exodus 22/2. Shooting a housebreaker in Texas gets public approval; in New York it gets a prison sentence. It seems that Texas is far more Biblical than New York.

Serial punishment: whenever one does wrong, he is not the only one to be punished. Exodus 34/7 warns that punishment will be inflicted upon his "children, and upon the children's children, unto the third and to the fourth generation."

Marriage outside the community effectively cuts both spouses off from the community; they cannot eat at the bride's father's table (Leviticus 22/12). Marriage is legal only within the ethnic community (Genesis 24/3); trans-ethnic (and certainly trans-racial) marriage is condemned (Ezra 9/12 and Nehemiah 10/30). Both participants in such a union may be legally killed (Numbers 25/1-9). Clearly, American society would be decimated if this rule were enforced.

Slavery: Leviticus 25/45-46 says that you may enslave the children of strangers who live among you. Others can also be enslaved. For example, a thief who cannot make restitution for what he has stolen should be sold into slavery. (Exodus 22/2) However one is enslaved, there is no Biblical basis for abolishing the institution.

Sexual discrimination: if a man seduces a married slave girl, she is to be whipped while he is to pay a small penalty (a sacrificial ram) to the priesthood. (Leviticus 19/20). In practical terms, a man is regarded as twice a woman (Leviticus 26/3-4). This is the same as Islamic Law. Sexual differentiation must be maintained so no cross dressing, thus presumably today's women should never wear masculine clothing. No more blue jeans for women! (Deuteronomy 22/5). Liking pure cotton and pure wood, without nylon addatives, I am happy that there is to be no mixing of materials in clothes. (Deuteronomy 22/11) but that regulation would play havoc with the rag trade.

Outcasts: Various categories of people whom most of us think should be protected and encouraged to realize their full potential in as meaningful a life as possible – and for whom we have written laws and have created charitable institutions are to be protected. Not so in the Old Testament. They are to be ostracized: in the community envisaged in the Old Testament, that means forbidding them from participating in religious observances. Thus, no one with a "blemish" can worship. This category of deprived or sick people includes (Leviticus 21/18-21) the blind, the lame, "he that hath a fl at nose, or anything superfluous, or a man that is brokenfooted or brokenhanded or crookbackt, or a dwarf, or that hath a blemish in his eye, or be scurvy, or scabbed, or hath his stones [testes] broken." Priests are given the task of checking the community and weed out the ill in order to ostracize them. (Leviticus 13-14)

Us against them: No pretense is made for concern with "mankind" or "all humanity." God is solidly on our (the Hebrew in the Old Testament) side against all the others. "I will send my fear before thee [the Hebrew people], and will destroy all the people to whom thou shalt come." (Exodus 23/27); "And I will send hornets before thee…"(Exodus 21/28); and you will be allowed to engage in sharp practice such as usury provided that you practice it only against outsiders. (Deuteronomy 23/19-20). This explains the enormity of the recent crime of the Jewish crooks who defrauded members of the Jewish community. Perhaps it also casts a light on the idea of the Jewish state: foreigners cannot be admitted "forever" into the community (Deuteronomy 23/3) so the only religiously feasible solution to the Palestine problem is the "two-state" pattern. In the one state, the non-Jews, the Arabs, can never achieve full membership. Well, there is a way they can: by waiting. A mixed Hebrew- Egyptian only has to wait three generations. (Deuteronomy 23/8) Negotiators take note! Almost that length of time has passed since 1948.

Animals: curious to the modern ear, if an ox gores a person, it is the ox that is to be stoned to death (Exodus 23/27); if a man (or a woman) forces an animal into an act of sex, the person and the animal are both to be put to death. (Leviticus 20/15-16)

Appearance: Much is made in the press today about Muslims growing great bushy beards. To many of us, this is the most evident symbol of Islam. In the immediate aftermath of the attack on the World Trade Center in New York in 2001, having a beard got an unfortunate Indian Sikh (thus, of course, a Hindu) attacked and lynched by an American mob who considered him to be a Muslim. Beards are not generally favored among Americans today, but the Old Testament orders believers: "Ye shall not round the corners of your heads, neither shalt thou mar the corners of thy beard." (Leviticus 19/27 and 21/5) That Sikh was more "Biblical" than most of us.

Witches are treated as actual, and the community is told, "Thou shalt not suffer a witch to live." (Exodus 22/18) So what the New England Puritans did in rooting out witches, as they decided some of their neighbors were, was in accordance with Biblical instruction.

As to government, the proper role and attitude of the moral person is obedience and silence: "Thou shalt not…curse the ruler of thy people." (Exodus 22/28) Some Americans, at least, would like to reinstitute this commandment, but it is clearly in opposition to the American Constitution.

Art and Sculpture: Exodus 20/4 enjoins "Thou shalt not make unto thee any graven image, or any likeness of anything that is in heaven above, or that is in the earth beneath, or that is in the water under the earth." This injunction was carried over into Islam, but, I believe at least most of us would agree, we are grateful that it has not deprived us of art and sculpture.

It would be fascinating to see the results if a poll were taken among American Fundamentalists today, without, of course, the Biblical references, to see how many of these injunctions would be regarded as just, reasonable, or even enforceable. Or, if enforced, how many of the Fundamentalists would themselves escape draconian punishment.

My hope for the first question – and hunch for the second – is that the answer would be "few."

November 15, 2005

The Neoconservative "Virtual Coup d'État"

THE SEPTEMBER 11, 2001 terrorist attacks on the World Trade Center in New York and the Pentagon in Washington D.C. brought to power in the US government a remarkable clique of ideologically-driven, intricately associated and carefully prepared men. The Israeli newspaper, *Haaretz*, identified them as "a small group of 25 or 30 neoconservatives, almost all of them Jewish, almost all of them intellectuals." Although appointed to office by the incoming Bush administration, so dramatic was the advent to supremacy of the neoconservatives that some have called it a virtual coup d'état.

To a degree unprecedented in the American political experience, the neoconservatives now guide the policies of President George Bush and his National Security Council; work in tandem with and under the patronage of Vice President Dick Cheney; virtually control the world's most powerful military establishment; and neutralize contrary opinions in the CIA and the Department of State. When they were unable, at least initially, to persuade American intelligence organizations to say what they wanted to hear, they founded their own "Office of Special Plans." It is on the neoconservative map and to their specifications that American foreign policy operates.

Working in conjunction with the Republican leadership in the Senate and House of Representatives, forming close and ties with what President Dwight Eisenhower called "the military-industrial complex," to secure massive funding for their "think thanks" and using the power of office to silence critics, the neoconservatives today form a virtual government within the American government. For men of such vast and unprecedented power, directing military campaigns around the world, affecting the economic relations among the nations and setting out a program intended to dominate the world of the twenty-first century, the neoconservatives are astonishingly still little known.

Who are these men? What motivates them? How are they linked together? How do they draw strength from the Bush administration in the White House, the Republican leadership in Congress and a powerful segment of American business? How have they managed to silence their opponents and to convince a majority of Americans that they are not radical revolutionaries but traditional conservatives? What are they now doing and what do they intend to do? These are the questions I set out to answer here.

When the Bush administration came into office, few observers paid much attention to the neoconservatives. Practically none were members of the traditional Washington "power elite." Unlike most of the Bush appointees, few came from the business world, some were former academics and, as mainly Jews, none were members of the clubs where much of Washington business is conducted. Outsiders they certainly were, but they had already been adopted by the men who would become key members of the administration. Vice President Dick Cheney and Secretary of Defense Donald Rumsfeld had served with some of them in the 1980s in the Reagan and first Bush administrations; then, in the 1990s, while out of office during the Clinton administration, they had worked together on projects aimed at shaping American policies for a return to power. In managing the transition from the Clinton to the Bush administration, Cheney used them as his agents and put many of them in key positions throughout the government.

Consequently, although few journalists or members of Congress paid much attention to them in the first months of the new administration, the neoconservatives were in position when the terrorist attack of September 11, 2001 gave them their opportunity. After the attack, they alone of all the men and women around the new president had a plan, were determined to carry it out and were in position to do so. Confused and frightened by the events, the inexperienced President Bush, encouraged by the Vice President and the Secretary of Defense, virtually turned over to them the reins of government. They avidly seized those reins and plunged immediately into a war of retaliation against the Taliban hosts of Usama bin Ladin'sal-Qaida movement.

The apparent (or at least initial) success of Afghan war tended to solidify their influence over President Bush and his team, and, despite their misgivings, over the military general staff. Even normally sceptical journalists were swept along. The neoconservatives not only seemed to have answers for all the presumed threats to American security but, because of the September 11 attacks, they had caught the wave of public opinion. The Afghan campaign evoked an instinctive patriotic response, was overwhelmingly popular in America and provided a reassuring demonstration of American power.

Useful as it was in consolidating their power, however, Afghanistan and the al-Qaida movement were never the central issues for the neoconservatives. From the first day after the September 11 attacks, as the clique's leader, Paul Wolfowitz, informed President Bush, their real target was the regime of Saddam Husain in Iraq. For them, Afghanistan was merely a first step, a sort of trial run, for what was projected to be an almost unlimited campaign – known among the military high command as "the long war" –with projected attacks on Iraq, Syria, Lebanon, Libya, Iran, Somalia and the Sudan. This was what they had been planning since the 1980s and finally were in position to begin to carry out.

To understand what they planned and why, I must introduce the individuals in the clique, show the sources of their inspiration and account for the intensity of their commitment to reshaping the Middle East and ultimately the whole of the Islamic world. And...beyond.

The first man to attract press attention was the newly appointed Deputy Secretary of Defense, Paul Wolfowitz. The instinct of the journalists was right: Wolfowitz was the most influential, most strategically placed and most experienced of the two dozen or so members of the group.

Born in New York City in 1943 of Polish Jewish parents, Wolfowitz went to Washington as a young man right out of college. Then, after a short government apprenticeship, he enrolled in graduate school at the University of Chicago. At Chicago he fell under the influence of two men who would set the ideological parameters of the whole neoconservative movement, the Cold War strategist Albert Wohlstetter and the then-little-known political scientist Leo Strauss.

Armed with a doctorate in political science from Chicago, Wolfowitz returned to Washington in 1972 for his first stint at the Pentagon. Already recognized as a young man of great ability and firm anti-liberal ideology by senior members of the Reagan administration, he was quickly promoted. In the crucial years from 1977 to 1980, he was made head of the State Department's Policy Planning Council. From that post, the first President Bush moved him to the post of assistant secretary of state for East Asian and Pacific Affairs and then sent him as American ambassador to Indonesia.

When Bill Clinton became president, Wolfowitz joined the Republican exodus from government. With his doctorate from Chicago, his wide government experience and his connections among the Republican Establishment, he was an attractive choice as dean of School of Advanced International Studies (SAIS) at Johns Hopkins University. SAIS proved to be a seedbed to prepare men of his persuasion for the Republican return to power under George W. Bush.

As a charter member of the Bush administration, Wolfowitz seems to have become an intimate friend of the President. Experienced, intelligent, a hard-liner and armed with a plan, he offered the administration a program that fit both its needs for a coherent foreign policy and its political leanings. Washington gossip had it that Bush flirted with the idea of naming him Secretary of Defense but, warned that he was too controversial for such a high profile post, made him deputy to the more "Establishment" Donald Rumsfeld, over whom, it was expected, his influence would be strong.

In an almost perfect theatrical scenario, Wolfowitz was in his office on September 11, 2001 when the Pentagon was hit by the third terrorist-hijacked aircraft. He had just told a visiting group of Congressmen that "we are in for some nasty surprises" from overseas enemies.

In response, Wolfowitz knew just what to do. In fact, he had single-mindedly planned what to do for over a decade. The attack gave him the opportunity. He took it. "That weekend, in front of the president at Camp David," wrote Sam Tanenhaus in the July 2003 *Vanity Fair*, "he would startle some officials by advocating an attack not on al-Qaeda's bases in Afghanistan but on Saddam Hussein's Iraq."

Wolfowitz was surprisingly outspoken on the reasons for the war with Iraq. While everyone else in the Bush administration focused on the presumed search for weapons of mass destruction, he dismissed that justification as simply "bureaucratic" – it was simply the one issue on which everyone could agree. Nor did he pay much attention to other then-current justifications such as Saddam's tyranny or the charge, already known to be spurious, that Saddam was supporting terrorism. Rather, he zeroed in on the key strategic issue, oil. At the Asia security summit in Singapore, he startled his audience by ascribing the war to the fact that Iraq was "swimming" in oil. As newsworthy as it was, it differed completely from what the administration was saying, his remark was not reported in the American press but was picked up only by two German newspapers. It was shocking, but, as we shall see, it was not the deeper reason he favored an attack on Iraq.

Less experienced and less coherent in his strategic thinking than Paul Wolfowitz, his friend and colleague, Richard Perle, was appointed chairman of the Pentagon's influential Defense Policy Board. Unlike Wolfowitz who was willing to devote himself entirely to government, Perle kept his hand in business. For him, that meant the arms trade. These activities were to involve him in a conflict of interest scandal, his second, which forced him to resign as chairman in 2003. The scandal was "papered over," in the Washington phrase, and he remains a member of the Board.

An ardent Zionist and personal friend of Israeli Prime Minister Ariel Sharon, Perle is also a member of the board of directors of The Jerusalem Post, a "resident fellow" of the American Enterprise Institute and a director of several other neoconservative lobbyist and policy organizations.

Like Wolfowitz, Perle was a protégé of Albert Wohlstetter with whom he had worked at the Pentagon-funded RAND Corporation in the 1960s. Moving to Washington, Perle took a different route from that followed by Wolfowitz. He worked as legislative aide to the most influential of the defense-oriented members of the Senate, Henry M. Jackson (whom Washingtonians called "the Senator from Boeing"). As Senator Jackson's aide, he drafted the "Jackson/Vanek Amendment" which made American trade with the Soviet Union dependent upon its allowing emigration of Russian Jews. This act made possible the emigration of Natan Sharanksy who is now deputy prime minister of Israel. That, in addition to other acts, cemented Perle's close relationship with the Israeli government.

During the Reagan administration, Perle moved from Capitol Hill to the

Pentagon where he became one of eleven assistant secretaries. There he quickly established a reputation as the most bellicose hardliner: in the last phases of the Cold War he was nicknamed "the prince of darkness." Colleagues have described him as a "one man wrecking crew of arms control negotiations."

During his time in office, Perle became enmeshed in his first conflict of interest, a pattern that was to mark his career. In this first brush with the law in 1983, he allegedly arranged an American arms contract for which service he was paid by an Israeli armaments manufacturer. Also, showing his affinities with Israel, Perle was suspected (but never formally charged) with passing classified documents to Israeli agents. A deputy, whose appointment he had arranged, Steven Bryen, was actually indicted by a grand jury on suspicion of espionage.

Wolfowitz and Perle have drawn the most attention from the press, but the other members of the neoconservative group, while not so well known to the public, collectively occupy what Lenin would have seen as the "heights of power" in the Bush administration.

Traditionally, in the American political system, the vice president played almost no role. In the Bush administration, however, Vice President Dick Cheney has been virtually co-president. In the transition to office of the administration, he placed most of the neoconservatives in office; then, once they were in office, he actively promoted their programs. In a series of public pronouncements, he argued for invasion of Iraq, charging that Saddam Husain was armed and ready to attack America and was working in league with Usama bin Ladin's terrorists.

When the established intelligence organizations found no proof for his accusations, he made unprecedented frequent visits to CIA headquarters to put pressure on analysts to come up with answers acceptable to him. More generally, his office, under the direction of his chief of staff, Lewis Libby himself a neoconservative, became the command post of the clique.

Meanwhile, at the Pentagon, two key neoconservatives orchestrated moves under Deputy Secretary Paul Wolfowitz. Douglas Feith, as under secretary, ranks just after Wolfowitz as the third highest official of the Defense

Department. Like other members of the clique, he is known to be close to the Israeli "hard right" and, while out of office, served as an adviser to then Prime Minister Binyamin Netanyahu. Working under him is Stephen Cambone as under-secretary of defense for intelligence who took the lead in the campaign to attack Iraq.

Working for Cambone, in turn, is one of the most important but least known of the neoconservatives, Abram Shulsky. Before it was clear that Vice President Cheney's pressure on the CIA would be successful, Shulsky was empowered to set up a new organization, the "Office of Special Plans," which aimed essentially to supplant the entire American intelligence evaluation system. Although never admitted, its task, effectively, was to prove the neoconservative charge, aggressively pushed by Vice President Cheney, that Saddam Hussein, in conjunction with his ally Usama bin Ladin, was poised to attack the US with a full arsenal of weapons of mass destruction. None of this has proved to be true, but it formed the justification for the invasion of Iraq.

In the State Department neoconservative John R. Bolton was appointed Under Secretary; his task, according to Washington gossip, was to neutralize Secretary of State General Colin Powell and to silence the State Department's own intelligence evaluation organization, the Bureau of Intelligence and Research. Bolton brought into office as his senior adviser another neoconservative, David Wurmser, who was also a sometime adviser to Israeli Prime Minister Benjamin Netanyahu. Mr. Wurmser moved over to the office of Vice President Dick Cheney in September 2003. His wife, Meyrav, an Israeli citizen, was co-founder (with Colonel Yigal Carmon, formerly in Israeli intelligence) of the Middle East Media Research Institute (MEMRI) which has acted in America as a propaganda outlet for the Israeli political "hard right."

Also at the State Department, Richard Haass was made director of the State Department's Policy Planning Council, a post in which he served until becoming, in 2003, president of the Council on Foreign Relations.

Meanwhile, at the White House, Elliot Abrams was put in charge of the Middle East at the National Security Council. Best known for his role in the Iran-Contra affair, one of the more sordid campaigns in recent American history, Abrams was charged in 1991 with two counts of withholding information from Congress; he pleaded guilty and was convicted but was pardoned by the first

President Bush. Perhaps because of this controversial background, the White House has kept him somewhat under wraps and will not allow the press to interview him. A long-time colleague and friend of Wolfowitz and Perle, he is married to the daughter of two of the movement's founders. As significant as his role in forming foreign policy, Abrams has also acted as a link between the neoconservatives and the Southern Christian Fundamentalists who support their policy toward Israel.

In the American political system, the "heights of power" also exist outside government in business, the academic community and ideologically receptive "think tanks." Among these influential actors move frequently and easily. One of the most important of these sometime officials, sometime publicists, has been James Woolsey, the former CIA director. Others like William Kristol, editor of the influential Neoconservative journal *The Weekly Standard*, are active supporters in the press.

Also playing a shadowy role has been another neoconservative, Zalmay Khalilzad. He alone was in position to be "the" expert on Afghanistan, but he was far more than a regional figure. Trusted by Vice President-elect Dick Cheney, he was assigned the highly sensitive task of placing the whole neoconservative group in power during the transition to the Bush administration.

An Afghan-American, Khalilzad is an anomaly among neoconservatives as he was born a Muslim. He may be described as the "odd man in." Son of a wealthy Pashtun family, Khalilzad studied in Kabul under royal patronage and then attended the American University of Beirut before doing graduate work at the University of Chicago. There, like Wolfowitz, he studied under the nuclear arms strategist, Albert Wohlstetter. After getting a doctorate in 1979, he briefly taught at Columbia with President Jimmy Carter's former National Security Council director, Zbigniew Brzezinsky. Then, in 1984, he got a one-year fellowship at the State Department where he worked with Wolfowitz at the Policy Planning Council. In the first Bush administration, Wolfowitz got him appointed assistant deputy undersecretary of Defense for policy. During Clinton's two terms, he left government and took up a post at the RAND Corporation where he founded the "Center for reater Middle East Studies."

While at RAND, Khalilzad became a consultant to the California oil company, UNOCAL, which was then attempting to get approval from the

Taliban government to construct a multibillion dollar gas pipeline across Afghanistan. Like another neoconservative, Richard Armitage, he lobbied the Clinton administration to take a softer line on the Taliban, writing in *The Washington Post* astonishingly that "The Taliban do not practice the anti-U.S. style of fundamentalism practiced by Iran." After the Taliban was implicated in the attack on US embassies in East Africa, UNOCAL ended its pursuit of the concession. Then Khalilzad abruptly changed his position and began calling Taliban Afghanistan a "rogue" state.

After the overthrow of the Taliban regime, Khalilzad was made special US envoy (effectively proconsul) to Afghanistan where he picked Hamid Karzai to be the Afghan ruler and cleared the way for him by more or less forcibly dissuading the former king to serve as an interim president, which was the desired option of the Afghan Grand National Assembly, the *Loya Jirga.*

Well before these events, Khalilzad began advocating the overthrow of Saddam Husain. His opportunity finally came in late 2001 when Vice President Dick Cheney got him appointed special assistant to the president for the Gulf area. That gave him a base of power in the National Security Council and from there he was appointed the president's "special envoy and ambassador at large for free Iraqis." In this position, he played a key role in the build-up to the invasion of Iraq and again served as a "king maker," fostering the campaign for Iraqi leadership of the neoconservatives' candidate, Ahmad Chalabi.

So rapidly did the Neoconservatives emerge and achieve power in the American government, that only now is their provenance or inspiration becoming clear. And since they form such a tightly knit group, it is possible to deal with them as a whole. The record shows four sources of inspiration:

The first source of inspiration was the Trotskyite Communist movement which some joined in their youth. As they got older, they jumped completely across the political spectrum from the extreme Left to the radical Right. In the jump, however, they retained a commitment to a version of one of Leon Trotsky's guiding ideas, that world politics could be shaped and controlled by "permanent revolution." His opponents, Trotsky thought, would never be able to mount effective opposition because they would be overwhelmed by an avalanche of insurrection. It was a compelling idea and the neoconservatives both adopted it and adapted it. In their hands, permanent revolution was transformed into "permanent war." As one member of the group, former CIA director James Woolsey, put it in a speech at UCLA on April 2, 2003, "This fourth world war, I think, will last considerably longer than either World Wars I or II did for us. Hopefully, not the full four-plus decades of the Cold War."

Permanent war has been embraced as the key element of the Neoconservatives' ideal American policy. Under the threat it poses and the actual destruction it entails, they believe, foreign opponents would be cowed or destroyed while domestic opponents would be unbalanced, carried along in a tide of events and silenced by the imperatives of patriotisim. War would thus give them what Trotsky thought revolution would give Communism: irresistible power.

The second source of inspiration on neoconservatives came from the work of a little-known professor of political science at the University of Chicago where Wolfowitz and Khalilzad studied. Leo Strauss, a German émigré, excited (and flattered) his protégés by his belief that he had found hidden meanings in Greek philosophy that could be understood only by a small elite — namely them. He also justified "the natural right of the stronger" which the neoconservatives later used to justify America's right to suppress any state that could challenge it. That is, through preëmptive war.*

It followed that, if war is requisite to a successful American policy, attempts at arms control would only weaken America. This conclusion came from the University of Chicago and RAND Corporation Cold War neoconservative strategist, Albert Wohlstetter. A determined believer in the threat of force, Wohlstetter is credited with coining the chilling phrase for his brand of foreign policy, "the delicate balance of terror." He is also said to have been one of the models for Stanley Kubrick's and Terry Southern's character "Dr. Strangelove."

* A decade after this paper was written, Anne Norton published her Leo Strauss and the Politics of American Empire (New Haven: Yale University Press, 2004) which is one ofthe better studies of the man, his ideas and the movement he inspired.

In addition to the commitment to permanent war and belief that they formed a small esoteric elite directing a policy of unilateral force, the neoconservatives are motivated by patriotism to Israel. And not just to Israel or to Zionism in general, they identify with the extreme Right of Israeli politics and the Zionist movement. In this, they were inspired by the radical Zionist leader, Vladimir Jabotinsky, who in the 1930s advocated employing "muscular Zionism" to conquer all of "Eretz Israel." Picked up by the Likud party, Israel's extreme Rightwing movement that grew out of the terrorist organizations Irgun Zeva'i Le'umi and Stern (LEHI), muscular Zionism is now personified by Israeli Prime Ariel Sharon. It is with him and his ideas, and not with such cosmopolitan and humane Israelis as Uri Avnery, that the American Neoconservatives identify themselves.

Closely bound together by these shared beliefs, the neoconservatives have established an interlocking series of memberships in well-financed, politically-engaged, pro-Israeli "think tanks." While the half dozen or so of these institutions are legally separate, their boards of directors, benefactors and appointees overlap. They are perhaps the supreme example of what in American business schools has come to be called "networking." Thus, a "scholar" of one may be a director or fellow of another, and individuals are often directors of two or more. This tight organization and outreach enables neoconservatives to be mutually reinforcing.

The largest of the group is the American Enterprise Institute (AEI) in Washington which in 2000 was said to work on a budget of $24.5 million. Richard Perle, Michael Ledeen, Joshua Muravchik, Michael Rubin and other neoconservatives are listed as "resident fellows" or "resident scholars" and active in it have been or currently are Vice President Dick Cheney and Secretary of Defense Donald Rumsfeld.

The Washington Institute for Near East Policy (WINEP) is somewhat smaller. In 2000, it received tax-deductable grants of $4.1 million. Its founding director was Martin Indyk who previously had been the research director of the leading pro-Israeli lobby, the American-Israel Public Affairs Committee (AIPAC). In 1993, hurriedly made an American citizen, Indyk became special assistant to President Clinton and "senior director" for the Middle East at the National Security Council. Later, he was made ambassador to Israel and assistant secretary of state for the Near East and South Asia. WINEP is now directed by Dennis Ross who had served as President Clinton's coordinator for the Middle East peace process. Among the fellows and staff it shares with other neoconservative institutes are Robert Satloff (director of policy), Patrick Clawson (director of research), Michael Rubin and Martin Kramer.

The Jewish Institute for National Security Affairs (JINSA), which was founded in 1976, runs on an annual budget of about $1.5 million. Virtually amalgamated with another group, the Center for Security Policy (CSP), it has an impressive board of directors including Vice President Dick Cheney and Neoconservatives Paul Wolfowitz, Richard Perle, Under Secretary of State John Bolton, Under Secretary of Defense Douglas Feith, Michael Ledeen, Former UN ambassador Jeanne J. Kirkpatrick, Stephen Bryen, Joshua Muravchik, Eugene Rostow, former CIA director James Woolsey plus a number of retired generals and admirals.

Perhaps no other group has so relentlessly campaigned for "regime change" in the Middle East, against arms control and in favor of the so-called "Star Wars" program as JINSA/CSP. Not surprisingly, it gets most of its funding from defense contractors, conservative foundations and far-Right individuals. It has placed nearly two dozen staff, fellows, directors and advisers in senior Bush administration positions.

The Hudson Institute was founded in 1961 by Herman Kahn who was then the leading advocate of nuclear war with the Soviet Union. It maintains an active program on the Middle East under the leadership of Meyrav Wurmser, whose husband David is the senior adviser to Vice President Dick Cheney. Richard Perle is one of its trustees.

The Middle East Forum, the smallest of the group, is also the most strident. It uses tax-deductable donations of about $1.5 million yearly to carry on a vigorous campaign in favor of the Likud government of Israel. The key members of its staff are also associated with the AEI and/or with WINEP. The Forum's director, Daniel Pipes, whom President Bush recently named to the Board of the United States Institute of Peace, organized a program known as "Campus Watch." The purpose of Campus Watch is to expose and attack American university professors who have been critical of Israel or American policy in the Middle East. His colleague, Martin Kramer (former director of the Moshe Dayan Center at Tel Aviv University and a fellow of WINEP), has broadened the attack to include the Department of State much as the old China Lobby attacked China specialists in the McCarthy era. Supported by this multiplicity of organizations and tightly bound ideologically, by friendship and even by marriage ties, the neoconservatives have made use of the opportunities given them by the September 11 attacks to achieve what former Under Secretary of State David Newsom has termed "a largely peaceful coup d'état." By "wrapping the group's embers in the flag" he went on, it has "created an atmosphere of intimidation on the basis of patriotism with the aim of muting criticism and contrary views."

Working under the auspices of Vice President Dick Cheney and Secretary of Defense Donald Rumsfeld, the Neoconservatives today form a powerful network extending throughout the American government which they have backed up, as I have shown, by an even more elaborate network of think tanks" in and around Washington. Operating as a virtual government within the government, we should ask, what do the neoconservatives want to achieve?

They have partially answered the question themselves not only in the actions they have recently espoused in the Bush administration but also in a sequence of policy papers they have written over the last fifteen years. Assembled by Joseph Cirincione for the Carnegie Endowment for International Peace, these papers form a graphic agenda for the war against Iraq and plans to engage in future wars. Because they affect the lives of people all over the world, they deserve the closest attention. The major documents are the following:

1) In 1992, infuriated by the first President Bush's halting of the first Gulf War, Paul Wolfowitz, then under secretary of defense for policy, supervised the drafting of the "Defense Policy Guidance" document. The objectives it set were to assure access to Persian Gulf oil, to prevent proliferation of weapons of mass destruction and to combat threats of terrorism. The document called for preëmptive attacks on actual or would-be rivals – that is, any nation that could challenge American preeminence — with the United States ready to act alone if "collective action cannot be orchestrated." The document so shocked Wolfowitz's colleagues that someone leaked it to *The New York Times*. Embarrassed, the administration retracted it. But, that was only a temporary setback. Today, the basic concepts have been incorporated in the "U.S. National Security Strategy"

document of September 2002.

2) In her book *Saddam Hussein's Unfinished War Against America*, neoconservative Laurie Mylroie popularized the neoconservative charge that Iraq carried out the 1993 World Trade Center bombing. Richard Perle endorsed the charge, calling the book "splendid and wholly convincing." While there is no evidence for the charge, it was the beginning of a concerted campaign to bring about an attack on Iraq.

3) In 1996 Richard Perle, Douglas Feith and David Wurmser joined in writing a paper for the newly elected Likud government of Israel calling for a "clean break" with policies of negotiating with the Palestinians and evacuating the occupied territories. Reaching outward, they urged that Israel should strike preemptively to weaken the government of Syria and overthrow Saddam Hussein.

4) In 1998, 18 neoconservatives including Elliot Abrams, Richard Armitage, John Bolton, Paula Dobriansky, Zalmay Khalilzad, Richard Perle and Paul Wolfowitz, many of whom later became key officials of the second Bush administration, joined by Donald Rumsfeld, wrote President Bill Clinton urging him to bring about the removal of Saddam Husain. In the year 2000, the "Project for the New American Century," organized by William Kristol and Robert Kagan, made bellicose recommendations which also have been incorporated in the U.S. National Security Strategy.

6) Immediately after the September 11 attacks, Paul Wolfowitz and other neoconservative officials urged President Bush to attack Iraq and helped arrange that the general staff of the armed forces begin planning that campaign.

On April 3, 2002, those neoconservatives not yet in government wrote President Bush saying, "You have declared war on international terrorism, Mr. President. Israel is fighting the same war…Israel's victory is an important part of our victory." They urged both unconditional support for Ariel Sharon's suppression of the Palestinians and for an immediate attack on Iraq.

While foreign affairs was the main focus of their activities, the neoconservative agenda had a domestic component. Its initial aim has been to silence critics by charging them as unpatriotic. However, a more complex set of aims is emerging. In the domestic campaign, the leading role has been played by the head of the Middle East Forum, Daniel Pipes, who, as I mention above, before being appointed by President Bush to the United States Institute of Peace, mounted "Campus Watch." Through a vigorous campaign, mainly on the internet, Campus Watch encouraged faculty members and students to report on the speech, teaching or political action of the 1,400 professors and the several thousand students of Middle East studies in American universities so that dossiers could be developed on them.

Some supporters of the neoconservatives took more aggressive action. When she was singled out for attack by "Campus Watch," Glenda Gilmore, a professor of history at Yale University, said "I know [about the campaign of harassment and intimidation] because I have been branded a traitor. I wrote an oped piece for the Yale Daily News and received death threats and rape wishes…" Others have reported what appear to be a well-orchestrated campaign of constant harassing telephone calls and letters.

The McCarthyite scheme Pipes began has now been taken up by the U.S. House of Representatives which, on October 21, 2003, unanimously passed a bill essentially along lines laid out by Pipes's colleague Martin Kramer (in his book Ivory Towers in the Sand). The bill, not yet approved by the Senate, would create a government board to monitor teaching in federally-funded academic centers. Approval by the Senate would be required to make the House bill law, but it has been enthusiastically endorsed by Senator Rick Santorum (R-Pa). Senator Santorum has written a bill with a name that only George Orwell could have imagined, "Ideological Diversity," that would cut federal funding for thousands of colleges and universities that permit teachers, students and student organizations to criticize Israeli policies. Santorum's Republican colleague from Kansas, Senator Sam Brownback, wants to go even further: he would create what would amount to an ideological police force, a federal commission, to investigate what he loosely terms anti-Semitism.

Real anti-Semitism, of course, is an ugly disease and deserves opprobrium. The neoconservatives and their allies, however, have used the charge as a sort of "weapon of mass destruction" to silence critics, even American Jewish critics, of Israelis and their policies. As some of those attacked have pointed out, no reasonable person would suggest that criticism of the Zimbabwe regime would open anyone to the charge of being "anti-black" or criticism of the Saudi Arabian government would make him anti-Arab. Moreover, it would be absurd to charge the many Israelis who vigorously criticize the government of Ariel Sharon with being anti-Semitic. But, in American politics, the charge of anti-

Semitism is both grave and difficult to refute.

Ironically, anti-Semitism has itself been a feature of neoconservatism. So hostile is Pipes to Arabs (who of course are also Semites) that he famously damned the "massive immigration of brown-skinned peoples, cooking strange foods and not exactly maintaining Germanic standards of hygiene." All Muslim fundamentalists, he went on, "must be considered potential killers."

Such moves as Messrs. Pipes, Kramer, Santorum and Brownback propose are bound to create, as did the earlier McCarthyism, an atmosphere of fear, mutual suspicion and the loss of the spirit of free inquiry which has been the pride and hallmark of the American academic world.

November 18, 2003

The Unending Neoconservative Crusade

THE NEOCONSERVATIVE POLICY on Iraq has been largely implemented. Where else might the Neoconservatives seek to commit American power? They have already staked out two targets, Syria and Iran.

The key man in each is Michael Ledeen who paradoxically has the same last name, with a slightly different orthography, as Usama bin Ladin. It was Ledeen who came up with the crudely-put but fundamental policy directive: "every ten years or so, the United States needs to pick up some crappy little country and throw it against the wall, just to show the world we mean business."[1]

"This doctrine of what they call preemption or preventive war," wrote the noted American historian Eric Foner,[2] "…is exactly the same argument that the Japanese used in attacking Pearl Harbor."

Syria is the "crappy little country" the Neoconservatives most love to hate. Syria is important to them because the Israeli government fears that it will be unable to impose its terms on the Palestinians while Syria remains a significant Arab power. Consequently, as Sharon and his colleagues see it, with Iraq now subdued, Syria should be next in line. This is the policy Richard Perle, Douglas Feith, third ranking official in the Defense Department, and David Wurmser, now key adviser to Vice President Dick Cheney, advocated in their 1996 "clean break" paper for the newly elected Likud government. It is in this context that the October 5th Israeli air strike against targets in Syria can be evaluated. Its purpose, obviously, was to warn the Syrian government not to support the Palestinian resistance movement.[3] We now know that the U.S. Department of Defense has infiltrated covert Special Forces "hunter killer" teams inside of Syrian territory[4] and that units from Iraq have made repeated forays across the frontier.

What about Iran? As Marc Perelman has written, "A budding coalition of conservative hawks, Jewish organizations and Iranian monarchists is pressing the White House to step up American efforts to bring about regime change in Iran...The emerging coalition is reminiscent of the buildup to the invasion of Iraq."[5] In the place occupied by Ahmad Chalabi as the Neoconservatives' candidate to rule Iraq, Reza Pahlavi, son of the former shah, has become the favorite to take power in Iran. For his part, the young pretender has established "quiet contacts with top Israeli officials...[including] Prime Minister Sharon and former Prime Minister Benjamin Netanyahu..."

As in the Iraq campaign, publicity for the new venture is being provided by William Kristol's Neoconservative journal, *The Weekly Standard.* More significant is that Michael Rubin, WINEP's specialist on ways to overthrow the current regime, has joined Abram Shulsky's "Office of Special Plans" to ensure that the intelligence reports substantiate the Neoconservative policy. Also active in the background is Michael Ledeen who has been arguing that the current Iranian regime is on the point of collapse. It just needed a push. America should give it, he said in a lecture at JINSAA on April 30, 2003: "the time for diplomacy is at an end; it is time for a free Iran, free Syria and free Lebanon."

Ledeen and other like-minded men have set up the "Coalition for Democracy in Iran" to gather the forces, funded by Congress, needed to bring about "regime change." Just as they advised President Bush that Iraqis would greet incoming American troops with flowers, so the Neoconservatives assert today that Persians will sing and dance in the streets.

The list of targeted countries does not end with Iran. Pakistan, Libya, Somalia and The Sudan have been mentioned by military planners. A trial balloon was even launched to see the reaction to a drive against Saudi Arabia.

Before he left the chairmanship of The Defense Policy Board, Richard Perle convened a meeting on July 10, 2002 to hear a briefing from an advocate of an attack on Saudi Arabia. Laurent Murawiec, from the RAND Corporation, described Saudi Arabia as "the kernel of evil, the prime mover, the most dangerous opponent" of the United States in the Middle East.[6] He recommended that "U.S. officials give it an ultimatum to stop backing terrorism or face seizure of its oil fields and its financial assets invested in the United States." The results were predictable: the Saudis immediately withdrew several hundred billion dollars from America and decided not to allow American troops and aircraft to operate against Iraq from Saudi territory.

Undaunted, the Neoconservative magazine, *The Weekly Standard,* published almost simultaneously with the briefing an article entitled "The Coming Saudi Showdown," and its message was picked up by the American Jewish Committee's magazine, *Commentary*, with an even more explicit article entitled "Our Enemies, the Saudis." But, perhaps partly because the Bush family and major business supporters of the Bush administration are deeply involved there, Saudi Arabia seems to have been dropped as an immediate target.

However, many potential targets remain.

North Korea was high on the list until the catastrophic cost of a campaign against it became clear. Since it is thought already to possess nuclear weapons, and forward units of its army are within artillery range of the South Korean capital, Seoul, it appears to have bought itself immunity from attack. Indeed, the roughly 30,000 American troops stationed there are more hostage than deterrent.

The lesson that at least some governments are likely to draw from the contrast between Iraq and Korea is that "regime survival" is to be gained by acquiring a nuclear weapon quickly and secretly. Owning a bomb is Korea's ticket to safety; getting caught while allegedly trying to get one was Saddam's death warrant; many believe that had he waited to attack Kuwait until he had a bomb, he might still be in power.

Iran today may be pondering these lessons as it reflects on its response to the Neoconservative agenda. It is probably not alone. Many other countries must be weighing their options. Whatever their immediate response, it is clear that the longrange effect is increased insecurity for the whole world.

Meanwhile, American troops are already committed in The Philippines in a protracted guerrilla war; are likely to be drawn more heavily into operations in Colombia; and today maintain bases in at least 14 African countries and dozens more in Central and South Asia, the Pacific and Latin America. American troops today actually serve in 130 countries. These are facts, but fantasies remain: the wilder ones are said even to include mainland China.

To turn fantasies into plans is nearly automatic: the job of staff officers of any army is to plan for future contingencies. To turn plans into action, however, requires major political decisions. Are such decisions even conceivable?

No one, of course, can possibly know. What we do know are two contradictory positions: on the one hand, the American military command has told the administration that the burden is unsustainable with conventional forces. It has begun to develop "usable" nuclear weapons for small wars.[7] This new policy, overturning a decade-long ban, has virtually sounded the death-knell to the bipartisan policy of phased nuclear weapons control. Almost as disturbing as this weapons trend is the Pentagon's newly announced policy of creating special military organization for "postwar stability operations."[8] The creation of such a standing force with its own headquarters presupposes a need for it, perhaps beyond Iraq and Afghanistan. "…it could be used for small-scale interventions in Africa and elsewhere," a government official told *The Washington Post* on November 24, 2003.

A slightly different approach has been taken by critics of the Neoconservativeled "Crusade;" it is to put American unilateralism aside and attempt to enlist the support of at least 70 countries. To date, the response has been meager. As public opinion polls have made clear, current American policy is deeply unpopular almost everywhere.[9] In an effort to counter this, at least with a few governments and to attempt to restructure $100 billion in Iraq's foreign debts, President Bush appointed former Secretary of State and Secretary of the Treasury James A. Baker III as his personal emissary. Before Baker had even had a chance to make contact with those heads of state he planned to see, however, Deputy Secretary of Defense Paul Wolfowitz undercut his position. Wolfowitz announced, allegedly without clearing his statement with the State Department, that those countries that had not supported American action in Iraq would not be eligible, on the grounds of "national security and national defense purposes," to bid on contracts to reconstruct the country.[10] This announcement, which was retroactively approved by President Bush, set off a storm of controversy around the world.[11] Unilateralism or limited multilateralism is clearly here to stay.

This American policy, however, may also be financially "unbearable" according to many economists including the respected investment banker, Felix Rohatyn."[12] As historians have pointed out what ultimately destroyed Rome and other empireswas not military defeat but financial collapse. In America, the agenda laid out by Neoconservative James Woolsey for a generation of "permanent war" has been estimated to cost at least $15 trillion.

Will President Bush find that unattractive if not unbearable?

The omens are not favorable.

In a speech at the American Enterprise Institute, he called the Neoconservatives "some of the best brains in our country..." But, his opinion could change. As he begins to see the degree of hostility their policies have engendered, as the casualty rate in Afghanistan and Iraq rises and as the American presidential elections draw nearer, perhaps he will find the Neoconservatives a political liability.

Ultimately, the American public and Mr. Bush must realize, as the conservative English journal, *The Economist*, editorialized, that the Neoconservatives are not conservatives. They are radicals. Their agenda adds up to a world-wide crusade. With all its historic anti-Muslim connotations, it is precisely the word most calculated to perpetuate movement down the path desired by the Neoconservatives, permanent, unending war.

Mr. Bush and his election advisers will have to decide whether the public will accept that path.

1. Quoted by Jonah Goldberg, "Baghdad Delenda Est, Part Two," *National Review Online*, April 23, 2002.
2. *Columbia Daily Spectator*, November 7, 2002.
3. *The International Herald Tribune*, October 6, 2003.
4. Julian Borger, "Israel trains US assassination squads in Iraq," *The Guardian*, December 9,2003.
5. Marc Perelman, *Forward*, May 16, 2003.
6. Thomas E. Ricks, *The Washington Post*, August 6, 2002.
7. William J. Broad, *The International Herald Tribune*, August 4, 2003 and Paul Harris, "Bush plans new nuclear weapons," The Observer, November 30, 2003.
8. Bradley Graham, "Pentagon Considers Creating Postwar Peacekeeping Forces," *The Washington Post*, November 24, 2003.
9. The results of the poll were not published in the American press. For them see Peter Preston, "Can might alone earn a nation love, trust?" *The Guardian*, December 10, 2002.
10. Jackie Spinner, "Only Allies to Help with Rebuilding," *The Washington Post*, December 10, 2003.
11. A summary of editorials from the world press was published in *The Guardian* of December 12, 2003.
12. *The Financial Times*, June 10, 2003. His article was not published in America. 13 May 2003.

THOUGHTS ON TORTURE

Guest Editorial on "Informed Comment"

DISPLAYS OF NAKED IRAQI prisoners being humiliated in American military prisons have shocked not only Arabs and Europeans but also most Americans. They need not have been surprised – torture is not new.

Widely practiced by the Germans during World War II, it was standard French procedure during the Algerian war. One of the most influential books on that war, written by Colonel Roger Trinquier, a French paratrooper, argued that torture is to "modern war" what the machinegun was to World War I. Horrified by what they learned was happening, French critics called torture the "cancer of democracy." Using it, the French not only destroyed their claim to legitimacy in Algeria but also nearly destroyed French civil life and almost provoked a civil war.

If there was a lesson to be learned by the Algerian experience, it certainly was not heeded.

Influenced by the French wars in IndoChina and Algeria – Trinquier's book was translated and made available by the CIA — American soldiers and "special forces" used torture in Vietnam. Israeli troops and security forces have employed it for years against the Palestinians. Routinely, almost casually, it is employed in prison systems throughout Africa, Asia and Latin America. It is more common in Europe than most would admit. From Greece, under the regime of the colonels, came a macabre episode: the men employed to torture prisoners, complaining of long hours at low pay, went on strike.

Studies of torture raise two questions that lie behind the horrifying images in the press in recent days: "does torture work?" and "why do governments do it?" If the objective of torture is to get information, as is usually said, the answer to the first question, does torture work, is "sometimes." The French in Algeria found that they could "break" a prisoner and find out where his colleagues were hiding or what kind of an operation was being planned. Often, of course, the person being tortured would just say what he thought his tormentors wanted to hear – anything to get them to stop. He knew that he was likely to be killed after he had been "debriefed." But they had ways to check what he said and, keeping him alive, increased his pain if he lied.

Even if torture often failed to get the sought-after information, it was still an attractive option for those seeking information. Why? I think there are two answers: first, security officers think it might work and they have few other options. Much more important and far more disturbing, I believe, is the second reason: Some circumstances almost demand brutality.

A century of careful medical and psychiatric studies tell us that the juxtaposition of absolute weakness and absolute power provokes violence. The bound and hooded Iraqi prisoners lying naked on the floor of Abu Ghraib prison invited attack.

So shocking is such a statement that few of us have wanted even to consider it. To deal with its implications requires us to reëxamine the very concept of our humanity. So to get around that inhibition, some scientists, like the Nobel Prize winner Konrad Lorenz, posed "our" problem to animals. What he found was that those animals that have "weapons systems," like the lion with its claws and fangs, have evolved to practice restraints. Had they not learned to curb the use of lethal force, their species might not have survived. So the winner in a fight between lions will make ferocious noises but will usually stop short of killing the lion he has just knocked down. In contrast, those creatures, like that symbol of peace, the dove, that do not have lethal weapons have not evolved to practice restraint. They did not need to. So they don't. Lorenz observed a dove actually torturing another to death.

Our evolution, students of violence assert, has made us more like doves than lions. True we have massive weapons systems but they are external; over the tens of thousands of generations of our evolution, our ancestors were not forced to incorporate them into our behavior. So, we are not like lions. When we see in the pictures of the Iraqi prisoners cowering on the floor, bound, hooded and defenseless we notice that the upright, armed and dominant guards do not show compassion. Rather, they feel stimulated to attack.

Surely, we say and would like to believe, these are aberrations. Normal people do not do such things. Alas, there is much evidence to the contrary.

Cultural, religious, ethnic and epochal differences do not seem to influence the willingness of human beings to torture others. Torture has been reported almost everywhere among peoples of all religions, cultures and historical experiences throughout recorded history. However, it does have a racial or ethnic dimension: men are more likely to torture people of a different color than their own kind. Setting them apart is often easy. In Vietnam, American soldiers derided yellow-skinned people as "gooks" and in Iraq, brown-skinned people as "ragheads;" Germans despised the dark-skinned Gypsies and Jews as *untermenschen*; Israelis treat brown-skinned Palestinians similarly and so on. Regarding the victim as unimportant because different makes it easier to attack him. Remember the phrase, "Asians feel no pain."

Can ways be found to prevent these deeply ingrained and pervasive horrors?

One that is generally ineffective, at least in the short term and probably even in the long term, is education. The Germans of the 1930s were certainly among the most educated people in the world; yet they herded their fellow citizens into the brutal concentration camps where they were often tortured to death. The French of the 1950s were a model for the rest of the world in their dedication to "culture," reason and intellect; yet some of their most educated and refined people were implicated in their sordid policies. Even more surprising, some Frenchmen who had fought in the underground against the Nazis to preserve French freedom, like Albert Camus, saw no incongruity in doing to the Algerians what the Nazis had been doing to them. The French too built concentration camps. And the record comes to challenge us. Clean-cut, decent American college graduates who felt strongly about civil liberties at home were prepared to do to Vietnamese what they abhorred in America. What they abhored in America is itself, of course, also grisly: we have only to look at photographs of the crowd of White American participants at the lynching of a black man to see how thin is the veneer of civilization.

So I think that the best we can say is that education is necessary but not sufficient.

Two actions offer some hope to those who wish to stop torture.

The first of these is to demand "transparency" in whatever prison systems are believed to be necessary everywhere. This means that we cannot close our eyes and ears to abuses as we naturally would prefer to do. Nor can we accept any justification for torture. Those who do it and those who authorize it must both know for certain that they will be held responsible for a crime against humanity. That is, to be clear, a crime against both the humanity of the victims and against us whose humanity they thus debase.

The second action is much more important because more likely to work. It is that we must make as a major goal of national policy the solution of situations that promote the use of torture. An obvious first step is one we have traditionally espoused but rarely sought to effect: it is to work toward a world which recognizes that a basic political right is that of self-determination. Unless or until this is at least approached, we can expect others to fight for it with every means at their disposal, including what we regard as terrorism, and that those who oppose them will similarly use the means at their disposal: guerrilla warfare/terrorism/"freedom fighting" will be met with various forms of suppression including torture. Only when it is no longer "needed" as a means of suppression will torture be put aside.

History shows us that this is what happens. Take just one example. After centuries of severe repression including torture of prisoners, England finally granted Irish independence. Torture then stopped because it was not longer useful.

A policy embodying the quest for self determination will not be easy to implement. Nor will the benefits appear quickly. There will be shortfalls and setbacks. But in evaluating such difficult actions as will be required, we must bear in mind that, however much some people will advocate the shortcuts that torture will seem to offer to avoid attacks or break terrorist cells, doing so not only will impact upon the victims but also brutalize those who employ or sanction it. That was the real lesson of Algeria. It should also be a lesson of Iraq. That is what the pictures from Iraq show us – not just the anguished faces of the prisoners but the gloating smirks of the torturers.

Lest those looks appear in our own mirrors, we simply and finally cannot "afford" torture.

May 6, 2004

Talk at Bennington College

I WANT TO TALK WITH you today for just an hour. To bring order into my remarks, I will divide what I have to say into four categories: where we are coming from; where we now are; where we are going; and what you can do about the conditions that will shape your lives.

First, Where we are coming from:

At the end of the Second World War, Americans had cause to be euphoric and we were. Most of us believed that the future was ours. Ours was the American Century.

The Cold War changed the world for both America and Russia. We like to think that we "won" the Cold War, but the history of events since it ended shows that we both really lost it. This is because of its impact on both Russian and American societies and economies. To match one another, we both were turned into militaristic states and our economies suffered. In America, we can trace our transformation – perhaps uniquely in history – to a single piece of paper. Paul Nitze's National Security Council Paper, "NSC 68" convinced President Harry Truman that we could sustain our economic growth and ensure full employment by applying John Maynard Keynes' emphasis on the role of government in the economy but apply it in the military or "security" sphere. President Truman signed it as a basic U.S. policy doctrine on September 30, 1950. This was a program that the wise American specialist on national policy, Chalmers Johnson, has termed "military Keynesianism." (His "blowback" trilogy should be required reading in every American college.)

Following the new strategy, the government used the power of the purse to divert our then efficient and productive civilian economy to the military. So profound was this change that by 1960s we were no longer competitive in manufacturing and distributing most civilian goods. Our civilian industrial plant was allowed to become obsolescent or even to deteriorate. Worse, our managerial skills, on which we had prided ourselves, atrophied. The new American business ethos no longer emphasized competition because military contracts were often awarded without bid and were frequently awarded at cost-plus.

While our industrial plant and managerial skills began to decay. Japan forged ahead. From Japan we bought our TV sets, our cameras, our computers, our cars. We were no long competitive in the world market. It is now estimated by the American Society for Civil Engineers that it would take $1.6 trillion just to bring our industrial plant and our supporting infrastructure back up to world standards. This was graphically demonstrated last week. As you probably read the automobile companies' executives have said that without massive government help they could no longer compete in the world market.

What happened was that we turned our skills and investments to military production: in the 1950s and 1960s, we were superb in weapons and space-related production but could no longer compete on civilian goods. We stopped trying to make many things our people wanted and were buying. Even those things we put out under American labels, like TV sets, were often just American wrappers on Asian components.

I watched this happen. I visited Japan in 1962 as a guest of the Japanese government. While there, I was taken on a tour of the Canon and Toshiba plants. I expected to see how cheap Asian labor was making possible the Japanese boom. What I saw was quite different. Labor was cheaper, it is true, but what really made the difference was automation, skilled technique, able management and intelligence.

Our companies didn't need these things: their market was increasingly our government. So why bother with making cameras or washing machines when you could make jet bombers or rockets. The profits were larger and distribution was no problem. Management could afford to be lax since mistakes could be repaired by overruns.

Even our universities fell into this trap. Getting government contracts was such an easy way to raise money. It was far easier than soliciting private support and it allowed expansion into new fields. Look at the budgets of even the private universities: Harvard, MIT, Chicago and many others came to rely on government subsidies for a large part of their expenditures and in return spent much of their intellectual energy on "security"-related studies. We even created new universities and dozens of research institutes for these activities. America was becoming a very different place than it was in 1945.

And the world began to see America in this new light. The America of 1945 was almost universally beloved — that is not too strong a term. When, as a young student, traveling through Asia and Africa, I was often in danger: everyone in a village would come nearly to blows to determine who could entertain me. Today, America is feared and hated in much of the world. Now, if I went back to those same villages, I would risk being shot.

Second, where we are:

To discuss where we are, I am going to have to use a number few of us – that is those of us not studying astronomy – ever heard before: trillion. When I was a student in the 1940s, I got more or less used to hearing the number million. Then when I went into the government, I had only just got used to billion. As I returned to academic life, I was astonished when trillion came along. It is still difficult for me to imagine a trillion dollars. You can think of it as a pile. If you stack up dollar bills, a trillion dollars will be miles high. But I would like to think of it in another way: a trillion dollars would provide health care for the 47 million Americans without it plus giving quality pre-school education to every American child and make college feasible for every American student. Just the interest on a trillion dollars (according to the World Bank) would eliminate starvation and malnutrition or provide primary education for every child on earth.

That speaks about our government's priorities. What about us? How do we treat our economy?

First of all, we do not save. Privately and governmentally, we just borrow. We borrow from each other. Our National debt went up 70% under Bush administration; we also borrow from foreigners. We had borrowed about $3 trillion as of a year ago; now our foreign debt is much more. Our projected government deficit for this year is $410 billion. Our children and grandchildren will inherit the debt of this last 8 years.

But you will hear, we are earning enough to cover it. Unfortunately that is unlikely. According to the chief of our Central Bank, the Federal Reserve, economic growth will stagnate or even fall; Over 6 out of each hundred Americans who are trying to find jobs are out of work. About that many more have given up trying. Americans are losing their houses in record numbers. About one in each five owes more on mortgages than his house is worth. That is, over ten million homeowners have lost their investments in their houses and foreclosures went up nearly 60 percent last year.

What has caused all this?

Partly it is our individual fault – visit the malls to see one part of the answer. The British were once derided as a nation of shopkeepers; we are a nation of shoppers. We are real "junkies" in our shopping for things we don't need.

But a part of the answer to our growing debt is our militarism: Our current Military budget is $541 billion. That is 58 cents of every dollar spent by US Government and it is more than the combined defense budgets of all other countries in the world and more than our combined spending on education, environment protection, justice administration, veterans benefits, housing assistance, transportation, job training, agricultural support, energy and economic development assistance.

We are told we need to spend this huge amount because our National Defense Strategy lays out our determination and "right" to make pre-emptive warfare, indeed to attack any country whose dominance even of its own neighborhood thwarts us. Coming into office in 2001 the Bush administration leaked information and that it was ready to "target" up to 60 other countries. Is this just posturing? Look at the sequence: the war in Afghanistan led to Iraq which led for the second time to Somalia and now has us attacking the territory of Pakistan and planning an attack on Iran. Are these necessary for our safety? Are we gaining or losing security by our involvement in them. I will briefly review them:

Consider, first, Afghanistan:

If anyone still thinks in historical terms, we should remember that the Afghans inflicted the worst defeat on the British Empire it suffered in the 19th century and they virtually wrecked the Soviet empire in the 20th. Are we more "successful?" With our overwhelming firepower, we have killed about as many Afghans as the Russians did, about one million, and needed far fewer soldiers to do it. So far we have suffered about 500 dead while they lost 15,000. Our invasion shattered what the Russians did not destroy of the Afghan economy. So the only remaining industry is the drug trade of which Afghanistan furnishes about 90% of the world's market. Our enemies, the Taliban, had banned it, but now they need the income they derive from it to fight us. And, sober observers report that the Taliban is returning both to favor and to geographical control. They are now not far from Kabul. Meanwhile, the warlords, whom the Taliban chased away and whom we have either supported or tolerated, are again running much of the country.

Consider, second, Iraq:
One and a half million Americans soldiers have served in Iraq. We now have about 140,000 men and women there. In addition, another group which few Americans have even heard about, also is there: we have some 180,000 private contractors in Iraq at a cost so far of $85 billion. Over all, the Iraq war has cost us through the end of this fiscal year $922 billion spent in direct (that is, in Congressionally-appropriated) outlays and perhaps $3 trillion in costs to our economy at home. These costs have been disguised from us by government borrowing from us (our national debt has risen 70%) and from foreigners (our government has borrowed from them more than $3 trillion).

But these are the trivial costs. The tragic costs are measured in blood and misery. We have now lost over 4,100 dead. Then there are the wounded. The Bush administration admits to about 25,000 wounded but that is wildly, even ridiculously, wrong: this year alone some 300,000 servicemen and –women are in treatment. The real total of wounded is probably at least 500,000 of whom over half have severe brain damage – concussions – which will cause memory loss, severe headaches and confused thinking, for the rest of many of their lives. They will be a burden on their families and communities. 22,000 of them tried to commit suicide this year. No one knows – yet – about the number of cases of cancer that will develop from the use of depleted uranium bombs and shells, but the numbers could be very high. In addition to the impact of these events on wives and children, just consider the cost of treating the wounded. The best guess is that, over their lifetimes, it will consume $1 trillion.

If you find these figures hard to believe, consider that from the effects of the 1991 Gulf War, which lasted only 100 hours, 300,000 men and women are now claiming disability payments.

Then consider the Iraqis: According to a study made by the Johns Hopkins School of Public Health, we or Iraqis in the conditions we have created have killed at least 600,000. That figure is as of two years ago. The figure today is perhaps over a million and we have made or helped to make about 3 million into refugees. The physical damage is literally beyond count but could be several hundred billion dollars.

More important is the "collateral" damage: we have shattered the cultural heritage of the world's oldest civilization, watching and doing nothing while its great antiquities museum was gutted and the national library trashed.

Worse we have destroyed the social contract between the people and authorities.

Let me dwell on this intangible issue: if any American city lost its social contract – a concept that our founding fathers and other 18th century philosophers well understood – the entire American army could not keep a semblance of order. That is what has happened in Baghdad. And we cannot control it with the world's most powerful army. The Neoconservatives advised our government that, by invading Iraq, we would create democracy. Instead, Iraq is a destroyed society.

We are told also that we are "winning" – whatever that might mean – and that the "surge" is working: But the fact is that while violence has died down somewhat – only 654 Iraqis were killed in May this year, making Iraq still the most dangerous country in the world – it is not more troops or a new strategy that have reduced casualties. It is the fact that neighborhoods have already been ethnically cleansed (so Iraqis are fighting less among themselves), we have built huge concrete barriers between them and we have drawn our troops back into secure bases from which they sally mainly in aircraft or tanks. These are tactical accommodations but do not lead to long-term solutions. In fact they lead in the opposite direction.

As even our former proconsul and current ambassador to the UN, Zalmay Khalilzad secretly wrote to President Bush, "the proposal to send more U.S.

forces to Iraq would not produced a long-term solution and would make our policy less, not more, sustainable." Mao Tse-Tung, Ho Chi Minh and Vo Nguyen Gap could have explained why: we have provided more targets and angered more natives. Our much-vaunted counterinsurgency ("CI" in the military acronym) is just a replay of what we did when we lost the Vietnam War; even the sales pitch is the same.

Consider, Third, Somalia:

Somalia had less to destroy than Iraq. It is a small country. Few of us have even heard of it except in the film "Black Hawk Down." There we were shown our decent young men trying to free the Somalis from a bunch of murderous, raping thugs, the warlords. We failed and President Clinton pulled the plug. We got out. The warlords came back. Then the Somalis did a remarkable thing: they got rid of the warlords themselves without our help. But we didn't like the way they did it. Like most Africans and Asians, they had given up on Marxism and had fallen back on religion. Their Islamic fundamentalism had some of the ugly features we have seen in Afghanistan. But we didn't care about that. What bothered us was that we feared that their Islam would be hospitable to the al-Qaida people. So we sicked our Ethiopian friends whose government is Christian and who have long wished to dominate Somalia, on them. Actually we didn't just urge them to attack their neighbor; we joined in on the attack, not only with money and arms but also with our own aircraft, ships and troops. So we destroyed the Somali Muslim government, the "Union of Islamic Courts."

Back to "Black Hawk Down:" on the heels of our forces and the Ethiopians came the same murderous, raping warlords, now more or less our allies. So Somalia today is a crippled society, but one that bitterly hates us. So bitter is their feeling against all foreigners that even aid workers are now targets. Somalia too is a destroyed society with a shredded social contract as a result of our actions. We did not create terrorism in Somalia – the warlords did that – but Somalis' hatred of them has now been redirected toward us.

Lastly, reflect on Terrorism:

Americans are obsessed by terrorism as a result of the September 11 attacks. There is, of course, reason to fear terrorism because of its unpredictability and randomness. But let us try to analyze it. Consider these facts:

• More Americans were killed by lightning and very many more by traffic accidents in the year of the attacks than by 9/11;

• We have never been opposed to "terrorism" as such. Our ancestors won the Revolution against the British using terrorism as a major tactic and we aided and abetted Afghan terrorism against the Russians in the 1980s. Then we renamed terrorists "freedom fighters" and, most important;

• Terrorism is a tactic used by the weak when they have no other recourse.

When a country is invaded and crushed, we should know from history, patriots take up arms. Regard the action of the Greeks and French in World War II, the Algerians against the French in the 1960s and our ancestors in the American Revolution. Since they were unable to defeat heavily armed military units, they resorted to hit and run tactics against the foreigners and terrorism against the waverers or Quislings in their own societies. Invaders nearly always face – and are usually defeated by – this fact. As the noted English expert on the Middle East, Patrick Seale, wrote: "Al-Qaeda did not exist in Iraq before America's criminally misconceived war. It was America's invasion and its continued occupation which gave Al-Qaeda the chance to plant itself in Iraq. Only when the U.S. finally withdraws from Iraq can Al-Qaeda be defeated there.... it is only in opposition to Western aggression that it gains popularity." Echo that for Afghanistan and Somalia and let it be a portent for Iran.

Third, Where we are going:

The Neoconservatives, who have set the foreign policy of the Bush administration, have called for what they call The Long War. They expect it to last about half a century, that is for most of your lives.

What is it? What will it do to our position in the world? What will it do to our laws and our concept of civil liberties? What effect will it have on our society and economy? What will it cost in terms of money?

• The core idea of neo-conservatism is that America, alone among world powers, has the strength, the wisdom and the right to impose its will upon all the nations of the world, in effect to remake them not in the American image, as we would define it, but as subordinate states within a new American security system. These concepts have been spelled out in numerous articles and speeches by prominent neoconservatives within and outside of government. The most important have also been embedded in the 2005 official "National Defense Strategy of the United States of America" which baldly states that "America is a nation at war [which] At the direction of the President…will defeat adversaries at the time, place, and in the manner of our choosing." That is, to engage in preemptive military strikes. Adversaries are variously described, but among the descriptions are those who seek to "limit our global freedom to act" and "dominate key regions" or "develop and use breakthrough technologies to negate current U.S. advantages in key operational domains." Broadly speaking, "Our role in the world depends on effectively projecting and sustaining our forces in distant environments where adversaries may seek to deny us access." In short, the official doctrine of America is world domination.

• Attempting to implement this doctrine now has us engaged in wars in Iraq, Afghanistan and Somalia. Inevitably, these military actions spill over into neighboring countries. Fighting in Afghanistan has caused in the last week attacks on targets in Pakistan (infuriating not only the pro-American government and causing it to close down our supply route to Afghanistan but also causing great popular anger while doing little or nothing to improve our position in Afghanistan). We can be sure that wherever we try to implement the neoconservative doctrine, we will lose allies and friends while entrenching and embittering those we attack.

• The effect on the American society is already pernicious. Our government has acquired the habit of lying to us (as it did on the Iraq war), of withholding information even from the Congress (as it has done on the Department of Defense expenditures), of setting aside the Constitution (as it has done on incarceration and torture of prisoners of war and on invasion of privacy of our own citizens by wiretaps in violation of the law) and in numerous other ways that would have shocked our ancestors. In short we have taken several steps toward the ghastly world described by George Orwell in his novel *1984*.

• It has polarized our society to a degree that makes intelligent debate on public policy nearly impossible and often dangerous and has so skewed our economy that, as I have pointed out, we spend more on military power than the rest of the world combined and more than we spend on all other public programs combined. Doing so, and refusing the admit the costs, have caused us to go deeply into debt, to allow our cities and schools to degrade and kept us from addressing the ultimate security issue of any free society, the health of our citizens.

• The cost we can project to implement the neoconservative program is literally staggering. Some estimates, which are probably underestimates, run to about double our gross national product, upwards of $20 trillion. Is this just a fantasy? A pipedream of a bunch of unbalanced, angry and frustrated neoconservatives?

I wish I could tell you that it is. Sadly, it is much more. For example, we now have nearly 1,000 U.S. military bases in other countries. We have the troops and weapons in place to act anywhere in the world. The Bush administration maintains publicly that it has the authority to do so. The previously operative law, the War Powers Resolution (P.L 93-148 of 1973), which was passed by Congress over the veto of President Nixon, limits the president's authority to commit American troops into hostile situations and requires him "in every possible circumstance" to consult with the Congress before so doing. In the aftermath of the September 11, 2001 attacks on the World Trade Center and the Pentagon, President Bush convinced the Congress to grant him full authority (P.L. 102-1 of September 18, 2001) to "use the Armed Forces of the United States as he determines to be necessary and appropriate in order to (1) defend the national security of the United States against the continuing threat posed by Iraq; and (2) enforce all relevant United Nations Security Council Resolutions regarding Iraq." President Bush has taken the position that this resolution gives him even wider authority over anywhere he deems a threat to exist. With this in mind, the Department of Defense, under Secretary Donald Rumsfeld, created a special secret force, said to number 55,000 men with a budget of about $80 billion, which does not have to report to Congress or even to civilian representatives of the Government, the ambassadors, but is authorized to carry out assassinations and even to overthrow governments. Members of this force were active in the Somalia invasion and are already said to be involved in covert activities in Iran. We learned on September 11, 2008 that some of them had been sent into Pakistan despite the refusal of its government to allow them.

It is, of course, possible to encourage proxies to act without committing American troops. This seems to have been the case in the recent crisis over

Georgia:

What happened in Georgia may be almost as much a lesson for America as what is happening in Iraq, Afghanistan and Somalia. The major difference is that an attack on Russia would cause a nuclear world war. Russia, under the Tsars, the Communists and Vladimir Putin, naturally was sensitive to what happened on its frontier – just as America, under the Monroe Doctrine, has always been in Latin America. Recognizing this strategic reality, James Baker, the first President Bush's secretary of state, promised the Russians that we would not move NATO ahead "even one inch." We have now moved it right into Russia's immediately neighborhood. I agree with Mr. Baker that this was not a wise move. But worse was to follow. You would have to read the press very carefully to learn that it was Georgia that attacked South Ossetia (whose citizens have Russian passports and which has been essentially independent for about 20 years). On August 7, Georgian President Mikheil Saakashvili ordered the attack when, he claims, he was given a "green light" by the Bush administration. Anticipating the move, the Russians reacted in their usual heavy-handed fashion. So we were furious. Vice President Dick Cheney rushed to Georgia to promise them a billion dollars in aid and after considerable diplomatic arm-twisting a NATO delegation to commiserate. But then, of course, nothing happened. We would not go to war with Russia to protect Georgia. Nor would NATO. So we created a crisis where none existed and both Georgians and the inhabitants of South Ossetia paid the bill in suffering.

Now look at what lies ahead in Iran

Two issues have dominated discussion of Iran – its alleged attempts to acquire nuclear weapons and its supposed intervention in Iraq. Of course, also, many people, particularly women, dislike its regressive social policies toward women. But, on the nuclear issue bear in mind two things:

• First, it was America that got Iran started toward nuclear weapons. As Jonathan Power wrote, "Lost somewhere in the mists of history is the knowledge that it was the pro-American Shah of Iran who initiated Iran's quest to build a nuclear bomb. And it was the anti-American revolution led by Ayatollah Khomeini that initially suspended work on the bomb." Also our most authoritative estimators of facts in foreign affairs, the National Intelligence

Council drawn from our 16 intelligence agencies, found unanimously last November that they had "high confidence" that Iran had no nuclear weapons and had no plans to attempt to build them.

• I obviously do not have access to all of the data available to intelligence community, but I have learned in my foreign affairs experience that to understand any other country's policies one must put himself, as it were, on the other side of the table, in the chair occupied by its leader. So what would I do if I were Ayatollah Ali Khamenei or President Mahmoud Ahmadinejad?

I would see that President Bush singled out three countries which he called "the Axis of Evil." Then he threatened them with "regime change." The Iranian leader would know that regime change is a euphemism for overthrowing their governments and killing their leaders. So what did America do? Iraq, which did not have nuclear weapons, was destroyed while North Korea, which did have nuclear weapons and so could not be safely attacked, was offered an aid program, money and food supplies. That leaves Iran. Never mind what a fanatical, ideologically driven wild man would do, but what would a rational, patriotic, practical Iranian leader do? No doubt he would try to acquire this ultimate defense tool as quickly and as secretly as he could. And, even if he is overthrown and killed, a successor could be expected to do the same. Even blowing up all the identified nuclear-related sites and killing all the nuclear-related technicians would only delay the process and guarantee that Iran will eventually get the bomb.

• Second, the Bush administration has charged that Iran was playing a significant role in thwarting our operations in Iraq – that is acting as we expected in our 2005 National Security Strategy Doctrine. But the US intelligence experts found that these charges were exaggerated or unproven.

Again, if I were an Iranian policy planner, I would urge that my government do what it could to make American lives there difficult. As an Iranian, I would react as an American would if a foreign power, which proclaims itself our enemy, were occupying Mexico. Imagine our reaction to that! In fact, we don't have to imagine. We just have to remember the Bay of Pigs operation against Cuba.

We are not yet in a full-scale war against Iran, but if we attack Iran with nuclear weapons, the estimates are that we will kill upwards of 3 million Iranians. Even that will not stop the war. What would follow would be a guerrilla war that would make Iraq look like a picnic. Iran has 150 thousand national guardsmen, already organized and fully equipped for guerrilla warfare – in 2003 Iraq had none at all – and Iran has a fleet of fast, highly maneuverable and lethal speedboats that will attack our fleet and, above all, oil tankers. On attacking Iran, the "free world" is not with us. Public opinion polls tell us that whereas at least the western Europeans used to regard us as the world's leader toward stability, many now think of us as a rogue nation. Americans would not use that term, but the latest polls in April this year show that 81% of us think that "things have pretty seriously gotten off on the wrong track." In my meetings with conservative business leaders, I find that practically all think that an attack on Iran would be insane. Many think that our brief role as the world's leader is nearly ended, that if the 20th century was the American century, the 21st will not be. Now, for the first time, we are even being turned down for further borrowing by the great sovereign wealth funds. They have come to regard us the way a bank does a customer whose assets are pledged, who is spending too much and who does not seem to be acting rationally.

In Conclusion: what must your generation do?

First, on public policy:

Our country must bring itself back from the binge we have been on. We need to be more modest. One of the best Marine Corps commander put it simply: "It used to be said that the side with the most guns won; today, the side with the most guns goes bankrupt." That is roughly where we are today. In his usual succinct way, Colonel Andrew Bacevich put it well: "America doesn't need a bigger army. It needs a more modest foreign policy…Modesty implies giving up on the illusions of grandeur to which the end of the Cold War and 9/11 gave rise. It also means reining in the imperial presidents who expect the army to make good on those illusions."

On the nuclear issue which I, from my intimate experience in the Cuban Missile Crisis, particularly worry about, we missed the opportunity to get a moratorium on nuclear weapons; instead we multiplied what we had to fantastic numbers, 30-40 thousand when a dozen would have blown up most of the world. The result was Russia set out to match us. China followed, then Israel working with South Africa, then India and Pakistan fearing one another, North Korea et al. Now we are on the brink of a new "surge." We are again building bombs and upgrading those we already have instead of trying to curtail them. This is exactly the opposite of what we need to do. Every new country adds new risks. Several more countries are on the brink of deciding to "go nuclear."

What we could do is to begin with ourselves and set an example for the world. From our (and the Russian) initiative, we should branch out. The most dangerous area is the Middle East so we should start there. We should push for a regional nuclear ban. Israel is the only nuclear power in the Middle East, and it will have to play the key role. Why should it? There are two obvious answers:
• The first is that the value of nuclear weapons to Israel is psychological rather than strategic. They were not used in the 1967 or 1973 wars or in the Lebanese war of last year. Moreover, Israel doesn't "need" them since it already has the most powerful army and air force in its neighborhood.

• All that Israel's possession of nuclear weapons does is to ensure that some of its neighbors will get them; so having nuclear weapons, far from being a source of security is today a source of insecurity. In a decade or so, no matter what happens in Iran, other Middle Eastern countries will acquire them. So it would be smart for the Israelis to take the leadership in removing them from the Middle East. We can help in various ways and should.

"Merchants of death" is what our more free-swinging ancestors called the international arms dealers. In 1934, Republican Senator Joseph P. Nye thought that the arms trade was so pernicious and dangerous that private dealers must be excluded and arms supply aboard, if any, must be reserved to the Federal government. Effectively it has been. But the result is the opposite of what Senator Nye wanted: the American government has become the world's largest dealer in arms. Last year we gave away or sold $14 billion worth of lethal weapons and support systems. We did this opportunistically both to offset some of our costs and to win friends among other governments, but the effects on human beings have often been disastrous. Even selfishly, we must reckon that some of the weapons were used to kill Americans.

We must end this pernicious policy which is destabilizing to world peace and order. We must get serious about the environment. What we have done so far is little more than a PR happening. If we really care, we should organize the effort we put into the Manhattan Project to acquire nuclear weapons in World War II and the Apollo Program we put into landing a man on the Moon. If we act on the environment the way we did in those programs, we could save our planet. And it is, after all, the only one we have.

We must demand government transparency and accountability. Today, the nonpartisan Congressional research organization has publicly admitted that it cannot find out how the Defense Department spends our money. Congress does not even demand that testifying officials take an oath to tell the truth, and all they get asked for are sound bites. The pathetic testimony of General David Petraeus is a good example. He never gave a clear answer to a single question on American overseas military actions, pathetic as the questions he was asked were.

We must reform the electoral system. Our country is literally up for sale. A typical representative spends at least half of his effective time raising money, that is, to put it bluntly, renting himself out to lobbyists. He turns over to his staff the chores of reading reports and books. So, the level of ignorance and corruption in the House of Representatives must be witnessed to be believed. To put it bluntly, Congress has become a whorehouse. Everyone is on the take. There are an average of 5 lobbyists for each congressman and money is the main topic of conversation. Few representatives of the people get beyond it. We must reform our educational system. By any standard it is appalling. Test scores of our students rank below most "Third World" countries. Studies by such organizations as The National Geographic show that few students even know where other countries are, much less who lives in them, what they think, what they want, how they earn their livings, etc. What passes in many universities as "education" is, in fact, merely job training? We pay our teachers poorly and get what we pay for. We do not apply standards to students – for many, the educational experience is merely a sort of enjoyable holding station between childhood and going out into the "real" world. As Thomas Jefferson warned us, "If a nation expects to be ignorant and free…it expects what never was and never will be."

Second, your individual tasks as citizens:

First, you must inform yourselves. Be curious. Be skeptical. Demand facts. Don't settle for sound bites. This is not easy. Governments since the time of the Roman Empire lulled their citizens with bread and circuses. Today, a government doesn't even need to do what Rome did. We lap up the pap put out by the pop stars of TV "news" programs as though it were gospel and allow ourselves to be guided by ignorant commentators. Hopefully you are getting in your education the ability differentiate real value from trash, real substance from pap. If you are not, you are wasting your time because developing standards is what education is all about.

Informing oneself is not easy. But it can be done. Everyone who has access to a computer can sample newspapers here, in Europe and Asia free just by typing in a few words. Anyone can sign on to a number of provocative and wide-ranging websites. Some of our public-minded fellow citizens do much of the job for us. At your request, they will send you what they manage to find. And anyone can ask his Congressman for government reports, most of which are reliable and readable, on all aspects of public policy.

Refuse to be marginalized. America has a long tradition of deprecating knowledge and distrusting excellence. But, the country has invested a great deal in educating you. You are national assets. And you owe the country the best you have. Do your jobs as citizens. Demand that your candidates tell you the truth and act with intelligence. Don't be a dummy. Be active. And don't just wait for the vote. Go out and carry your thoughts to your fellow citizens and your candidates. Again, that powerful tool, the Internet, can be used as a giant lever for democracy. You can reach everybody.

Participate. You cannot afford to sit back and do nothing. If you do, you are almost certain to pay for your laziness. A democracy is not a holding company to be run by a board of directors. You are stockholders. Your life and your well-being are at stake. If you care about them, protect them. After you inform yourself, make your voice heard and put your actions where your mouth is. Be a leader. Get your generation into action. Together you are strong.

Our future is in your hands. This is your country, your world, and your time. Make this the first day of the rest of your lives.

Comments on Other Books by William R. Polk

The United States and the Arab World

"Dr. Polk maintains the detachment of the scholar, the fairness of the judge."
—Crane Brinton (Harvard University, editor of The American Foreign Policy Library)

"Exactly that solid, illuminating synthesis we have long lacked, and which men studying and acting in public affairs ought to read first about the Arab World."
—Manfred Halpern (Princeton) *The Middle East Journal*

"It is the depth of Professor Polk's historical and cultural presentation and the breadth of his economic, social, and political analysis that distinguish this volume from the plethora of journalistic commentary on the subject and make of it a true 'classic.'"
—Edwin Reischauer (Harvard University, and former ambassador to Japan)

"An authoritative and lucid interpretative history."
—*Annals of the American Academy of Political and Social Sciences*

Neighbors and Strangers: The Fundamentals of Foreign Affairs

"A splendid achievement." — Brian Urquhart (former UN Under-Secretary-General)

"a brilliant, fascinating analysis of war and statecraft from ancient times to the latest head-line...done with superb scholarship."
— Roger Hilsman (former Assistant Secretary of State, Columbia)

"...a massive, ambitious and reflective work, huge in concept and scope...Polk is equally adept in handling defense, trade, intelligence and diplomacy..."
—Thomas Hughes (President emeritus of the Carnegie Endowment for International Peace)

“A work of great learning, clear thought and logical presentation.”
— John Campbell (former director of studies of the Council on Foreign Relations)

“A wise, learned, and graceful work that constitutes a superb introduction to the origin and logic of the principal areas of transaction among political collectives – defense, trade, espionage, and diplomacy.” — *Foreign Affairs*

“William Polk has compressed a lifetime of scholarship, diplomacy, travel and inspired writing into this thoughtful, sometimes whimsical, but never boring account of how human beings have behaved toward each other from Neanderthal times to the nuclear age.
—*The International Herald Tribune*

“a highly learned and very readable book…”
— *Times Higher Education Supplement*

The Birth of America

“dazzling social history of early America…Polk…is a masterful storyteller ”
— *Publishers Weekly*

Understanding Iraq

”…by far the most absorbing and disturbing of the many recent books [and] has the authority that comes from formidable knowledge.” —*The Economist*
“Polk's compact book should be required reading…” —*The Washington Post*
“Polk's history…reads like a portent…The effect is haunting.” —*Publishers Weekly*

“…a sober and informed account of Iraq's history, culminating in a compelling critique of the U.S. intervention there.” —*Foreign Affairs*
“head and shoulders above other analyses…Candid, concise, and highly recommended.” —*Booklist*

“The author could hardly be more expert…”
—*Journal of the American Foreign Service Association*

Understanding Iran

"This is an extraordinary book by an extraordinary author…It portrays masterfully and humanely the evolution of the complex realities of Iranian history and culture and their profound impact on contemporary Iran and its relations with the United States."
—Professor R.K. Ramazani in the *Middle East Journal*

"…the most cogent, objective and informed view of the Iranian policy problem yet written." —Ambassador William G. Miller, Woodrow Wilson Center.

"A great scholar's brilliant appreciation of Iranian culture and history."
—Dr. Khodadad Farmanfarmaian, former head of the economic development authority of Iran.

"This is an easy read with a very big payoff…If you know someone in the United States government dealing with the Iran or the Middle East, give that peron this book; the prospects of American policy success vis-à-vis both could go up considerably."
—Ambassador Chas W. Freeman, Jr., former assistant secretary of defense for international security affairs.

"…a story that anyone who cares about America and Iran should read."
—*The Washington Post.*

"engrossing and penetrating…"
—William H. McNeill, former president of the American Historical Association, winner of the National Book Award.

"William Polk brings that rare combination of both scholarship and policy experience to his fascinating study of what makes Iran tick."
—Graham E. Fuller, former vice chairman of the US National Intelligence Council.

"William R. Polk['s last] four books constitute a graduate course on the contemporary and historical Middle East."
—Ambassador Robert V. Keeley, *The Foreign Service Journal.*

Violent Politics

"A must-read for all thinking Americans." —Former Senator George S. McGovern "William Polk's masterful and succinct history of eleven insurgent wars is the best available antidote to the U.S. counterinsurgency strategy in Iraq that de-couples war and politics. Polk re-couples them through the prism of historical experience."

—William E. Odom, Lt. General, USA, Rtd. 'This is a 'must-read'

—Congresswoman Lynn Woolsey (D-Ca), House Foreign Affairs Committee.

"There will be few more important books for the next president of the United States to read than William Polk's Violent Politics."

—John Brademas, President Emeritus, New York University, former member for twenty-two years of the U.S. House of Representatives.

The Elusive Peace: The Middle East in the Twentieth Century

"I can't remember a better general book on the whole region." —The New Statesman "William Polk, a professional in history and diplomacy ... manages to simplify without distorting the region's problems of war and peace, of wealth and poverty, and of adaptation to the modern world, setting them against a background of political and cultural history.

—*Foreign Affairs*

www.ingramcontent.com/pod-product-compliance
Lightning Source LLC
LaVergne TN
LVHW020523100826
845148LV00010B/1319

* 9 7 8 0 9 8 2 9 3 4 0 0 5 *